JOYCE CAROL OATES

WHERE I'VE BEEN AND WHERE I'M GOING . . .

"In Olden Times, When Wishing Was Having . . ."

Joyce Carol Oates examines classic fairy tales as expressions of
women's deepest fantasies and fears—and explores how such writers
as Shirley Jackson, Anne Sexton, Angela Carter, and Margaret Atwood artfully subvert the traditional depictions of romance with wit,
cynicism, and eloquently rendered rage.

"Haunted Sylvia Plath"

Oates investigates the work of the internationally acclaimed poet and
what distinguished her as an artist.

"Lost in Boxing"

A longtime observer of the sport, Oates draws provocative parallels
between professional boxing and our society by exploring the limits
of violence, discipline, and sportsmanship.

"Edward Hopper's Nighthawks, 1942"

Entering the dreamlike world of Edward Hopper's quintessentially
American masterpiece, Oates brings her sensitivity, passion, and insight to a fascinating essay on its artistic and emotional power.

Joyce Carol Oates is the author of numerous novels, including *My
Heart Laid Bare*, *Man Crazy*, and *We Were the Mulvaneys* (available in
Plume editions). Her most recent novel is *Broke Heart Blues*, forthcoming from Dutton in July 19   author of several
collections of short stories, poetry   t-
erary awards, Ms. Oates is the F   o-
fessor of Humanities at Princeto

JOYCE CAROL OATES

WHERE I'VE BEEN, AND WHERE I'M GOING

Essays, Reviews, and Prose

A PLUME BOOK

PLUME

Published by the Penguin Group

Penguin Putnam Inc., 375 Hudson Street, New York, New York 10014, U.S.A.

Penguin Books Ltd, 27 Wrights Lane, London W8 5TZ, England

Penguin Books Australia Ltd, Ringwood, Victoria, Australia

Penguin Books Canada Ltd, 10 Alcorn Avenue, Toronto, Ontario, Canada M4V 3B2

Penguin Books (N.Z.) Ltd, 182–190 Wairau Road, Auckland 10, New Zealand

Penguin Books Ltd, Registered Offices: Harmondsworth, Middlesex, England

First published by Plume, a member of Penguin Putnam Inc.

First Printing, July, 1999

10 9 8 7 6 5 4 3 2 1

 REGISTERED TRADEMARK — MARCA REGISTRADA

LIBRARY OF CONGRESS CATALOGING-IN-PUBLICATION DATA:

Oates, Joyce Carol

Where I've been and where I'm going : essays, reviews, prose / by Joyce Carol Oates.

p. cm.

ISBN 0-452-28053-2

I. Title.

PS3565.A8W45   1999

814'.54—dc21   98-45234
                                                                          CIP

Printed in the United States of America

Set in Garamond no. 3

Designed by Eve L. Kirch

BOOKS ARE AVAILABLE AT QUANTITY DISCOUNTS WHEN USED TO PROMOTE PRODUCTS OR SERVICES. FOR INFORMATION PLEASE WRITE TO PREMIUM MARKETING DIVISION, PENGUIN PUTNAM INC., 375 HUDSON STREET, NEW YORK, NY 10014.

for Samuel Hynes, and for Edmund White

CONTENTS

III. "The Madness of Art": Essays and Introductions

IV. Where I've Been, and Where I'm Going: Prefaces, Afterwords

PREFACE

These essays, reviews, and prose pieces, predominantly written during the past several years, represent a wide variety of subjects linked by a few abiding themes: the role of the artist in society and in extremis, the beguiling mystery of literary creation, the often ironic distance between the work of art and its very human creator. My love of reading, and of thinking, brooding, dreaming about what I've read, predates my love of writing, and was certainly the stimulus, from early childhood onward, for writing itself. If my first beloved books were Lewis Carroll's *Alice's Adventures in Wonderland* and *Through the Looking-Glass*, these classic fantasies have been probable guides for my life as both a reader and a writer: as Alice bravely plunges down the rabbit hole into Wonderland, or eases through a mirror into the uncanny Looking-Glass World, so the reader, and the writer, plunge into wonderlands of the imagination.

And what a pleasure, for a writer of prose fiction, poetry, and drama, to speak in a direct, unmediated voice; a voice that's my own, and not that of a fictional character's; a voice addressing itself to a presumably like-minded audience, on varied, impersonal subjects that are not my own invention. As a critic my primary hope is to engage the reader in a kind of conversation, to provoke thought and appreciation of books and their elusive makers. A collection of prose pieces can constitute, however obliquely, a writer's journal, a record of where I've been, and where I hope to go. Even the impersonal is stamped with the personal, and "ideas" can be fueled by the most intense and private of emotions.

—Joyce Carol Oates
June 1998

They who are to be judges must also be performers.
—Aristotle

I

WHERE IS AN AUTHOR?

Where Is an Author?

The artist's life is his work, and this is the place to observe him.
—Henry James

It all came together between the hand and the page.
—Samuel Beckett (on the composition of
Waiting for Godot)

W hy do we write? Why do we read? Why is "art" crucial to
    human beings?

The engine that gives its mysterious inner life to a work of art
must be the subterranean expression of a wish, working its way to the
surface of narrative. In fairy tales and legends, the "wish" is often explicit: for a rendering of justice rare in life, for romance in the face of
improbability, for a happy ending. In a more sophisticated art, the
"wish" may be so buried as to be unacknowledged by the artist, or
even repudiated. "Never trust the artist," D. H. Lawrence warned in
his iconoclastic *Studies in Classic American Literature* (1923). "Trust
the tale. The proper function of a critic is to save the tale from the
artist who created it." Often, writers don't know what they're writing
until they've completed it. For some of us, the composition of any
sustained, structured work would not be possible if there wasn't a secret code or connection between the story (or what we call for lack of
a more precise term "story") and an interior, hidden pattern. A sense,
in a way visual, of the story's trajectory: where it begins, where it
ends, its dominant images and tone. Though the act of writing can be
emotionally volcanic, a white-hot frenzy in the initial process of creation, in its later stages, those of revision, recasting and restructur-
ing, it is the most icy-cold of activities. "So cold, so icy, that one
burns one's fingers on him! Every hand that touches him receives a

shock. That is why some think he is burning hot." This aphorism of Friedrich Nietzsche's suggests the formalist's self-conception: the self as viewed from within. To present emotionally dynamic material is to confess that one *has felt*, and perhaps extremely, but is *not now feeling*, emotion.

Is the artist, by temperament, a perpetual antagonist to the crowd? the state? the prevailing ethos? This collision of the ethical/tribal/familial world and the world of the individual; the world of the individual soul and the universe of sheer numbers—"laws" of nature: This is the drama that arrests me, and haunts me, in life as in writing; in reverie, most keenly during insomniac fugues when "I" seems to dissolve, and an impersonal kernel of being, primarily one of inquiry, emerges. (For me, these fugues began in early adolescence.) In asking, like Lewis Carroll's child-heroine Alice, *Who am I?* am I really asking *Who, or what, is this "I" that asks this question, asked repeatedly, with such hope, yet perhaps futilely, through human history?* Is this "I" unique—or is it in essence identical with the multitude of other "I"s?—as we are presumably composed of identical matter, turn and turn about, mineral deposits from the stars of how many trillions of years ago, in varying compositions, except never varying in our temporality: "Oh Life, begun in fluent Blood, / And consummated dull!" (Emily Dickinson, 1130, c. 1868)

Or is this, too, a fiction?—an artfully constructed and sculpted wish? In the collision of the personal and the impersonal, in the arena where language and silence touch, the possibility of art arises like flame.

In 1969, the influential if much-misunderstood Michel Foucault published a speculative essay, "What Is an Author?" A kind of thought-experiment, generated perhaps more by political bias than disinterested aesthetic inquiry, this famous essay considered the ontological status of the writer; one might say, undermined it. (Yet only in theory, for since Foucault's time no writers, including theorists of the Foucault school, have surrendered their names on the spines of their books, nor their advances and royalties. As in hothouse plantings, bibliographies of even obscure writers flourish; but the plantings are discreetly fenced off from one another, and named.) Still the debate over what is called "authorial presence" continues, and has not been resolved, for, in such debates, it is language, or a critical vocabulary, that is at stake, and not a quantifiable reality. Roland Barthes and Jacques Derrida have argued, though not this succinctly, for the "death of the author"—the theoretical claim that "there is nothing outside the text"—"there is no center or integrated core from which we can say a piece of literature issues." (There is no Mozart from whom the music issues; there is the Mozartian text, which shares with other Mozartian texts certain characteristics, like voiceprints, or fingerprints, but no essential identity.)[1]

One might stand the theory on its head, as in a phantasmagoric scenario in which any and all things written by a "historic individual" (with name, fingerprints, DNA, etc.) are part of the oeuvre of the writer; not merely the revised, polished hardcover books he/she has nurtured into being with such determination. Certainly, collectors of manuscripts act upon this assumption, appalling to the writer: They are willing to pay high sums of money for minor work, juvenilia, letters tossed off in unguarded moments, mere jottings—for, one might argue, these are the truer testaments of the elusive self, because unmediated. If you are a writer of reputation you may argue eloquently, like T. S. Eliot, that art is in fact the "extinction of personality"; nonetheless, any original manuscript of yours, in your own inimitable hand, any embarrassing love letters, diary entries, in Eliot's case anti-Semitic and misogynist pornographic fantasies, will be worth far more than any chastely printed book with your name stamped on the spine. For human beings seem to honor instinctively the individual sui generis, despite philosophical theories arguing the nonexistence of individuals. To escape the prison house of identity, writers have often fled to pseudonyms in the hope that the text will be, simply, a text, with an anonymous-sounding name attached to which no prior assumptions accrue. To begin again!—to be born again!—not as an author, but purely as a text!

Yet it's symptomatic of our profoundly secularized era that, French theory and the "New" Historicism to the contrary, any and all biographical data can be applied to the writer as a "historic" individual; nothing too obscure, too mundane, too trivial, too demeaning is ruled out as an instrument of illumination into the writer's motive.

(A well-regarded academic-literary journal recently printed an essay on Sylvia Plath's last poems interpreted in the light of premenstrual tension, for instance.) Massive contemporary biographies, bloated with unedited taped interviews, bury their ostensible subjects beneath a vertiginous mass of data, and the writer's forlorn plea *The artist's life is his work, and this is the place to observe him* is ignored. Yet, most writers will acknowledge that they do not inhabit their books—the more clinical term is "texts"—once they have completed them; they—we—are expelled from them like any other reader, for the act of composition is time-bound, and time is an hourglass that runs in one direction only. To consider the text as an art work is to acknowledge that there can be nothing outside the text. Authorial intentions have long been dismissed from serious critical consideration, though outside the lecture hall there may be intense, gossipy interest in such old riddles as the nature of Henry James's wound, did an individual named "Shakespeare" write the body of work attributed to "Shakespeare" or is someone else "Shakespeare," is the "I" of the next poem you read the poet or an invented persona? As Michel Foucault reasonably asks, "What difference does it matter who is speaking?"

What difference does it make to know that Marcel Proust was a homosexual? Does this biographical information alter the text of Proust's great novel?—does it expand the text?—detract from the text?—qualify, or enhance, its greatness? Can it be argued that Oscar Wilde's *The Picture of Dorian Gray*, written by a homosexual, is a more subtle, codified work of fiction than the identical novel would have been had Wilde been heterosexual? No matter the plea embodied in the question "What difference does it make?" it seems, in fact, to make a difference to most readers.

For the feminist critic, it makes a considerable difference to know that the text has been authored by a woman: For a woman's discourse will presumably differ from a man's, even if the texts are identical. If the author is a woman, her text has very likely been generated by "female rage"; her art work may be intimately related to her body. To protest against such narrow corseting of motive is to deny one's gender-identity. Far from erasing identity, this popular strategy of criticism has reenforced identity by means of gender. Does a woman, in fact, possess a special language, distinct from male language? Or is it purely Woman, and no individual, who possesses such a language? And what of the "androgynous" artist? As a writer, and a woman, or a woman, and a writer, I have never found that I was in possession of a special female language springing somehow from the female body, though I can sympathize with the poetic-mystic yearning that might underlie such a theory. To be marginalized through history, to be told repeatedly that we lack souls, that we aren't fully human, that we're "unclean," therefore can't write, can't paint, can't compose music, can't do philosophy, math, science, politics, power in its myriad guises—the least of our compensations should be that we're in possession of some special gift brewed in the womb and in mother's milk. For the practicing woman writer, feminist/gender criticism can be wonderfully nurturing, for obvious reasons: Texts by women are read attentively and sympathetically; "lost" writers are continually rediscovered, and wrongly dismissed writers (Kate Chopin, for instance) are given the respectful scrutiny they deserve. On the most practical level, as the feminist critic Elaine Showalter has said, "The best thing the feminist can do for women's writing is to buy women's books."

Yet this criticism, for all its good intentions, can be restrictive as well, at least for the writer who is primarily a formalist, and for whom gender is not a pressing issue in every work. (As a writer who happens to be a woman, I choose to write about women, and I choose to write from the perspective of women; but I also choose to write about men, and I choose to write from the perspective of men; with the confidence that, dissolving myself into the self of a fictitious other, I have entered a dimension of consciousness that is not my own in either case, and yet legitimate.) Surely it is an error to reduce to a genitally defined essence any individual, whether a woman or a man; for the (woman) writer, it is frustrating to be designated as a "woman writer"—a category in relationship to which there is no corresponding "man writer."

To return to the question "Where is an author?"—we might say, with Henry James, that the artist's life is his work, yet this is not quite the same thing as saying that the artist's work is his life, for of course it can be only part of that life, and possibly, for some artists, even the gifted, not the most valued part of that life. We might argue that there must be an ontological distinction between the writer-as-creator-of-texts and the living person, the medium of the art. The work is thus the artist. The artist is a component of an aesthetic object, a product, printed or processed or in some way made into an artifice—"artificial." The individual is born of nature, but the artist is born of that individual, yearning to transcend the merely "natural" and to make complete that which, existentially, is forever incomplete, unrealized. We might argue that all books, fiction, poetry, nonfiction, have been created by pseudonymous selves in the process of that creation, and if the name on the dust jacket is identical with the historic name, that is not the same thing as saying that the name on the dust jacket *is* the historic individual.

Where is the author?—in the work, of course.

Which is not to say that the author of the author (i.e., the historic self) doesn't exist too; at least provisionally.

NOTES

1. Wolfgang Amadeus Mozart is our paragon of genius. This letter suggests the genius as oddly passive, a vessel to be filled from the unconscious.

When I am, as it were, completely myself, entirely alone, and of good cheer . . . it is on such occasions that my ideas flow best and most abundantly. *Whence* and *how* they come, I know not; nor can I force them. . . .

When I proceed to write, the committing to paper is done quickly enough, for everything is . . . already finished. . . . But why my productions take from my hand that particular form and style that makes them *Mozartish*, and different from the works of other composers, is probably owing to the same cause which renders my nose so large or so aquiline, or, in short, makes it Mozart's, and different from those of other people. For I really do not study or aim at originality. (trans. Edward Holmes)

Yet Mozart's most dazzling compositions are readily identified as of his musical era; for even a genius is a child of his time.

"In Olden Times, When Wishing Was Having . . .": Classic and Contemporary Fairy Tales

1.

> Whatever is an exit from that country . . . cannot be an
> entrance.
> —John Crowley, "The Green Child"

The fairy tale, as a literary/cultural genre, has traditionally been associated with women; and women have, in different times and in distinctly different ways, impressed upon these tales the nature of their deepest fantasies. The fairy tale of tradition has been imaginatively transformed, in recent decades, into what might be called the "revisioned" fairy tale, in which the archetype is retained but given, by individual artists, a distinctly contemporary interpretation.

Distinguished archivists like the pioneering Charles Perrault (whose *Histoires ou contes du temps passé* appeared in 1697), Jacob and Wilhelm Grimm (whose *Die Kinder-und Hausmärchen* appeared in various volumes, 1812–57), and Hans Christian Andersen (whose collections appeared 1857–72) have been male, but most of the material they collected was provided by women. It is one of these extraordinary sources that Wilhelm Grimm speaks of so warmly in the preface to an early Grimms' edition:

[This woman] retains fast in her mind these old sagas—which talent, she says, is not granted to everyone. She recounts her stories thoughtfully, accurately, with uncommon vividness and evident delight—first quite easily, but then, if required, over again, slowly, so that with a bit of practice it is possible to take down her dictation, word for word.

The very expression "fairy tale" calls to mind a quintessential female sensibility: The tales are "old wives' tales," "Mother Goose tales." The association has long been an ambiguous one, not altogether flattering to women, and frequently disturbing.

For the term "fairy tale" is itself ambiguous. Sometimes it is frankly pejorative, dismissive. Its received connotation has to do with benign, rather brainless fantasy: *And they lived happily ever after.* But many fairy tales are nightmares of senseless cruelty and violence (as in "The Girl Without Hands" a father chops off his daughter's hands to save himself from the devil—and this, one of the "good" fathers in the Grimm collection); and the terms of "happiness" in others (Hansel's and Gretel's reconciliation with the father who had left them to die in the forest, for instance; the torture-death of Snow White's wicked stepmother) are problematic to say the least. Girls and women are the uncontested property of men, to be handed over by their fathers to virtually anyone the father favors—a murderous/cannibal Robber Bridegroom, a "frightful Beast," the devil himself. The father's wish seems to include the daughter's reflexive response, as if the two were not two but one: When the craven father of "The Girl Without Hands" tells his daughter what he must do to save himself from the devil, the daughter meekly replies, "Dear Father, do with me what you will, I am your child." Simply to be *female* is to be without volition, identity.

In the great majority of the tales, to be a heroine in even a limited sense requires extreme youth and extreme physical beauty; it would not be sufficient to be merely beautiful, one must be "the greatest beauty in the kingdom," "the fairest in the land" (as Snow White's famously jealous stepmother demands for herself). Young, maturing girls like Snow White, Cinderella, and the White Bride of "The White Bride and the Black Bride" (Grimm) are the natural targets of the homicidal envy of older women; ubiquitous in the tales are "wicked stepmothers" who conspire to injure or kill their beautiful stepdaughters. (If there is a fairy tale in which a stepmother befriends her stepdaughter, or even treats her decently, I seem to have missed it.) Even Sleeping Beauty, whose mother loves her, attracts the animus of a wicked (female) fairy, for her possession of a "bright resplendent beauty [that] had somewhat in it luminous and divine" (Perrault). The lot of women in a patriarchal society that privileges them as valuable possessions (of men), or brands them as worthless and contemptible, made it inevitable that women should perceive other women as dangerous rivals; that there are so many "step" mothers in the tales suggests how frequently women died in childbirth or as a consequence of constant childbearing; how frequently they were replaced by younger wives. Even for princesses like Sleeping Beauty, the optimum marriage age is fifteen or sixteen.

Though fairy tales, like ballads, to which they are closely related, are a communal folk art of the uneducated, nonliterate class, they are politically and morally conservative to a degree that seems puzzling. Caste goes unquestioned even in such picaresque, spirited tales as "Puss-in-Boots"; individual merit is rarely celebrated except in terms of the fixed social order. Contrary to popular assumptions, Cinderella, for instance, is not a commoner but a girl of aristocratic birth whose misfortune has been to lose her mother; when her father remarries, as fathers inevitably do, she finds herself displaced in the household by a cruel stepmother and stepsisters, made into a chargirl ("Cinderella": "of the cinders"). To interpret "Cinderella: or, The Little Glass Slipper" as a populist rags-to-riches romance is to totally misinterpret its fundamental story, which has to do with the putative injustice of denying one of aristocratic birth her rightful privilege, and with the drama of disguised worth; though Cinderella sleeps in a chimney corner, is forced to wear rags, and is abused by the females in her household, nonetheless she is "a hundred times handsomer than her sisters" in their costly attire. Her physical self, including her small, dainty, beautiful feet, is the expression of her aristocratic virtue, and so she will be recognized by her prince because such virtue will assert itself; how very different from a tale in which a cinder girl, or match girl, or beggar girl is plucked for romance by a nobleman. In a crucial sense fairy tales work to subvert romantic wishes, for they repeatedly confirm "order" and redress dislocations of privileged birth while leaving wholly unchallenged the hierarchical basis for such privileging. Amid the countless tales exalting the aristocrat over the commoner, "The Princess and the Peas" is a rarity in its suggestion of satire. In the most commonly known version, popularized by Hans Christian Andersen in 1835, aristocratic hyperesthesia is celebrated tongue-in-cheek: A self-declared princess is put to a secret test by her prospective mother-in-law, a queen; sleeping on a bed of twenty mattresses and twenty featherbeds laid upon three peas with such discomfort that, in the morning, she complains that her body is black and blue with bruises—proof to the queen and her son that she is the genuine article, a true princess fit to marry a prince, "for it was quite impossible for any but a true princess to be so tender." Hans Christian Andersen, of working-class origins, concludes the tale with a slyly ironic aside: "Now was not that a lady of exquisite feeling?"

Few fairy tales, however, are so playful as "The Princess and the Peas," nor do they suggest subversive attitudes; the world as it appears is not to be questioned, still less resisted. "Progress" in the social-evolutionary sense would be anathema to the fairy-tale atmosphere of fateful resignation and what might be defined as a causeless consequence: Your fate is deserved because it happens to you, it doesn't happen to you because it's deserved. All "good" heroines accept their fate passively, unquestioningly. To express even normal distress at being viciously mistreated would be in violation of the narrow strictures of fairy-tale "goodness."

For fairy-tale heroes and heroines are children, and the fairy tale derives from the childhood of the race when there would seem to have been, for most people, no coherent sense of "history"; only an unchanging, static present encompassing an infinite cycle of seasons. The very concept of "history"—the male province of deliberation, analysis, action, acquisition, and control—springs from a grasp of individual self-determination, not mindless passivity and acquiescence. The traditional fairy tale begins *Once upon a time*—bland, blurred, stereotypical language that thwarts the more vigorous intellectual desire to know *when, where, how, why*. And *who*: For while recorded history is a chronicle of specific rulers and their governments, a complex mosaic of individual names, dates, allegiances, careers, the fairy-tale world is ahistoric and timeless, politically static, its abbreviated dramatis personae a perennial cast of kings, queens, princes, and princesses; there are wealthy men and poor men, merchants, hunts-men, wood-cutters, millers; there are beautiful daughters, handsome young men, and wicked stepmothers (before the Grimms' discreet al-terations, some of these were wicked natural mothers). Beyond this, characterization does not exist; of the growth, development, and evo-lution of human personality there is none. (Except in those instances in which a vain princess repents of her ill-treatment of a disguised prince or wicked stepsisters repent of their ill-treatment of a stepsis-ter who has married a prince.) Of course there are fairies—good, wicked—and "godmothers" (though rarely godfathers); there are gi-ants, ogres, talking beasts of every species, including bears who are likely to be bridegrooms and talking cats likely to be helpers. There are always wolves, and wolves are "bad."

Many a fairy tale turns upon a secret word-formula or a secret, highly potent name: To utter "Rumpelstiltskin" is to save the life of one's baby. To have access to a magic knapsack and hat (as in the Grimm tale "The Knapsack, the Hat, and the Horn") or to a cloak of invisibility (as in the Grimm tale "The Twelve Dancing Princesses") is to save one's own life and to reap great riches. As in Ovid's great poem *The Metamorphoses*, there are abrupt, magical changes: Young men become swans, or ravens, or boarlike beasts and frogs yearning for human love to redeem them; sometimes, though rarely, as in Hans Christian Andersen's "The Swineherd," a disguised, begrimed prince will reveal himself in anger to the princess he would have mar-ried, and reject her. In Andersen's famous tale "The Little Mermaid" a cruel bargain requires that the heroine relinquish her siren's voice in return for a human shape and human love on earth—a disturbing parable of women's place in the world of men. (To be different in any respect, for a woman, or even to be suspected of "difference" is dan-gerous by fairy-tale logic, for the categories of women are few, and divisive: in the cruel, darkly comic cautionary tale "Clever Elsie" [Grimm], a mentally defective girl is boasted to be clever, married off by her father under false pretenses, and soon shut out of her house by her disgruntled husband, who has outfitted her with bells.) As in

Homer's *Iliad* and *Odyssey* the fairy tales are filled with fantastical interludes in which benevolent or malevolent beings of supernatural origin intrude in human affairs, with the astonishing omnipotence of parents exerting their power in an infant's life. Above all, human beings are surrounded by invisible forces that cannot be controlled but which, if one knows the secret rite or word-formula, can be placated, like the Judeo-Christian patriarch-god.

(How odd it seems to us, in fact, that the European fairy-tale world coexisted with a powerfully institutionalized and politicized state religion; an essentially anti-Christian, pagan world populated with mysterious nonhuman beings like fairies, trolls, and witches who ceaselessly involve themselves in the affairs of mankind. The Grimm brothers collected a number of Christian fairy tales under the title "Children's Legends" which are about such holy figures as Saint Joseph, the twelve apostles, the Virgin Mary, the Christ child, and God Himself; little-known tales lacking the dramatic force and arresting images of the more traditional tales.)

What is troubling about the fairy-tale world and its long association with women is precisely its condition as mythical and stereotypical, a rigidly schematized counterworld to the "real"; an enchanted, or accursed world, whose relationship to reality is analogous to that of our dreams to our waking lives. As if the province of women must be unreal, trivial. As if women are fairy-tale beings yearning for nothing more than material comforts, a "royal" marriage, a self-absorbed conventional life in which social justice and culture of any kind are unknown. Which helps to account for why fairy-tale endings are nearly always absurd. For instance,

> . . . As they spoke a splendid carriage drove up with eight beautiful horses decked with plumes of feathers and golden harness, and behind rode the prince's servant, . . . then all set out fully of Joy for the Prince's kingdom; where they arrived safely, and lived happily a great many years.
>
> ("The Frog Prince")

And a magnificent princess alighted from the coach and went into the mill, and this princess was the little tabby-cat whom poor Hans had served for seven years. . . . [She] took her faithful Hans and set him in the coach, and drove away with him. They first drove to the little house which he had built with the silver tools, and behold it was a great castle, and everything inside was made of silver and gold; and then she married him, and he was rich, so rich that he had enough for all the rest of his life. After this, let no one ever say that anyone who is silly can never become a person of importance.

("The Poor Miller's Boy and the Cat")

In the yet more transparent wish-fulfillment fantasy "The King of the Golden Mountain" (Grimm), a king takes revenge on his unfaithful queen and a court of kings, princes, and councillors by brandishing a magic sword and uttering the words "All heads off but mine!" with the immediate gratifying result—"All the heads rolled on the ground, and he alone was master, and once more King of the Golden Mountain."

2.

> Beauty is a simple passion,
> but, oh my friends, in the end
> you will dance the fire dance in iron shoes.
> —Anne Sexton, *Transformations*

Of course, I've been unfair to the very nature of the fairy tale: It *is* crude, it *is* transparently wishful, it does reflect the unquestioned prejudices of a conservative patriarchal folk culture. Yet fairy tales contain an incalculably rich storehouse of mysterious, luminous, riddlesome, and ever-potent images, a vast Sargasso Sea of the imagination. Though characterization is minimal, plots are bold and original; if endings often have a hasty, perfunctory quality, nonetheless fairy tales can encompass in the space of a few fluid passages complete miniature narratives. Like the folk ballads, the tales spring from a diverse and anonymous communal source, mysterious in their origins as language itself.

Jacob and Wilhelm Grimm believed that the myths of ancient

times had descended first into heroic legend and romance and finally into folktales with an appeal to children. Before the Grimm brothers it was fashionable to revise and "improve" the tales to make them pleasing to an educated reading public, but after the Grimms began to publish their monumental work respect for the oral folk source was observed; it would come to be considered a violation of principle to alter the purity of the fairy-tale source. Only in recent times has the fairy tale been reclaimed by writers and artists for their own imaginative and frequently subversive purposes. Such experimental, postmodernist work draws upon tradition while boldly "revising" it, often from a feminist perspective, as in the work of Anne Sexton (*Transformations,* 1971) and Angela Carter (*The Bloody Chamber,* 1979).

Anne Sexton's brilliantly inventive poetry sequence retells sixteen classic fairy tales, among them "Snow White and the Seven Dwarfs," "Rumpelstiltskin," "Rapunzel," "Cinderella," "Red Riding Hood," "The Frog Prince," "Hansel and Gretel," and "Briar Rose (Sleeping Beauty)"; it is also the confessional document of "a middle-aged witch, me." The poems are notable for their characteristic Sexton flights of romantic lyricism, black comedy, and bittersweet irony; each poem is preceded by an autobiographical preface—"Take a woman talking, / purging herself with rhymes, / drumming words on a typewriter, / planting words in you like seed grass." ("Iron Hans") "Snow White" faithfully recapitulates the fairy tale in contemporary / vernacular language: "The dwarfs, those little hot dogs, / walked three times around Snow White, / the sleeping virgin. They were wise / and wattled like small czars." Unlike Donald Barthelme's droll metafiction *Snow White,* Sexton's poem does not explore the sexual possibilities of a virgin residing with (male) dwarfs; Sexton's Snow White is a virgin even after her nominal marriage to a faceless prince, a younger version of the wicked stepmother who dies in the dance of red-hot iron shoes: "Meanwhile Snow White held court, / rolling her china-blue doll eyes open and shut / and sometimes referring to her mirror / as women do." Sexton's feminism is radical enough to expose and condemn the deadly "femininity" of women who refuse to acknowledge their masculine, aggressive selves: "Inside many of us / is a small old man / who wants to get out . . . / one part papa, / one part Doppelgänger." ("Rumpelstiltskin") Cinderella's tale is "that story"—made banal by familiarity and repetition, yet never entirely believable:

> Cinderella and the prince
> lived, they say, happily ever after,
> like two dolls in a museum case
> never bothered by diapers or dust,
> never arguing over the timing of an egg,
> never telling the same story twice,
> never getting a middle-aged spread,
> their darling smiles pasted on for eternity.
> Regular Bobbsey Twins.
> That story.

"Red Riding Hood" is the most complex of the poems in *Transformations*, freely mixing the poet's anguished personal life ("And I. I too. / Quite collected at cocktail parties, / meanwhile in my head / I'm undergoing open-heart surgery") with the familiar tale of Little Red Riding Hood deceived and devoured by the wolf and saved by the fortuitous intervention of the huntsman ("It was a carnal knife that let / Red Riding Hood out like a poppy, / quite alive from the kingdom of the belly"). The poem is an anti-lyric, heavy with irony, able to make little of the overfamiliar tale, which resolves itself all too easily in a "happy" ending:

> Those two remembering
> nothing naked and brutal
> from that little death,
> that little birth,
> from their going down
> and their lifting up.

"The Frog Prince" is an occasion for a hallucinatory stream-of-consciousness linking the poet's confused inner life with the symbolic Other, the Frog: "My guilts are what / we catalogue. / I'll take a knife / and chop up frog." Not the Frog as Prince but the Frog simply as Frog captivates her.

Frog has no nerves.
Frog is as old as a cockroach.
Frog is my father's genitals.
Frog is a malformed doorknob.
Frog is a soft bag of green.

The moon will not have him. . . .

Once Frog becomes Prince, the poem ends abruptly; as in "Hansel and Gretel" the fairy tale swiftly dissolves like a bad dream, with a coda in which the poet speaks ironically: "Their mother, / you'll be glad to hear, was dead." Sexton's most personal identification seems to be with "Briar Rose (Sleeping Beauty)," whose experience parallels the poet's own wavering pilgrimage "from Bedlam and part way back" (the title of her first book of poems, 1960): "Consider / a girl who keeps slipping off, / arms limp as old carrots, / into the hypnotist's trance, / into a spirit world / speaking with the gift of tongues. / She is stuck in the time machine, / suddenly two years old sucking her thumb, / as inward as a snail, / learning to talk again. / She's on a voyage." Sexton's Briar Rose, saved by her prince, is released from the prison of catatonic sleep only to fear normal sleep forever, dependent upon ". . . the court chemist / mixing her some knock-out drops / and never in the prince's presence." The poem's elliptical revelation is a shocking one: Briar Rose has been sexually molested by her king-father, a "theft" committed upon her as a child.

There was a theft.
That much I am told.
I was abandoned.
That much I know.
I was forced backward.
I was forced forward.
I was passed hand to hand
like a bowl of fruit.
Each night I am nailed into place
and I forget who I am.

Daddy?
That's another kind of prison.
It's not the prince at all,
but my father
drunkenly bent over my bed,
circling the abyss like a shark,
my father thick upon me
like some sleeping jellyfish.
What voyage this, little girl?
This coming out of prison?
God help—
this life after death?

A nightmare ending of the boldly revisionist *Transformations*, this plea from the child-self, locked in the heart of the adult woman. *Is this life after death?* may well have been the plea of Sexton's life, and Briar Rose/Sleeping Beauty the poet's most poignant expression of her suffering.

In Angela Carter's similarly iconoclastic collection of stories, *The Bloody Chamber*, a lush, fevered prose style expresses the exoticism of the fairy-tale world in a way that, ironically, the pedestrian, service-able prose of the fairy tales themselves did not. (Angela Carter, a scholar/translator of Perrault's *Histoires ou contes du temps passé*, defined their essence as "heroic optimism," the principle that makes possible "happy" endings.) A postmodernist fantasist, an experimenter in form and voice, Carter created for her tales a florid, self-conscious, over-wrought prose, as in these musings of the seventeen-year-old virgin bride of Bluebeard: "I felt so giddy as if I were on the edge of a precipice; I was afraid, not so much of him, of his monstrous presence, heavy as if he had been gifted at birth with more specific *gravity* than the rest of us, the presence that, even when I thought myself most in love with him, always subtly oppressed me. . . . No. I was not afraid of him; but of myself. I seemed reborn in his unreflective eyes, reborn in unfamiliar shapes. I hardly recognized myself from his description of me and yet, and yet—might there not be a grain of beastly truth in them? And, in the red firelight, I blushed again, unnoticed, to think he might have chosen me because, in my innocence, he sensed a rare talent for corruption." The "talent for corruption" in fairy-tale virgins is one of Carter's most provocative revisionist-feminist themes, often equated with food, drink, perfumes, and flowers, in sensuous prose: "the reeling odor of a glowing, velvet, monstrous [rose] whose petals had regained all their former bloom and elasticity, their corrupt, brilliant, baleful splendor." ("The Lady of the House of Love")

In Carter's revision of the Bluebeard legend, the collection's title story, the virgin-bride of the murderous marquis is saved, in an unexpected ending, by her own mother, a huntswoman who arrives at just the right moment: "You never saw such a wild thing as my mother, with her hat seized by the winds and blown out to sea so that her hair was her white mane, her black lisle legs exposed to the thigh, her skirts tucked around her waist, one hand on the reins of the rearing horse while the other clasped my father's service revolver. . . . And my husband stood stock-still, as if she had been Medusa, the sword still raised over his head as in those clockwork tableaux of Bluebeard you see in glass cases at fairs"—to fire a single bullet through his forehead. (A ridiculous ending, perhaps, but no more ridiculous than any other fairy-tale ending, the feminist Carter seems to be saying. And why not, for once, feminist wish-fulfillment?) In Carter's similarly lush, sensuous revision of "Beauty and the Beast," titled "The Courtship of Mr. Lyon," the mythical marriage of innocent virgin and good, decent beast evolves into ordinary domestic marital happiness: Mr. and Mrs. Lyon walk in the garden; the old spaniel drowses on the grass, in a "drift of fallen petals." (How welcome, for once, a fairy-tale ending that subverts the fantastic altogether.) In an artful variant of this marriage tale, "The Tiger's Bride," a female sexuality emerges passionately from a lifetime of repression, conquering "nursery fears made flesh and sinew; earliest and most archaic of fears, fear of devourment. The beast and his carnivorous bed of bone and I, white, shaking, raw, approaching him as if offering, in myself, the key to a peaceable kingdom in which his appetite need not be my extinction." Beauty craves Beast as Beast craves Beauty; in erotic union, female and male are perfectly conjoined: "And each stroke of his tongue ripped off skin after successive skin, all the skins of a life in the world, and I left behind a nascent patina of shiny hairs. My earrings turned back to water and trickled down my shoulders; I shrugged the drops off my beautiful fur."

Carter's females are hardly "good" girls but complex, morally ambiguous individuals, not to be defined or predicted by gender, as in
"The Company of Wolves": "See! sweet and sound she sleeps in
granny's bed, between the paws of the tender wolf." And females can
be as cruelly rapacious as males, in "The Snow Child" (in which a
decadent nobleman's wife conspires in his brutal rape and murder of a
young girl, the "child of his desire"); and "The Werewolf," in which,
unexpectedly, the grandmother herself is the wolf against whom the
shrewd young virgin must defend herself with her father's knife and a
public denunciation of her grandmother to neighbors: "They knew
the wart on the hand at once for a witch's nipple; they drove the
old woman, in her shift as she was, out into the snow with sticks,
beating her old carcass as far as the edge of the forest, and pelted
her with stones until she fell down dead." The tale ends abruptly
with the girl (never identified as Red Riding Hood) moving into
her grandmother's house and "prospering." *The Bloody Chamber* revels
in such startling reversals, dramatic surprises that suggest the tales'
schematic intentions rather more than they evolve from a graceful
conjunction of character and tale itself.

Like Sexton's more slapdash, idiomatic poems, Carter's prose fictions recapitulate familiar fairy-tale forms from radical angles of perspective. Sexton's women are trapped in their legends like puppets on
strings, while Carter's are more realized as protagonists, willful and
often perverse creations who define themselves against their seemingly prescribed fates. Not "heroic optimism" after all but "defiant
self-dramatization" most accurately describes the mood of *The Bloody
Chamber.*

Following the innovative tactics of Sexton and Carter, a number of
writers, both female and male, though predominantly female, have
experimented with revisioning the fairy tale in recent years. Though
her story is not derived from a specific source, Rachel Ingalls's novella
Mrs. Caliban is clearly of the fairy-tale/wonder-tale mode, notable for
its matter-of-fact tracing of a companionable love affair between a
housewife and a "frogman"—a creature six feet seven inches tall, indigenous to the Gulf of Mexico. Ingalls's fantasy is compelling for
being so realistic as prose, unlike Angela Carter's baroque fantasies;

though weakened by a hurried, rather sketchy denouement, in which the woman's unfaithful husband dies in a car crash, *Mrs. Caliban* has the melancholy, bittersweet air of a romance that has come to no significant resolution, but simply ends with the departure of the frogman-lover.

Like Ingalls's alien being, the mysterious green-skinned children of John Crowley's "The Green Child" (collected in Crowley's slender volume of fabulist tales, *Antiquities,* 1993) have come from a world, or a counterworld, to which they can never return: ". . . from a land below the earth [where] there is always twilight. Whatever is an exit from that country . . . cannot be an entrance." This enigmatic tale of children who have lost their way out of their own world and are exiled in another opens: "This story is recorded by Ralph of Coggeshall and by William of Newbridge, both of whom say it took place in their time, in the middle of the twelfth century, in West Suffolk." The mode of narration is resolutely undramatic, however astonishing the events narrated. One of the green-skinned children, a boy, dies of malnourishment; the other, a girl, survives, able to consume human food and, in time, losing most of her green color—"though her eyes remained large and strangely golden, like a cat's, and she never grew to proper size." Like most of the tales of *Antiquities*, "The Green Child" invites symbolic interpretation while pressing for no obvious meaning; nor does it move to a dramatic resolution, inviting us to ponder the mystery of "fairy" children as they might have been perceived in an authentic historic setting. The surviving girl marries, but

> . . . if there were children, and children of those children, so that in some way that green land elsewhere and also the distant bright country glimpsed across the wide river entered our plain human race, it must surely be so diluted now, so bound up and drowned in daylight and red blood, as not to be present in us at all.

Some of our most distinguished contemporary writers have drawn imaginatively upon archetypal fairy tales, interpreting them in a distinctly feminist manner. Jane Smiley's *A Thousand Acres*, for instance, is a realistically rendered revisioning of Shakespeare's *King Lear*, itself a bold revision of an ancient Anglo-Saxon legend (in which not daughters but sons "betray" the aging former king); in Smiley's interpretation, the tragic action derives not from the experience of the tyrannical, self-absorbed father, a Midwestern farmer whose ambition has been to own "a thousand acres," but from the largely repressed, debilitating experience of his three daughters, who have been victims of their father's incestuous lust. (Significantly, the old man never acknowledges his brutal exploitation of his daughters, never repents.) Margaret Atwood's *The Robber Bride* is an ebullient, rather farcical modern-day variant of the nightmare tale of female victimization, and her more realistically depicted short story "Bluebeard's Egg" conflates variants of the classic Bluebeard legend, including a little-known version that predates Perrault. In this variant, not a key but an egg is the object of Bluebeard's temptation of his young wife. At the conclusion of Atwood's story we are left to contemplate with the betrayed and now frightened housewife-heroine her mysterious husband, a surgeon, who in his impenetrable maleness would seem to be, himself, Bluebeard's egg: "This is something the story left out, Sally thinks: the egg is alive, and one day it will hatch. But what will come out of it?"

In Shirley Jackson's curious version of the Bluebeard legend, "The Honeymoon of Mrs. Smith" (subtitled "The Mystery of the Murdered Bride"), a story never published during the author's lifetime but probably written in the early 1960s, the murderous husband's seventh wife "Mrs. Smith" is mysteriously, maddeningly passive in her role as victim, as the Bluebeard figure is himself passive. The author seems to be suggesting in this enigmatic, rather low-keyed tale that the Bluebeard archetype of the murdering husband/helpless bride repeats, and repeats, and repeats through history; individuals lack all volition, caught in the impersonal cycle of murderer and victim, sexual psychopath and bride. The story ends:

"A week of marriage was too much for you," [Mr. Smith] said, and patted her hand. "We'll have to see that you get more rest."

Why does it take so long, why *does* it take so long? Mrs. Smith thought . . . and turned and said to her husband, "Well?"

"I suppose so," Mr. Smith said, and got up wearily from the couch.

A. S. Byatt's "The Story of the Eldest Princess" mimics the quest motif of fairy tales and legends by following the episodic fortunes of a princess who seems to know that she is "caught in a story" not of her own devising; her encounter with an old woman (fairy godmother) instructs her to find a way out by realizing that "many things may and do happen, stories change themselves, and these stories are not histories and have not happened." In "Ursus Triad, Later" by Kathe Koja and Barry N. Malzberg, the tale of "Goldilocks and the Three Bears" is transmogrified as a hallucinatory erotic fantasy of Goldilocks's sexual subjugation to the bears, her masochistic accommodation to violation by the nonhuman: "You wanted to be filled? their postures asked her as they came upon her. Then *be* filled. To bursting." The innocent virgin becomes, through sexual degradation, Queen of the Bears, "the queen of the magic forest and the empty house, daughter of the night born to gambol in stricken and ecstatic pleasure . . . to pour and fill and to become." Beneath the classic fairy tale of a child blundering into a house not her own, a self-annihilating fantasy.

That the artful revisioning of fairy tales has become a popular genre is attested by the commercial success of a series of anthologies edited by Ellen Datlow and Terri Windling with such titles as *Black Thorn, White Rose*; *Snow White, Blood Red*; *Ruby Slippers, Golden Tears*. Among these stories is a variant of "Beauty and the Beast" titled "The Beast," by Tanith Lee, in which the inner, secret bestial nature of a handsome princelike lover is revealed at his death; a variant of "Hansel and Gretel" by Gahan Wilson updates the fairy tale to the Depression, conjoining it with a parable of wealth, privilege, and exploitation in which brother and sister coolly supplant the malevolent witch who would destroy them. Kathe Koja's "Waking the Prince" reverses stereotypical male activity and female passivity in a narrative that moves in parallel time dimensions, one quaintly fairy-tale and the other achingly contemporary. "The Huntsman's Story" by Milbre Burch is an anti–fairy tale about a psychotic serial killer and a child victim (Polly Klass) abducted by a parolee with a lengthy criminal record and murdered in California several years ago. The deep melancholy of the narrative excludes all magical transformations, the sleight-of-hand of elevated language:

She followed him mutely, not out of literary convention, but because he bound her mouth with duct tape. . . . No seven small men to befriend her. When it's time, there will be six pallbearers. The huntsman came unbidden.

It is instructive to note that the contemporary fairy tale in its revised, re-imagined form has evolved into an art form that subverts original models; from the woman's (victim's) perspective, the romance of fairy tales is an illusion, to be countered by wit, audacity, skepticism, cynicism, an eloquently rendered rage.

NOTES

Works consulted in the preparation of this essay are:

The Complete Grimm's Fairy Tales (Pantheon, 1972)

The Classic Fairy Tales, edited by Iona and Peter Opie (Oxford University Press, 1992)

From the Beast to the Blonde: On Fairy Tales and Their Tellers by Marina Warner (Farrar, Straus, & Giroux, 1994)

The Complete Poems of Anne Sexton (Houghton Mifflin, 1981)

Burning Your Boats: The Collected Short Stories by Angela Carter (Holt, 1995)

Mrs. Caliban by Rachel Ingalls (The Harvard Common Press, 1983)

Antiquities by John Crowley (Incunabula, Seattle, 1993)

A Thousand Acres by Jane Smiley (HarperCollins, 1991)

Bluebeard's Egg by Margaret Atwood (Houghton Mifflin, 1986)

Just an Ordinary Day by Shirley Jackson (Bantam, 1996)

Caught in a Story: Contemporary Fairy Tales and Fables, edited by Christine Park and Caroline Heaton (Vintage, England, 1992); contains "The Story of the Eldest Princess" by A. S. Byatt

Off Limits: Tales of Alien Sex, edited by Ellen Datlow (St. Martin's Press, 1996); contains "Ursus Triad, Later" by Kathe Koja and Barry N. Malzberg

Ruby Slippers, Golden Tears, edited by Ellen Datlow and Terri Windling (William Morrow, 1995)

The Aesthetics of Fear

The oldest and strongest emotion of mankind is fear, and the oldest and strongest kind of fear is fear of the unknown.
—H. P. Lovecraft, "Supernatural Horror in Literature"

There are far worse things awaiting than death.
—*Dracula* (Tod Browning's film, 1931)

Why should we wish to experience fear? What is the mysterious appeal, in the structured coherences of art, of such dissolving emotions as anxiety, dislocation, terror? Is fear a singular, universal experience, or is it ever-shifting, undefinable? We can presume that the aesthetic fear is not an authentic fear but an artful simulation of what is crude, inchoate, nerve-driven, and ungovernable in life; its evolutionary advantage must be the preparation for the authentic experience, unpredictable and always imminent. In times of war and social upheaval, suicide is reported to be virtually unknown, for life, the merest shred of life, becomes infinitely precious. (The troubled Bruno Bettelheim, who eventually committed suicide at the age of eighty-six, remarked that his year in Buchenwald and Dachau was the only time in his life when he was free of thoughts of suicide.) In authentically fearful times, the aesthetic fear is redundant. As Shakespeare's Edgar remarks in *King Lear*, "The worst is not / So long as we can say, 'This is the worst.' "

In the earliest of our consummate art works of fear, Homer's *Iliad* and *Odyssey*, composed nearly three thousand years ago and in many ways strikingly contemporary, a primitive and continuous brutality is made "aesthetic"—that is, palliative and negotiable—by the poet's highly stylized language. In Homer's terms: How is one to confront fear? How is one to emerge a "hero"? The Greeks who constituted

Homer's audience would surely have recoiled in horror from scenes of actual brutality like those celebrated in the poems, as we would, but the strategy of the poems is to present horror through the prism of a reflective consciousness; moreover, the *Iliad* and the *Odyssey* present prehistory, a mythic time now past; we understand that by the time of the poem's composition the warrior-heroes of the Trojan War are long dead, and even Odysseus the man of twists and turns has died his incongruously peaceful, gentle death. All that has happened has happened: ". . . hurling down to the House of Death so many sturdy souls, / great fighters' souls, but made their bodies carrion, / feasts for the dogs and birds." (*Iliad*, Book 1, 3–5. Translated by Robert Fagles.) The *Odyssey* is similarly retrospective though much looser in structure than the *Iliad*, picaresque and seemingly improvised in its succession of vivid, cinematic adventures; its horrors are more primitive than those of the *Iliad*, many of them the actions of monsters: the man-devouring Cyclops, the cannibal giants of Laestrygonia, the fantastical Scylla ("the yelping horror, / . . . twelve legs, all writhing, dangling down / and six swaying necks, a hideous head on each, / each head barbed with a triple row of fangs, thickset, / packed tight—armed to the hilt with black death!") and equally "awesome" Charybdis. Yet the most haunting horror of the *Odyssey* is probably, for most readers, the House of Death, where "burnt-out wraiths of mortals make their home"; ghosts emitting "high thin cries / as bats cry in the depths of a dark haunted cavern." The two Odysseyan visits to the underworld of bodiless, brain-damaged wraiths are disturbing in ways difficult to explain; evoking, perhaps, those dream-locked fugues of paralysis when we are neither fully unconscious nor conscious, knowing ourselves in a dream state yet unable to wake, our "souls" trapped in useless bodies. (Some stroke victims are believed to experience this living hell.) It's an unexpected moment in the *Odyssey* when the heroic Achilles, the hero of the Trojan War, now a ghost, says bitterly to the still-living Odysseus, "I'd rather slave on earth for another man— / . . . than rule down here over all the breathless dead"—so repulsive is death that the Greeks' highest value, the glory of the warrior-hero, is repudiated by the most celebrated warrior-hero of them all.

In Ovid's *Metamorphoses*, an approximate thousand years later, a

similarly prehistoric, mythic world is evoked, characterized by nearly
continuous scenes of brutality, violence, and horror. A kind of cosmo-
logical ether or amniotic fluid seems to contain all living things so
that, destroyed in our current form, we are merely transformed (by
the caprice of gods) into another form; yet terror is real enough,
physical humiliation, dismemberment, agony. Ovid's world is both
hallucinatory and matter-of-fact. No matter how frequently we read
the story of "guiltless" Actaeon we're struck by the meta-horror of
the young hunter's fate when turned by Diana into a stag: "There is
one thing only / Left him, his former mind." (Book 3, 204–5. Translated by Rolfe Humphries.) The peculiar Ovidean sadism of this
story resides in the irony of Actaeon's pursuit and dismemberment
by his own faithful hounds: "Blackfoot, Trailchaser, Hungry, Hurri-
cane, / Gazelle and Mountain-Ranger, Spot and Sylvan, / Swift Wing-
foot, Glen, wolf-sired, and the bitch Harpy / With her two pups . . . /
Tigress, another bitch, Hunter, and Lanky, / Chop-jaws, and Soot,
and Wolf, with the white marking / On his black muzzle, Moun-
taineer and Power, / The Killer, Whirlwind, Whitey, Blackskin,
Grabber, / And others it would take too long to mention . . . / [They]
lacerate and tear their prey, not master, / No master whom they
know, only a deer." Evoked with similarly vivid images is the rape
and mutilation of the virgin Philomela by the "savage" Tereus, who,
to prevent his victim informing on him, cuts out her tongue: "The
mangled root / Quivered, the severed tongue along the ground / Lay
quivering, making a little murmur, / Jerking and twitching, the way
a serpent does / Run over by a wheel, and with its dying movement /
Came to its mistress's feet. And even then— / It seems too much to
believe—even then, Tereus / Took her, and took her again, the injured body / Still giving satisfaction to his lust." To revenge this
atrocity, Philomela's sister, Tereus' wife and the mother of his son,
commits an atrocity of her own: she cuts up the boy "still living, still
keeping something of the spirit" and feeds him to his unknowing
father, who, eating, is "almost greedy / On the flesh of his own flesh."
At last Philomela, Procne, and Tereus are metamorphosed into birds
bearing appropriate characteristics—blood-colored feathers, a sword-
like beak. Human beings, victims and victimizers alike, frequently

become birds in Ovid; and beasts; trees, flowers, fountains, and streams; rocks and stone; or, like Echo, the most subtle of metamorphoses, "voice only." What seems to elude them is common humanity: No one is changed into another person. At the conclusion of this remarkable work of horror mitigated by art, Ovid speaks in his own voice: "Now I have done my work. It will endure, / I trust, beyond Jove's anger, fire and sword, / Beyond Time's hunger . . . Part of me, / The better part, immortal, will be borne / Above the stars . . . / I shall be read, and through all centuries, / . . . I shall be living, always." The motive for art is bound up with a childlike wish to be immortal; what is the "aesthetic of fear" but the vehicle by which fear (of mortality, oblivion) is obviated? At least temporarily.

In these great works of the ancient world, existential horror would seem to be the result not of human volition and responsibility but of mere chance: the cruel caprice of gods. We are struck by how often anxiety is attached to acts of eating and of being eaten: devoured by monsters or by one's own kind. The *Odyssey* might be seen, from a certain perspective, as a succession of meals devoured by ravenous jaws. Our earliest fears are associated with being hungry and being fed and with our mothers' nourishing presence, or lack of it; since as helpless infants we can't feed ourselves, we must *be fed*, as mere mouths. This involves an agent, seemingly godlike, beyond our comprehension and control yet bound to us by the deepest physical intimacy. So the gods of antiquity are but "immortal" versions of mortal men and women, bizarre extended families ruled by figures of ambivalence like Zeus. To the more modern sensibility, post-Ovid, imbued with a Manichean/Christian metaphysics, it isn't chance but "evil" and its personification in Satan that tempts mankind into sin—thereby taking his immortality from him. The phenomenon of Dracula and the vampire legend generally can only be understood as a melding of ancient, that is pagan, and more modern, Christian anxieties: not simply that we are the hapless victims of absurd, violent, dehumanizing, and dismembering fates, to be devoured and dissolved back into brainless nature, but that, succumbing to the vampire's temptation, we are complicit in our own fate. Something in us wants to be seduced, violated, transformed; our innocence, like our virginity, torn

from us. The ancient world posits atrocities *out there*; the Christian-
ized world posits atrocities *in here*, in the soul. Dracula, the quasi-
human villain of Bram Stoker's mythopoetic novel of 1897, is clearly
akin to Satan, and to Bluebeard, the malevolent European nobleman
celebrated through centuries in fairy tales and folk ballads, who
courted and won any number of virginal young brides, bringing
them to his castle, forbidding them to enter a certain chamber—
which of course the young brides do, and must, each in turn, accursed
by her own curiosity, like Eve eating the apple and like Pandora opening the box that contains the world's ills. The victim is
to blame—isn't this always the case, especially when the victim
is female?

Count Bluebeard is no ordinary brute and murderer, of whom, in
fairy tales and ballads, there is no short supply, but a seducer, like
Satan. The story of "La Barbe-Bleue" was recorded by Charles Perrault in his monumental *Histoires ou contes du temps passé*, 1697. The
first English translation was by Robert Samber, 1729, and became
the basis for numerous woodcut illustrations of a popular sensational-
ist nature. In the Perrault version, the Blue Beard, as he is called, is finally killed by the brothers of one of his young wives; he leaves no
heirs, and so she inherits all his wealth—a happy ending, apparently.
Yet, in popular legend, Bluebeard continued to thrive even as his
bride-victims multiplied, doomed to anonymity. Do Bluebeard's
wives—do Dracula's victims—*want* to be violated, to be victims?—
to align themselves not with Christ but with Christ's nemesis, Satan?
No—but yes. Apparently, yes. In Bram Stoker's *Dracula*, which
would come to be the most popular of all English fin-de-siècle stories
for film, Jonathan Harker speaks for many a victim of romantic
supernatural forces in saying, in a passionate outburst near the conclusion of the novel, "Do you know what the place is? Have you seen
that awful den of hellish infamy—with the very moonlight alive
with grisly shapes, and every speck of dust that whirls in the wind a
devouring monster in embryo? Have you felt the Vampire's lips upon
your throat?" Harker's actual experience in the count's castle has been
significantly different, and here we have the heart of the vampire's
secret, unspeakable appeal. Harker has been approached in his sleep
by one of Dracula's sisters, a "fair girl" with "honey-sweet" breath in

which there is a faint scent of a "bitter offensiveness, as one smells in blood." She bends over his motionless form, gloating;

> there was a deliberate voluptuousness that was both thrilling and repulsive, and as she arched her neck she actually licked her lips like an animal, till I could see in the moonlight the moisture shining on the scarlet lips and on the red tongue as it lapped the white sharp teeth. Lower and lower went her head as the lips went below the range of my mouth and chin and seemed about to fasten on my throat. Then she paused, and I could hear the churning sound of her tongue as it licked her teeth and lips, and could feel the hot breath on my neck. Then the skin of my throat began to tingle as one's flesh does when the hand that is to tickle it approaches nearer—nearer. I could feel the soft, shivering touch of the lips on the super-sensitive skin of my throat, and the hard dents of two sharp teeth, just touching and pausing there. I closed my eyes in a languorous ecstasy and waited—waited with beating heart.

The powerful appeal of the Gothic world is that its inhabitants, who resemble civilized and often attractive men and women, are in reality creatures of primitive instinct. Gratification is all, and it is usually immediate—to *wish* is to *act*. Yet more magically, our own ethical behavior is suspended, for any means are justified in destroying the vampire. We ourselves can become savages in a good Christian cause. The most revealing episode in *Dracula* is the most luridly erotic and misogynist: the killing of Lucy Westenra's vampire-self by the men bent upon "saving" her. Here, a communion of blood brotherhood is enacted that parodies the Christian ritual of purification and atonement. The virginal Lucy, it seems, has died; a vampire-Lucy has taken her place, Dracula's bride; she is a "nightmare" with pointed teeth, a bloodstained, voluptuous mouth, the entire "carnal and unspirited appearance" a devilish mockery of the former Lucy's purity; naturally she must be killed, but according to ritual. Led by the insufferably righteous vampire expert Van Helsing, the men place the point of a stake over the slumbering Lucy's heart, recite a prayer for the dead, and strike in God's name; with these spectacular results:

The Thing in the coffin writhed; and a hideous, blood-curdling screech came from the opened red lips. The body shook and quivered and twisted in wild contortions; the sharp white teeth champed together till the lips were cut, and the mouth was smeared with a crimson foam. But Arthur never faltered. He looked like a figure of Thor as his untrembling arm rose and fell, driving deeper and deeper the mercy-bearing stake, whilst the blood from the pierced heart welled and spurted up around it. His face was set, and high duty seemed to shine through it; the sight of it gave us courage so that our voices seemed to ring through the little vault.

And then the writhing and quivering of the body became less, and the teeth seemed to champ, and the face to quiver. Finally it lay still. The terrible task was over. . . .

There, in the coffin lay no longer the foul Thing that we had so dreaded and grown to hate that the work of her destruction was yielded as a privilege to the one best entitled to it, but Lucy as we had seen her in her life, with her face of unequalled sweetness and purity.

Where except in a Gothic dimension in which "high Christian duty" mingles with violent sexual sadism might such an episode occur? The stake pounded into the female vampire's heart is "mercy-bearing"—the entire procedure performed in the name of God the Father—as if rape and death, the particular province of the male aggressor, might be a kind of absolution. Since the "sacrifice" is in the service of religion, it might even be portrayed as altruistic. And if vampirism is erotic experience, we see how a woman must be punished, at least in Stoker's Victorian terms, for the awakening of her forbidden sexuality.

In the Gothic imagination, the unconscious has erupted and has seeped out into "the world." As if our most disturbing, unacknowledged dreams had broken their restraints, claiming autonomy. The profane and the sacred become indistinguishable: Dracula, immortal so long as he is infused with the blood of living creatures, becomes for certain of his victims a perversely life-bearing force, ironically not unlike the Christian savior. For those whom he blesses, he can transform into vampires like himself. This is the unique vampire attraction, one might say; very different from the fates of those simply devoured, and digested, by such monsters as the Cyclops. The most striking aspect of Tod Browning's film *Dracula* (1931), famously starring Bela Lugosi, is its grave, ritualistic, sacerdotal quality. Here, Count Dracula is no quasi-human bat-faced creature with a fetid breath, as in the crude Stoker novel, or an alarmingly Semitic buck-fanged hook-nosed rodent as in the silent German film by F. W. Murnau *Nosferatu* (1922). (Though in all respects, as a work of visually poetic art, the Murnau film is far superior to the film by Browning.) Instead, Dracula is an elegant European gentleman, a reincarnation of the fatally charming Blue Beard; his formal evening wear, high starched collar, and long black cape suggest the vestments of a Catholic priest, as do his carefully choreographed movements and the studied precision with which he speaks English, as if it were a very foreign language. (Lugosi memorized his lines phonetically.) Where in the Murnau film Dracula is subhuman and lacking all attraction, indeed a carrier of bubonic plague like any infected rat, in the Browning film Dracula is heightened as a charismatic screen presence. There is a brilliant audacity in aligning vampire and priest, for in Catholic ritual the priest celebrating the Mass drinks the "blood" of Christ (diluted red wine) out of a chalice, as the congregation prays, in the solemn moments leading to the dramatic sacrament of Holy Communion when communicants come forward to receive from the priest, on their tongues, a consecrated wafer representing the body of Christ. Until fairly recent times, the priest intoned at this moment, in Latin, *Hic est corpus Christus*. This is the body of Christ.

Protestants, Jews, believers of other faiths may find it difficult to comprehend, or frankly preposterous: the Roman Catholic Communion does not offer to communicants a mere symbol of Christ's body and blood but, through the mystery of "transubstantiation," that very body and blood. Christ's Last Supper as recorded in the Gospels is a symbolic ritual in a way that the Catholic Communion is not.

What are we to make of these charismatic fantasy figures, vampire and savior? Vampire-as-savior? Count Dracula and Jesus Christ? To merely categorize them as fantasies, springing from childlike, if not infantile, wishes for immortality, is too schematic, reductive. Personifying "evil"—like personifying "good"—is a human attempt to exert control over the incalculable and impersonal forces of nature of which (though we imagine ourselves superior because we possess the gift of language) we are a part, but only an infinitesimal part. Bram Stoker wrote *Dracula* in the waning years of the nineteenth century, in a time of intellectual and religious crisis; like Lewis Carroll in the very different but equally mythopoetic *Alice's Adventures in Wonderland* and *Through the Looking Glass* of some years before (1865, 1872), Stoker was dramatizing the clash of Darwinian evolutionary theory with traditional Christian-humanist sentiment. (Of course, Christianity triumphs at the melodramatic conclusion of *Dracula*—this is the obligatory Victorian happy ending.) In the austere Darwinian model of our beleaguered Earth, the individual counts for virtually nothing; only the species matters, the replication of DNA; yet, as we humanists are informed by our scientist colleagues, to our dismay, if not to our surprise, even the species doesn't really count—more than 99 percent of all species that have ever existed on Earth are now extinct. What does this seem to predict for our aggressive, fear-ridden, and paranoid species? In the benign Christian model, however, the individual is all: Christ died for each of us, as individuals, and we are redeemed by His sacrifice. If this is a fantasy, shared, in other terms, with other religions, it's at least an imaginative one, a powerful antidote to the "aesthetic of fear."

To return to the question: Why should we wish to experience fear, if only aesthetically? Why do we wish as a species to approach the unspeakable, the unknowable, the vision that, like Medusa with her horrific head of serpents, will prove unbearable? In H. P. Lovecraft's Gothic classic "The Rats in the Walls," this forbidden vision is given a lurid Boschean grandeur as the story's doomed protagonist experiences a revelation in "those grinning caverns of earth's center where Nyarlathotep, the mad faceless god, howls blindly in the darkness to the piping of two amorphous flute-players." In other words: madness. The total disintegration of mind and language: our humanity. "The Rats in the Walls" ends with a brilliantly realized devolution of the protagonist as he regresses through stages of consciousness represented by stages of the English language, back through Middle English, Old English, to mere bestial grunts—and cannibalism. Classic Gothic literature asks: How human are we? How deep is our humanness? Is the vampire a monster, or is the vampire a natural extension of our human-animal selves? Anxiety arises when we ponder to what degree we share in the civilization to which we belong. The most extreme "fall" is to revert to vampirism/cannibalism, violating the taboo against eating human flesh but also the taboo of acknowledging that the eating of human flesh is a possibility; looking upon one another as not spiritual beings but mere meat. To succumb to such a revelation is, in Lovecraft's cosmos, to succumb to madness; for sanity collapses at this crucial point. As Lovecraft says in his parable-like "The Call of Cthulhu,"

> The most merciful thing in the world . . . is the inability of the human mind to correlate all its contents. We live on a placid island of ignorance in the midst of black seas of infinity, and it was not meant that we should voyage far.

What we most fear, I suggest, is not death; nor even physical anguish, mental decay, disintegration. We fear most the loss of meaning. To lose meaning is to lose one's humanity, and this is more terrifying than death; for death itself, in a coherent cultural context, always has meaning. It is the anxiety of the individual that the very species may become extinct in our complicity with the predator— the cannibal/vampire—within. These fears, these anxieties, these recurring and compulsive nightmares, so powerfully dramatized by artists of the tragic and the grotesque through centuries, are not aberrations of the psyche but the psyche's deepest and most profound revelations. The aesthetics of fear is the aesthetics of our common humanity.

Art and Ethics?
—The (F)Utility of Art

Nothing beyond the State, above the State, against the State. Everything to the State, for the State, in the State.

—Benito Mussolini

All art is quite useless.

—Oscar Wilde

The issue for the artist, of course, is: whose ethics? whose morality? whose standards of propriety? whose community? whose censors? whose judges?—prosecutors?—jailers?—executioners? whose State?

The customs of the tribe may seem to outside witnesses to be as arbitrary as language itself—language, in which words for *things* are understood to be *not-things*—but, within the tribe, they are rarely negotiable. Still less are they violable by the individual except at great risk. (As the distressing case of Salman Rushdie has made clear.) Whatever "taboo" is, out of what chthonian darkness it arises, one thing about "taboo" is clear: You violate it only at a price. The reigning ethics of a society is the stone wall against which the individual may fling himself, to no avail—or be flung, and broken. As the poet Frank Bidart says in one of his poems from *In the Western Night: Collected Poems 1965–90*:

1. Man is a MORAL animal.
2. You can get human beings to do anything—IF you convince them it is moral.
3. You can convince human beings anything is moral.

Even if one does not incur the wrath of the authorities, or, in a "free" democracy like our own, the wrath of elected or self-appointed censors, the artist's relationship to ethics is always problematic, paradoxical. Always there is the question not only of whose ethics but the issue of art's purpose in the community: If art exists as a medium by which "ethical" messages are conveyed, an implicit morality sanctioned, why trouble with "art" at all? Why the ambiguous—and ambagious—strategies of "art"? "If I had a message," Ernest Hemingway is said to have said, "I would send a telegram." This witty rejoinder makes us laugh, suggesting as it does a naive question or an impertinent demand; yet, in more elevated quarters, where the artist is not under attack but indeed may be highly respected, it is common to encounter questions of "theme," "vision," "worldview," as if such might be extracted from the body of the artist's work; as if such were somehow distinct and separable from the experience of the art work itself, available for a sort of economical freeze-drying. *What was your purpose in writing this? What were you trying to convey? Is this how you see the world?*

In the artist's own experience, of course, art is fundamentally indefinable, unsayable; there is something sacred about its demands upon the soul, something inherently mysterious in the forms it takes, no less than in its contents. Henry James's metaphor of the art of fiction as a "dim underworld, [a] great glazed tank of art" in which "strange subjects float" is a compelling one, in the parable-like story "The Middle Years," as is his rhapsodic insistence upon the essential "madness" of art at the conclusion of that story. Here is a contemporary novelist, Marilynne Robinson:

> The novel cherishes what is unuttered, uncountenanced, uninvolved—the heart's darkness and bitterness. It will not embarrass the guiltiest secret with revelation. All sorts of questions flourish in this murky atmosphere. What is the self? How does identity take shape? . . . What is guilt and how is it to be borne in the absence of justice or expiation? These questions change as soon as they are put into words because they have their most profound meaning as sensation, in aching discomforts like loneliness, awkwardness, emptiness, and dread.

All writers know this truth: *things change as they are put into words because they have their most profound meaning as sensation,* the heart's passion and conviction prior to any linguistic effort to explain, express, summarize, dramatize. We *know*—before we comprehend the terms of our very *knowing.* We violate the beautiful subtleties of our art by speaking reductively of it, yet how else can we speak of it, at all? Or perhaps we cannot, and should not, except in the very terms of art:

> Tell all the Truth but tell it slant—
> Success in Circuit lies
> Too bright for our infirm Delight
> The Truth's superb surprise
> As Lightning to the Children eased
> With explanation kind
> The Truth must dazzle gradually
> Or every man be blind.

(Emily Dickinson, 1129, c. 1868)

"Art" does after all suggest "artifice"—even "artificial." Certainly it stands in a pertinent relationship to "nature"—"natural." But the enemies of art deny this metaphysical distinction, equating what is metaphorical with their perception of what is "real," as if a photograph of a landscape were the landscape, or a word the very thing or concept it indicates, with the power, too, to do harm. And the artist's power to question authority, expose hypocrisy and fraud has always evoked fear in the custodians of the State.

Yet the artist is the perpetual antagonist of what is fixed and "known"—what is "moral," "ethical," "good." If it is suggested, however obliquely, that the artist should do x, y, z, he or she instinctively responds, like Stephen Dedalus of *A Portrait of an Artist*, "I will not serve." In its earliest energies in the individual, art is likely to be expressive of adolescent rebellion, for the typical artist begins in adolescence, defining him- or herself against family, authority, a world of elders.

The voice of rebellion runs through our classic American literature, which is on the whole a youthful, idiosyncratic, defiant voice. It is the voice of which Melville approves so passionately in Hawthorne's *Mosses from an Old Manse*: "There is the grand truth about Nathaniel Hawthorne. He says NO! in thunder; but the Devil himself cannot make him say *yes*." Unheroic in every way except the most crucial is Melville's Bartleby the Scrivener, whose response to every reasonable suggestion put to him is the terse "I would prefer not to"—Bartleby, formerly of the Dead Letter Office in Washington, who eventually, like Kafka's Hunger Artist, starves to death out of sheer stubborn isolation from mankind. Our most subversive poetic voice of the nineteenth century is surely Emily Dickinson, whose stubborn sense of her own worth sustained her through the composing of 1,775 remarkable poems, most of them unpublished and unknown during her lifetime. Dickinson was the only member of her family not to declare herself a Christian; her quick, sly observations on the subject of God suggest a skeptic's detachment and bemusement:

> Drowning is not so pitiful
> As the attempt to rise.
> Three times, 'tis said, a sinking man
> Comes up to face the skies,
> And then declines forever
> To that abhorred abode,
> Where hope and he part company—
> For he is grasped of God.
> The Maker's cordial visage,
> However good to see,
> Is shunned, we must admit it,
> Like an adversity.

(1718, ?)

This is hardly the sort of genteel ladies' verse, whether written by female or male poets, likely to have been published in general-interest magazines like *The Atlantic Monthly* in Dickinson's time. Nor

> God is indeed a jealous God—
> He cannot bear to see

That we had rather not with Him
But with each other play.

(1719, ?)

The very look of Dickinson's poetry on the page, its breathless word
clusters that suggest not the ponderousness of polished lines but the
rapid flight of thought, is boldly iconoclastic; her slant rhymes, perverse off-rhythms and fading or broken-off cadences suggest a virtual
meta-poetry, a poetry of a heightened self-consciousness, starkly contemporary with our own time. This is a poetic imagination capable of
expressing, in the most compact space, the most expansive emotions.
Dickinson's "I"-narrator is both an individual of singular ferocity
and a representative figure, most frequently, though not exclusively,
female:

They shut me up in Prose—
As when a little Girl
They put me in the Closet—
Because they liked me "still"—
Still! Could themself have peeped—
And seen my Brain—go round—
They might as wise have lodged a Bird
For Treason—in the Pound— . . .

(613, c. 1862)

—the "female" is trapped within the "feminine." There is evidence in
certain of the poems that, for all her reclusiveness, Emily Dickinson had
a sense of her own genius; she inhabited so intense and all-consuming
an interior world, how could an "exterior" world compete?

In other, seemingly rawer poems, turbulence is the subject itself;
the mind's terrifying autonomy, the poet's self-surrender to passion,
dissolution, madness—

The Brain, within its Groove
Runs evenly—and true—
But let a Splinter swerve—
'Twere easier for You—

To put a Current back—
When Floods have slit the Hills—
And scooped a Turnpike for Themselves—
And trodden out the Mills—

(556, c. 1862)

The quintessentially *visible* poet of rebellion is the dandy; the androgyne; the celebrant of fin-de-siècle excess who, in the style of Baudelaire, Huysmans, flouts not only authority but good taste, prudence, "common" sense. Who else but Oscar Wilde is our exemplar?—he who made the observation that, when giving a public lecture, it is not what one says but what one wears that matters. (Touring the United States and Canada in 1882, lecturing to promulgate "beauty," Wilde chose his eye-catching costumes with care: a great green coat that fell past his ankles, collar and cuffs trimmed with sealskin; another coat lined with lavender silk; shirts with wide Lord Byron collars; brightly colored neckties and handkerchiefs; black velvet suits with puffed upper sleeves and frills of fine lace; knee breeches, black hose, patent leather shoes with bright buckles.) As Wilde's mentor Walter Pater offered a "vision" in *Studies in the History of the Renaissance* (1873) to "regard all things and principles . . . as inconstant modes or fashions"—"to burn always with this hard, gem-like flame, to maintain this ecstasy"—to realize "the truth of aesthetic culture . . . as a new form of the contemplative life"—"for art comes to you proposing frankly to give nothing but the highest quality to your moments as they pass, and simply for those moments' sake"—so Oscar Wilde, with a self-publicist's flair for the provocative, pushes aestheticism to a sort of inverted, or perverted, ethics. "Lying, the telling of beautiful untrue things, is the proper aim of Art," Wilde says in "The Decay of Lying"; and, more famously elsewhere, in the prologue to *The Picture of Dorian Gray* (1891), "No artist has ethical sympathies. An ethical sympathy in an artist is an unpardonable mannerism of style. . . . Vice and virtue are to the artist materials for an art. . . . Those who go beneath the surface do so at their peril. . . . All art is quite useless."

In "Modern Fiction," in *The Common Reader* (1919), Virginia Woolf states boldly that "any method is right, every method is right, that expresses what we wish to express, if we are writers." This is the very soul of Modernism, the declaration of the artist's independence from all prescribed forms of art: the virtual elimination of any awareness of, let alone concession to, a community of readers, an audience whose sympathies should be courted. The artist constitutes his own audience and, in Goethe's terms, is the sole inhabitant of his universe. Voice, style, sheer language become subject: "What seems beautiful to me, what I should like to write, is a book about nothing, a book dependent upon nothing external, which would be held together by the strength of its style," writes Flaubert in a letter of 1861. The self-determining artist becomes an obvious enemy of the State, less in political terms than in moral terms, for nothing so arouses the fury of the puritan temperament as a violation of "taboo"; through history, from the time of Homer to the very present, depictions of violent acts of savagery can be accommodated in art in a way that depictions of sexual acts of even "normal" proportions evidently cannot. The censorious American missionary spirit empowered a crusader named Anthony Comstock, founder of the New York Society for the Suppression of Vice in the waning years of the nineteenth century, to arrest writers, publishers, and booksellers for "violating community standards of Christian decency"; this, the virulent puritanism, whose "democratic" power should not be underestimated, interfered with the publication of various editions of Whitman's *Leaves of Grass*, all but banned Kate Chopin's *The Awakening* in 1899, and destroyed Chopin's career; eviscerated Theodore Dreiser's *Sister Carrie*, banned Joyce's *Ulysses*, served summonses upon booksellers as recently as the late 1950s (in Syracuse, New York) for stocking Lawrence's *Lady Chatterley's Lover*; and threatens writers, publishers, and booksellers at the present time. The hatred of the most reactionary citizens for those citizens perceived as "free-thinking"—as enemies—is always astonishing to the artistic temperament, for it seems so disproportionate to our perception of our own power, political or otherwise. One violates "ethics"—whatever, in the community, "ethics" precisely *is*—at one's own risk.

From other quarters, in different epochs, have come other demands upon the imaginative artist, other expectations of the uses to which individual talent might be put. From the ideological camp of Mussolini et al. on the Fascist right, from the ideological camp of Marx, Lenin, Trotsky, et al. on the Communist-Socialist left, the insistence is that art is a function of society; the artist's soul belongs to the State. And if the artist rebels?—the State can respond with censorship, imprisonment, exile, death. Plato, lover of the Good, nonetheless argued for the banishment of the poet from his idealized totalitarian Republic; by his own cruel logic, how could he have disapproved of the execution of Socrates? Always there have been artists who are themselves ideologues, and some of these are major talents; George Orwell, for instance, who declared that his work was written "*against* totalitarianism and *for* democratic Socialism." In this context, it is not surprising that other artists reacted with aristocratic disdain. In his essay "Art as Establisher of Value," Wallace Stevens boldly remarks, "I might be expected to speak of the social, that is the sociological or political, obligation of the poet. He has none." Vladimir Nabokov snubbed "ideas" entirely: "Mediocrity thrives on 'ideas.' " His loathing of idea-mongers, as he called them, like Dostoyevsky, Gorki, Mann, Orwell, Freud ("Dr. Froid," "that Viennese quack"), and his reaction against didactic, "realistic" art have their basis in personal, if unarticulated, politics of an extreme conservative nature. (Nabokov detested and seems to have feared homosexuals, for instance; thus "homosexuals," as he imagines them, are portrayed with contempt in his work as signs or symbols of disease.) For Nabokov, a work of fiction is only justified if it supplies "what I shall bluntly call aesthetic bliss" (Afterword, *Lolita*). Echoing one of his masters, Walter Pater, Nabokov remarks in his memoir *Speak, Memory* that pleasure in such moments arises from the conscious savoring of details, of colors, textures, patterns, designs: when "mortality has a chance to peer beyond its own limits." Words are worlds; the world can only be apprehended through the Word. Ordinary reality "begins to rot and stink unless it is transformed by art."

Nabokov's influence was most prevalent in the sixties and seventies, inspiring any number of bright, inventive, iconoclastic younger writers, most of them male. The flattening of fiction's landscape to two dimensions, as in a Magritte painting, and the insistence upon fiction's total lack of relationship to "reality" had its most eloquent polemicist in William Gass, who argues in *The World Within the*

World that poetry is "cathartic" only for the unserious; therapy through art is a "delusion"; a character in a novel is "any linguistic location in a book toward which a great part of the text stands as modifier." The ideal book, therefore, following Flaubert, would have only one character: language itself. Witty and provocative as this aesthetic stance is, its limitations are obvious. Postmodernism—self-reflexive fiction—metafiction—the "Literature of Exhaustion"—"fabulism": Confronted with so many voices trumpeting the Wildean premise that all art is quite useless, the reader is tempted to turn aside from experimental fiction altogether. Younger writers, particularly those whose experience of America differs significantly from the largely unexamined experience of the dominant majority, of white male heterosexuals of the middle, educated class, have returned to other forms of fiction, poetry, and drama. Race, gender, class emerge as perspectives of vision as well as subjects and "issues"; the work of our gifted contemporaries, too rich, too diverse, too many to even begin to name, frequently combines experimental method with storytelling of a traditional sort, "poetic" and "realistic" simultaneously.

If we persist, we come full circle. The shifts and currents of prevailing aesthetics are a great Möbius strip, forever turning upon itself; stimulated by, and reacting against, and again stimulated by the politics of the time. If we are told that art is only for the State, we rebel; if we are told that art is useless, futile, we rebel; we are creatures of self-determination, yet creatures of our time, deeply connected with one another, nourished by one another, defined by one another, in ways impossible to enumerate. Consider, for instance, the Belgian Surrealist René Magritte, creator of "anti-art" images in the 1920s and '30s; the dedicated experimentalist who claimed that, for him, art was a "lamentable expedient" by which thought might be produced. Magritte's most characteristic canvases are thought-parables, paradoxes unrelated to the visual world and explicable solely in terms of ideas (in one famous painting, for example, a canvas depicting a landscape is set before a window opening out upon the "real" landscape; in another famous painting, *The Treachery of Images,* a pipe is displayed above the caption *This is not a pipe*). Magritte rejected as worthless the kind of art designed to evoke emotion in the viewer, as well as art displaying painterly effects. During the Nazi occupation of Belgium, however, the artist found himself suddenly painting in a different mode. Where his art had always been flat, his images generic, monotonic as wallpaper, in this phase of his career, which lasted from the spring of 1943 to 1946, Magritte's canvases erupted in color; the tone of his paintings became bright and joyful; his brushwork took on an Impressionistic quality. In this "Renoir period," Magritte obsessively painted warm, sensuous figures, images clearly intended to evoke emotion, even eroticism. Magritte, the most cerebral of artists, believed that this work was in reaction to the Nazi tyranny and the horror of war: "My work is a counter-offensive."

The artist as perpetual antagonist; the artist as supremely self-determined; the artist as deeply bonded to his or her world, and in a meaningful relationship with a community—this is the artist's ethics, and the artist's aesthetics.

The Romance of Art:
Four Brief Pieces

The Romance of Art

> We dream—it is good we are dreaming—
> It would hurt us—were we awake—
> But since it is playing—kill us,
> And we are playing—shriek—
>
> What harm? Men die—externally—
> It is a truth—of Blood—
> But we—are dying in Drama—
> And Drama—is never dead—
>
> —Emily Dickinson (531, c. 1862)

In a world most accurately and unsentimentally described as a ceaseless storm of Darwinian struggle, for survival as individuals, and for survival as species, in which countless individuals die as the consequence of "natural" predators (the most virulent being microscopic, invisible to the unassisted eye), and of primitive political and religious beliefs (the deaths of Nazi victims, for instance, estimated to be as many as sixteen million men, women, and children, the deaths of Communist victims under Stalin estimated to be as many as twenty million, and yet more millions victims of Chinese Communist ideology—and these horrors in the twentieth century alone)—it is clear that "art" is a frail vessel, an enterprise of a communal sort, dedicated to the proposition that *the individual matters*; indeed, dedicated to the celebration of the individual, in the face of nature's indifference. Tragedy's grandeur is exclusively of the individual in his or her anguished nobility; the tragic hero or heroine suffers, but does not suffer pointlessly, or without eloquence and redeeming insight. On the brink of self-extinction, Shakespeare's Othello continues to command the stage: "Soft you; a word or two before you go. / I have done the state some service, and they know't— / No more of that. I pray you, in your letters, / When you shall these unlucky deeds relate, / Speak of me as I am; nothing extenuate, / Nor set down aught in malice. Then must you speak / Of one that lov'd not wisely but too well; / Of one not easily jealous, but being wrought, / Perplexed in the extreme; of one whose hand, / Like the base [Indian], threw a pearl away / Richer than all his tribe. . . ." (*Othello,* V.ii) The raging despair of Lear at the death of his daughter Cordelia is at once the despair of a great, if flawed, nobleman and the despair of any parent, or any bereaved person contemplating the most profound and intransigent mystery of our lives: ". . . No, no, no life! / Why should a dog, a horse, a rat, have life, / And thou no breath at all? Thou'lt come no more, / Never, never, never, never, never." (*Lear,* V.iii) Profound and intransigent as this mystery is, it is utterly natural, too; it *is* the very signature of Nature.

How readily then, with dreamlike logic, the artist by tradition identifies himself with the materials of his art, which make a claim for "immortality" in defiance of mortality; granted, the individual artist may pass away, but the form of his art, its unique essence, endures. The poets of the Renaissance, of whom Shakespeare is of course the exemplar, seem to us obsessed with what they call "mutability"—the terror of "Devouring Time"; the subterranean theme of Shakespeare's love sonnets is the proposition that the merely mortal be *willed* immortal by way of art's strategems. "So long as men can breathe or eyes can see, / So long lives this, and this gives life to thee." (Sonnet 18) "Yet do thy worst, old Time: despite thy wrong, / My love shall in my verse ever live young." (Sonnet 19) "Your monument shall be my gentle verse, / Which eyes not yet created shall o'er-read, / And tongues to be your being shall rehearse, / When all the breathers of the world are dead; / You shall live (such virtue hath my pen) / Where breath most breathes, even in the mouths of men." (Sonnet 81) The rawer impulse, so sheerly wished, yet so adamantly pronounced, is that, of course, the artist transcends his finite self by way of great and enduring art; it is his, or her, *most valuable* self, consequently "immortal." The analogue with religious redemption is evident: In religion, the "soul" transcends the body, if the believer has conformed to the belief system, and may abide forever with God, in another dimension of being. For those to whom "art" is "God," it can only be "art" that redeems. In the self-pronounced cynic, such sudden revelations are astonishing to us, as, for instance, in the epilogue to that most surreal, hallucinatory, blackly comic and inexhaustibly imaginative work the *Metamorphoses* of Ovid, when the poet drops the mask of art to confide: "Now I have done my work. It will endure, / I trust, beyond Jove's anger, fire and sword, / Beyond Time's hunger. The day will come, I know, / So let it come, that day which has no power / Save over my body, to end my span of life / Whatever it may be. Still, part of me, / The better part, immortal, will be borne / Above the stars; my name will be remembered / Wherever Roman power rules conquered lands, / I shall be read, and through all centuries, / If prophecies of bards are ever truthful, / I shall be living, always." (Translation by Rolfe Humphries) A cri de coeur as passionate as Stendhal's famous prophecy: "I have drawn a lottery ticket whose winning number is: to be read in 1935."

If one feature of romance is its willful defiance of what is perceived to *be*, in the most common commonsensical of meanings, we must acknowledge that the greatest art is "romance"; the fantasy of autogenetic immortality is both childlike and an abiding obsession of genius. Consider an odd, provocative remark of Goethe's: "Is one man alive when others are alive?" Meaning that, is one "being" possible if others, differing from it, are also possible? (We note in passing the valiant machismo of such a proposition. How strangely would it ring on our ears if the lament were "Is one woman alive when others are alive?") In *The Book of Laughter and Forgetting*, Milan Kundera quotes Goethe approvingly, and adds: "By writing books, the individual becomes a universe. . . . And since the principal quality of a universe is its uniqueness, the existence of another universe constitutes a threat to it. . . . A person who writes books is either all (a single universe for himself and everyone else), or nothing. And since *all* will never be given to anyone, every one of us who writes is *nothing*. Ignored, jealous, deeply wounded, we wish the death of our fellow man." (Perhaps Kundera, fleeing Communist-totalitarian Czechoslovakia in 1975, absorbed and carried with him certain of the assumptions of the "totalitarian" imagination: the prescribed, closed universe in which rank and power determine worth.) The impulse to write Kundera defines as "graphomania," a pathology linked to the desire for immortal life: ". . . Everyone has trouble accepting the fact that he will disappear unheard of and unnoticed in an indifferent universe, and everyone wants to make himself into a universe of words before it is too late." In a pluralistic democracy like ours, self-expression has never seemed quite so megalomaniac, nor so pathological: How few of us would rejoice in "being alive" if others were not also "alive"! We are rather more likely to define art as subjectivity, and perhaps the highest and most abiding form of subjectivity; each voice, each talent, each visionary consciousness, each *spiritual phenomenon*, equal to all others, as legitimately positioned within the world. If we define art, too, as a form of sympathy, echoing both George Eliot and D. H. Lawrence, two very different moralists of English prose fiction, we have no difficulty extending the boundaries of the (artist) self to include other selves; in fact, we wish to include other selves, we yearn to know them, to learn from them and to be transformed by them; we would languish without them. The abiding fantasy that art may provide a sort of extra-terrestrial and -temporal haven for the artist is most comically and most touchingly parodied by, of all self-absorbed artists, James Joyce, in the opening chapter of *Ulysses*, in which, with customary irony, young Stephen Dedalus strolls alone, musing: ". . . Books you were going to write with letters for titles. Have you read his F? O yes, but I prefer Q. Yes, but W is wonderful. . . . Remember your epiphanies on green oval leaves, deeply deep, copies to be sent if you died to all the great libraries of the world, including Alexandria? Someone was to read them there after a few thousand years. When one reads these strange pages of one

long gone one feels that one is at one with one who . . ." And Stephen
breaks off with a shrug, as we are invited to, strolling with him.

In the Darwinian drama of history and of nature, then, art is romance; its focus upon the individual, or related groups of individuals, is immensely flattering to the precarious human ego. In place
of the *muteness* that is nature we substitute the musical cadences of
our greatest invention, language. In place of the *amorality* of nature
we substitute moralities of all sorts, including that most civilized
of all genres, the "comedy of manners"—in which individuals are
minutely, fastidiously measured against the ephemeral criteria of
parochial societies' mores, fashions, trends. The brute struggle for
physical existence is not so much denied as, in Emily Dickinson's
terms, co-opted into the drama: "And Drama—is never dead—."
The world beyond the human is given a comfortingly foreshortened
perspective, except in rare instances, in the coldly elegant fiction of
Paul Bowles, for example, or in the elemental allegories of the now
rather underrated Jack London; *we* are in the foreground, *we* matter,
immensely. The background blurs out into faceless, anonymous humanity: into landscape itself, misty and unchartable as the perimeters
of our dreams.

First Principles

The primary intentions of art, and of the artist, are perhaps no
more than two.

(The intentions of this writer, at least.)

They are: the creation of an aesthetic object to exist in the world as
rightfully as any other object; and, the appeal to an audience, or community, or nation, or an entire world, that, by way of this aesthetic
object, these individuals might be moved to human sympathy—that
"enlargement of sympathy" of which D. H. Lawrence speaks in his
commentary on the novel.

1. The creation of the aesthetic object: whatever its type or genre,
a variation upon a strict imitation of life or action (in Aristotelean
terms, "mimesis"); an aim of originality, in concept and execution;
a (possible, private) relationship with other, previous works by the

same artist, as in a continuous dialogue, or tapestry, created over a period of years, if not a lifetime. The writer's subject-within-a-subject is of course language; not *what* is said, but *how* it is said, with what "art." The creation of the object (in this case, writing) is an *aesthetic* activity. Yet it utilizes metaphor and mimesis that are part of a common language. (As Odysseus Elytis remarked: "Landscape is not simply the sum of specific trees and mountains, but a complex signifier, an ethical power mobilized by the human mind.") The intention of the artist is to make of *common* material an *uncommon* artifact. Even where language is employed with virtuoso inspiration, the basic material is shared by all who speak the language. Its existence does not displace any other; allowing even for the finitude of space in which to "store" works of art, greatly magnified in our electronic era, the wonder of art is that it *is* democratic: No novel negates another, no poem extinguishes another. Are we most alive when others are alive in us?

2. The second principle has to do with evoking in the audience or community a sympathetic response. Or any response. This signals the movement outward—it is an ethical gesture, not purely aesthetic. Aristotle, presumably defending poetry against Plato's rigid strictures against the useless excitation of the art, argued that it does in fact have use; its effects are "cathartic"—hygienic, one might say, curative. Emetic? Tragedy is the only genre discussed in detail in the *Poetics*, analyzed by Aristotle in terms that have become virtually universal: the aim of tragedy is declared to be the "purging" of the soul by arousing and then exhausting the passions of pity and terror. The poet is only an imitator (of things as they are, things as they are imagined to be, or things as they ought to be), but his power is to evoke the wonderful, the mysterious and sublime—one might say, the X in the equation, which ordinary discourse can never quite explain, nor yet anticipate. But the art work is contextual, and social; it cannot be but historical. Of course, it frequently happens that the community is not engaged by the art work, and, if it is, not in the way that the artist had wished. Horrific examples abound, one of the more recent being the response of Muslim fundamentalists to Salman Rushdie's novel *The Satanic Verses*—the issuing of a ritual *fatwa*, or death sentence. How many artists through the centuries have been, and continue to be, persecuted for their art—arrested,

tried, fined, imprisoned, executed—"censored"—"banned"; how many critic-legislators have argued, like Plato, that the imaginative arts are dangerous to the State, and must be strictly regulated, simply because they are imaginative. (How chillingly contemporary this passage from Plato's *Laws* sounds to our ears, after more than twenty-three centuries: "No poet shall write any poem that conflicts with what, in accordance to the public standard, is right and lawful, beautiful and good; nor show his compositions to any private individual until they have been submitted to the appointed judges in these matters, and to the guardians of the law, and been officially approved." [VII, 801. Translation by Lane Cooper.]) In a relatively lighter vein, consider the ironic misfiring of Upton Sinclair's *The Jungle*, a crusading Socialist novel of 1906. The young writer had hoped to reform the dehumanizing social structure in which his immigrant protagonist is forced to work, in the Chicago stockyards and slaughterhouses; with a journalist's sharp, unsparing eye, Sinclair included numerous vivid scenes exposing the filthy conditions of the meatpacking industry, based upon his firsthand experience. As a Socialist, he had believed he might move American citizens to sympathy for the immigrant workers who were cruelly exploited, exhausted, and frequently crippled or killed, in any case soon discarded by their capitalist employers. When *The Jungle* was published, it did indeed create a sensation overnight: Americans were sickened and outraged, not by the exploitation of their fellow citizens, but by Sinclair's graphic descriptions of meatpacking. (Readers who may have long forgotten most of *The Jungle* will yet recall how rodents, rodent feces, and an occasional worker fall into open, steaming vats in the meatpacking factory, to go "out into the world as Durham's [i.e., Armour's] Pure Leaf Lard.") President Theodore Roosevelt summoned Sinclair to the White House, and, with admirable speed, Congress passed legislation intended to regulate the industry—the sanitary outrages, that is. Virtually no interest in workers' rights was evinced. Years later Upton Sinclair observed ruefully, "I aimed for the heart of America, and hit its stomach instead."

Sympathy encompasses a wide range and diversity of human emotions, of course. Perhaps no one has expressed art's fundamental principles more eloquently and succinctly, after all, than Aristotle, in his discussion of *mimesis*, which, under the dramatic exigency of, or by way of the artificial concentration of, unity (of time, place, theme, characters, subject, language, "spectacle") arouses emotions in an audience, breaking down the barrier between the "imagined" and the "real." This is Samuel Coleridge's "willing suspension of disbelief"—but there is always something magical about it, a submission surely unwilled. The Aristotelean concept of *catharsis*, or the purging of emotion, is less persuasive, and certainly ambiguous; but of the arousal of sympathy in an audience and the resulting link between artist and community, the rebirth of the artist *in* the community's response, there seems to me to be little doubt. These are the magical powers of art, as true for us as for Aristotle and his contemporaries.

Transformations of Play

All my life I've been fascinated with the mystery of human personality. Who are we?—so diverse, yet, perhaps, beneath diversity, so much akin? Why are we here? And where *is* here? The mystery of human existence shades into the mystery of physical matter itself and the questions that abide are those of the ancient philosophers: Why is there something and not instead nothing? What is the purpose of consciousness, and of human inquiry, itself?

When we begin as writers, of course, it's out of a fascination with language; with the mysterious sound, music, power of words. The sense of subterranean meanings beneath public discourse. The sense of the unpredictable, the playful, and the ungovernable; the inexpressible as it defines itself, through us, in language. As children, we acquire a talismanic power by imitating the speech of our elders; what begins as mimesis evolves into what we realize, one day, glancing about ourselves in wonder, is—what? Life itself? The most seemingly conscious of artists acknowledges his subordination to *discovery*:

> . . . In fashioning a work of art we are by no means free, we do not choose how we shall make it but . . . it pre-exists us and therefore we are obliged, since it is both necessary and hidden, to do what

we should have to do if it were a law of nature—that is to say, to discover it.　　　　　　　　　　　　　　　　　　　(Marcel Proust)

What begins in childlike wonder and curiosity becomes, with the passage of time, if we persist in our devotion (or delusion), a "calling"; a "profession." Almost without knowing what we do, we find ourselves in places we've never been, nor even anticipated. We come into contact with worlds, and with people, utterly foreign to us. In doing so, in turn, we become other people; we mature into those adults of the world we'd so admired, in our youth. If we are very fortunate, we participate in a mystical evolution of the human spirit itself; that "enlargement of sympathy" of which George Eliot and D. H. Lawrence spoke in such idealistic terms.

But what are the origins of the impulse Wallace Stevens calls the "motive for metaphor"?—the motive to record, transcribe, invent, speculate? The late William Stafford says in a poem,

So, the world happens twice—
once we see it as is;
second, it legends itself deep,
the way it is.

The crucial word here is "legends" with its suggestion of storytelling; a secondary creation over and above the existential experience of the world in which we find ourselves. To experience seems not quite enough for us, we want to know what we've experienced; we yearn to analyze it, debate it, even, at times, doubt and refute it. "There is an ancient feud between philosophy and poetry," Socrates is noted as stating, in Book X of Plato's *Republic*, but is perhaps a way of saying that there is a continuous dissatisfaction in mankind with things as they are said to be; a continuous yearning for the playfulness of the imagination.

I suggest several theories of the genesis of art:

1. Art originates in play—in improvisation, experiment, and fantasy; it remains forever, in its deepest instincts, playful and spontaneous,

an exercise of the imagination analogous to the exercising of the physical body to no purpose other than ecstatic release.

2. Art is fueled by rebellion: the need, in some amounting to obsession, to resist what *is*; to defy one's elders, even to the point of ostracism; to define oneself, and by extension one's generation, as new, novel, ungovernable. Virtually all artists begin as children or as adolescents; in adolescents, the need to break away from the past is as powerful as the drive to reproduce the species. "I have lived some thirty years on this planet," Henry David Thoreau says, with typical modesty, in the first chapter of *Walden*, "and I have yet to hear the first syllable of valuable or even earnest advice from my seniors. They have told me nothing, and probably cannot tell me anything. . . ." The unfairness, the very inaccuracy of such a declaration strikes the necessary chord of youthful revolt.

3. Art is a means of memorialization of the past; a recording of a rapidly vanishing world; a means of exorcising, at least temporarily, the ravages of homesickness. To speak of "what is past, or passing, or to come"—in the most meticulous language, thereby to assure its permanence; to honor those we've loved and learned from, and must outlive. The writer who most keenly evokes a landscape, a way of life, a gathering of people is likely to be one who has been exiled from his birthright. In time, even his (or her) rebellion shifts to a bittersweet sense of loss; even hurt, anger, chagrin become priceless emotions, bound up with the energies of youth.

4. The artist is born *damned*, and struggles through his (or her) life to achieve an ever-elusive redemption, by way of art; a sense of one's incompleteness or inadequacy fuels the instinct for ceaseless invention, as in an extension of the very self's perimeters. The visual artist "makes art" that one can see, literally; this physical matter becomes part of the artist's identity. As the Puritans lived in dread of being damned by God, Whose grace they could not assume, still less call down upon themselves through prayer or good works, so the artist seems to cast about for a way of re-creating himself in aesthetic terms that are also spiritual terms. Like William Butler Yeats he "makes and unmakes" his soul. His art works may be subordinate to an idea or a vision; they may be said to constitute a single work, comprehensible, if then, only in retrospect.

* * *

In the beginning, for the child, there is only life, and consciousness; "play" is indistinguishable from both. No child, not even the prodigy Mozart, "plays" for professional purposes, nor even to define himself as talented, a worthy object of others' attention. Though uttered in somber adulthood, describing the genesis of *Waiting for Godot*, Samuel Beckett's offhand remark "It all came together between the hand and the page" is illuminating.

When I'm asked, as sometimes I am, when did I know I "wanted to be a writer," my reply is that I never "knew" I wanted to be a writer, or anything else; I'm not sure, in fact, that I "want" to be a writer, in such simplistic, abstract terms. A person who writes is not, in a sense, a "writer" but a person who writes; he (or she) can't be defined except in specific terms of texts. Elsewhere I've stated that "JCO" is not a person, nor even a personality, but a process that has resulted in a series of specific texts. What is perceived as product by others is process from the artist's perspective. My earliest, most vivid memories have to do not with any "self" (I think that young children must have very blurred, shifting images of themselves) but with drawing and coloring with crayons; inventing play worlds, or what might be called secondary worlds; or, as philosophers might term them, "counter-factual worlds."

Why?—to what purpose? No doubt child psychologists have speculated on the phenomenon of children's imaginations and the extraordinary energy invested in play, and surely it has to do with testing the perimeters of the self and of "reality," and, of course, imitating adult models. But the fact remains that it is a mysterious activity, exciting, fascinating, unpredictable. Like Lewis Carroll's heroine Alice, the child plunges willfully down the rabbit hole, or through the looking glass, into another dimension. This "other dimension" is a counterworld into which only one individual has access: ". . . The artist needs only this: a special world to which he alone has the key." (André Gide) The counterworld both mirrors the "real" world and distorts it; in it, you both are, and are not, yourself . . . the most primary, if unacknowledged, fact of artistic creation.

Recall the thrilling openings of the Alice books! In John Tenniel's famous drawings, their intricate shadings so evocative of the dream

state, a partly dematerializing Alice is seen pushing through a drawing room mirror in *Through the Looking Glass*; she re-emerges in a
world less tidy than the one she'd known, but far more interesting—
for everything, here, is *alive*. Chess pieces have metamorphosed into
kings, queens, knaves of singular ferocity; flowers not only speak, but
debate with passion; "snapdragonflies," "rocking horseflies," "bread-
and-butterflies," fawns tame as house pets, animal-human figures
out of childhood mythology—all participate in Alice's adventure in
this "curious" country that is England, yet marked off like a great
chessboard.

> "It's a huge game of chess that's being played—all over the
> world—if this *is* the world, you know. Oh, what fun it is! How I
> *wish* I was one of them! I wouldn't mind being a Pawn, if only I
> might join—though, of course, I should *like* to be a Queen best."

Alice's excited enthusiasm is that of a child about to embark upon the
adventure of life, beginning as a Pawn and ending (in theory, at least)
as a Queen. Alice is an epic heroine with whom any child can identify; sometimes reckless, sometimes rather shy; at all times questing,
inquisitive. "Curiouser and curiouser!" she exclaims. The world *is* curiouser and curiouser, the more we plunge into it. Lewis Carroll's
counter-factual worlds shade into nightmare, informed by a subtle
subtextual theme of Darwinian evolution—"survival of the fittest"—
that takes its most graphic expression in the numerous instances of
eating in the Alice books. (Eating is surely an infant's preoccupation,
and it's said that "being eaten" is a dark fantasy of childhood.) The
conclusion of *Through the Looking Glass* suggests terror narrowly
averted, as Alice wakes from a scene of impending disaster; about to
be crowned Queen, as she'd wished at the outset of her adventure, she
discovers, at the celebratory banquet, that "Something's going to
happen!" How familiar, in its essence, the dream logic that stands
expectation on its head, reverses anticipation to horror within an
instant:

> And then . . . all sorts of things happened in a moment. The
> candles all grew up to the ceiling. . . . As to the bottles, they each

took a pair of plates, which they hastily fitted as wings, and so, with forks for legs, went fluttering about in all directions. . . .

At this moment Alice heard a hoarse laugh at her side, and turned to see what was the matter with the White Queen, but, instead of the Queen, there was the leg of mutton sitting in a chair. "Here I am!" cried a voice from the soup tureen, and Alice turned again, just in time to see the Queen's broad, good-natured face grinning at her for a moment over the edge of the tureen, before she disappeared into the soup.

There was not a moment to be lost. Already several of the guests were lying down in the dishes, and the soup ladle was walking up toward Alice's chair. . . .

Alice can escape from, by waking from, the nightmare prospect of being eaten; the adventures through the looking glass, like the adventures down the rabbit hole, involve intense emotion, but the child-heroine is never seriously in danger. One "plays" at adult life in such classic childhood fantasies but can revert back, virtually at will, to a waking world, one's parents' home, where all is safe and controlled.

Then there are those gifted, blessed or accursed children who are themselves, in childhood, geographers of the imagination. It is probably not a rarity, the child-fantasist who develops his or her imagination consistently, but it is rare that we know of it, at least in much detail. Consider the extended, ingeniously labyrinthine counterworlds of the Brontë children—Charlotte, Anne, Emily, and their ill-fated brother Branwell. These precocious children, motherless and isolated in a rural English parsonage, their household dominated by an eccentric father with a predilection for melodramatic violence—a soldier manqué who had ended up, unfortunately for him, a country parson—created by way of communal storytelling two fantasy lands: Gondal (the invention of Emily and Anne: a fictitious island in the Pacific bearing a distinct resemblance to rural Haworth) and Angria (the invention of Charlotte and Branwell: an imaginary African country conquered by the British). Many years later, Charlotte designated a gift of their father's of twelve wooden soldiers as "the origin of our plays"—ordinary toys that sparked the children's imaginations to such extraordinary heights.

The Brontë children confabulated plays, mimes, games, and serial adventure stories; eventually, tales of Gondal and Angria were recorded in "Little Magazines"—tiny books filled with italic handwriting meant to resemble print. These remarkably detailed chronicles of imaginary lands were not short-lived preoccupations of childhood, to be abandoned at puberty: Charlotte wrote her final Angrian story at the age of twenty-three, and Anne and Emily continued their Gondal saga until they were twenty-six and twenty-seven respectively. Under the pseudonym "Currer Bell," Charlotte Brontë published *Jane Eyre* in October 1847, when she was thirty-one years old; under the pseudonym "Ellis Bell," Emily Brontë published *Wuthering Heights* in December 1847, when she was twenty-nine. (Emily would die a year later.) Has the transformation of private loneliness and childhood isolation into enduring works of art ever been more triumphant than this? The memorialization of childhood fantasy re-imagined as adult passion and "fate"?

No one has written more intimately of the writerly impulse than John Updike, in his autobiographical *Self-Consciousness*, which focuses upon a self's points of consciousness—the very points at which (by way of skin, breath, speech and its impediments, yearning for transcendence) a child-self becomes defined. In the chapter "Getting the Words Out," in which Updike examines his stuttering, he theorizes that his writing has its origin in relationship to breath. And language is visual, too: Updike's wooden ABC's were "alphabetical symbols stamped on blocks . . . [marking] the dawn of my consciousness." Updike's mother wanted passionately to be a writer herself, yet did not succeed while Updike was growing up; his memory of hearing her type hour after hour, shut away in a room to which he wasn't allowed entry: "The sound of her typing gave the house a secret, questing life unlike that of any of the other houses up and down Philadelphia Avenue" (Shillington, Pennsylvania, in the 1930s). The child John discovered to his astonishment and hurt that "in my mother's head there existed, evidently, a rival world that could not co-exist with the real world of which I was, I had felt, such a loved component." *Writing* was clearly an adult, even a secret, preoccupation; it presented itself initially to the child John as a matter of graphic symbols, the literal type of newsprint and the "marvel of reproduced imagery" of comic strips. Updike was mesmerized by the world of popular culture, including Walt Disney's cartoons and cartoon strips; he speaks of "dead pulped paper quickened into life by . . . Dick Tracy or Captain Easy or Alley Oop." A love of comic strips blossomed into a love of copying them onto blank paper and even onto plywood, setting them in rows on his bedroom shelf. Updike's verbal virtuosity, the painstaking craft of his prose, has its genesis in these early acts of devotion: "The very crudities and flecked imperfections of the [cartoon] process and the technical vocabulary of pen line and crosshatching and benday fascinated me, drew me deeply in, as perhaps a bacteriologist is drawn into the microscope and a linguist into the teeming niceties of a foreign grammar."

It is instructive to note, in passing, that the fantasies of childhood, whether self-invented or acquired by way of popular culture, parallel, in essence, the fantasies of the race. Not "realism" (a convention most people believe to be primary) but a kind of "surrealism" is the mode of storytelling that seems to have predated all others. Legends, fairy tales, ballads, the earliest of preserved drawings and other works of "primitive" art are not at all realistic but magical, with claims of divine or supernatural origin; of course, they are anonymous. As if, on so dreamlike a level of human consciousness, we are identical and the intrusive "individuality" of more modern times is not yet a problem. As beat and melody underlie the most formally intricate works of poetry, so romance underlies prose fiction, and is perhaps indistinguishable from it. All writers—all artists—may be classified as romantics, for the very act of creating, *and of caring passionately enough to create,* is a romantic gesture. What begins as child's play ends, not ironically so much as rather wonderfully, as a "vocation," a "calling," a "destiny"—even, above a certain income level, a "respectable profession." But the origins of the impulse remain tantalizingly mysterious, and we no more understand them, for all our exegesis and our science, than we understand our dreams.

As witty Alexander Pope has said, in *Epistle to Dr. Arbuthnot:*

Why did I write? what sin to me unknown
Dipt me in Ink, my Parents', or my own?
As yet a Child, nor yet a Fool to Fame,
I lisp'd in Numbers, for the Numbers came.

(By "numbers," Pope meant rhythm and rime.)

For the numbers came: This marks about the extent of our knowledge of "creativity," in 1740 or today.

The Artist as Perpetual Antagonist

No artist tolerates reality.   —Friedrich Nietzsche

A proposition: In the human imagination, lodged deep in that inaccessible and unfathomable and surely wordless strata of consciousness of which our (recalled, articulated) dreams are but fleeting reflections, two forces contend. The self is divided, in perpetual conflict. Historically, we know that "civilization" is the most precarious of constructs, its parts forever finding reasons to make war with one another: For it is not issues that cause war, but the desire to "war." To quote Nietzsche again, "In times of peace, the warlike man makes war with himself." The most passionately unified, the most thrillingly inspired of nations, tribes, communities, families are those with a potent enemy.

It has been observed that there are two opposed currents in Western thought, derived from the ancient Greeks, which formally reflect the division in the human imagination: the first, articulated by Parmenides (c. 515 B.C.), the second, by Heraclitus (c. 540–c. 480 B.C.).

For Parmenides, truth and "reality" combine in motionless, perfect Being: unitary, unchanging, absolute.

For Heraclitus, appalled by this vision, the primordial substance of the universe is fire, and water is the symbol of life in perpetual flux.

Virginia Woolf writes in her diary for January 4, 1929: "Now is life very solid or very shifting? I am haunted by the two contradictions. This has gone on for ever; will last for ever; goes down to the bottom of the world—this moment I stand on. Also it is transitory, flying, diaphanous. I shall pass like a cloud on the waves. Perhaps it may be that we change, one flying after another, so quick, so quick, yet we are somehow successive and continuous we human beings, and show the light through. But what is the light?"

Ontology and metaphysics. Being in repose, Being in flux. Here is the primary opposition, *which is a mode of perception* from which the myriad of oppositions that embody religion, politics, culture, history, aesthetics, ethics, sexual relations, "morals" derives.

The challenge for the artist is to accommodate and express these warring contentions in images capacious and powerful enough to contain both.

The challenge for the artist is to fulfill his or her destiny as the perpetual antagonist: the one who questions what others believe they believe; the one who questions even the role of art and artists.

"Zero at the Bone":
Despair as Sin and Enlightenment

What mysterious cruelty in the human soul, to have invented despair as a "sin"! Like the Seven Deadly Sins employed by the medieval Roman Catholic Church to terrify the faithful into obedience, despair is most helpfully imagined as a mythical state. It has no quantifiable existence; it "is" merely allegory, yet no less lethal for the fact. Unlike other sins, however, despair is by tradition the sole sin that cannot be forgiven: It is the conviction that one may be damned absolutely, thus a refutation of the Christian savior and a challenge to God's infinite capacity for forgiveness. The sins for which one may be forgiven—pride, anger, lust, sloth, avarice, gluttony, envy—are all firmly attached to objects of this world, but despair seems to bleed out beyond the confines of the immediate ego-centered self and to relate to no desire, no-thing. The alleged sinner has detached himself even from the possibility of sin as a human predilection, and this the Church as the self-appointed voice of God on earth cannot allow.

Religion is organized power in the seemingly benevolent guise of the "sacred," and power is, as we know, chiefly concerned with its own preservation. Religion's structures, its elaborate rituals and customs and scriptures and commandments and ethics, its very nature, objectify human experience, insisting that what is *out there* in the world is of unquestionably greater significance than what is *in here* in the human spirit. Despair, surely the least aggressive of sins, is dangerous to the totalitarian temperament because it is a state of intense inwardness, thus independence. The despairing soul is a rebel.

So, too, suicide, the hypothetical consequence of extreme despair, has long been a mortal sin in Church theology, in which it is equivalent to murder. Suicide has an element of the forbidden, the obscene, the taboo about it, as the most willful and the most defiantly antisocial of human acts. While thinkers of antiquity condoned suicide, in certain circumstances at least—"In all that you do or say or think, recollect that at any time the power of withdrawal from life is in your hands," Marcus Aurelius wrote in the *Meditations*—the Church vigorously punished suicides in ways calculated to warn others and to confirm, posthumously, their despair: Bodies were sometimes mutilated, burial in consecrated soil was of course denied, and the Church, ever resourceful, could confiscate goods and land belonging to suicides.

Yet how frustrating it must have been, and be, the attempt to outlaw and punish *despair*—of all sins.

(In fact: Is "despair" a pathology we diagnose in people who seem to have repudiated our own life agendas, as "narcissism" is the charge we make against those who fail to be as intrigued by us as we had wished?)

At the present time, despair as a "sin" is hardly convincing. As a state of intense inwardness, however, despair strikes us as a spiritual and moral experience that cuts across superficial boundaries of language, culture, and history. No doubt, true despair is mute and unreflective as flesh lacking consciousness; but the *poetics* of despair have been transcendentally eloquent:

> The difference between Despair
> And Fear—is like the One—
> Between the instant of a Wreck—
> And when the Wreck has been—
>
> The Mind is smooth—no Motion—
> Contented as the Eye

Upon the Forehead of a Bust—
That knows—it cannot see—

(Emily Dickinson)

This condition, which might be called a stasis of the spirit, in which life's energies are paralyzed even as life's physical processes continue, is the essence of literary despair. The plunging world goes its own way, the isolated consciousness of the writer splits from it, as if splitting from the body itself. Despair as this state of keenly heightened inwardness has always fascinated the writer, whose subject is after all the imaginative reconstruction of language. The ostensible subject *out there* is but the vehicle, or the pretext, for the ravishing discoveries to be made *in here* in the activity of creating.

Literary despair is best contemplated during insomniac nights. And perhaps most keenly savored during adolescence, when insomnia can have the aura of the romantic and the forbidden; when sleepless nights can signal rebellion against a placidly sleeping—unconscious—world. At such times, inner and outer worlds seem to merge; insights that by day would be lost define themselves like those phosphorescent minerals coarse and ordinary in the light that yield a mysterious glimmering beauty in the dark. Here is the "Zero at the Bone" of which Emily Dickinson, our supreme poet of inwardness, writes, with an urgency time has not blunted.

My first immersion in the Literature of Despair came at a time of chronic adolescent insomnia, and so the ravishing experience of reading certain writers—most of them, apart from Dickinson and William Faulkner, associated with what was called European existentialism—is indelibly bound up with that era in my life. Perhaps the ideal reader *is* an adolescent: restless, vulnerable, passionate, hungry to learn, skeptical and naive by turns; with an unquestioned faith in the power of the imagination to change, if not life, one's comprehension of life. To the degree to which we remain adolescents we remain ideal readers to whom the act of opening a book can be a sacred one, fraught with psychic risk. For each work of a certain magnitude means the assimilation of a new voice—that of Dostoyevsky's Underground Man, for instance, or Nietzsche's Zarathustra—and the permanent altering of one's own interior world.

Literary despair, as opposed to "real" despair, became fashionable at mid-century with a rich, diverse flood of English translations of European writers of surpassing originality, boldness, and genius. Misleadingly linked by so-called Existentialist themes, these highly individual writers—among them Dostoyevsky, Kafka, Kierkegaard, Mann, Sartre, Camus, Pavese, Pirandello, Beckett, Ionesco—seemed to characterize the very mission of literature itself: never in the service of "uplifting," still less "entertaining," but with a religious ideal of penetrating to the most inward and intransigent of truths. Despair at the randomness of mankind's fate and of mankind's repeatedly demonstrated inhumanity was in a sense celebrated, that we might transcend it through the symbolic strategies of art. For no fate, however horrific—as in the graphically detailed execution of the faithful officer of Kafka's great story "In the Penal Colony," or the ignominious execution of Joseph K. of Kafka's *The Trial*—cannot be transmogrified by its very contemplation; or redeemed, in a sense, by the artist's visionary fearlessness. It is not just that despair is immune to the comforts of the ordinary—despair *rejects* comfort. And Kafka, our exemplary artist of despair, is one of our greatest humorists as well. The bleakness of his vision is qualified by a brash, unsettling humor that flies in the face of expectation. Is it tragic that Gregor Samsa is metamorphosed into a giant cockroach, suffers, dies, and is swept out with the trash?—is it tragic that the Hunger Artist starves to death, too finicky to eat the common food of humanity?—no, these are ludicrous fates, meant to provoke laughter. The self-loathing at the heart of despair repudiates compassion.

My generation, coming of age at the very start of the sixties and a national mood of intense political and moral crisis, is perhaps the last American generation to so contemplate *inwardness* as a romantic state of being; the last generation of literary-minded young men and women who interiorized the elegiac comedy of Beckett's characters, the radiant madness of Dostoyevsky's self-lacerated God-haunted seekers, the subtle ironies of Camus' prose. I doubt that contemporary adolescents can identify with Faulkner's Quentin Compson of *The Sound and the Fury* as, a Harvard freshman, he moves with the fatedness of a character in a ballad to his suicide by drowning in the Charles River—"People cannot do anything that dreadful they cannot do anything very dreadful at all they cannot even remember tomorrow what seemed dreadful today," Quentin's alcoholic father tells him, as if urging him to his doom. For even tragedy, in Faulkner's vision of a debased twentieth-century civilization, is "second-hand."

That this is a profound if dismaying truth, or an outrageous libel of the human spirit, either position to be confirmed by history, seems beside the point today, in a country in which politics has become the national religion. The Literature of Despair may posit suicide as a triumphant act of rebellion, or a repudiation of the meanness of life, but our contemporary mood is one of compassionate horror at any display of self-destruction. We perceive it, perhaps quite accurately, as misguided politics; a failure to link *in here* with *out there*.

For Americans, the collective belief, the moral imperative is an unflagging optimism. We want to believe in the infinite elasticity of the future: what we *will*, we can *enact*. Just give us time—and sufficient resources. Our ethos has always been hard-core pragmatism as defined by our most eminent philosopher, William James: "truth" is something that happens to a proposition, "truth" is something that works. It is a vehicle empowered to carry us to our destination.

Yet there remains a persistent counterimpulse; an irresistible tug against the current; an affirmation of those awkward truths that, in Melville's words, will not be comforted. At the antipode of American exuberance and optimism there is the poet's small, still, private voice; the voice, most powerfully, of Emily Dickinson who, like Rilke, mined the ideal vocabulary for investigating those shifting, penumbral states of consciousness that do, in the long run, constitute our lives. Whatever our public identities may be, whatever our official titles, our heralded or derided achievements and the statistics that accrue to us like cobwebs, this is the voice we trust. For, if despair's temptations can be resisted, surely we become more human and compassionate; more like one another in our common predicament.

There is a pain—so utter—
It swallows substance up—
Then covers the Abyss with Trance—

So Memory can step
Around—across—upon it—
As one within a Swoon—
Goes safely—where an open eye—
Would drop Him—Bone by Bone.

(Emily Dickinson)

The self's resilience in the face of despair constitutes its own transcendence. Even the possibility of suicide is a human comfort—a
"carrion" comfort. In the Jesuit Gerard Manley Hopkins, extreme
states of mind are confronted, dissected, overcome by the poet's shap-
ing language:

I am gall, I am heartburn. God's most deep decree
Bitter would have me taste: my taste was me;
Bones built in me, flesh filled, blood brimmed the curse.

Selfyeast of spirit a dull dough sours. I see
The lost are like this, and their scourge to be
As I am mine, their sweating selves; but worse.

("I Wake and Feel")

Not, I'll not, carrion comfort, Despair, not feast on thee;
Not untwist—slack they may be—these last strands of man
In me ór, most weary, cry *I can no more*. I can;
Can something, hope, wish day come, not choose not to be.
But ah, but O thou terrible, why wouldst thou rude on me
Thy wring-earth right foot rock? lay a lionlimb against me? scan
With darksome devouring eyes my bruisèd bones? and fan,
O in turns of tempest, me heaped there; me frantic to avoid thee
    and flee?

("Carrion Comfort")

These poems are among the most unsettling ever written; yet, in
the way of all great art, they so passionately transcend their subject as
to be a statement of humankind's strength, not weakness.

Art and "Victim Art"

The very concept of "victim art" is problematic. Only a sensibility unwilling to grant full humanity to persons who have suffered injury, illness, or injustice could have invented so crude and reductive a label.

There is a long and honorable tradition of art that bears witness to human suffering, but this is not "victim art" as the current term would have it, still less an art that manipulates or intimidates its audience to a perverse degree. (Though you might argue that all art, in particular the conventional and pleasing, has the goal of affecting an audience's emotions.) That a human being has been in some way "victimized" doesn't reduce his or her humanity, but may in fact amplify it.

This issue, with its numerous political implications, emerged in a maelstrom of response to a controversial non-review of Bill T. Jones's dance *Still/Here* by the veteran dance critic Arlene Croce in *The New Yorker* (January 1995). The non-review, paradoxically titled "Discussing the Undiscussable," began: "I have not seen Bill T. Jones's *Still/Here* and have no plans to review it." The critic's objection to *Still/Here* was that the dance piece, which integrated video and audio tapes of AIDS and cancer victims, was, for her "beyond criticism"; it was a prime example of "victim art"—a "raw art . . . deadly in its power over the human conscience" and part of a larger "pathology in art" that seeks to manipulate audiences' feelings of sympathy, pity, intimidation, terror. By the end of the polemical essay, Arlene Croce was lashing out indiscriminately at "issue-oriented" art (a thinly veiled slap at Tony Kushner's AIDS epic *Angels in America*) and all "mass-produced art of the twentieth-century" (encompassing not only commercial television but the "grisly" Holocaust film *Schindler's List*); she acknowledged her resentment at being "forced" to feel sorry for "dissed blacks, abused women, [and] disfranchised homosexuals."

For the conservative *New Yorker* dance critic, this "pathology in art" began with the anarchic freedoms of the sixties (anti–Vietnam War protest, blacks' and women's rights agitation) and flourished in the eighties when hitherto marginalized ethnic-minority and gay Americans began to be awarded N.E.A. and other grants for their creative work. Bill T. Jones was perceived as a threat from the start, as a radical black/gay artist who seemed peculiarly immune to harsh criticism from Establishment voices. ("When I blasted an early work of his with the phrase 'fevered swamps,' he retaliated by using the phrase as the title of a piece," Ms. Croce complained.)

Response to "Discussing the Undiscussable" was immediate, and vociferous. A flurry of letters, both pro and con, to *The New Yorker*, columns and editorials in *Time, Newsweek*, the *Village Voice*, and elsewhere; and renewed, embittered debate between "conservatives" and "liberals" about the changing nature of art. As with the controversial Mapplethorpe obscenity trial of several years ago, crucial questions have been raised of both aesthetics and morality; the role of politics in art, and the role of the professional critic in assessing art that integrates "real" people and events in an aesthetic framework.

Why should authentic experience, in art, render it "beyond criticism"? Consider great memoirist work like Dostoyevsky's *The House of the Dead*, American slave narratives by ex-slaves like Frederick Douglass and Harriet Jacobs, the witness-bearing testimonies of Holocaust survivors Primo Levi, Elie Wiesel, Aharon Applefeld, Tadeusz Borowski, poetry by Nelly Sachs, Paul Celan, and numerous others.

The Diary of Anne Frank, the young Dutch Jew who died in Bergen-Belsen in 1945, is hardly the document of a mere victim, any more than the powerful elegy "The Ship of Death," D. H. Lawrence's last poem, written on his deathbed. We have poems of psychic disintegration that are nonetheless poems of transfiguration by Gerard Manley Hopkins, Emily Dickinson, Sylvia Plath. We have certain of Dorothea Lang's photographs—"Damaged Child," for instance. The portraits of tragically exhausted migrant workers, of Walker Evans. The strange, isolated, painfully human subjects of Diane Arbus. The Buchenwald photographs of Margaret Bourke-White, who considered herself a witness, an emissary: "To understand another human being you must gain some insight into the conditions that made him what he is." Consider the graphic depictions of the oppressed by Goya and Hogarth and Käthe Kollwitz, the lyric tenderness of Edvard Munch's *The Sick Child* and *Spring*, which depict the artist's dying young sister. There are tortured self-portraits by Egon Schiele, Frida Kahlo, Francis Bacon. There are heartrendingly powerful works of drama, Eugene O'Neill's *Long Day's Journey into Night*, Tennessee Williams's *A Streetcar Named Desire*, Edward Albee's *Who's Afraid of Virginia Woolf?*, Sam Shepard's *Buried Child*, Marsha Norman's *'Night, Mother*, Scott McPherson's *Marvin's Room*, among notable others, that deal with extremes of emotional distress—but how imaginatively, and how differently from one another!

Of recent dramatic works that utilize "real" material most effectively, Emily Mann's *Still Life* and *Execution of Justice* are exemplary, and have had an obvious influence upon Anna Deavere Smith's one-woman documentary-performances, *Fire in the Mirror* and *Twilight: Los Angeles 1992*. Romulus Linney's controversial *Two*, a play about the trial of Hitler's second-in-command, Goebbels, incorporates film footage from Nazi extermination camps into its action; once the "real" is experienced by the audience, the stage sophistry and devious charm of Goebbels are irrevocably shattered.

What is particularly revealing in Arlene Croce's position is a revulsion for art with "power over the human conscience." But what is wrong with having a conscience, even if one is a professional critic? If art is too "raw" to be reviewed, shouldn't it be witnessed, in any case, as integral to cultural history? (Surely the critic cares for art even when it isn't for "review.")

The counterminings of tragedy are more subtle than those of

comedy. It is an absurd expectation that, in the face of suffering, the afflicted should invariably "transcend" their fates. Sometimes, yes: Dostoyevsky seems truly, by his account, to have embraced his destiny and experienced a mystic oneness with God (in an epileptic's ecstasy?). But hardly Samuel Beckett, Primo Levi, Tadeusz Borowski. Many of our human stories end, not in triumph, but in defeat. To demand that victimized persons transcend their pain in order to make audiences feel good is another kind of tyranny.

To declare some works of art "non-art" presupposes a questionable authority. "It's art if I say it is," Humpty-Dumpty declares in *Alice's Adventures in Wonderland*, and while we're meant to laugh at his smugness, Alice's creator, Lewis Carroll, meant more than a joke.

Art is a mysterious efflorescence of the human spirit that seems not to have originated in a desire to please or placate critics. At the juncture of the communal and the individual, in ancient cultures, "art" sprang into being: The individual artist expressed the communal consciousness, usually of a "divinely" inspired nature. The scribes of the Hebrew Bible and the New Testament were extraordinary storytellers and gifted craftsmen of narrative, but their tales were presumed not to be of their own invention. The earliest visual artists may have been visionaries but their visions were surely not private ones; their art is anonymous, for the concept of "individual" did not yet exist.

At the point at which the individual begins to detach himself from the collective, the artist begins to achieve what we call "identity"; art may still be in the service of the nation or the tribe, but it has the unmistakable stamp of personality upon it, and may be highly original. Consider the remarkable paintings of the late-fifteenth-century Flemish Hieronymus Bosch, set beside conventional Christian iconographic art of his era, and earlier: how bold, how bizarre, how hallucinatory Bosch's great altarpieces *The Garden of Earthly Delights*, *The Hay Wagon*, *The Temptation of Saint Anthony*, *John the Baptist in the Desert*—if ever there was a brilliant "pathology of art," Bosch is our patron saint. The exquisite mosaics and frescoes of the Byzantine-Roman world, in the service of an impersonal religious piety, blend together in their harmony (or blandness), once one has seen the eruption of sheer genius in a visionary like Bosch. Where was the critical intelligence that could have begun to assess Bosch in his time, let alone presume to prescribe his art?

The earliest sustained work of literary criticism in Western culture is Aristotle's *Poetics* (c. 335–22 B.C.), believed to be primarily a defense of tragedy and the epic as they were attacked by Plato in *The Republic*. Where Plato saw drama as disturbing and disruptive to the well-run state, and argued that the poet should be banished from it, Aristotle argued that drama's more profound effects are beneficent and purgative, and that the poet is a valuable citizen of the republic. The *Poetics* is a meticulously descriptive, not a prescriptive, work; Aristotle based his theory of catharsis upon works of drama he had seen by Aeschylus, Sophocles, Euripides, and others. More than two thousand years after it was written, the *Poetics* remains our greatest single work of aesthetics.

Out of this seminal work by one of the world's great imaginative minds, however, there came to be, in subsequent centuries, as interpreted by less imaginative minds, a set of rigid rules meant to prescribe how drama must be written, else it is "not art." So Neoclassic dogma decreed that art insufficiently "Aristotelian" was not art. Even Voltaire, the inspired demolisher of others' delusions, rejected Shakespeare as barbaric because he did not conform to Neoclassic principles of unity. The English critic Thomas Rhymer might have thought he'd wittily disposed of Shakespeare's *Othello* by calling it "much ado about a handkerchief." Samuel Johnson, the greatest critic of his time, felt obliged to reject such masterpieces as Milton's *Lycidas* and *Samson Agonistes* for violations of Neoclassical decorum. (Yet Johnson was not so blind as to reject Shakespeare, for whose genius he was willing to stretch Aristotle's principles, choosing to interpret Shakespeare's drama as something he could call a "mirror of life.") Nahum Tate, English poet laureate of the early eighteenth century, "corrected" the insufficiently uplifting ending of *King Lear*, providing Cordelia with both life and a husband, Kent; this popular stage version ran into the 1830s.

Through the centuries, through every innovation and upheaval in art, from the poetry of the early English Romantics to the "Beat" poetry of the American 1950s, from the explosion of late-nineteenth-century European Modernist art to the Abstract Expressionism of mid-twentieth-century America, professional criticism has exerted a primarily conservative force, the gloomy wisdom of inertia, interpreting the new and startling in terms of the old and familiar; denouncing as "not art" what upsets cultural, moral, political expectations. Why were there no critics capable of comprehending the superb poetry of John Keats, most of it written, incredibly, in his twenty-fourth year?—there were not, the reviews Keats received were savage, he was dead of tuberculosis at the age of twenty-five. When, in 1862, Emily Dickinson sent several of her characteristic poems to one Thomas Wentworth Higginson, an *Atlantic Monthly* man of letters on the lookout for "new genius," her hopes were dashed by the smug sensibility of an era: Higginson was a traditionalist confronted by poetry as radical for its times as Cézanne's landscapes would have been in provincial New England. Is this poetry at all? Higginson wondered. Imperfectly rhymed, its metrics spasmodic, punctuation eccentric. "Remarkable, though odd . . . *too delicate*—not strong enough to publish." Walt Whitman's *Leaves of Grass*, privately printed in 1855, received only a few enthusiastic reviews—Whitman's pseudonymous own. Otherwise, poet and book were denounced, and would be denounced for decades, vilified as "obscene." So too Kate Chopin, whose elegantly written novel *The Awakening* brought her arguably the most violent critical opprobrium ever endured by an American artist. Our most beleaguered American Modernist writer, William Faulkner, long a target for jeering, uncomprehending reviews (his principal nemesis was the influential Clifton Fadiman, writing for *The New Yorker*, greeting one after another of Faulkner's great novels with unflagging and gleeful scorn), emerged at last to international acclaim and a Nobel Prize by way of the effort of French literary critics, and the support of the American critic and man of letters Malcolm Cowley. Only after his canonization by the Nobel Prize did Faulkner begin to receive enthusiastic reviews here at home—though, of course, his finest work was long behind him.

When, in 1913, European Modernist art came to the United States for the Armory Show, there was an opportunity for American art and cultural critics to assess the new, innovative art that had swept Europe by storm. Instead, professional critics, like the general public, from Teddy Roosevelt on down, received the work of Gauguin, van Gogh, Cézanne, Matisse, Picasso, Braque, and Duchamp with cheerful derision. Roosevelt publicly noted that Duchamp's *Nude Descending a Staircase* resembled a Navajo blanket; the most popular description of the painting was "an explosion in a shingle factory." Matisse's thirteen canvases drew the most savage reviews, and the artist had the honor of being hanged in effigy in Chicago, by students at the presumably conservative Art Institute.

Of course there have been exceptions to this dismaying history. An exemplary critic comes immediately to mind: Clement Greenberg, the early, for years the sole critic championing the ridiculed work of Jackson Pollock. There was the intrepid Frank Budgen, preparing the critical groundwork for understanding James Joyce. There was the *Times'* drama critic Frank Rich, elucidating the difficult art of Stephen Sondheim. One can name individuals here and there, but these are likely to have persisted in the face of their fellow critics' inclination for what is known, what is safe, what is "traditional." One might expect, after so spotty a record, more hesitancy, more modesty on the part of critics. Yet the censorious-conservative impulse remains: to define art, to appropriate art, to "protect" art from apparent incursions of disorder; even from artists themselves.

If this is indeed an era, as Arlene Croce charged in "Discussing the Undiscussable," when critics seem "expendable," the news will not be greeted as a disaster in all quarters. Criticism is itself an art form and like all art forms it must evolve, or atrophy and die. There can be, *pace* the conservative battle cry of "standards," no criticism for all time, nor even for much time. Ms. Croce's cri de coeur may be a landmark admission of the bankrupcy of the old critical vocabulary, confronted with ever-new and evolving forms of art. New critics for new art.

On Fiction in Fact

In the famous opening of Mark Twain's *The Adventures of Huckleberry Finn*, we're assured by the narrator, Huck Finn, that the novel that precedes it, *The Adventures of Tom Sawyer*, "is mostly a true book, with some stretchers." This caveat lector is comically applied by a fictitious character to a work of prose fiction in which he himself is featured, but it might as reasonably be applied to the amorphous genres of "nonfiction," "history," and "memoir" as well. Especially today, in an electronic era in which staggering quantities of facts are available, many of us feel, as readers, that we can trust the truth of only a fraction of what we read, even when it's presented as "true" by seemingly reputable writers and publishers.

(Except when we read fiction or poetry, whose truth is understood to be metaphorical, and not literal; subjective, and not objective.)

"Interesting—if true" is a skeptical phrase that might be an epigraph for our time. A platoon of fact checkers might attest to the individual truths of facts, but what of facts that have been "selected out," what of a writer's bias, or blindness, or determination to discover, as the distinguished and intrepid biographer of Henry James, Leon Edel, prescribed for the biographer, "the figure in the carpet"— that is, the hidden story of the subject's life, known only to the astute biographer? No matter if the subject's life might not have conformed to a pattern or a story, the task is to find it; what rare biographer would admit that his subject lacked a narrative shapeliness? Between an honest-but-dull book and a not-entirely-honest but lively book, let alone a potential best-seller, how many biographers would hesitate?

In any case, language by its very nature tends to distort experience. With the best of intentions, in recalling the past, if even a dream of the previous night, we are already altering—one might say violating—the original experience, which may have been wordless and was certainly improvised. Contemporary biographies and memoirs that purport to replicate conversations and nuances of behavior across decades are clearly fictional in technique, if not in essence. (Yet, thinks the skeptic, why not in essence? Can a true statement be composed of a succession of false syllables?) Putative eyewitnesses in criminal cases are notoriously unreliable, yet juries are powerfully, sometimes lethally, persuaded by their testimonies; people will adamantly swear to the truth of something that didn't in fact happen, and will refuse to change their minds even when their mistakes are pointed out to them. It would be a rare memoirist, with a winning style as well, who could transcend the limitations of our error-prone species or resist the commercial lures of "faction" ("fact" plus "fiction")—the "polishing" or "enhancing" or "rounding of corners to make a better narrative" (John Berendt's euphemism in describing his writing process in the best-selling *Midnight in the Garden of Good and Evil*).

And there is the self-protective instinct in all texts in which the "I" is intended to speak directly to the reader. In Friedrich Nietzsche's aphorism: " 'I did this,' says memory. 'I cannot have done this,' says my pride, remaining inexorable. Eventually, my memory yields."

Writing is an art and art means artifice, the artificial. That we are keenly aware of this today is a testimony to our higher standard of truth, no less than to our diminished expectation of encountering it. Our contemporary predilection for "nonfiction" in the form of that most notional of all genres, "memoir," is perhaps a testimony to our desperate wish that some truth of the spirit be presented to us, though we know it's probably invented. We want to believe! *We are the species that clamors to be lied to.*

* * *

The truth of one era becomes, as if by an artist's sleight of hand, the mythology of subsequent eras. What was sacred becomes secular. Our impassioned ancestors must have intended such books as the Hebrew Bible and the New Testament to be historical documents, bearing literal truth, not the compendia of legends, folktales, prose poems, prophecies, miracle tales, and hallucinatory ravings they seem to many readers, including "believers," today. In Puritan New England, Cotton Mather's massive *Magnalia Christi Americana* (The Great American Works of Christ, 1702) was once read as divinely inspired history, but can now be read only as an epic encyclopedia of early New England as seen from the elevated, Biblical perspective of the most revered and intolerant of Puritan ministers. It was a Puritan conviction that history was in fact the biography of saints—Puritan saints. Our earliest American memoirs are exclusively religious, the autobiographical confessions of faith offered as qualification for church membership. One would hardly expect from these documents any measure of objectivity, yet, in their time, they were presumably models of the newly evolving genre of "life-writing."

At least in theory, a diary or a journal may be a fairly accurate record of an individual's life, but any memoir or autobiography that is artfully shaped, didactically intended, divided into sections, and narrated with a retrospective omniscience is a text, and therefore an artifact. It may contain elements of truth, but its very organization belies the messiness and myopia of real life. Slave narratives tended to follow certain patterns of narration, often consisting of a "before" and "after" (escaping from slavery), like tales of religious conversion or a repudiation of a vice like the consumption of alcohol. Such classic American works as Benjamin Franklin's *Autobiography* (1771–90), Henry David Thoreau's *Walden* (1854), and Henry Adams's *The Education of Henry Adams* (1907) read as highly calculated literary inventions in which ideas are principles of organization and much of "real" life is omitted; Thoreau's prose in particular has been painstakingly written and rewritten, a mosaic of meticulously observed nature vignettes conjoined with an impassioned polemic, and both imposed upon a single year at Walden Pond near Concord, Massachusetts—though Thoreau lived in his cabin there for two years, and lived a historic life very different from the idealized, rather bodiless and monastic life he presents. Thoreau, who disapproved of fiction ("One world at a time"), was as masterful a creator of his own mythic image as Mark Twain, Jack London, Ernest Hemingway would be of theirs in subsequent generations.

Yet who would wish *Walden* and other classics altered in the interest of "truth"?

In *Sojourner Truth: A Life, a Symbol* (1996), the historian Nell Irvin Painter discusses the "resistance" she encountered from graduate students, fellow scholars, and admirers of Sojourner Truth when she presented a respectfully revisionist portrait of the ex-slave and abolitionist preacher Truth, one of the two most famous African-American women of the nineteenth century (the other is Harriet Tubman). Far from welcoming Painter's discoveries regarding the historic Truth, audiences who heard her speak were disgruntled; even other historians slighted her findings, preferring the earlier, "mythic" Truth to the complex, flawed, and very human woman whom Painter movingly presents in her biography. Yet the final chapter is titled "Coda: The Triumph of a Symbol" and here Painter seems to reassess her subject and, by extension, the process of creating history itself: "Sojourner Truth belongs to a company of 'invented greats' (like Jesus and Joan of Arc). . . . The symbol of Sojourner Truth is stronger and more essential in our culture than the complicated historic person. . . . The symbol we require in our public life still triumphs over scholarship."

Not all historians or readers of history will agree with Painter that "symbol" is more valuable than history, or truth. But it's illuminating to see this intellectual problem, which is also a moral problem, so cogently discussed. Where myth and truth contend, where the "rounding of corners to make a better narrative" and facts are at odds, we must learn to make our way as skeptics. The books our society publishes must be the books we deserve, suited to the moral ambiguity of our species.

II

"I Had No Other Thrill or Happiness": Reviews, Review-Essays, Journalism

F. Scott Fitzgerald Revisited

The Love of the Last Tycoon: A Western by F. Scott
Fitzgerald, edited by Matthew J. Bruccoli
(Cambridge University Press)

Fitzgerald and Hemingway: A Dangerous Friendship
by Matthew J. Bruccoli (Andre Deutsche Ltd.)

Scott Fitzgerald: A Biography
by Jeffrey Meyers (Macmillan)

The most minor of "major" American writers, F. Scott Fitzgerald (1896–1940) yet retains a perennial fascination, which his imminent hundredth anniversary will surely enhance. Rarely is a literary figure so seemingly exemplary in the most terrible, tragi-pathetic of ways. William Hogarth might have chronicled the Fitzgerald saga as *The Wunderkind's Progress*: at first we see the twenty-four-year-old Fitzgerald, a boyishly handsome Princeton dropout, being celebrated in New York literary circles as the "voice of his generation" for his best-selling first novel, *This Side of Paradise* (1920); next we see young Fitzgerald waltzing with his bride, dazzlingly beautiful Zelda Sayre, an Alabama debutante who consented to marry him only after he became rich and famous; next, a kaleidoscopic blur of parties, dances, speakeasies, gay and giddy and manic celebration, the "Jazz Age" (given its name by Fitzgerald—"the most expensive orgy in history"; of which Scott and Zelda were indefatigable icons); next we see what the moralist would call the "morning after"—a chronically hungover Fitzgerald turning out as rapidly as possible "horrible junk" (his description) for *The Saturday Evening Post* while Zelda continues to carouse, an edge of mania now to her twenties-flapper gaiety; next comes Fitzgerald's first, very public and very humiliating failure, his play *The Vegetable* (1923); next, as in a rapid film collage, years of drunken, childish, disorderly, and increasingly self-destructive behavior on the part of both Fitzgeralds in Europe and at home, as Fitzgerald, unable to maintain his household on $36,000 a year, twenty times the income of the average American of the time, continues to churn out inferior work ("I now get $2000 a story and they grow worse and worse. . . .") while publishing with great hope, but to cruelly disappointing sales, the novel generally considered his single masterpiece, *The Great Gatsby* (1925)—even as Zelda becomes increasingly disturbed, tries to kill herself, and begins the pattern of hospitalization, release, and again hospitalization that will continue for the remainder of her life; we see the one-time darling of the Jazz Age a sodden, broken, bewildered alcoholic in the somber decade of the Great Depression, managing to publish what will be his last completed novel, *Tender Is the Night* (1934), again to disappointing sales; we see Fitzgerald baring his soul for both attention and cash, in *The Crack-Up* (1936)—"In a real dark night of the soul it is always three o'clock in the morning, day after day." At last we see Fitzgerald, burnt out in his early forties, still drinking heavily yet determined to make money in Hollywood by turning out screenplays, for which he seems to have had no aptitude, nonetheless by sheer exhaustive effort managing to write approximately one half of a novel to be published posthumously as *The Last Tycoon* (1941), considered in some quarters an unfinished masterpiece. Out of print even in the United States at the time of his death (of a heart attack, aged forty-four), Fitzgerald could not have foreseen the remarkable resuscitation of his reputation that would come a decade later. The last royalty check he received from his publisher, Scribner, in 1940, was for $13.13.

It was Scott Fitzgerald who famously remarked, "There are no second acts in American lives." In fact, as Fitzgerald's checkered saga bears out, there are many acts in a life dominated by an explosive initial success, and there are likely to be numerous posthumous epilogues.

As a success, Fitzgerald was vain, boorish, shallow, exhibitionistic, and a trial to his friends (Ernest Hemingway, for instance, was so upset by Fitzgerald's drunken behavior, he refused to give Fitzgerald his Paris address). As a failure, forced to look inward like his alter ego

Dick Diver of *Tender Is the Night*, and obsessed to the end of his life with the mentally ill Zelda, Fitzgerald matured, acquiring qualities of stoicism, heroism, even, like the sacrificial Gatsby, a tragic dignity. (Compare Fitzgerald's commitment to Zelda with the callous indifference with which Hemingway sloughed off his wives as well as friends, like Fitzgerald, who had helped his career.) Fitzgerald's Jewish protagonist, Monroe Stahr, the eponymous "last tycoon," is a man so haunted by the memory of his dead wife that he falls in love with a young Englishwoman who physically resembles her, replicating Fitzgerald's emotional bond with Zelda; Stahr, modeled as well after the legendary film producer Irving Thalberg, the "boy wonder" of Hollywood of the 1920s, is potentially Fitzgerald's most subtly drawn male portrait, which, had the author lived, would very likely have grown in depth and significance as Fitzgerald reworked the novel in his typically layered, fastidious manner. (Fitzgerald was a fanatic revisionist, as his manuscripts show. *Tender Is the Night*, for instance, went through more than seven drafts.)

The Love of the Last Tycoon: A Western is a new edition, in fact an intriguing new text altogether, assembled by Matthew J. Bruccoli, general editor for the Cambridge Edition of the Works of F. Scott Fitzgerald and author of the richly detailed, highly regarded biography of Fitzgerald, *Some Sort of Epic Grandeur*. Consisting of 129 pages of Fitzgerald's work-in-progress, 222 pages of facsimile pages and notes by the editor, and a lengthy and informative introduction, *The Love of the Last Tycoon* is intended partly as a corrective to the misleading and "cosmeticized" edition assembled by Fitzgerald's old friend and former Princeton classmate Edmund Wilson, which was published as *The Last Tycoon: An Unfinished Novel* in the year following Fitzgerald's death. (Typical of Wilson's proprietary manner is the very choice of the title *The Last Tycoon*—Wilson's title, not Fitzgerald's. According to Bruccoli, Fitzgerald left two surviving titles-in-progress, *Stahr: A Romance* and the one Bruccoli has chosen. Fitzgerald's manuscripts and related documents are housed in the Firestone Library Rare Books and Special Collections Department at Princeton University.)

W. H. Auden once remarked dryly that a writer judges other writers by their published works but would wish to be judged himself on the basis of what he might have written had he lived a little longer. So too Scott Fitzgerald would have wished to be judged on the projected excellence of his Hollywood novel, the labor of which filled him with such exhilaration and despair, and very likely contributed to his death. In March 1938, he wrote to his Scribner's editor, the now legendary Maxwell Perkins: "I have a grand novel up my sleeve. . . . It would be short like 'Gatsby' but the same [sic] in that it will have the transcendental approach, an attempt to show a man's life through some passionately regarded segment of it." At a later date, Fitzgerald acknowledged anxiety to Perkins: "if it were known [that he is embarking upon a Hollywood novel, or a novel about Irving Thalberg] it would be immediately and unscrupulously plagiarized. . . ." According to Fitzgerald's lover at the time of his death, the gossip columnist and self-described "purveyor of glamour" Sheilah Graham, with whom he'd been involved since arriving in Hollywood in 1937, Fitzgerald had "satirically" considered yet another title, *The Last of the Tycoons*, hoping it would "sound like a movie title and completely disguise the tragi-heroic content of the book." At the time of his death Fitzgerald left seventeen episodes of a projected thirty, in addition to numerous pages of notes, drafts, outlines. The work, Bruccoli explains, was developing slowly through Fitzgerald's characteristic process of composition by "accretion" and there is no reason to conclude that any passages are in a final state, nor even that Fitzgerald had decided upon the novel's ending. (The ending he'd tentatively had in mind was Monroe Stahr's unexpected death in an airplane crash—an eerie prefiguring of Fitzgerald's own collapse.) The facsimile pages in this edition show fragments of prose with many emendations and sections crossed out, a puzzle of many disparate parts, clearly a temptation to the scholarly temperament for assembling, interpreting, "editing." Though the scholar as a type has often been irreverently portrayed in literature—consider George Eliot's ironic portrait of Casaubon in *Middlemarch*, still more Vladimir Nabokov's savagely comic portrait of Charles Kinbote in *Pale Fire*—one has the sense, in reading Professor Bruccoli's description of his editorial principles and procedures, of the scholar as historian, archaeologist, guardian, acolyte, clairvoyant; the scholarly pursuit as an ethical commitment, though it is rarely heralded as such.

How to assess a work so far from completion as *The Love of the Last Tycoon: A Western?* It seems unfair, indeed unethical, to bring to bear critical expectations upon a work-in-progress, still less one that was giving its author so much anguish as this. But the exaggerated claim that the work is an "unfinished masterpiece"—"Fitzgerald's most mature piece of work," as Edmund Wilson called it—does require examination. Where Monroe Stahr is the subject, *Tycoon* is consistently interesting, like those passages in Part II of *Tender Is the Night* that focus upon Dick Diver's career as a physician, and his brooding inner life, in contrast to the hedonistic, affable, aimless extrovert he'd seemingly become as the husband of a wealthy, mentally unstable woman. Stahr is the first portrait in our literature of a filmmaker as an artist (of sorts) as well as a canny, even unscrupulous business executive; he is Jewish, a novelty for Fitzgerald's Catholic upbringing, and therefore an exotic, an unknown; like his real-life model, Irving Thalberg (aged nineteen, Thalberg, a high school dropout, was a secretary-stenographer in the New York office of Universal Pictures; aged twenty, in 1919, he was managing the California studio), and like the twenty-four-year-old Scott Fitzgerald of 1920, Stahr is an astonishing prodigy, seemingly blessed with good luck. At the same time, Stahr is seemingly accursed, for he has lost his wife, whom he loved deeply (in real life, Thalberg was happily married to the actress Norma Shearer), and he has a heart condition that dooms him to an early death, though he is addicted to work as a panacea for loneliness: "Fatigue was a drug as well as a poison and Stahr apparently derived some rare almost physical pleasure from working lightheaded with weariness. It was a perversion of the life force. . . ." He is a pitiless and bemused manipulator of others' ambitions who hires as many as three pairs of writers to work independently (that is, without knowing of the others) on a single screenplay; he has no sentimental respect for the artist's "integrity," and fires employees at will. He states bluntly, without irony, "I don't read" and has never heard of the great, gloomy historian Oswald Spengler (whose fashionable treatise *The Decline of the West*, published in English 1926–28, had made a profound impression on Fitzgerald). At the same time, Stahr is a gifted natural storyteller, as his deft, brilliantly improvised parable of "making movies" indicates, as told to a befuddled Englishman novelist–turned screenwriter named Boxley (modeled upon Aldous Huxley, who did in fact attempt screenwriting), who doesn't, even so, quite get it. Unexpectedly, Stahr is a romantic; a man who falls in love with an unknown woman's face, and pursues the woman until he has won her—or so it seems. The purveyor of film fantasies becomes caught up in a fantasy of his own in an awkwardly executed interlude that reads almost as cinematic parody: "Stahr's eyes and Kathleen's met and tangled. For an instant they made love as no one ever dares to do after. Their glance was closer than an embrace, more urgent than a call." Yet more painful is the slickly romantic dialogue Fitzgerald invented for the lovers against the idyllic backdrop of a drive along the Pacific Ocean in the rain, as if with Claudette Colbert and Clark Gable in mind.

It was Fitzgerald's hope to sell the novel for $15,000 for first serial rights to *Collier's*, an arrangement that fell through when the editor rejected early chapters as "pretty cryptic." And perhaps a certain ambiguity of motives—the desire to make money and the desire to recoup his sullied reputation as a writer of serious literature—irrevocably marred Fitzgerald's conception of the work. Nor do the projected melodramatic elements, among them the bizarre improbability of the gentlemanly Stahr contracting for the murder of a labor organizer who is a threat to the studio, bode well for a plausible, integrated plot.

The most serious flaw in *The Love of the Last Tycoon: A Western* is suggested in the title's awkward self-consciousness. Fitzgerald seems not to have known whether the novel would be ironic or romantic; whether he should be parodying his material or treating it with dogged seriousness. This confusion of tone and intention is a consequence of Fitzgerald's fatal choice of narrative perspective, for though the novel purports to be about Monroe Stahr, a person of substance, it is in fact told by a breathless young woman—a "girl," as she calls herself—named Cecelia, daughter of a business partner of Monroe Stahr's. Replicating the mawkish adolescent infatuation of Rosemary of *Tender Is the Night* with handsome Dick Diver, Cecelia confesses that she is in love with Stahr, whom she has known all her life. Why filter the consciousness of a novel about adults through the uncritical gushing consciousness of an immature girl?—a not very convincing girl, at that? Where for *The Great Gatsby* Fitzgerald chose a narrator of maturity, intelligence, and irony, as well as moral innocence, having modeled *Gatsby* on Joseph Conrad's *Lord Jim* and *Heart of Darkness*, which so brilliantly employ the mordant storyteller Marlow, he seems for some inexplicable reason to have believed that the adolescent female mode of wide-eyed adulation would pump up his "tycoon"-hero in the reader's eyes:

> . . . I ran into Monroe Stahr and fell all over him, or wanted to. There was a man any girl would go for, with or without encouragement. . . . From where he stood (and though he was not a tall man it always seemed high up) he watched the multitudinous practicalities of his world like a proud young shepherd, to whom night and day never mattered. He was born sleepless without a talent for rest or the desire for it.

(One wants to inquire how many proud young shepherds does Cecelia know? Or, for that matter, Scott Fitzgerald?) Cecelia's coy, movie-script-seductive dialogue with her dream man constitutes some of the worst prose Fitzgerald ever wrote, whether for *The Saturday Evening Post* or otherwise. "Pretty cryptic" must have been a kindly euphemism. Yet more distractingly, Fitzgerald is locked into telling his complex story from Cecelia's intellectually limited position, and is forced to interrupt the narrative occasionally, as at the start of section fifteen: "This is Cecelia taking up the story." Admirer of Joseph Conrad's work as Fitzgerald purportedly was, he seems not to have assimilated the master's technique.

The most original novel about Hollywood remains Nathanael West's *The Day of the Locust*, published in 1939, when Fitzgerald was still grappling with the unwieldy material of *Tycoon*. Fitzgerald's own most fully realized novel remains *The Great Gatsby*, written when he was only twenty-eight; an intensely felt, dramatically rendered and uniquely American tale of the destruction of naive idealism. His most beautifully realized short stories are "Babylon Revisited," "Winter Dreams," and the unsentimental, unsparing, relatively unknown "An Alcoholic Case," told from the perspective of a nurse hired to care for a severely alcoholic "well-known cartoonist, or artist, whatever they call themselves," who collapses at the story's end:

> She stared at his handsome face, weak and defiant—afraid to turn even half-way because she knew that death was in that corner where he was looking. She knew death—she had heard it, smelt its unmistakable odor, but she had never seen it before it entered into anyone, and she knew this man saw it in the corner of his bathroom: that it was standing there looking at him. . . . It shone there . . . crackling for a moment as evidence of the last gesture he ever made.

"I talk with the authority of failure—Ernest with the authority of success," Fitzgerald remarked, with characteristic self-disparagement, at a time when the men's early fortunes had reversed; Hemingway's rapid ascent as the preeminent American writer of the era paralleling, with ironic symmetry, Fitzgerald's decline to virtual extinction by the late 1930s.

From their initial meeting in Paris, in 1925, when Fitzgerald was twenty-nine and famous as the handsome young chronicler of the Jazz Age, and Hemingway was twenty-six, his early book of stories, *In Our Time*, months from publication, each man was emotionally engaged with the other; not as rivals initially but rather more as brothers of a sort, young men passionately committed to the writer's life. Almost immediately, however, their relationship became lopsided: Though Fitzgerald helped Hemingway find a publisher and sympathetic editors, and was extraordinarily generous in offering first-rate critical advice, and even cash, he naively adopted Hemingway as his "literary conscience"—"my kind of idealist"; while Hemingway smugly assumed his own superiority as a writer and a "manly" man, and condescended to Fitzgerald. His sneering portrait of Fitzgerald as a failed writer in "The Snows of Kilimanjaro" was deeply wounding to Fitzgerald, though it did not destroy their friendship. After Fitzgerald's death, which Hemingway seemed sincerely to mourn, he nonetheless became a conduit for numberless demeaning, vicious, and probably inaccurate anecdotes about Fitzgerald, the most notorious included in the pseudo-reminiscence *A Moveable Feast* (posthu-

mous publication, 1964). Fitzgerald seems cannily to have anticipated the betrayal of his friend, noting in his journal, in 1937, that
he'd met with Hemingway only four times in eleven years—"Not
really friends since '26."

Fitzgerald and Hemingway: A Dangerous Friendship reprints the
entirety of the writers' saved correspondence, with helpful commentary by Professor Bruccoli: twenty-eight letters or telegrams from
Fitzgerald, twenty-nine from Hemingway. This is a fascinating
record of a "dangerous" friendship—dangerous, in any case, for Fitzgerald, who persisted in defining himself disadvantageously with
Hemingway. Yet Fitzgerald's excellent suggestions for revisions of
Hemingway's novels, including *The Sun Also Rises* and *A Farewell to
Arms*, surely contributed to the novels' literary success, whether or
not Hemingway would have wished to acknowledge the fact. (Hemingway learned from Fitzgerald even as he irritably annotated in a
margin of one of Fitzgerald's letters, "Kiss my ass EH.") On his side,
Hemingway never gave Fitzgerald critical advice except after the fact
of publication: "I liked [*Tender Is the Night*] and I didn't like it. . . .
Goddamn it you took liberties with peoples pasts and futures that
produced not people but damned marvelously faked case histories.
You, who can write better than anybody can, who are so lousy with
talent that you have to—the hell with it." Fitzgerald's replies are
usually dignified, if a bit subdued; sometimes somewhat defensive—
"The theory of it I got from Conrad's preface to *The Nigger*, that the
purpose of a work of fiction is to appeal to the lingering after-effects
in the reader's mind. . . ." (June 1, 1934; p. 174) At other, less rever-
ent times, the men exchange macho banter of the sort presumably associated with companionable drinking:

Dear Ernest:
    . . . Please write me at length about your adventures—I hear you
were seen running through Portugal in used B.V.D.'s, chewing
ground glass and collecting material for a story about Boule players; . . . that you have finished a novel a hundred thousand words
long consisting entirely of the word "balls" used in new group-
ings; that you . . . dress always in a wine skin with a "zipper" vent
and are engaged in bootlegging Spanish Fly. . . . *Now I Lay Me* is a

fine story—you ought to write a companion piece, *Now I Lay Her*.
Excuse my bawdiness but I'm oversexed. . . .

> Always Afftly,
> Scott
> (Dec. 1927; p. 93)

To which Hemingway replies with yet more ebullient machismo:

Dear Scott—

Always glad to hear from a brother pederast. You ask for the
news. Well I have quit the writing game and gone into the pimp-
ing game. They have been purifying Paris and running all the former and well known pimps out and it has left a big lack. . . . I
have lined up a fine lot of girls "les girls" a french word and when
you and the Mrs. Come over in the Spring I will be able to offer
you some very interesting reductions.

. . . There was no money in Spanish fly so I gave up the Spanish
fly game. . . . You are right about the spanish wine skin and I find
it very comfortable but it has nothing so unhemanish as a zipper. I
have to watch myself that way and deny myself many of the [*sic*]
little comforts like toilet paper. . . . Any time I use any of these
people begin to shout that old Hem is just a fairy after all and no
He man ha ha. . . .

> yrs. always,
> Ernest
> (Dec. 1927; pp. 94–95)

A correspondence between two parties seems to acquire its own
textual life, at least in retrospect, like a narrative composed by a
third, invisible party.

The last letter in the correspondence is Fitzgerald's, written in
November 1940, a month before his death, congratulating Hemingway on *For Whom the Bell Tolls*, a runaway critical and commercial
success—"I envy you like hell and there is no irony in this."

What a diverse community are biographers. There are the pioneers who spend years heroically, sometimes quixotically, involved

in original research of their subjects—sifting through manuscripts, documents, letters, "memorabilia" out of trunks, attics, archives; risking quarrels with the subject's proprietary relatives and ex-lovers, not to mention lawsuits. There are the second-generation biographers who speak of "building upon" the work of the pioneers, adding new discoveries and pressing new interpretations, often taking issue with their predecessors. Then there are the scavenger biographers, who, coming belatedly to their subjects, when the labor of research is more or less over, cobble together books from others' books, recycling tales many times told, frequently tending toward the scurrilous and the sensational in the hope of making their books, if not significant, saleable.

Of the making of books and memoirs related to F. Scott Fitzgerald there is seemingly no end. Each sad, sordid, demeaning tale has been recounted dozens of times: "There is a surprising amount of evidence about Fitzgerald's sexual organ and sexual performance," the most recent biography, by Jeffrey Meyers, notes deadpan, preparatory to recycling this possibly factitious anecdotal material another time. (The Tale of Fitzgerald's Penis derives from *A Moveable Feast*, in which Hemingway recalls his friend's anxiety that his penis might be undersized, as Zelda charged, and Hemingway's generous offer to compare organs in a café men's room in Paris, 1931. This tale has been told and retold so many times it has acquired the patina of a Biblical parable.) In fairness to biographers, Fitzgerald may be said to have struck the first dissonant chord himself with his painfully confessional *The Crack-Up*, which shocked and disgusted Hemingway. ("It was a terrible thing for [Scott] to love youth so much that he jumped straight from youth to senility," Hemingway wrote Perkins, in 1936.) In 1951, the first Fitzgerald biography, Arthur Mizener's *The Far Side of Paradise*, was published to much attention and controversy, for its relentless scrutiny of the Fitzgeralds' private lives; revised in 1965, this is still the most compelling of the numerous biographies, with a dramatic freshness that time has not dulled. Other biographies and memoirist accounts steadily followed, sensational (and best-selling), among them Sheilah Graham's *Beloved Infidel* (1958), an intimate and self-serving account of Graham's relationship with Fitzgerald in Hollywood in the waning, dimming, desperate last years of his life. (In all, Graham would publish a staggering seven books about her love affair with Fitzgerald, plus numerous interviews, which does suggest the risk of cohabiting with a gossip columnist. After Fitzgerald's death, Graham discovered a photograph of her in his bedroom with the words "Portrait of a Prostitute" scrawled on the back.) Other, more substantial books on Fitzgerald are by Andrew Turnbull, Scott Donaldson, James Mellow, Henry Dan Piper, and Matthew J. Bruccoli, noted above. The definitive book on Zelda Fitzgerald is the feminist-revisionist *Zelda* by Nancy Milford, and Mary Gordon's introduction to *The Collected Works of Zelda Fitzgerald* is highly recommended.

Coming so belatedly, Jeffrey Meyers's *Scott Fitzgerald* would not seem to be a promising venture. It contains a two-page discussion of Fitzgerald and Edgar Allan Poe, and several rather inflated pages of material about an ephemeral love affair Fitzgerald allegedly had with an Englishwoman named Bijou O'Connor in 1930, but is otherwise a sort of *Reader's Digest* of previous biographies. Yet again the familiar facts, quotes, anecdotes, ironies; the much-reproduced photographs. A section on Fitzgerald-Hemingway is engagingly written, though again none of it is new, and Meyers produces no remarkable insights. Perhaps, fifty-five years after his death, Fitzgerald's delicate bones have at last been picked clean?

Raymond Chandler:
Genre and "Art"

Stories and Early Novels
by Raymond Chandler (Library of America)

Later Novels and Other Writings
by Raymond Chandler (Library of America)

The powerful appeal of certain forms of "genre" stems from an apparent simplicity that, in the hands of inspired practitioners, rises to a kind of classic purity. There is an element of the parable, the fairy tale, even the ritual that subtextually fuels such brilliant variants of genre as Henry James's *The Turn of the Screw*—a ghost story in the English tradition of which its author spoke with unusual disdain, virtually dismissing it as an inferior work. The abiding appeal of Edgar Allan Poe's hallucinatory tales of the arabesque and grotesque springs from their fevered, defiant unreality; the boldness with which, in appropriating the well-trodden Gothic tale, in particular the fables of E.T.A. Hoffmann, for his own commercial purposes, Poe jettisoned all semblance of individual psychology and sociological "realism" in the service of another kind of vision. Only in his notebooks, in particular the remarkable prose pieces edited and published as *The American Notebooks*, is Nathaniel Hawthorne a realist; his novels and short stories are purposefully of the genre of "romance," ingeniously contrived moral allegories that yield numerous interpretations. In the preface to *The House of the Seven Gables*, Hawthorne helpfully defines not just the art of the romance but by implication all genre fiction:

When a writer calls his work a Romance, it need hardly be observed that he wishes to claim a certain latitude, both as to its

fashion and material, which he would not have felt himself entitled to assume had he professed to be writing a Novel. The latter
form of composition is presumed to aim at a very minute fidelity,
not merely to the possible, but to the probable and ordinary course
of man's experience. The former—while, as a work of art, it must
rigidly subject itself to laws, and while it sins unpardonably so far
as it may swerve aside from the truth of the human heart—has
fairly a right to present that truth under circumstances, to a great
extent, of the writer's own choosing or creation.

All of Herman Melville's fiction is a variant of romance in these
Hawthornian terms. More subtle and ambiguous is the appropriation
of the journal genre by Henry David Thoreau in *Walden*, an artfully
composed and semi-fictionalized portrait of "Henry David Thoreau"
as a hero free of all personal history and identity. Mark Twain's *Huck-
leberry Finn* is imagined as a companion to *Tom Sawyer*, a picaresque
boy's book in which distinctly adult truths are discovered. Oscar
Wilde's *The Picture of Dorian Gray* is a morality play of which
William Hogarth's *The Rake's Progress* is a visual analogue. Jonathan
Swift's *Gulliver's Travels*, Mary Shelley's *Frankenstein*, Robert Louis
Stevenson's *Dr. Jekyll and Mr. Hyde*, H. G. Wells's *The Island of Dr.
Moreau*, *The Time Machine*, *The War of the Worlds*, George Orwell's
Animal Farm—all are appropriations of highly entertaining genres in
the service of moral or political polemics. George Du Maurier's *Trilby*
is a unique work in which a Gothic tale emerges fantastically yet
somehow convincingly out of what had seemed a realist-memoirist
novel. (*Trilby* happens also to have been the first modern American
runaway best-seller.) In such idiosyncratic works, "genre" hardly de-
means genius but provides its very channel of expression. Consider
the minutely observed, psychologically motivated, historically accurate "realist" novel of which Orwell's *Animal Farm* is the swift,
brilliant, beast-fable equivalent, and you begin to appreciate the extraordinary power genre writing can possess. In the right circumstances, genre moves swift as a Thoroughbred at the starting gate,
leaving far behind the good, diligent, faithful beast shackled to a cart
heaped with "the real."

Sigmund Freud's *Studies in Hysteria* is the classic model of a popular modern genre, the "case study," which purports to be a retrospective analysis of some species of pathology in which the physician is the detective and the patient is the victim, the one usually male and the other frequently female or a male somehow emasculated. Oliver Sacks is the most gifted contemporary practitioner of the genre, and has developed it along lines that deviate considerably from Freud's. Vladimir Nabokov's *Lolita* is subtitled *The Confession of a White Widowed Male*, and the voice of Humbert Humbert is that of the mock-penitent confessing his crimes and claiming moral insight after passion has run its course—in the most revered Augustinian tradition. Each of Nabokov's novels is at once sui generis and genre-bending: *Pale Fire* is a tour de force of mad academic scholarship in which footnoted commentary overwhelms its ostensible subject; *The Real Life of Sebastian Knight*, *Invitation to a Beheading*, *King, Queen, Knave*, *Transparent Things* are variants of mysteries, as the autobiographical *Speak, Memory* is a work of artful self-invention, like Thoreau's very different *Walden*, presented as "memoir." A genre indigenous to American popular literature is the variously named "Gothic," "horror," "occult," or "dark fantasy," directly descended from Poe, containing such disparate practitioners as Charlotte Perkins Gilman ("The Yellow Wallpaper" is a brilliant feminist reinterpretation of Poe's "mad" narrator), Ambrose Bierce, H. P. Lovecraft, August Derleth; and, in more recent decades, Paul Bowles, Tennessee Williams, Ursula K. Le Guin, John Crowley, Steven Millhauser, Jonathan Carroll, Thomas Liggoti, Barry N. Malzberg, Kathe Koja, and Joanna Scott, as well as best-selling writers like Stephen King, Anne Rice, Peter Straub, and R. L. Stine, whose novels sell tens of millions of copies. This genre divides thematically into two overlapping categories: works in which supernatural forces figure, manifested literally as monsters or symbolically as "compulsions" in presumably normal people, and works in which obsessive sexual predators stalk their victims. The former might be defined as essentially a juvenile mode, the latter its adult equivalent.

Erotic horror is a subgenre that shades into hard-core pornography in which victims, usually but not exclusively female, are stalked, terrorized, raped, tortured and mutilated and murdered without end in a grotesque parody of "real life"—the "war of the sexes." Genitalia are lethal weapons in the one sex, passive and sometimes compliant objects of desire in the other. The turgid, cerebral fantasies of the Marquis de Sade are presumably the classic models for this genre, and the elegantly written *The Story of O.*, by "Pauline Réage," is its masochists' Bible. In such works the human body is a magic theater of insatiable, cruel experimentation that usually ends in death for the victim. The perpetrator of evil is rarely apprehended or punished. Brett Easton Ellis would seem to have been parodying this genre in *American Psycho*, though it was difficult to tell; Paul Theroux would seem to have been deftly exploiting it in *Chicago Loop*. The lushly overdone vampire sagas of Anne Rice are primarily erotic horror, as Bram Stoker's *Dracula*, though Victorian chaste on its surface, is erotically charged throughout. Contemporary dark fantasy has become a genre in which erotic relations are explored in vivid, metaphorical terms, frequently against the nightmare backdrop of an implicit curse or apocalyptic doom (the spectre of AIDS, unnamed); far from being escapist fiction, a number of these parable-like tales are painfully resonant for our time, collected in anthologies edited by Ellen Datlow bearing such titles as *Alien Sex*, *Off-Limits*, *Blood Is Not Enough*, and *Little Deaths*. (A frequently reprinted practitioner of the genre is Lucy Taylor, whose *Unnatural Acts*, a gathering of feminist-Sadean excess, is aptly named.) Erotic horror and dark fantasy are the antithesis of the genre known as "romance"—by tradition the most popular and lucrative of all genres, with an exclusively female, uncritical readership.

The genre most indigenous to American literature is the "mystery-detective," descending directly from Edgar Allan Poe's tales of ratiocination—"The Purloined Letter," "The Murders in the Rue Morgue," and "The Mystery of Marie Roget," in which the Parisian detective C. Auguste Dupin ingeniously solves mysteries that have stymied ordinary minds. Out of Poe's "The Gold Bug," surely one of the world's most tedious mysteries, has sprung the vast flood of codes, ciphers, secret messages, "clues" that are the stock-in-trade of the genre, reaching an apogee of the absurd in the crammed and contrived Ellery Queen mysteries of the 1930s. (The clue-crammed mystery is enjoying a spectacular resuscitation currently, however, as a consequence of recent discoveries in forensic science, including DNA tracing; in such adventures, scientific detection has supplanted arm-chair speculation by amateur sleuths, and the puzzle-solver can as readily be a woman as a man, as in the best-selling murder mysteries of Patricia Cornwell, a former pathologist.) Brilliant variants are Jorge Luis Borges's *Ficciones* and Umberto Eco's *The Name of the Rose* (in which a blind librarian named "Borges" is the very villain), which pay homage to the genre while transcending it.

Yet more native to America, the "hard-boiled mystery-detective" genre with its realistic, usually contemporary urban settings con-forms only partly to Hawthorne's dictum regarding romance: "It must rigidly subject itself to laws" and "sins unpardonably" if it swerves from "the truth of the human heart." In fact, the genre is a demonic anti-pastoral in which "laws" of probability are continu-ously defied, and its primary truth is that men and women, though more frequently women, if they are beautiful, are rotten to the core. The influence of Chandler and his mentor, Dashiell Hammett, has been ubiquitous in the genre, a readily recognizable cluster of styles, attitude, atmosphere, and tough, succinct dialogue. Contemporary practitioners of the genre, as gifted as Chandler and Hammett, are James Ellroy and Michael Connelly, both of whom write about crime and passion in Los Angeles. These noir romances transfer readily into film since they are cinematically imagined, structured so that periodic eruptions of action and violence, and not narrative language, form the skeleton of the work. When in doubt, Chandler breezily advised the writer of such fiction, bring in a man with a gun.

By contrast, in the British detective mysteries that Chandler scorned, by Agatha Christie and others, action and violence are virtually nonexistent, subordinated to clever repartee and genteel puzzle-solving. A corrupt social order, the very premise of American mystery-detective fiction, is rarely indicted in the conservative Brit-ish tradition, even in the relatively sophisticated police procedurals of Ruth Rendell and P. D. James. "Realistic" variants of the genre would have to be official police detective mysteries, for private detec-tives are rarely involved in authentic crime cases, and would have no access, in contemporary times, to the findings of forensics ex-perts. In recent decades the police procedural has effloresced into an enormously popular subgenre, worldly wise yet not wholly cynical, crammed with up-to-date information and "colorful" characters; though invariably formulaic in outline, the police procedural can be richly inventive within its perimeters and strongly atmospheric, as in the novels of Joseph Wambaugh (a former policeman), James Lee Burke, and the prolific Ed McBain (Evan Hunter), with their appealing, macho, thoroughly professional detective protagonists.

> Honesty is an art.
> —Raymond Chandler, "The Simple Art of Murder"

While the romance genre, for women, is universally reviled, the mystery-detective genre, so transparently its equivalent for men, has long enjoyed a privileged cult status. What are the secret wishes this genre's elaborately contrived scenarios fulfill? What are its subterranean assumptions, its blood beliefs? Who is the solitary hero-savior, bearer of sacred seed that never replicates itself in mere flesh?—for detectives, of course, have no progeny. Raymond Chandler, high priest of his own cult, passionately proclaims:

> . . . Down these mean streets a man must go who is not himself mean, who is neither tarnished nor afraid. The detective . . . must be this kind of man. He is the hero, he is everything. He must be a complete man and a common man and yet an unusual man. He must be, to use a rather weathered phrase, a man of honor, by instinct, by inevitability, without thought of it, and certainly without saying it. He must be the best man in his world and a good enough man for any world. . . . He will take no man's money dishonestly and no man's insolence without a due and dispassionate revenge. He is a lonely man and his pride is that you will treat him as a proud man or be very sorry you ever saw him.
>
> ("The Simple Art of Murder")

In life, the private detective is likely to be a failed or fired police officer, and the antithesis of Chandler's romantic icon; in fantasy, the detective is a kind of savior, all that other men are not, the object of their envy, adulation, and desire. The detective is the wish-fulfillment icon of the (male) reader of the genre, as the heroine of romance is the wish-fulfillment icon of the (female) reader of the genre. Significantly, he isn't a sexual predator, for women often fill him with revulsion, but he's the very essence of male virility. It isn't so much that his gun suggests a magical phallus but that he himself *is* the magical phallus, inextinguishable. Though, as Philip Marlowe the wisecracker, he declines even the rudiments of personal charm, a sardonic adolescent among disapproving adults, he enjoys a remarkable access to the (scorned) world of wealth, privilege, power, political authority; he is constantly summoned to the homes of wealthy strangers who plead with him to help them; he learns the most intimate and sordid secrets of men and women whose elevated social positions, under normal circumstances, would ensure that his path never cross theirs. Sometimes, improbably, yet wonderfully, he finds himself in a position to offer spontaneous aid to one of their kind, as in the curious opening of *The Long Goodbye*— "The first time I laid eyes on Terry Lennox he was drunk in a Rolls-Royce Silver Wraith outside the terrace of The Dancers." Private investigator, private "eye": The fantasy figure of Chandler's detective is not unlike that of an "invisible" man or a supernatural being with faerylike powers of observation, intuition, mobility, survival. Philip Marlowe is repeatedly "sapped" on the head with blackjacks or gun barrels, shot at, beaten, kicked, choked, drugged, trussed up and left for dead, yet he invariably recovers, and sometimes within the space of a few minutes takes his "dispassionate" revenge on one or another of the caricatured thugs and bit players who populate, like vermin, the Los Angeles/"Bay City" sets of Chandler's novels:

> I giggled and socked him. I laid the coil spring on the side of his head and he stumbled forward. I followed him down to his knees. I hit him twice more. He made a moaning sound. I took the sap out of his limp hand. He whined.
>
> I used my knee on his face. It hurt my knee. He didn't tell me whether it hurt his face. While he was still groaning I knocked him cold with the sap.
>
> (*Farewell, My Lovely*)

Where in a realistic or "literary" novel there is no expectation that the protagonist, however deserving, will triumph, or even survive, in such genre works there is a tacit contract between writer and reader guaranteeing that the detective will triumph, as the life force itself must triumph.[1] In this sense even the "hard-boiled" American detective novel is a British "cozy"—we are given to know that we are in safe hands, we need not fear chaos or the defeat of our deepest desires. The promise of the mystery-detective novel is that its beginning, its very opening statement, is simultaneously its ending, the terror of ambiguity resolved.

In *The Long Goodbye*, Philip Marlowe breaks his usual reticence about himself to boast quietly:

> I'm a licensed private investigator and have been for quite a while. I'm a lone wolf, unmarried, getting middle-aged, and not rich. I've been in jail more than once and I don't do divorce business. I like liquor and women and chess and a few other things. The cops don't like me too well, but I know a couple I get along with. I'm a native son, born in Santa Rosa, both parents dead, no brothers or sisters.

Philip Marlowe was fired for "insubordination" from a district attorney's office, but it isn't clear that he has a law degree; nor does he seem to have trained as a policeman. He has never married because he dislikes "policemen's wives." When we first meet him in *The Big Sleep* (1939), he is thirty-three years old and his fee is twenty-five dollars a day plus expenses; by the time of *The Long Goodbye* (1954), he is forty-two years old and his fee has risen to forty dollars a day plus expenses. This is a striking, manly man whom women adore, usually in direct proportion to his disdain: Poor little druggie rich girl, twenty-year-old Carmen Sternwood of *The Big Sleep* introduces herself to him by giggling, "Tall, aren't you?" and "Handsome too" and "You're cute," as she pretends to faint back into his arms, within seconds of their initial meeting, and later so defiles his bachelor bed by waiting for him in it naked, that he "tore the bed to pieces savagely." Her older, married sister Vivian cries, "My God, you big dark handsome brute! I ought to throw a Buick at you." Marlowe is repeatedly suggested to be tall, dark, handsome; he is mistaken for a prizefighter; even the chaste, sensible Anne Riordan of *Farewell, My Lovely*, a journalist and the daughter of a policeman, is painfully smitten with him. The most gorgeous seductress of all the Marlowe adventures, the elusive Velma of *Farewell, My Lovely*, in her guise as the wife of the wealthy, rather moribund Mr. Grayle, is immediately attracted to him, or gives that flattering impression:

> "What's your name?"
> "Phil. What's yours?"
> "Helen. Kiss me."
> She fell softly across my lap and I bent down over her face and began to browse on it. She worked her eyelashes and made butterfly kisses on my cheeks. When I got to her mouth it was half open and burning and her tongue was a darting snake between her teeth.

There is the "dream blonde" Eileen Ward of *The Long Goodbye*, a seemingly steadfast, loyal wife, so beautiful and desirable in Philip Marlowe's eyes that he can describe her only as "unclassifiable, as remote and clear as mountain water, as elusive as its color"——she too eventually succumbs to hysterical lust, a specifically female frenzy:

> When I faced her she was already falling towards me. So I caught her. I damn well had to. She pressed herself hard against me and her hair brushed my face. Her mouth came up to be kissed. She was trembling. Her lips open and her teeth opened and her tongue darted. Then her hands dropped . . . and the robe she was wearing came open and underneath it she was naked. . . .
> "Put me on the bed," she breathed.

And so on. There are many such instances, but Marlowe always escapes, sacred seed unspilled.

If a cult figure of enviable sexual allure, forever driving the labyrinthine streets of Los Angeles in search of what his creator calls, in his most famous essay, "The Simple Art of Murder," a "hidden truth," Philip Marlowe is also a "common man or he could not go among common people"; he would seem to be a vessel of American egalitarianism, the very voice of democracy: "He has a range of awareness that startles you, but it belongs to him by right, because it belongs to the world he lives in." Yet here is a sampling of the words, fairly obscene by contemporary standards and surely repugnant in Chandler's era, that fall casually and frequently from Philip Marlowe's lips: "nigger," "shine," "fag," "queen," "Jewess," "Mex," "greaseback," "wetback," "Jap." In this Caucasian-macho landscape, "a pansy has no iron in his bones, whatever he looks like." Marlowe's wisecracks are sometimes indistinguishable from ethnic slurs: "[You're] cute as a Filipino on a Saturday night." A minor character in *The High Window* is "a big burly Jew with a Hitler mustache and pop eyes." Like the Los Angeles smog of which he speaks so knowingly, Marlowe's misogyny permeates the novels; yet it's with a supreme lack of self-consciousness that he informs us repeatedly of his aversion for the female: "It's so hard for women—even nice women—to realize their bodies aren't irresistible." And, bluntly: "Women make me sick." The noir tradition has it that women are evil and disgusting if they are sexual beings; if they are not sexual beings, they scarcely exist. The Caucasian male of a certain macho sensibility is the arbiter of all values, morals. Such males understand one another instinctively; when they meet, their bonding is immediate and unquestioned, sealed with the sacrament of serious drinking,[2] like the curious, almost mystical brotherly bonding between Marlowe and the misogynous alcoholic Terry Lennox, the "war-hero"–kept husband of a rich, promiscuous woman who gets herself shot in the head and her beautiful face battered beyond recognition amid the preposterous pretzel plot of *The Long Goodbye*. Marlowe the fastidious homophobe never questions his own infatuation with Lennox, though the reader is likely to be puzzled. The two men understand each other so intuitively, commonplace social rituals are not needed: "We didn't shake hands. We never did. Englishmen don't shake hands all the time like Americans and although [Lennox] wasn't English he had some of the mannerisms." The profile of the ideal American-Caucasian male turns out to be, upon closer examination, that of an English-Caucasian male. Can it be that Marlowe, the common man, is really a frightful snob? Misogynous, racist, a homophobe, something of an anti-Semite?

A writer's worst nightmare is to envision his life's work out of print, on the brink of oblivion; a writer's second-worst nightmare is to envision his life's work reprinted in its virtual entirety, in one or two dense, dispiriting volumes, early and inferior and miscellaneous work jammed together with "major" work. Raymond Chandler is the first popular genre writer to be canonized by the Library of America, reprinted in the uniformly presented, "authoritative" series that includes our great American classics, and then some (not just Jack London's novels, for instance, but his dogged social commentary; not just Henry James's fiction, but his voluminous reviews, essays, travel sketches, and musings). The imprimatur of the Library of America is at once immortalizing and embalming; in Chandler's case, there is something ludicrous about the very packaging of his mystery-detective novels in such a scholarly format, yearning as they do for separate publication, preferably in paperback, with suitable melodramatic-romantic covers. Footnotes! The grave scholarly editing of "texts" originally published in *Black Mask*, *Dime Detective*, *Detective Fiction*, dismissed by their creator as "trash"! How Chandler would have laughed, bemused as he was by literary pretension.

> I'm just a fellow who jacked up a few pulp novelettes into book form. How could I possibly care a button about the detective story as a form? All I'm looking for is an excuse for certain experiments in dramatic dialogue. To justify them I have to have a plot and situation; but fundamentally I care almost nothing about either. All I really care about is what Errol Flynn calls "the music," the lines he has to speak.
>
> (from a letter to Frederick Lewis Allen, May 7, 1948)

Still, the decision of the editors of the Library of America to pack in so much of Chandler's early, inferior work with his major novels (*The Big Sleep*, *Farewell, My Lovely*, *The High Window*, *The Little Sister*, *The Long Goodbye*) was not a felicitous one. The thirteen "pulp" stories from the mid-1930s that open volume 1 present a challenge for the most sympathetic reader:

> "This is a gun, buddy. It goes boom-boom, and guys fall down. Want to try it?"

"Do that again and I'll put a slug in your guts, copper. So help me I will."

(from "Blackmailers Don't Shoot")

Steps sounded on the walk.
A harsh voice rasped: "Everybody out! Mitts in the air!"

(from "Smart-Aleck Kill")

Repeatedly the terms "shamus," "sleuth," "gumshoe" are used, by caricatured thugs, villains, and "coppers." As if the very genre of the mystery-detective were played out, in 1935, before Chandler began his career as a novelist.

How much better to begin with *The Big Sleep*, Chandler's first substantial work of fiction. One is tempted to describe it as his first mature work—but in fact Chandler was forty-five when he sold his first pulp story, and fifty-one when *The Big Sleep* was published, to enthusiastic reviews and encouraging sales in both the United States and England. Though the novel, like other novels of Chandler's, was partly "cannibalized" (Chandler's term) from the early stories, the language Chandler invented for it, the "voice" of Philip Marlowe, strikes an entirely different note. This is noir landscape, and, yes, crudely caricatured females will appear, but the prose rises to heights of unself-conscious eloquence, and we realize with a jolt of excitement that we are in the presence of not a mere action tale-teller but a stylist; a writer with a vision. The wish-fulfillment fantasy that fuels the mystery-detective genre is the wish to penetrate facades, to know secrets forbidden to ordinary mortals, and the private "eye" takes us to such places and describes what he/we see in such a way that the "seeing" is both information and sensation:

The path took us along to the side of [Mr. Sternwood's] greenhouse and the butler opened a door for me and stood aside. It opened into a sort of vestibule that was about as warm as a slow oven. He came in after me, shut the outer door, opened an inner door and we went through that. Then it was really hot. The air was thick, wet, steamy and larded with the cloying smell of tropical orchids in bloom. The glass walls and roof were heavily misted and big drops of moisture splashed down on the plants. The light had an unreal greenish color, like light filtered through an aquarium tank. The plants filled the place, a forest of them, with nasty meaty leaves and stalks like the newly washed fingers of dead men. They smelled as overpowering as boiling alcohol under a blanket.

With the exception of *Farewell, My Lovely*, Chandler's major novels are distinguished by striking initial scenes. The very reader who has vowed never again to squander time on another mystery-detective novel, having swallowed the increasingly convoluted and improbable twists of plot of a previous mystery-detective novel, is nonetheless drawn into a new adventure, captivated by Chandler's seductive prose. Before the absurdities and *longueurs* of plot explication, a sense of mystery, of romantic yearning! *The High Window* with its opening shot of the Murdock house in Pasadena and its reiterated images of windows from which terror-struck men fall, or are pushed; *The Lady in the Lake*, which begins with Marlowe entering a richly atmospheric office building (so like Edward Hopper's paintings of melancholy sepia-toned offices) and ends with images of a drowned woman floating in a lake and a man's broken body in a smashed car deep in a canyon; *The Little Sister*, which begins with a close-up of Marlowe's own office, into which evil comes in the least likely "little-sister" guise; *The Long Goodbye* with its romantic evocation of a shadow-brother of Marlowe's amid a glitzy Los Angeles night life—these brilliant if brief flights are touchstones of Chandler's talent, even as the novels that encase them are invariably disappointing, clogged with unwieldy incidents, unassimilated emotions, puppetry in place of characterization. *Farewell, My Lovely*, despite its inspired title, is a wretched novel until the eighth chapter, at which, mysteriously, yet in true erratic Chandleresque style, it springs into life, acquiring an intelligence, a perspective, even a measure of depth. Chandler's "experiments in dramatic dialogue" have an air of the hit or miss about them; some of his chapters read as if unedited. The author, who boasted of having had a classical education (at Dulwich College, England), was perhaps bored with the exigencies of "plot" required of melodrama; in any case, he was not a gifted craftsman, yoking characters together by sheer force of coincidence, or by way of the organic, carefully imagined plot webs of his younger and in some ways more gifted contemporary Ross MacDonald (see *The Chill*, *The Goodbye Look*, *The Moving Target*). In his "Twelve Notes on the Mystery Story," Chandler argues defensively, "The perfect detective story cannot be written. The type of mind which can evolve the perfect problem is not the type of mind that can produce the artistic job of writing." (Had Chandler not read Dickens?—the brilliantly riddlesome *The Mystery of Edwin Drood*? And what of the ingenious plot of Henry Fielding's *Tom Jones*, a "detective" story of a unique kind?) As Chandler practiced it, the mystery-detective story is an admittedly second-rate art. The tangled trails Marlowe follows, replete with false leads, switchbacks, dead ends, begin to fade immediately after the mysteries are "solved," like emotionally charged, confusing dreams after the sleeper has awakened. In this genre more than in any other, anticipation is all; revelation, virtually nothing.

What is most appealing about Chandler is his characteristic tone, which is that of the bemused, neutral observer. Marlowe's is the poet's—or the misanthrope comic's—eye for the precise metaphor, packing information in a figure of speech, an aphorism or a one-liner, a wisecrack. Who but Marlowe would note that a disingenuous woman client pushes his meager retainer in bills across his desktop "very slowly, very sadly, as if she was drowning a favorite kitten." Who but Marlowe would observe of a middle-aged blowsy woman that her voice "dragged itself out of her throat like a sick man getting out of bed" or that "suspicion climbed all over her face, like a kitten, but not so playfully." Sometimes the similes, the forced wit, veer out of control and Marlowe seems to be parodying Chandler's very "music": "I got up on my feet. I was as dizzy as a dervish, as weak as a worn-out washer, as low as a badger's belly, as timid as a titmouse, and as unlikely to succeed as a ballet dancer with a wooden leg." Classic Marlowe one-liners spin off the page with apparent ease, though surely planted in the texts the way Emily Dickinson's brilliant phrases were planted in her poems and letters: "She was cute as a washtub." ". . . He looked about as inconspicuous as a tarantula on a slice of angel food cake." "You boys are as cute as a couple of lost golf balls." "[He] had hair the color of the inside of a sardine can." Typically hung over, Marlowe notes of himself in the midst of a vexing adventure, "I drove back to Hollywood feeling like a short length of chewed string. . . . Inside my head thoughts stuck together like flies on flypaper. . . . An hour crawled by like a sick cockroach." Unsurprisingly, Marlowe's taste in music is conservative: "I was . . . listening to Khachaturyan working in a tractor factory. He called it a violin concerto. I called it a loose fan belt and the hell with it." Like his taste in women: "A girl in a white sharkskin suit and a luscious figure . . . wobbled her bottom over to a small white table and sat down beside a lumberjack in white drill pants and dark glasses. . . . He reached over and patted her thigh. She opened a mouth like a fire-bucket and laughed. That terminated my interest in her. I couldn't hear the laugh but the hole in her face when she unzipped her teeth was all I needed." Failed irony is mere sarcasm; sarcasm frequently juvenile insult. Chandler works this vein fairly consistently through his short stories and novels, assuming a like-minded sexual disgust in his (male) readers.

At other times, Chandler allows Marlowe a more intellectual, occasionally lyric sensibility. The detective observes of a suspicious character, "[His story] seemed a little too pat. It had the austere simplicity of fiction rather than the tangled woof of fact"—an observation that, considering Chandler's snarled plots, is a comic understatement. There is a shamelessly nostalgic, sentimental ode to bars in *The Long Goodbye*, too lengthy to quote here; even longer and more rhapsodic is an ode to blondes beginning "There are blondes and blondes," cleverly setting the scene for the "dream-girl" Eileen Wade, for whom Marlowe will feel so gallant an attraction. From time to time Marlowe drops his cynicism entirely and speaks in what is surely his creator's unmediated voice:

I used to like this town. . . . A long time ago. There were trees along Wilshire Boulevard. Beverly Hills was a country town. Westwood was bare hills. . . . Hollywood was a bunch of frame houses on the interurban line. Los Angeles was just a big dry sunny place with ugly homes and no style, but goodhearted and peaceful. . . . People used to sleep out on porches.

Except for bouts of heavy drinking, suicidal depression, and an occasional mental crisis, Raymond Chandler's life bore little resemblance to the fantastical noir world of his imagination. He seems to have felt self-conscious, even apologetic of his "diffident" personality, in contrast to the heroic Marlowe—that "simple alcoholic vulgarian" with "as much social conscience as a horse." He was born in 1888 in Chicago and after his alcoholic father abandoned the family, he and his mother lived in various cities in the United States and England, where Chandler was educated. In 1918, he enlisted in the Canadian army, and was sent to France, where he fought in the trenches ("Once you have had to lead a platoon into direct machine-gun fire, nothing is ever the same again") and was wounded and discharged with the rank of acting sergeant. Like many writers, Chandler seems to have been unsuited for any other career, having tried, in a desultory fashion, journalism and business (bookkeeping, auditing). Unmarried, he lived with his mother until 1924; he was thirty-six when she died of cancer, and immediately married a woman named Cissy Pascal, who was fifty-four years old. His life with Cissy was itinerant and disorganized, marked by severe alcoholism and erratic behavior on Chandler's part. He seems to have been compulsively unfaithful to her, at least initially, but after her death in 1954 he broke down completely. "For thirty years, ten months and four days, she was the light of my life, my whole ambition. Anything else I did was just the fire for her to warm her hands at," Chandler wrote to his English publisher Hamish Hamilton, shortly before attempting suicide. Chandler's mood swings, self-loathing, and the sheer dull doggedness of his alcoholism suggest the best-selling novelist Wade of *The Long Goodbye*, whom Marlowe is hired to protect and who is finally murdered when, in effect, Marlowe is looking the other way, by the very "dream-girl" Eileen. Chandler was a chronic drunk, yet, like his creation Marlowe, he persevered for a remarkably long time, living to the age of seventy-one, writing virtually to the end and on his very deathbed proposing to Helga Greene, his literary agent. (Sentimentally, or shrewdly, Greene accepted.)

In addition to the pulp stories and the major novels, the Library of America volumes contain Chandler's last, not very inspired novel *Playback* (1958), written when his store of one-liners and similes had

been depleted; the screenplay for the celebrated noir film *Double In-
demnity* (1944), adapted from the bare-bones novella by James M.
Cain in collaboration with Billy Wilder ("an agonizing experience,"
Chandler recollected), which was nominated for an Academy Award;
several provocative essays, of which the rueful "Writers in Hollywood" is as timely today as when it was written decades ago;[3] and a
selection of letters written fairly late in Chandler's life, after 1945.
The chronology of Chandler's life and notes provided by Frank
MacShane, the leading Chandler biographer and scholar, are brief
but helpful. What is badly needed for the edition is an introductory
essay of some depth, an overview of the mystery-detective genre and
an assessment of Chandler's seminal place in it; still more, a balanced
assessment of Chandler's significance, if any, in American literature.
Chandler's employment of Hemingway (whom he rather gracelessly
parodies in *Farewell, My Lovely*) might well be investigated. The phenomenon of Raymond Chandler raises an interesting question: Can
one be a "major" figure in a "minor" field?—a "great" writer in a
genre in which there is very little competition for "greatness"?[4]
There has always seemed an element of special pleading in Chandler
criticism, as if the flaws and infelicities in his novels were somehow not relevant. Is the canonization of Chandler by the Library of
America a sentimental gesture, a quirky misstep? Or is this decision
to extend the definition of "American classic" to include a practitioner of the "hard-boiled mystery-detective" school an imaginative
one, opening possibilities for the publication of other popular, much-
adored writers who have excelled in their respective genres? H. P.
Lovecraft ("Gothic horror"), Ray Bradbury ("fantasy," "science fiction"), Ayn Rand ("prophecy," "romance") come immediately to mind.

In a letter of January 7, 1945, to a literary associate, Chandler
remarked,

All I wanted when I began was to play with a fascinating new language, and trying, without anybody noticing it, to see what it
would do as a means of expression which might remain on the
level of unintellectual thinking and yet acquire the power to say
things which are usually only said with a literary air. I didn't really
care a hell of a lot what kind of story I wrote; I wrote melodrama

because when I looked around me it was the only kind of writing I saw that was relatively honest. . . .

One would not know from this disingenuous avowal that Chandler's contemporaries and near-contemporaries were, among others, Sherwood Anderson, Ernest Hemingway, Willa Cather, Jean Toomer, F. Scott Fitzgerald, Zora Neale Hurston, Eugene O'Neill, William Faulkner, Richard Wright, Langston Hughes, William Carlos Williams, T. S. Eliot, Lillian Hellman, Tennessee Williams. Melodrama is not an "honest" mode of fiction, though, to give Chandler his due, he may have thought so.

NOTES

1. How unexpected, then, that the private investigator Walter Downs, of Cornell Woolrich's *Waltz into Darkness*, is shot and killed by his own client midway through the novel! But Downs is not the novel's hero, only a minor character; the novel's very flawed hero is the murderer-client.

2. If passages devoted to drinking, and smoking, were removed from Chandler's oeuvre, as from Hemingway's, the volumes required for their work would shrink considerably. Like his creator, Philip Marlowe is clearly an alcoholic, though one with superhuman powers of durability. The hard-drinking detective seems to have been a cliché from the start, yet one beloved by Chandler, who might have despaired of characterizing his hero otherwise. By 1949, in Ross MacDonald's deftly Chandleresque *The Moving Target*, his private eye Lew Archer declines an offer of a drink from a client: "Not before lunch. I'm the new-type detective."

3. "There is no such thing as an art of the screenplay," Chandler states in "Writers in Hollywood." Yet, however his experience as a screenwriter was disappointing, Chandler was unusually well served by Hollywood. Three films were made of *Farewell, My Lovely* (one titled *Murder, My Sweet*) and one of *The High Window* (titled *Time to Kill*); *The Big Sleep*, starring Humphrey Bogart, was extremely successful. A CBS radio series, *The Adventures of Philip Marlowe*, was broadcast in 1948. Chandler's collaboration with Alfred Hitchcock on the screen adaptation of Patricia Highsmith's *Strangers on a Train* ended with Chandler's dismissal by Hitchcock in 1950.

4. Of Chandler's contemporaries, Cornell Woolrich (1903–1968) is a

striking, idiosyncratic talent writing in a very different noir vein; less formulaic than Chandler, and more experimental in terms of voice, form, theme. Unlike Chandler, he did not create a series detective with whom readers could identify from book to book. Each of his novels differs significantly from the others: *I Married a Dead Man* (1948) is a dreamy first-person confession that reads like a fairy tale of fantastic coincidences and improbable episodes in an undefined American city; the more ambitious historical suspense novel, *Waltz into Darkness* (1947), is a lavishly detailed account of a New Orleans businessman's seduction by a femme fatale con woman who leads him into a life of crime in turn-of-the-century America. Woolrich is the author of *Rear Window*, *Phantom Lady*, *The Bride Wore Black*, and *Into the Night*; his short stories have titles like "Vampire's Honeymoon," "Graves for the Living," "I'm Dangerous Tonight," "The Street of Jungle Death." A master of "psychological horror," Woolrich too has become a cult figure since his death, though never achieving Chandler's prominence and commercial success. Like Chandler he was a despondent alcoholic who drank himself to death; he died a recluse.

Of Chandler's younger contemporaries and heirs, Ross Macdonald (1915–1983) is outstanding. His private detective Lew Archer shares kindred traits with Philip Marlowe and is perhaps no less a figure of (male) fantasy; but the California milieu through which he travels on his dogged quest for truth (it is really "mercy" Archer seeks, not "justice"— but "justice" is what he finds), a suburbanized America populated by seemingly ordinary people, will strike the reader as realistic in ways Chandler's does not. Lew Archer has learned from Philip Marlowe the arresting power of the well-turned simile, but in Archer's voice language is more artfully restrained, less forced and outrageous and inclined to insult. Macdonald's *The Chill*, which investigates a mystery involving a man whose mother is his wife—or is his wife his mother?—suggests the author's fascination with Chandler's private life. Where Chandler's crammed and confusing mysteries are largely a matter of coincidence, motivated by human greed and rarely plausible when explained, Macdonald's mysteries are thoughtfully plotted family dramas in which a malevolent past erupts into the present. A classically tragic, or a Freudian, determinism is the key to Macdonald's finely honed puzzle novels, which might be recommended even for readers with a temperamental aversion to the mystery-detective genre.

René Magritte: Art Contra Art

Magritte by Jacques Meuris, translated by J. A. Underwood (The Overlook Press)

Magritte is a great painter, Magritte is not a painter."
This provocative statement, made by a poet friend of René Magritte, suggests the ambiguity of both Magritte's coolly cerebral art and the response to his art. The controversial Belgian Surrealist, who was born in 1898, died in 1967, and left behind a massive body of work (more than 1,200 finished paintings, in addition to drawings, photographs, and sculptures) is certainly a major European artist of the twentieth century; yet so schematic, willed, and "anti-art" are his most characteristic canvases, one might argue that he was not an "artist" in the traditional sense at all.

Indeed, Magritte often expressed contempt for art: "What needs painting," he said, "is confined to a thought that can be expressed by painting." And: Painting is a "lamentable expedient" by which thought might be expressed. The emphasis, unusual in a visual artist, is upon *thinking*, not feeling, for Magritte vehemently rejected as "not worth looking at" the kind of art designed to evoke emotion, as well as classical art designed to display pictorial effects. Influenced by Max Ernst, Marcel Duchamp, above all by Giorgio de Chirico, open to iconoclastic new aesthetic theories developed by Italian Futurism, Cubism, French Surrealism, and abstract art, the gifted young Magritte quickly established his characteristic style in the 1920s and spent the remainder of his long, steady, workmanlike career refining that style. An artist friend, Suzi Gablik, remarked that Magritte was a true Baudelairean hero "who amused himself all alone" and who lived hypothetically, as if he doubted the existence of the external world; Jacques Meuris, the French art historian who has written this new, highly detailed, and handsomely produced study of Magritte's work, remarks that the very enterprise of attempting to analyze Magritte is paradoxical, since the artist's work celebrates mystery—that which is "undecodable."

René Magritte's canvases are readily recognizable in museums and galleries everywhere. His images are dreamlike, but the dreams, unlike those of, say, Balthus, whom Magritte superficially resembles, are flat, even banal, like wallpaper or cutouts—in some cases, they are intended to represent cutouts. Some have become famous, more have become notorious; most have been repeated by the artist, recurring in works over long periods of time, with subtle but significant modifications. There is *Rape* (1935, 1948)—a woman's naked torso represented as if it were her face, complete with flowing "feminine" hair; there is *Girl Eating a Bird* (1927, 1946)—a neatly dressed schoolgirl calmly eating a living bird, her mouth, hands, and starched white collar splattered with blood; there is *The Fair Captive* (1931, 1965)—a trompe l'oeil in which a painter's canvas, set in the foreground of a landscape or skyscape, so fastidiously reproduces its subject as to be virtually indistinguishable from it. One of Magritte's most provocative contributions to art is his series of "conceptual" paintings—*The Treachery of Images* (1928–29, 1948), for instance, in which a pipe is illustrated above the caption "Ceci n'est pas une pipe." ("This is not a pipe.") And *The Key of Dreams* (1930, 1936)—illustrations of a horse (identified as "the door"), a clock face (identified as "the wind"), a pitcher (identified as "the bird"), and so forth. More painterly in execution, and, in fact, dramatically beautiful, as if in defiance of Magritte's own credo, are later canvases, of the 1950s and 1960s, that depict eerily floating boulders in realistic skies (*The Battle of the Argonne*, 1959; *Castle in the Pyrenees*, 1961) and massively enlarged natural objects—a green apple filling an entire room (*The Listening Room*, 1958), an enormous multifoliate rose filling an entire room (*The Wrestler's Tomb*, 1961).

(If these titles seem oddly related to their subjects, it is because, in true Dada fashion, they frequently have no logical relationship at all. Magritte invited his writer friends to think up captions for his finished paintings, and the spirit of their collaboration was ingenious, playful, and provocatively misleading.)

The focus of Magritte's art is always upon mystery, paradox, self-contradiction; sometimes parody. Admirers of art who unconsciously seek a Muzak for the eyes (pretty Impressionist landscapes, for instance) recoil from Magritte's icily manipulated images, which are blatantly invented, "painted," in spatial relationships that exist only in the artist's imagination. An art of such studied distance and detachment does not draw the viewer in, but excludes him: One thinks of Brecht's adversarial theater of alienation, of the arbitrary and often absurdist terms of discourse of such experimental writers as Borges, Dürrenmatt, Ionesco. These are not imaginative artists who seek in any way to reproduce our experience of the world, but to subvert our experience of the world, to make us think, and, perhaps, by way of thinking, re-imagine the world. In such landscapes, all objects are "objects"—man is not dehumanized, but exposed as a mere term in the equation of existence. Magritte's familiar male figures, for instance, are often pictured from the rear or in silhouette, flat as cardboard cutouts, in conservative suits and bowler hats. (Magritte, in disguise as a bourgeois, typically wore a bowler hat.) Magritte's female figures, though based upon his wife, Georgette, are blandly generic nudes, frequently lacking heads. It is unsurprising to learn that Magritte, along with Duchamp, had a considerable influence upon Pop, Op, and Conceptual art in America, though he had little admiration for these movements, and dismissed them as lacking in poetry and originality—"infinitely less bold" versions of Dada.

Considering this, it is startling—and deeply moving—to learn that, in the final years of his life, Magritte was painting canvases that, though without sentiment, might be called haunting—even beautiful. His untitled, unfinished work of August 1967, on his easel at the time of his death, depicts a shadowy horseman approaching a warmly lit but featureless house in a country setting, at dusk, yet with an immense sky eerily illuminated—a striking work very different from Magrittean art, and suggestive of, say, the poetic mysticism of the American Albert Pinkham Ryder.

This volume of Magritte's work includes nearly four hundred photographs, among them large and elegantly reproduced color plates. The critical commentary by Jacques Meuris is helpful and often illuminating; faced with the paradoxical task of decoding an artist who seems to have actively resisted being decoded, Meuris takes on the challenge gamely, though, obliged to "explain" certain images, he falls back upon inevitable platitudes and clichés—"In distinguishing between the imaginary and imagination, the artist was also, particularly in this painting (*Man of the Open Sea*, 1926), distinguishing between very different value concepts: the imaginary is a chimera, while imagination is a faculty that nourishes thought." And: "It often happens . . . that looking at a painting by Magritte claims only the exclusive attention of the look. There is never an explanation." Meuris's study is strongest in its discussion of Magritte in relationship to art history and in its generous use of letters, memoirs, and other material by Magritte and his contemporaries. If, even with its marvelous reproductions, it is not the definitive work on René Magritte, it is only because, though drawing upon her ideas, it lacks the intellectual and intuitive brilliance of Suzi Gablik's *Magritte* (1985). And, in a work so studded with, and dependent upon, outside sources, an index would have been a good idea.

But this is a valuable book, a work of art in itself, of special interest to all admirers of experimental twentieth-century art.

After the Road:
The Art of Jack Kerouac

The Portable Jack Kerouac,
edited by Ann Charters (Viking)

Jack Kerouac: Selected Letters, 1940–1956,
edited by Ann Charters (Viking)

Whom the gods would destroy, they first make famous.

Very like the young, brash, prodigiously gifted George Gordon, Lord Byron, who woke one morning in London, in 1812, to find himself famous, and the trajectory of his brilliant and fated life set before him, so too did the brash, prodigiously gifted, not-so-young (thirty-five-year-old) Jack Kerouac wake one morning in New York, in September 1957, to find himself a literary celebrity, and the course of his less brilliant but equally fated life set before him. From such rocket launchings, there can be no return to the safe harbor of obscurity.

The occasion of Byron's meteoric fame was the publication of *Childe Harold's Pilgrimage,* Cantos I and II; the occasion of Kerouac's, the publication of his second novel, *On the Road,* which was blessed with the unlikely imprimatur of the *New York Times* in one of those fluke-hype reviews that can determine not just an artist's career but his or her subsequent life. Dismissed by other reviewers as subliterary trash, *On the Road* was declared by the *Times'* reviewer not just an "authentic work of art" and a "major novel" but "an historic occasion." Yet more: "The most beautifully executed, the clearest and most important utterance yet made by the generation Kerouac himself named 'beat.' " Wild! "Zen Lunacy"! (Few except literary insiders could appreciate the delicious irony of this review, itself something of a historic occasion: It was written by a young substitute named Gilbert Millstein, filling in for the vacationing, famously conservative regular reviewer Orville Prescott, who would surely have loathed *On the Road*, if he'd condescended to read and review it at all.)

Both *Childe Harold* and *On the Road* are, of course, "pilgrimages": the former an account, in elaborate Spenserian stanzas, of a highly self-absorbed and romantic-minded young man's travels in such exotic places as Portugal, Spain, Albania, and Asia Minor; the other an account, in rhapsodic, first-person, head-on "spontaneous prose," of a young man's travels across the United States hitchhiking and in the manic company of the charismatic Dean Moriarty (in life, one Neal Cassady, an autodidact/ex–reform school kid from Denver). Byron's Childe Harold is a transparency through which the twenty-four-year-old poet speaks his mind and his heart with self-dramatizing bravura; Kerouac's Sal Paradise is a twenty-five-year-old aspiring writer identical in most respects with Kerouac, word-obsessed, yearning, a blend of Huck Finn and Walt Whitman and Thomas Wolfe persona, wild to experience "the purity of the road" and "perform our one and noble function of the time, *move*." Both young pilgrims are force fields of romance and youthful ardor, emblematic of their very different, yet kindred, eras; Kerouac's Sal Paradise is the more rawly adolescent, if not juvenile, yet possessed of an irresistible, undauntable *enthusiasm* that fairly leaps off the page, inviting the reader to participate, as in the incantatory breathless poetry of Whitman.

> What is that feeling when you're driving away from people and they recede on the plain till you see their specks dispersing?—it's the too-huge world vaulting us, and it's good-by. But we lean forward to the next crazy venture beneath the skies.
>
> (*On the Road*)

And there is a faint echo, too, of what might be called the innocent solemnity of Twain's Huck Finn, the in-transit "I" open to ever-new adventures, ever-new mysterious and fascinating fellow Americans.

> Meanwhile the young blond fugitive sat the same way; every now and then Gene leaned out of his Buddhistic trance over the

rushing dark plains and said something tenderly in the boy's ear. The boy nodded. Gene was taking care of him, of his moods and fears. I wondered where the hell they would go and what they would do. They had no cigarettes. I squandered my pack on them, I loved them so. . . . We zoomed through another crossroads town, passed another line of tall lanky men in jeans clustered in the dim light like moths on the desert, and returned to the tremendous darkness, and the stars overhead were pure and bright because of the increasingly thin air as we mounted the high hill of the western plateau. . . . And once I saw a moody whitefaced cow in the sage by the road as we flitted by.

(On the Road)

Jack Kerouac, self-designated "madman bum and angel" as much resembles Byron's friend and fellow wanderer Percy Shelley as he does Byron, in his combination of narcissism and idealism, passionately fueled by religious-mystical yearning: not the sublime Neoplatonism of the young expatriated English romantic but the American-styled Buddhism, San Francisco—based, of the Beat fifties and sixties. (Kerouac, of French-Canadian family background, was a lapsed Roman Catholic who would retain, through his life, theistic-Christian imagery: In an alcoholic stupor recorded in his 1962 novel *Big Sur*, his alter ego Jack Duluoz hallucinates a cross.) The sentiment of Whitman's "I tramp a perpetual journey" underlies the exhilarated, defiant mood of young-male pilgrimages generally; the conviction of a special destiny, a special dispensation, not only literary but spiritual, recurs through history, forever new, or new-proclaiming, and forever a threat to youth's vigilant elders.

Of course, the differences between the English poets and the American chronicler of "confessional picaresque memoirs" is considerable. Both Byron and Shelley would develop brilliantly as poets, following their precocious debuts; both are geniuses of the English language, though hardly geniuses of their lives. (Byron died, utterly worn out, aged thirty-six; Shelley, in a sailing accident so reckless as to seem near-suicidal, at thirty.) Kerouac's prose seems scarcely to have developed at all, reaching a peak of fevered lyricism in *On the Road* that reappears, at decreasing intervals, through his career. Neither Byron nor Shelley, no more than Kerouac, would have required the Rimbaudian admonition to "systematically derange" their senses in the service of their art. Is it ordained by culture, or biology, that so many romantic young-male talents burn themselves out by way of alcohol, drugs, sexual promiscuity, sexual experimentation? Jack Kerouac, if no genius, was one of those prodigious prodigies (not unlike Jack London) whose talent comes to seem, in retrospect, very much a matter of imaginative vigor, physical recklessness, the energies of youth, and an adolescent disdain for self-censure and the wise, boring constraints of his elders. In a flood of prose—millions of hyperthermic words!—Kerouac would squander his writerly gifts as he would, in sexual liaisons fleeting as those of fruit flies, squander his seed. He did not believe in remorse, nor even in revision. From the evidence of his "true-life novels" and letters, it seems that Kerouac could not have written as he did, with such a zestful lack of inhibition, perhaps could not have conceived of the grandiloquent project of a life's work, the Duluoz Legend, without the neurophysiological jolts of alcohol and drugs. *On the Road*, which did indeed make him a legend, was written at approximately the speed it can be read, on a single sheet of taped-together Chinese art paper forming a 150-foot roll through Kerouac's typewriter; it required a manic energy surge of twenty days. (Only think if Kerouac had had a word processor: He might have written *On the Road* in a fraction of that time.) In the 1968 novel *The Vanity of Duluoz*, the narrator speaks ruefully of those years, the forties: ". . . The drugs, the morphine, the marijuana, the horrible Benzedrine we used to take . . . by breaking open Benzedrine inhalers and removing the soaked paper and rolling it into poisonous little balls that made you sweat and suffer. . . . My hair had begun to recede from the sides. I wandered in Benzedrine depression hallucinations." (As early as 1944, aged twenty-two, a friend of drug users Allen Ginsberg and William S. Burroughs from their undergraduate days at Columbia College, Kerouac was hospitalized for thrombophlebitis from Benzedrine overuse.)

Still, *On the Road* came to be written, at whatever cost, enshrined in Beat legend as an ecstatic experience, the first triumph of what Kerouac called "spontaneous prose"; the "new literature" that would make all previous literature obsolete. Its famous bout of composition would be quickly bested by other manic bouts by the dervish-author: the writing of *The Subterraneans* in three uninterrupted days and the writing of the stage adaptation of *On the Road* in a single night. (Of *The Subterraneans*, published in 1958, it can be said that it is the finest literary work of its length ever written in three days, on a kitchen table. Of the play, only that it seems not to have been produced by its hopeful off-Broadway producer.) Kerouac's lengthy, effusive letters to such friends as Ginsberg, Burroughs, John Clellon Holmes, the West Coast poets Gary Snyder and Philip Whalen, and above all his "long-lost brother" Neal Cassady are of the same prose texture as much of his fiction; so doggedly self-absorbed as to be exhausting to read, though surely written in fiery outbursts of energy. Kerouac's football-player stamina kept him going for years, though he might lose as much as ten pounds in a single writing session and was left drained, depleted, depressed, and even suicidal afterward. Violent mood swings more and more characterized his life as he rapidly aged.

Our response to Kerouac's novels is largely our response to Kerouac's emotions. And to the "characters"—the "Dharma Bums" and others—who arouse those emotions to fever pitch. The great, and apparently sexually unconsummated love of Kerouac's life was the slightly younger Neal Cassady, a "jailkid" from Denver whom he first met in 1947 and who took him on the road—literally—in 1948, in a brand-new Hudson, driven from New York City to New Orleans and from there to San Francisco. Neal Cassady is "Dean Moriarty" of *On the Road*, a wild man you would not wish to encounter rushing toward you on a two-lane country highway. Sometimes Moriarty drives naked, insisting that his passengers disrobe too; he is invariably drunk or stoned; or both; isn't above casual theft (from poor folk) or frenzied sex; given to yelling "Oh man, what kicks! . . . You know I'm hotrock capable of everything at the same time and I have unlimited energy" and "Now we're going to get our kicks!"

At dusk we were coming into the humming streets of New Orleans. "Oh, smell the people!" yelled Dean with his head out the window, sniffing. "Ah! God! Life!" He swung around a trolley. "Yes!" He darted the car in every direction looking for girls. "Look at *her*!" . . . We bounced in our seats. "And dig her!" yelled Dean, pointing at another woman. "Oh I love, love, love women! I think women are wonderful! I love women!" He spat out the window; he groaned; he clutched his head. Great beads of sweat fell from his forehead from pure excitement and exhaustion.

(*On the Road*)

(What of the real-life Neal Cassady, with whom, too, Allen Ginsberg immediately fell in love?—and William S. Burroughs found mesmerizing? A handsome lad, son of a skid row derelict in Denver, who by the age of twenty-two had stolen five hundred cars, been arrested ten times, convicted six times, spent fifteen months in jail. An aspiring writer, like Kerouac, yet even more expansive in his grandiloquence than Kerouac. A manic womanizer, a timeless drinker and carouser. He smoked marijuana, took amphetamines. Yet, what physical prowess: He could throw a football seventy yards, run a hundred yards in less than ten seconds, broad-jump twenty-three feet, and masturbate five or six times a day, every day.)

Kerouac's narrator Sal Paradise explains his boyish idolization of this "young Gene Autry"—"a sideburned hero of the snowy West" and certain others:

. . . They danced down the streets like dingledodies, and I shambled after as I've been doing all my life after people who interest me, because the only people for me are the mad ones, the ones who are mad to live, the ones who never yawn or say a commonplace thing, but burn, burn, burn like fabulous yellow roman candles exploding like spiders across the stars and in the middle you see the blue centerlight pop and everybody goes "Awww!"

(*On the Road*)

Virtually all of Kerouac's novels from *On the Road* onward (his first novel, *The Town and the City*, as its title suggests inspired by Thomas Wolfe, appeared in 1950, and is not part of the Duluoz Legend), notably *The Subterraneans* (1958), *The Dharma Bums* (1958), *Visions of Cody* (1959), *Doctor Sax* (1959), *Big Sur* (1962), *Desolation Angels* (1965), and *Vanity of Duluoz* (1968), are, like the metafictional experiments of the sixties and seventies, as much about the process of creation as their ostensible subjects. In each novel, a Kerouac alter ego, variously named "Sal Paradise," "Ti-Jean" (Kerouac's family nickname for him), "Jack Duluoz," and "Ray Smith," has picaresque adventures on the road, with his delirious "beat" ("beatific") friends, with unfailingly gorgeous and sexually compliant women, in a vertiginous rush of eidetically vivid settings like New York, New Orleans, San Francisco, Seattle, Denver, Tangiers (there is a memorable interlude in *Desolation Angels*, in the company of the brilliantly sinister junky "Bull Hubbard," a.k.a. William S. Burroughs), Saint Petersburg, El Paso, Mexico City, Juarez, Los Angeles, Oakland, Berkeley; in the wilds of Big Sur, in a remote fire-watch station in the Cascade Mountains, on Mount Matterhorn (there is a wonderfully narrated mountain-climbing interlude in *The Dharma Bums*, in the company of the California poet-Buddhist "Japhy Ryder," a.k.a. Gary Snyder). Each of the novels is a first-person narrative in the process of being recalled, and written, by the alter ego, in the "sheer joy of confession," as Kerouac named it in his essay "Essentials of Spontaneous Prose": ". . . A kind of new-old Zen Lunacy poetry, writing whatever comes into your head as it comes . . . 'without consciousness' in semitrance. . . . Never afterthink to 'improve.' " To say that Kerouac's work is uneven is simply to say that it is Kerouac's work.

Most of the novel excerpts and prose pieces of *The Portable Kerouac* contain inspired passages, lyric language riffs emulating jazz improvisation, set beside passages that are not so inspired. Kerouac is capable of scintillating speech and also of speech undifferentiated as a gravel truck unloading. The story "Good Blonde" (originally published in *Playboy*) and the essay "On the Road to Florida" (in the company of the photographer friend Robert Frank) are exceptions to Kerouac's usual unstoppered flow, being conventionally structured, and extremely readable. There are set pieces of sustained drama, sharply recalled episodes of boyhood angst in the "gloomy book-movies" of *Doctor Sax*, an opium overdose (in the company of the indefatigable "Bull Hubbard") in *Desolation Angels*, a surreal, final hitchhiking stint from Big Sur to Monterey in *Big Sur*, a blackly comic nightmare interlude with a distraught woman named Billie who threatens to kill herself and her young son if the alcohol-dazed

"Jack Duluoz" refuses to love her, also in *Big Sur*. Kerouac is capable of humor both lunatic and ironic, "goofy" (a favorite Beat word) and chilling. His boy-romantic's eye can be as shrewd as Nathanael West's:

Sunset and Vine!—what a corner! Now there's a corner! Great families off jalopies from the hinterlands stood around the sidewalk gaping for sight of some movie star and the movie star never showed up. When a limousine passed they rushed eagerly to the curb and ducked to look: some character in dark glasses sat inside with a bejeweled blond. "Don Ameche! Don Ameche!" "No George Murphy! George Murphy!" They milled around looking at each other. Luscious little girls by the thousands rushed around with drive-in trays; they'd come to Hollywood to be movie stars and instead got all involved in everybody's garbage. . . . Handsome queer boys who had come to Hollywood to be cowboys walked around wetting their eyebrows with hincty fingertip. Those beautiful little gone girls cut by in slacks in a continuous unbelievable stream; you thought you were in Heaven but it was only Purgatory and everybody was about to be pardoned, paroled, powdered and put down; the girls came to be starlets; they upended in drive-ins with pouts and goosepimples on their bare legs. . . . Hollywood Boulevard was a great screaming frenzy of cars; there were minor accidents at least once a minute; everybody was rushing off toward the farthest palm . . . and beyond that there was desert and nothingness.

("The Mexican Girl")

In *The Dharma Bums*, a pricking of Beat-Buddhist pretensions:

. . . I went over to an old cook [in a Chinatown, San Francisco, restaurant] and asked him, "Why did Bodhidharma come from the West?"

"I don't care," said the old cook, with lidded eyes, and I told Japhy and he said, "Perfect answer, absolutely perfect. Now you know what I mean by Zen."

The terrifying lucidity of a true Zen epiphany, in a retreat in Raton Canyon, Big Sur, as "Jack Duluoz" tries to meditate, to regain some measure of his lost, pre–"King of the Beatniks" innocence:

> . . . But I remember seeing a mess of leaves suddenly go skittering in the wind and into the creek, then floating rapidly down the creek towards the sea, making me feel a nameless horror even then of "Oh my God, we're all being swept away to sea no matter what we know or say or do"—And a bird on a crooked branch is suddenly gone without my even hearing him.

> (*Big Sur*)

As for connecting with a similarly notorious elder writer:

> —"No!" I almost yell, "I mean I'm so exhausted I don't wanta do anything or see anybody"— (already feeling awful guilt about Henry Miller anyway, we've made an appointment with him about a week ago and instead of showing up . . . at seven we're all drunk at ten calling long distance and poor Henry just said "Well I'm sorry I don't get to meet you Jack but I'm an old man and at ten o'clock it's time for me to go to bed. . . ."

> (*Big Sur*)

Failure can be nurturing for an artist, as his work is gaining strength and inward authority; success, particularly premature success, can be devastating. The impulse is to quote F. Scott Fitzgerald in this context: "There are no second acts in American lives." In fact, we know that there are innumerable acts in the lives of Americans, but for the life touched by "fame" there is usually one spectacular first act followed by others considerably less spectacular that must nonetheless be lived. Kerouac, long accustomed to the vicissitudes and camaraderie of a marginal literary existence, began to crack up almost immediately after the publication of *On the Road*; his canonization as spokesman for a new Beat Generation assured him an ineradicable identity that would follow him to the grave, and beyond. His drinking and drug-taking escalated. His friendships foundered. His "love" affairs became ever more desperate and short-lived. (Impotence, a result of chronic alcoholism, did not help.) His relationships with editors, always uneasy, worsened under the strain of his megalomania, for of what service is even a brilliant editor like Malcolm Cowley to a compulsive writer who believes "As it comes, so it flows, and that's literature at its purest"? Celebrated by the media in one season, Kerouac was virulently, viciously, jeeringly, and indefatigably assailed by the media in seasons to follow. Yet he had his "fans"— stoned acolytes of *On the Road*—whom he feared and despised and who followed him everywhere they could. Our vision of Kerouac, provided by Kerouac himself, is of a man rapidly aging before our eyes, as in a horror film. By the time of his notorious *Paris Review* interview of 1967, ill, alcoholic, embittered, and incoherent, Kerouac would have revised (that is, repudiated) his personal emotional history:

> Oh the beat generation was just a phrase I used in the 1951 written manuscript of *On the Road* to describe guys like Moriarty who run around the country in cars looking for odd jobs, girlfriends, kicks. It was thereafter picked up by West Coast leftist groups and turned into a meaning like "beat mutiny" and "beat insurrection" and all that nonsense; they just wanted some youth movement to grab onto for their own political and social purposes. I had nothing to do with any of that. I was a football player, a scholarship college student, a merchant seaman. . . .

Politically reactionary, anti-intellectual, distrustful of a new "Pepsi generation of twisting illiterates" and even of anti–Vietnam War agitation, Kerouac retreated, to live in cramped quarters in Saint Petersburg, Florida, with his aging, ailing mother. He was himself aged and ailing, though only in his forties. His life was late-night drunken telephone calls, days of television, fits of writing on a manuscript tentatively titled *The Beat Spotlight*. In February 1968, he learned that Neal Cassady was dead, aged forty-one, of a lethal combination of tequila and Seconals. Kerouac survived him only briefly, dying in October 1969, aged forty-seven. He collapsed in front of the television set, drinking and writing in his notebook, eating from a can of tuna fish, watching "The Galloping Gourmet."

* * *

Ann Charters, author of *Jack Kerouac: A Life*, clearly a devotee of the Kerouac legend, has assembled a highly readable *Portable Kerouac* and an intermittently engaging *Selected Letters, 1940–1956*. The anthology would have been strengthened by including the whole of *On the Road* and omitting Kerouac's poems—his "pomes," as he called them. As it is, some of *On the Road*'s strongest passages, including the wry, memorable ending, are missing. Still, the *Portable Kerouac* is an attractive gathering. Charters is too loyal to Kerouac, or too diplomatic, to acknowledge the obvious: that such a volume allows for judicious editing of the kind that, in life, Kerouac so disdained.

If the letters are of lesser interest, this is primarily because Kerouac's life so intimately fed his fiction that to have read the fiction is to already know the life in a more urgent, distilled form. Also, the writer's chronic self-absorption and the sheer length of his musings become repetitive and wearing. To his old friend and sometimes rival Allen Ginsberg, Kerouac confessed: ". . . My art is more important to me than anything . . . I've long ago dedicated myself to myself." The most warmly effusive (and lengthy) letters are, of course, to Neal Cassady, to whom Kerouac poured out his heart as if writing to a mirror-self, rehearsing the nostalgic novels *Doctor Sax*, *Visions of Gerard*, *Maggie Cassidy*. Kerouac even offered to type Cassady's voluminous "scrawls" out of a passion for pure writing: "It's the work itself, I want, I want to see the ordered sentences, typed up neat on perfect pages under a soft lamp, wild prose describing the world as it raced through my brain and cock once. . . ." Cassady never replied to Kerouac's offer.

Unfortunately, the *Selected Letters* ends in 1956, shortly before the publication of *On the Road*, the turning point in Kerouac's career and life. Though it contains hundreds of letters to family members, Kerouac's first wife, Edith Parker, editors, literary acquaintances (among them Alfred Kazin, whom Kerouac seems to have besieged with manuscripts and requests) as well as to the real-life models of his fictional characters, most of the letters are to the same small gathering of people upon whom Kerouac was emotionally fixed. Clearly, to have been drawn into the personal mythology of the man's orbit was to remain enshrined there for years. The letters, for all their rhapsodizing on life, writing, Buddhism, do not demonstrate a striking intelligence, still less a particularly original imagination, but they throw off sparks of raw, coruscating emotion very like the thrumming narrative energy of the fiction. The most interesting are to Ginsberg, whom Kerouac admired as a poet and an intellectual, yet could not resist chiding; often swerving, in the course of a seemingly friendly letter, into sudden hostility:

> . . . The quality of my friendship for you is far purer than yours could ever be for me. . . . There's nothing that I hate more than the condescension you begin to show whenever I allow my affectionate instincts full play with regard to you; that's why I always react angrily against you. It gives me the feeling that I'm wasting a perfectly good store of friendship on a little self-aggrandizing weasel.
>
> (September 6, 1945)

And condescension:

> . . . Don't study Greek and Prosody at Berkeley get away from this Pound kick. Pound is an Ignorant Poet—how many times do I have to tell you that it's a Buddhist, AN EASTERN FUTURE ahead—Greeks and Poem styles are child's play. . . . The Greeks are a bunch of ignorant cocksuckers as any fool can plainly see. . . . I like Dickinson and Blake. . . . But even they are Ignorant because they simply don't know that everything is empty IN AND OUT IN TEN THOUSAND INFINITE DIRECTIONS OF THE UNDISTURBED LIGHT . . . please, Allen, wake up. . . .
>
> . . . All's I need is a drink . . . I drink eternally. Drink always and ye shall never die. Keep running after a dog, and he will never bite you; drink always before the thirst, and it will never come upon you. . . .
>
> (July 14, 1955)

(Despite Kerouac's boorish behavior toward him in the late 1960s, Ginsberg would prove a patient and loyal friend.)

Beneath Kerouac's manic intensity there seems to have been a fatalistic passivity. His self-sabotaging conviction that writing must be "spontaneous" and innocent of "afterthink to improve" rests upon the untenable assumption that impulse is superior to reflection, and that the first words to fly into one's head are inevitably superior to the second, or the third, or fourth. Indeed, all artists know that any act of reflection, revision, or re-imagining is as "active" and "spontaneous" as the initial act; to have subsequent thoughts about one's work is invariably to place oneself in an advantageous position vis-à-vis that work. "Not that the story need be long," Henry David Thoreau wisely said, "but it will take a long while to make it short."

The evidence of Jack Kerouac's oeuvre is that, for all its flaws, it, and he, deserved to have been treated better by the censorious "literary" critics of his time. Certainly, Kerouac was dismissed as a "beatnik" by many commentators who had not troubled to read his work, still less to read it with sympathy. *The Portable Kerouac*, so capably edited by Ann Charters, will be seminal in a re-evaluation of Kerouac's position in the literature of mid-twentieth-century America, a richly varied affluence of "high" and "low" art that permanently changed the course of our fiction. The era is distinguished by tales of mordant flight from domesticity: Paul Bowles's cult novel *The Sheltering Sky* (1949) bounded by John Updike's *Rabbit, Run* (1960). Between, such disparate works as J. D. Salinger's *The Catcher in the Rye*, Norman Mailer's *The White Hipster*, Allen Ginsberg's *Howl*, William S. Burroughs's *Naked Lunch*, and Vladimir Nabokov's *Lolita*. *On the Road* is a classic of the era to set beside these.

Haunted Sylvia Plath

The Haunting of Sylvia Plath
by Jacqueline Rose (Virago Press)

What a compelling argument against suicide, the melancholy example of Sylvia Plath! This immensely gifted and ambitious poet, thirty years old, in a paroxysm of domestic unhappiness, emotional crisis, and physical breakdown, gassed herself in the depths of a bitter winter in London 1963, shortly after having written a number of extraordinarily powerful poems—the very poems, white-hot, venomous, self-lacerating, that would make her posthumous fame. (These were gathered into Plath's second book, *Ariel*, 1965, in an arrangement by Plath's literary executor and husband, Ted Hughes, that has been faulted by critics for violating the poet's own intention: Hughes, from whom Plath was separated at the time of her death, admitted that he had left out some of "the more personally aggressive poems . . . and might have omitted one or two more had [Plath] not already published them herself in magazines—so that by 1965 they were widely known.")

Plath's suicide may have been, as some have theorized, rather more a gesture toward suicide than an act of absolute self-annihilation, a desperate wish that, by cruelly punishing herself, she might punish others, particularly her estranged husband, Hughes. It is impossible—indeed, unseemly—to speculate about such a matter, but Plath had in fact attempted suicide some time before, in adolescence, and had been saved; this resuscitation would have felt to her like a resurrection, confirming her (our?) unconscious conviction of immortality. Plath's most characteristic poetry celebrates an intensely romantic view of death (as in "Edge": "The woman is perfected. / Her dead / Body wears the smile of an accomplishment. . . .") that evokes it as a magic principle of purification and abstraction, and, no doubt, revenge upon one's enemies, not as a principle of decay or mere physical deadness. Its romance too is with the defiant uttering of those things that should not be uttered, nor even thought; if Plath has become an icon of sorts for some—in Jacqueline Rose's words, a "shadowy figure whose presence draws on and compels" it is not likely to be because of the high quality of her poetry, but because of the taboos she is perceived as having broken, and the sensationalism of her death, the bitterness of the feud with Hughes, the posthumous and sordid controversy.

What irony, as savage as any evoked in Plath's most mordant poetry!—not only did her act of suicide destroy a remarkable talent, but, since Plath had not yet signed divorce papers, it legally delivered over her work, so precious to her—a considerable body of poems, stories, journals yet unpublished—to the very people Plath had surely wished to punish, Ted Hughes and his sister Olwyn, whom Hughes named literary executor of Plath's estate in his place. Given this legal imprimatur, Hughes has been within his rights in destroying the final volume of Plath's journals and in freely censoring other work to remove the "intimacies" and "nasty bits" he finds offensive; since permission to quote from copyrighted material must be obtained from the Plath estate, critics and biographers must conform, or give some initial promise of conforming, to the estate's strictures. Just as we prize our own privacy—which is to say, our control of others' images of us—conversely, we are frustrated and alarmed by others' attempts to control their privacy, particularly when these attempts are successful. Jacqueline Rose is not the first commentator on Sylvia Plath to have entered into conflict with Ted and Olwyn Hughes, but she may well be the first to have detailed the experience in print, in this book's most passionately argued chapter ("The Archive"), and to relate the Plath controversy to theoretical issues of who "owns" another's work; who controls "facts"; is there a "singular truth" of a historical nature to which all other speculation must conform; who defines another's "real self," which in Rose's words, "can surely have meaning only as *self*-definition, as a self-defining of self"? (This, in response to Hughes's imperial statement that only the poems he has so judged are the work of Plath's "real self"—her other writings are "waste products.") Rose notes wryly that, at one point, not only do the Hugheses censor Plath and what they can of commentary on Plath directly, but Plath's mother, Aurelia, in assembling her determinedly upbeat collection of letters from Sylvia, *Letters Home* (1975), which omits letters and passages that might reflect poorly upon the mother-daughter relationship, in an effort to correct "cruel and false caricatures" promulgated by Sylvia Plath in her work, is forced, in turn, to conform to further cuts in these letters demanded by Ted and Olwyn Hughes. On all sides people claiming to know Sylvia Plath's "real self" and what "really happened" feel obliged to correct "false" texts—the locus of falsity being, of course, Plath, and not her censors.

In Rose's words,

> The problem is then compounded by the way the process of editing, specifically in relation to the *Journals*, strikes at the corpus of the writing in the most vulgar, physical sense. . . . Scholars who go to Smith College [where the Plath archive is located] . . . are presented with a text part original, part publisher's typescript . . . with the latter at various points literally cut to pieces—pages with sections cut out in the middle, other lines made illegible by heavy black ink, sections ringed in red and marked "cut." Faced with this, it is not difficult to see how this editing could be regarded as violation—"corps morcelé"—body in bits and pieces.

The Plath estate denounced *The Haunting of Sylvia Plath* as "evil" and threatened legal action; Rose's interpretation of a poem of Plath's, "The Rabbit Catcher," was said by Ted Hughes to be, "in some countries, 'grounds for homicide.' " Of Linda Wagner-Martin, author of *Sylvia Plath: A Biography* (1988), Hughes fulminated, "She's so insensitive that she's evidently escaped the usual effects of undertaking this particular job—i.e., mental breakdown, neurotic collapse, domestic catastrophe—which in the past has saved us from several travesties of this kind being completed."

For the record, Jacqueline Rose's analysis of "The Rabbit Catcher," like most of the literary analysis in this book, is both temperate and convincing; Wagner-Martin's biography is a model of sensitivity and tact.

The Haunting of Sylvia Plath is less a unified work than a compendium of engagingly written articles, part literary politics, part theoretical, somewhat doggedly psychoanalytical, speculation. The critic sets as her task the hope to "find a way of looking at the most unsettling and irreducible dimensions of psychic processes which [Plath] figures in her writing without turning them against her—without, therefore, turning her into a case." The tendency for commentators on Plath has been to split into two groups—those who would pathologize the poet, reducing her art to symptoms; and those who would stress the representative nature of her work, particularly in terms of a repressive patriarchal society. Rose focuses upon the primary processes of Plath's imagination, with some emphasis upon Plath's contextual position—as a poet with a keen sense of her craft, and an agenda for professional success. In this she succeeds admirably, though there is a sense throughout the book, in even those chapters devoted to a purely literary-psychoanalytic approach, of a stormy adversarial atmosphere; a need to protect, defend, explain, redeem the poet against a field of detractors. So much negative, carping, small-minded criticism, duly recorded, and taken so seriously!—it is as if Jacqueline Rose is unaware of the fact that all writers of originality and significance arouse hostile attention—this, in fact, is a warning signal that they are original and significant.

Indeed, the space given to a somber recounting of "negative" criticism has the inadvertent effect (inadvertent because Rose is hardly antagonistic to her subject) of obscuring the fact that, from the first, Plath received highly respectful criticism from first-rate commentators; an early volume, *The Art of Sylvia Plath*, 1970, contains contributions by Charles Newman, Richard Howard, Mary Ellmann, John Frederick Nims, M. L. Rosenthal, and set a tone of quality for subsequent work. To focus upon the poet's angry detractors, even to expose the anti-feminist or anti-female bias of their remarks, is to suggest that these critics are somehow more important than the others. (Or, at least, more exciting: "Would it be going too far," Rose inquires, "to suggest that Plath has generated a form of 'psychotic' criticism?")

The very title, *The Haunting of Sylvia Plath*, and the book's opening gambit ("Sylvia Plath haunts our culture") strike the ear as excessive. If by "culture" one means "London literary culture" racially and economically delimited, this might be so; otherwise, it is too capacious a notion. Even among practitioners of poetry in, for instance, the United States, where the number of poets is almost exactly equivalent to the number of readers of poetry, though it is probably a bit higher, Sylvia Plath is often conflated with Anne Sexton and other women poets; the work of women writers is cheerfully muddled in the popular imagination, like their names and "tragic" histories. Plath's accomplishment as a literary artist transcends the parochial, just as the passion that underlies her art is refined by painstaking craftsmanship. Plath is most helpfully linked not to the demeaning disputes of her milieu but to such powerful predecessors as Theodore Roethke, T. S. Eliot, Dylan Thomas, above all Emily Dickinson.

Ambition, like talent, is a gift. In some, it is a prodigious gift. Without it, talent itself may quickly wither, or content itself with easy and repeated successes. One of the most significant facts about Sylvia Plath, which Jacqueline Rose rightly emphasizes, is that, far from being at the mercy of a wayward, demonic psyche, Plath was, from earliest adolescence, determined to be a writer—a writer of consequence. She was willing to work tirelessly learning the forms of poetry, the strategies of prose fiction. She set out to dismantle the stories of Frank O'Connor—"I will imitate until I can feel I'm using what he can teach." (Quoted in Ted Hughes, introduction to *Johnny Panic and the Bible of Dreams*, by Sylvia Plath, 1979.) She learned from Wallace Stevens and James Thurber; from *Seventeen*, *The New Yorker*, and *The Ladies' Home Journal*. Her journal is rife with self-admonitions, pep talks, plots. This voice may not be the "real" Sylvia Plath, but it is a wonderfully appealing, forthright voice:

First, pick your market: *Ladies' Home Journal* or *Discovery? Seventeen* or *Mlle*? Then pick a topic. Then think.

Sent it off to *The Sat Eve Post*: start at the top. Try *McCall's*, *Ladies' Home Journal*, *Good Housekeeping* . . . before getting blue.

I want to hit *The New Yorker* in poetry and the *Ladies' Home Journal* in stories, so I must study the magazines the way I did *Seventeen*.

I will slave and slave until I break into those slicks.

If the "blood-jet" of poetry, as Plath would later call it, came with tremendous, unbidden power, whatever mysterious force it was that generated the voices of prose had to be coaxed, flogged. In the journal, Plath notes, with typical ingenuousness,

I need a master, several masters. Lawrence, except in *Women in Love*, is too bare . . . in his style. Henry James, too elaborate, too calm and well-mannered. Joyce Cary I like. . . . Or J. D. Salinger. But that needs an "I" speaker, which is so limiting.

Where another critic might have quickly glossed over such remarks, as demeaning to the high seriousness of her subject, Jacqueline Rose argues that this too is a legitimate voice of Plath's. Writing in journals, letters, a novel (*The Bell Jar*, to be published under the pseudonym Victoria Lucas, in 1963), short stories, poems, Plath created a diversity of voices that "enter into an only ever partial dialogue with each other which it is impossible to bring to a close. To which of these voices are we going to assign an absolute authority?" It is futile, Rose says, to seek a "singular, monologic reading" of Plath.

One of the attractive qualities of *The Haunting of Sylvia Plath* is the author's thoroughness in researching the women's magazines of Plath's era to which she had pinned such naively high hopes. *The Ladies' Home Journal*—alternately an object of "desire, critique, and identification"—is discovered to be, like other publications of its genre, not so predictable as one might think: Much of the material dealt with marital unhappiness and female problems of one kind or another, though the core of women's existence, marriage and motherhood, was never questioned. Rose includes too some chilling excerpts from Philip Wylie's now-forgotten best-seller *Generation of Vipers*

(1942), a pathological diatribe of misogyny that helped to shape the consciousness of the era in which Plath came of age; Rose quotes some equally misogynous, if more pretentious, pseudomythology from Robert Graves's *The White Goddess*, which Plath, under Ted Hughes's tutelage, was reading in the mid-1950s: " 'The White Goddess is anti-domestic; she is the perpetual "other woman," and her part is difficult indeed for a woman of sensibility to play for more than a few years, because the temptation to commit suicide in simple domesticity lurks in every maenad and muse's heart' "; and, " 'Woman is not a poet: she is either a Muse or she is nothing.' " The ironic, combative tone of Plath's most celebrated poetry is surely, in part, the result of her need to define herself as both poet and woman in the face of such stultifying sexist clichés.

Admirable in passion and integrity as *The Haunting of Sylvia Plath* is, the book is nonetheless an uneven affair; rather more, as I've suggested, a compendium of articles, with fluctuations of tone, purpose, density, and pacing, than a single coherent work, as if it were written over a period of time and subsequently spliced together. This is not a criticism in itself, for there is no special virtue in consistency, but the book's chapters do not seem to follow from one another; the strengths of one are abandoned as another theme emerges, and the narrative thread that connects them is not always evident. A culminating chapter is badly needed, for the book breaks off abruptly with an odd quotation from Marguerite Duras's *La Douleur*, to the effect that a writer identifies with all her characters, good and evil, and a very old journal entry of Plath's. The reader feels the book gain strength and momentum as it proceeds, but its effect is seriously dissipated in the final, overlong chapter, which examines Plath's famous (notorious?) poem "Daddy" as if it were not a poem so powerful and direct as to be, in essence, immediately comprehensible to any reader of moderate intelligence but a strand of DNA in need of meticulous decoding for an audience of unenlightened laymen. More than thirty pages of background and exegesis to "explain" Plath's poem, by a circuitous route that involves the usual chorus of "outraged" critics, papers presented at the 1985 Hamburg Congress of the International Association of Psychoanalysts, Holocaust commentary, Nazism, William Styron's *Lie Down in Darkness*, and much more—to provide us with innocuous or even doubtful conclusions: "I read 'Daddy' as a poem about its own conditions of linguistic and phantasmic production." And, wonderfully "lit.-crit." in its breathless revelation, of a kind to stun fellow theorists:

> This is the father as godhead, as origin of the nation and the word—graphically figured in the image of the paternal body in bits and pieces spreading across the American nation state: bag full of God, head in the Atlantic, big as a Frisco seal. Julia Kristeva terms this father *"Père imaginaire,"* which she then abbreviates "PI." Say those initials out loud in French and what you get is "pays" (country or nation)—the concept of the exile. Much has been made of Plath as an exile, she goes back and forth between England and the United States. . . .

Elsewhere in the book, particularly in an analysis of Plath's "Poem for a Birthday," the author takes us through punctilious classroom exercises in literary exegesis, which, though well-intentioned, and informed by an overall intelligence and generosity of spirit, have a numbing effect—like making one's way, with mincing steps, through a tide of glue, so that, by the time one gets to where one is going, not only has one forgotten where one began, but when, and why.

Such devout attention to her every word would surely have pleased Sylvia Plath, however displeased she would be regarding the current state of the Plath "archive." For this was the brilliant, gifted, impatient, forever scheming young woman who complained in her journal, "It is sad only to be able to mouth other poets; I want someone to mouth me."

The Enigmatic
Art of Paul Bowles

So Far from Home (1993) brings together in a single volume the rich and unexpectedly variegated achievement of a major American writer whose "American-ness" is invisible in his work, yet a constant point of reference. Like Ernest Hemingway, whose imagination was aggressively stimulated by the self-defined role, and the romantic adventure of the role, of the expatriate, the voyager into the human soul by way of "foreign" peoples and landscapes, Paul Bowles realized his genius by "getting as far away as possible" from home as a young man, as he says in *Without Stopping*, his autobiography; like Hemingway, he fashioned a writerly voice, early on in his career, perfectly suited to the subject matter he would claim as his own. Both writers began their careers with first novels that achieved immediate celebrity, or notoriety, and commercial success: Hemingway's *The Sun Also Rises* (1926) was published when the author was twenty-seven years old; Bowles's *The Sheltering Sky* (1949) was published when the author was thirty-eight years old—but had already had a brilliant career as a composer, music critic, and poet. *The Sun Also Rises* became the very voice of the "Lost Generation" of American expatriates living in Paris in the 1920s, and *The Sheltering Sky* became a cult novel, a stark, ironic, uninflected drama of existential absurdity and fate.

A writer's language is more than merely a vehicle of communication, of course. It is predominately music created by the rhythm and texture and cadence of words. In the earliest stories, Paul Bowles wrote with the chill omniscient ease of fable—"A Distant Episode," for instance, first published in *Partisan Review* in 1946, unfolds with the horrific calm of a legend, or dream, in which a fate both impersonal and ordained becomes the lot of an American professor of linguistics in Morocco. (The ironic significance of the professor's specialty is an integral part of the story, appropriate to a pitiless world in which, at least in metaphor, the punishment fits the crime.) Bowles's voyager is unnamed, only the Professor; he is both an allegorical figure and a succinctly characterized individual, very likely an alter ego of the author's, like the doomed principals of *The Sheltering Sky* and the isolated Pastor Dowe at Tacaté. The Professor's fate is *not* death—his fate is, horribly, to exist, in a sense, beyond death; to survive as consciousness, bereft of the human. A captive of an outlaw tribe of the Sahara, the Professor perversely lives on, and on, and in the story's mordant climax:

> The tiny inkmarks of which a symphony consists may have been made long ago, but when they are fulfilled in sound they become imminent and mighty. So a kind of music of feeling began to play in the Professor's head, increasing in volume as he looked at the mud wall, and he had the feeling that he was performing what had been written for him long ago. . . .

The Professor has become, unknown to him, a "holy maniac." He runs out into the desert to become "a part of the great silence out there beyond the gate."

"A Distant Episode" is one of those stories, like Poe's "The Tell-Tale Heart" or Kafka's "In the Penal Colony," that, once read, can never be forgotten—even if one should wish to forget it.

Bowles's first gathering of stories, *The Delicate Prey* (1950), a number of which are included in this volume, became too, notably for young writers, a cult book. Published at a time when "the short story" was a fastidiously crafted mannerist genre in which the mores of middle-class Caucasian Americans were subjected to microscopic examination—"A tempest," as Hortense Calisher wittily observed, "in a very small teacup"—*The Delicate Prey* offended, astounded, impressed readers in both the United States and England, and became something of a succès de scandale. Significantly, its dedication page read: "For my mother, who first read me the stories of Poe."

Virtually all of Bowles's fictional work might be so dedicated. Though differing in obvious ways from Poe's insular, claustrophobic, and wildly surrealist tales, as much in their coolness of language as in their keenly recorded camera's-eye observations of Morocco, Mexico, South and Central America, Bowles's fictional works share with Poe's the imagination of nightmare; a simplicity of vision that would seem to predate history; a sense that a man's or a woman's character is fate, and that both are impersonally prescribed. The demonic self-destructive urges to which Poe gave the memorable name "the imp of the perverse" are ubiquitous in Bowles's worlds. From the earliest stories and novels through the new novella set in the Niger River valley, *Too Far from Home*, we encounter men and women, travelers from America, at the mercy of buried wishes experienced as external fate. Indeed, in his 1980 preface to *Let It Come Down*, originally published in 1952, Bowles speaks bluntly of his hero Dyar as a "nonentity, a victim," with a personality "defined solely in terms of situation."

Readers coming to Paul Bowles for the first time are invariably startled by the *uncanniness* his fiction exudes. We are habituated to writers who identify with their characters and whose aim is to maneuver us into an identification with them too. We are habituated to writers whose preoccupations are with human affairs—family crises, politics, marriages, comedies, or tragedies of manners. We may be disoriented by a writer whose focus of attention is not upon human beings but upon primitive forces—land—or cityscapes—that express themselves through human beings. The humanist tradition that most educated readers share does not accommodate itself readily to ironic perspectives; we wish to believe, even in the face of Darwinian logic, that the individual matters, and matters greatly. In Bowles's imagination, no such tradition is honored, nor even evoked except ironically. Tennessee Williams, himself the object of passionate attack for his work, warned Bowles, after having read "The Delicate Prey," that he would be considered a monster if he published it. Yet in such monstrousness, such an antiheroic downscaling of man's spiritual possibilities, is there not, oddly, a kind of modesty?—a most reasonable modesty?

The hapless Pastor Dowe, for instance, deluded in his worthy Protestant mission to bring the "truth" of Jesus Christ to unregenerate South American Indians, realizes one day that the place his church has sent him is "outside God's jurisdiction." The seemingly civilized American husband of "Call at Corazón" detaches himself from hideousness by fixing his attention "upon the given object or situation so that the various elements, all familiar, will regroup themselves. Frightfulness is never more than an unfamiliar pattern": this recipe, as he calls it, allows him to abandon his alcoholic wife to an unspeakable fate in the South American jungle. In "At Paso Rojo" a young Mexican woman surrenders to the atmosphere of brutality that surrounds her and discovers a kinship with spiders living in the crevices of her bedroom walls; in "Allal," a kif-besotted boy is transmogrified into a snake that experiences "the joy of pushing his fangs" into two men before he is killed. In "The Circular Valley," perspective is outside the human altogether: We experience the valley, and human visitors to the valley, through the restive consciousness of the "Atlajala," a demonic spirit capable of passing into sensate creatures:

> It would become one of the swallows that made their nests in the rocks beside the waterfall. In the burning sunlight it would plunge again and again into the curtain of mist that rose from far below. . . . It would spend a day as a plant louse, crawling slowly along the under side of the leaves, living quietly in the huge green world down there which is hidden forever from the sky. Or at night, in the velvet body of a panther, it would know the pleasure of the kill. Once . . . it lived in an eel at the bottom of the pool . . . ; that was a restful period, but afterward the desire to know again the mysterious life of man returned—an obsession of which it was useless to try to rid itself.

Even in first-person narratives like "Pages from Cold Point" the reader feels distanced from the speaker, to whom and around whom things happen with an eerie, dreamlike inevitability. In *Too Far from Home*, the narrator is an unstable woman, in retreat from a disastrous marriage, who, without knowing what she does, evokes a curse on two young fellow Americans visiting the Niger River valley; in turn, she is herself under the spell of a black servant—in this place where "blacks were the real people and . . . she was the shadow, and . . . even if she went on living here for the rest of her life she would never understand how their minds worked."

Bowles's epigraph to Book 1 of *The Spider's House* (1955) might be an epigraph to all his fiction:

> I have understood that the world is a vast emptiness built upon emptiness. . . . And so they call me the master of wisdom. Alas! Does anyone know what wisdom is?
>
> (Song of the Owl, *The Thousand and One Nights*)

And then there are Paul Bowles's numerous nonfiction works in which his voice, his first-person persona, is so strikingly different from the voice, or voices, of the fiction.

In the scrupulously observed travel essays collected under the exotic title (from, in fact, Edward Lear) *Their Heads Are Green and Their Hands Are Blue: Scenes from the Non-Christian World* (1963), in the elegantly composed "lyrical history of Morocco" *Points in Time* (1984), in the resolutely unsensational *Without Stopping* (1972) and *Days: Tangier Journal 1987–89*, and in letters and interviews, Paul Bowles emerges as a dispassionate analyst of culture and of his own life. Temperamentally antithetical to, for instance, Ernest Hemingway and countless fellow writers whose supreme fiction is their self-created image, Bowles declares himself *not* a mythmaker; his efforts are to clarify, not obfuscate. His intelligence is a beacon that illuminates but does not blind, as in the sharply observed anthropological passages in the travel essays; in the autobiographical *Without Stopping*, his tone is one of earnest bemusement with the circumstances of his life and of life generally—"Things don't happen. It depends upon who comes along."

So uninflected in tone and so noncommittal in revealing "secrets" is *Without Stopping*, that Bowles's longtime friend William Burroughs remarked that it might more accurately be titled *Without Telling*. Yet Bowles's account of his long, crowded life is generous with information; he is unsparing in the melancholy details, for instance, of his life as a child. (He was born on December 30, 1910, the only son of a Long Island dentist and his wife: His relations with his abusive father, a thwarted violinist, were always strained. The father had allegedly tried to kill him as an infant and never ceased monitoring and restricting his behavior, with the result that at the age of eleven Bowles "vowed to devote my life to his destruction, even though it meant my own—an infantile conceit, but one which continued to preoccupy me for many years.")

Great memoirs are carefully orchestrated works of art, like Thoreau's *Walden*; they are no more "authentic" than works that announce themselves as fictional texts, though they may contain (or appear to contain) historical veracity. Bowles's memoirs are bluntly direct and honest, for the writer perceives that what he recalls is not an actual event, but merely a memory of the last time the event was recalled; for Bowles, this sort of writing is a kind of journalism, devoid of the strategies of art. His role is to undercut speculation, for instance, about his lengthy expatriated life in Tangier, by saying that he did not choose to live in Tangier permanently—"It happened." Similarly, in his autobiography, as in his life, there is little drama because there was no struggle: "I hung on and waited. It seems to me that this must be what most people do."

Bowles's egoless detachment from his own life has allowed him, through the decades of his career, to cast a cold eye upon the world and his own position within it. How significant then that he did find a permanent home in a part of the world that to the American sensibility would indeed seem like a region outside God's jurisdiction—a region where nothing, save the Infinite, is real.

Jean Stafford:
Biography as Pathography

Jean Stafford: A Biography
by David Roberts (Little, Brown)

Though this has been an era of magisterial biographies by such
writers as Leon Edel, Richard Ellmann, Joseph Frank, Judith
Thurman, and Justin Kaplan, among others, it has also evolved a new
subspecies of the genre to which the name "pathography" might usefully be given: hagiography's diminished and often prurient twin. In
the traditional biography the subject is usually substantial enough to
support high claims for his or her cultural significance; the spirit of
the times may also be examined, as a way of presenting and comprehending the subject. Thus, for instance, in Ellman's posthumously
published life of Oscar Wilde the story of Wilde and the history
of his epoch dovetail; Frank's immensely ambitious biography-in-
progress of Dostoyevsky is a fact-filled, analytical study of the novelist in the social and political context of nineteenth-century Russia.

By contrast, pathography typically focuses upon a far smaller canvas, sets its standards much lower. Its motifs are dysfunction and disaster, illnesses and pratfalls, failed marriages and failed careers,
alcoholism and breakdowns and outrageous conduct. Its scenes are
sensational, wallowing in squalor and foolishness; its dominant images are physical, and deflating; its shrill theme is "failed promise," if
not outright "tragedy." Biographies of writers as varied as Robert
Frost, Ernest Hemingway, John Berryman, Dylan Thomas, Katherine Anne Porter, Tennessee Williams, and now of the novelist and

short story writer Jean Stafford so mercilessly expose their subjects, so relentlessly catalogue their most private, vulnerable, and least illuminating moments, as to divest them of all mystery save the crucial, and unexplained: How did a distinguished body of work emerge from so undistinguished a life? In some notorious pathographies (Lawrence Thompson's *Robert Frost*, for instance) a true malevolence seems to be the guiding motive. As in a court of law to which the (deceased) defendant has no access, a trial of sorts is launched; evidence damningly presented; the testimonies of old friends, acquaintances, rivals, and enemies honored. When, in a 1952 interview, Jean Stafford made the remark that "Irony is a very high form of morality," she could hardly have anticipated the painful sort of irony represented by *Jean Stafford: A Biography.*

David Roberts, whose three previous books have been on the outdoors, has written a seemingly well-intentioned but numbingly repetitive and emetic life of Jean Stafford that falls into pathography's technique of emphasizing the sensational underside of its subject's life to the detriment of those more scattered, and less dramatic, periods of accomplishment and well-being. Jean Stafford, who died in 1979, was the author of a small, circumscribed, exceedingly fine body of fiction who had the misfortune to succumb to alcoholism and was unable to complete a major novel upon which she had labored intermittently (and, it would seem, despairingly) for more than twenty years. Instead of granting Stafford the singularity of her achievement—the highly regarded novels *Boston Adventure*, *The Mountain Lion*, and *The Catherine Wheel* and some two dozen superbly crafted short stories—the biographer chooses to sound, from virtually his first page, the clarion call of "failed promise"; his claim is that "the causes of Stafford's decline are several and elusive" and that "for all the excuses she loved to make, at the deepest level she knew that she had no one to blame but herself." Thus pathography's unmistakable slant, emphasis, tone.

Never considering that early praise lavished upon Jean Stafford upon the occasion of her first novel, *Boston Adventure*, in 1944, might have been journalistic hyperbole—*Life* excitedly heralded the twenty-eight-year-old author as "the most brilliant of the new fiction writers"—Roberts judges most of Stafford's adult life in terms of its "decline" and grants to her twenty-odd years of alcoholic crises as much weight as the earlier, productive years. Surely this is unfair? And surely wrong-headed? Where a judicious biography might diplomatically round off a consideration of its subject's career when the career is more or less over, summarizing years of fitful dissolution in a brief space, the pathography shifts into high gear, becoming a repository of illnesses and disasters and disappointments, primarily because evidence—letters, documents, witnesses' testimonies—is abundantly available. Admirers of Jean Stafford's writing will be dismayed at the demeaning images this biography yields: Stafford in various stages of public and private drunkenness; Stafford in Payne Whitney, and—thirty-four times!—in New York Hospital; Stafford tripping over her cat and falling downstairs drunk; or vomiting into her purse; or glimpsed through a window by a friend, passed out cold; Stafford hallucinating in Grand Central Terminal; Stafford as a "fag hag" in East Hampton; Stafford as a "battered, bruised, drunken old woman" of whom, in 1973, one of her oldest friends declares: "I was very happy to turn my back on her." Yet more offensively, the biographer claims to detect a thread of syphilitic infection through most of Stafford's life, speculating upon circumstantial evidence that she contracted the disease in 1936, while studying in Heidelberg, and that the disease radically affected her entire life. Suicidal moments are duly noted; cruel, unsparing testimony by numerous witnesses is provided. The menu of ailments and paranoid fantasies escalates, ending finally, mercifully, in death by cardiac arrest at the age of sixty-three, after a severe stroke had left Stafford aphasic. Is there no defense, no way of eluding such protracted exposure? As Oscar Wilde once observed, the prospect of biography "adds to death a new terror."

Jean Stafford was born in Covina, California, in 1915, and grew up in Boulder, Colorado, where she attended the University of Colorado; after leaving home—initially to study philosophy in Heidelberg— she set herself passionately in opposition to her family, and seems to have mythologized her relations with them. She would afterward boast that she had left home at the age of seven, and friends observed how "desperately" she wanted to be an orphan. Her early literary heroes were Proust and Thomas Wolfe. She so despised her mother's optimistic, platitudinous nature that she kept a notebook of her mother's clichés and transcribed her mother's letters to her with jeering annotations, to be sent to her friends. Her father was "brutal" and may have been a bit mad: He was an obsessive, unpublished writer, a would-be Western novelist and autodidact who did not support his family but labored for a prodigious thirty years on an incomprehensible crank analysis of government deficit spending. Eerily, Jean Stafford's later career would recapitulate John Stafford's: she was to work for twenty-four years on "A Parliament of Women" and left behind a miscellany of fragments—in her biographer's blunt words, "a mess." (Yet out of these fragments her editor Robert Giroux assembled one of her most powerful short stories, "An Influx of Poets.")

Stafford's ill-advised marriage to Robert Lowell seems too to have recapitulated certain elements of her relationship with her father. She immediately recognized the young poet's emotional instability, so fearing his "pathological" nature and his capacity for violence that she considered getting an injunction against him—yet marrying him anyway, after an automobile accident caused by Lowell's careless driving left Stafford critically injured. Her reason: Although at times Stafford hated Lowell, "he does what I have always needed to have done to me and that is that he dominates me." And this "dominating" seems to have included physical abuse.

A difficult marriage followed, described in letters to Peter Taylor and Stafford's old friend Robert Hightower (with whom she was to correspond forty years), and dramatized in such poignant stories as "A Country Love Story" and "An Influx of Poets." Though Stafford documented a near-strangling episode shortly before her and Lowell's separation, their divorce in 1948, after eight years of marriage, seemed to have permanently unmoored her: There would be two other marriages (to Oliver Jensen, a *Life* editor, and to A. J. Liebling, the *New Yorker* writer), but Lowell was clearly the passionate center of her life. Even her writing, about which she had once been so ambitious, lost its meaning:

I know this, Cal, and the knowledge eats me like an inward animal: there is nothing worse for a woman than to be deprived of her womanliness. For me, there is nothing worse than the knowledge that my life holds nothing for me but being a writer. . . . In your letter you say that you hope I will be recognized as the best novelist of my generation. I want you to know now and know completely that that would mean to me absolutely *nothing*.

Though Roberts doesn't make the connection, it is interesting to note how, decades later, in Stafford's derisive polemical pieces against feminism—including the notorious "review" of Susan Brownmiller's study of rape that has Stafford seemingly defending rapists against their accusers—the essence of what might be called Stafford's masochism would be given an angry eloquence. If men are born to be "brutal" and to "dominate," surely it is perverse for women to object, and to unify their objections in political activism? As Roberts notes, Stafford expended her creative energies in later years by writing crankily amusing satirical pieces for magazines and even condemnatory letters to strangers. Among her last published essays were serio-comic indictments of the contemporary world for *Esquire*, the *New York Times*, and *Vogue*.

Jean Stafford's novels and short stories, however, are entirely free of polemics. Mere opinions do not engage her. If there is some writerly concern with excessive drinking, and bizarre behavior, and "bad characters"—*Bad Characters* being the title of one of her story collections—the writing remains precisely honed, the sensibility intelligent and seemingly impartial. Among Stafford's many strengths as a writer of fiction are a sharp poetic eye for the telling detail—the memorialized antique sleigh that becomes the very vehicle of madness in "A Country Love Story," the doomed capuchin monkey Shannon of "In the Zoo"—and an authorial voice that ranges from the sinewy and vernacular to the coolly detached. If Stafford learned from Mark Twain on the one hand and from Proust, Henry James, and Virginia Woolf on the other, these lessons were fully assimilated. In certain of her mature work the author's voice is both immersed in the narrative and hovering above it, as in a ghostly meditation in which all action, all life, is retrospective. It might be said of Stafford at the peak of her powers as Stafford says of the disfigured accident victim

Pansy of "The Interior Castle": "Pansy felt horror, but she felt no pity."

Of Stafford's three well-received novels only *Boston Adventure* (1944), her first, sold well—it was in fact a best-seller, with 400,000 copies in print; and this despite the novel's literary manner, its resolutely old-fashioned language that advances the narrative by slow grudging degrees. *The Mountain Lion* (1947) and *The Catherine Wheel* (1952), by contrast, both possess the sharpness of dramatic focus and the economy of style of superior short stories, and may have sold poorly because of their very excellences. Though one would not want to stigmatize Stafford by suggesting that she is a "writer's writer," these novels, particularly *The Mountain Lion*—a subtly and brilliantly realized tragedy of adolescence, told in a remarkably graceful and seemingly artless voice—were, and remain, highly regarded by other writers, and substantiated early claims for Stafford's gifts. Awards and honors came to her in plenty, including a number of O. Henry prizes, inclusion in *The Best American Short Stories*, and, in 1970, the Pulitzer Prize for her *Collected Stories.* Perhaps more important, the novels and the collected stories are all in print today, and a collection of Stafford's essays and reviews will soon be published. In the light of these achievements the charge of "failed promise" seems singularly unjust. Must every writer aspire to being George Eliot, Dickens, Tolstoy?

When not reiterating Stafford's frustrations with writing and her astonishing medical history—has anyone save Jean Stafford, aged forty-seven at the time, ever answered "yes" to all but one or two questions on a medical history form?—not to mention her alcoholic breakdowns, and when not pursuing the motif of the "secondary syphilis" infection, David Roberts writes of his subject with compassion and intelligence. He has clearly done a good deal of reading (the correspondence with Hightower alone is 591 manuscript pages) and has talked to many witnesses. He does not avoid the biographer's penchant for scrutinizing works of art for what they might yield of the life, as if sifting for bone fragments, nor does he attempt to place Stafford in a context of the literature of her time. Some of his claims strike the ear as merely promotional. Did Stafford discover or invent the mode of fiction in which she wrote, or is it simply the mode of psychological realism we have come to call "traditional"?—inherited from Joyce, Chekhov, James, Conrad, above all Flaubert. And if Stafford is, in his opinion, "her generation's outstanding investigator of abandonment, voluntary exile, and self-estrangement," perhaps some consideration of the work of Stafford's gifted and possibly more original coevals—for example, Flannery O'Connor, Katherine Anne Porter, John Cheever, and Robert Lowell himself—might have been provided. The intense focus upon the merely personal (and physical) leaves the account claustrophobic and airless, like a sickroom. No biographer is compelled to follow his subject into disintegration.

The most memorable parts of *Jean Stafford: A Biography* belong, not surprisingly, to Stafford herself. Beyond a certain point in her life, like her one-time friend and fellow "failure" Delmore Schwartz, Stafford seems to have channeled her writerly brilliance into her correspondence; the letters quoted are wonderfully astute, unsparing, funny, wicked, illuminating. Only Evelyn Waugh has outdone Jean Stafford in terms of sheerly venomous humor. There is a hilarious account of a committee meeting at the American Academy–Institute of Arts and Letters, of which Stafford was a member, and yet a more hilarious letter of 1974 that begins "Not long ago I had a scandalously bad meal at Craig Claiborne's and haven't accepted any invitations anywhere since then" which must be read to be believed. Treated generously by *The New Yorker* for many years after the magazine had stopped publishing her fiction, Stafford nonetheless said "terrible things" about the editors; she teased the literary world about the contents of her fourth novel, hinting that it was close to completion when in fact it was not—"A well-known American poet, with whom I was once closely associated, is petrified. And well he should be! I am cutting up the poets to a fare-thee-well." Her writing students at Columbia were "cretinous"; at Penn State, "cretinous" and "loutish." Occasionally she relented, confiding in Eve Auchincloss, "I am growing meaner by the hour and I bitterly regret that I did not prick this sac of simon-pure venom long ago." Yet Stafford was unsentimental about herself and cast a very cold eye upon the cornucopia of ailments that settled upon her in middle age; she told Wilfrid Sheed, in 1976, that she didn't mind dying, "but emphysema is such an *uncomfy* way to do it."

Jean Stafford's most inspired act of venom was posthumous. As a way of taking revenge upon the many friends and East Hampton neighbors who had tended to her over the years of her decline, she willed her estate to her cleaning woman, and named her literary executor, in Robert Giroux's place, though the woman had never read Stafford's work and was minimally educated. (This, scarcely a week after "An Influx of Poets" had appeared in *The New Yorker*, as a consequence of Giroux's creative editing.) For years afterward Stafford's friends speculated over her motive—which was surely one of the reasons she did it. If the fiction writer's imagination is not aired in her craft it will manifest itself in other ways.

David Roberts concludes *Jean Stafford: A Biography* by confessing that his "fondest fantasy" is that readers unfamiliar with Stafford's work might put down his book and say, "What an interesting woman. I wish I'd known her." Given this pathographical portrait, would it not be more reasonable to hope that readers turn to her books instead? For a writer's life *is* his or her books. As Henry David Thoreau once said, in the hope of discouraging an admirer from visiting him, "You may rely upon it, you have the best of me in my books."

To Bedlam: Anne Sexton

Anne Sexton: A Biography by Diane Wood
Middlebrook (Houghton Mifflin)

Because Anne Sexton's reputation seems to be bound up irrevocably with that school, or mode, or habitude of poetry called "confessional," it is helpful to state at the outset that much of lyric poetry through the centuries has been frankly and unapologetically confessional. Shakespeare's sonnets, the love poems of John Donne, work by poets as diverse as Wordsworth, Shelley, Yeats, D. H. Lawrence, indeed even Emily Dickinson, when decoded—all wrote intimately, and all wrote magnificently. The test in judging poetry, if one feels obliged to judge it, is not its content so much as the beauty or power or technical brilliance with which poetry is written. In charging that Anne Sexton is "confessional" and that the "confessional" is in some generic way repugnant, one is probably saying instead that the degree of artistry in some of Sexton's poems is at fault. But the "confessional" as a tradition is surely legitimate.

Of American poets of recent decades, only Allen Ginsberg has rivaled Anne Sexton as a figure of intense controversy; a media figure of a kind "too much aware of . . . the audience"—to quote from Sexton's English editor at Oxford University Press, Jon Stallworthy, in 1972. Only Ginsberg seems to have evoked such extreme responses from readers and critics, and such excitement and adulation from large, sympathetic audiences for public readings. These are poets who would seem to have stepped out from behind the mask of poet or writer to reveal themselves naked, on display. Apparently lacking, or repudiating, the usual strategies of subterfuge, Ginsberg and Sexton, and a few others, transcend, in their best poetry, the very confines of the "self," and seem to speak for numberless others who have had their experiences. Diane Middlebrook aptly quotes a fan of Sexton's: "I don't read poetry, but I read Anne Sexton."

Of course, when the poetry is less than successful, the "confessions" may simply appal, or bore. The remarkable technical achievement of Sexton's early books *To Bedlam and Part Way Back* (1960) and *All My Pretty Ones* (1962), which produced poems that packed a considerable dramatic wallop, gave way, over the intense, often manic eighteen-year career the poet rode like a roller-coaster, to poems that seem rather more raw sketches for poetry; glimmering with passion and images but repetitive, overassertive, verging at times upon self-parody. (As in much of *The Book of Folly* [1972], *The Death Notebooks* [1974–the year of Sexton's suicide], and the posthumously published *The Awful Rowing Toward God* [1975], *45 Mercy Street* [1976], *Words for Dr. Y.* [1978].) Dianne Middlebrook's sympathetic but resolutely unsentimental biography charts the trajectory of Sexton's life and career from early formalism to late disintegration, making the case for the observation the poet Maxine Kumin made at the time of Sexton's death, that, suicidal as she was, prone to alcohol and drug addiction, Sexton would have disintegrated long before 1974 had it not been for the discipline and solace of poetry, and, not least, the ego-gratifying public response her poetry received. Unlike Sylvia Plath, whom in obvious ways Sexton resembles, Sexton did not die at the height of her powers. No doubt, this was partly why she chose to die, so very deliberately, at the age of forty-five; after dozens of suicide attempts of varying degrees of seriousness.

(Sexton carried "kill-me" pills in her purse, the very brand of powerful barbiturates she had taken from her parents' medicine cabinets after their deaths. Her final act was well planned: Fortified by alcohol and pills, wearing her mother's fur coat, Sexton died of carbon monoxide poisoning in the garage of her home. Two days before, she had given a tumultuously acclaimed reading at Goucher College.)

Diane Wood Middlebrook, herself a poet, spent ten years researching this intelligent, sensitive, at times rather harrowing biography;

which is, fortunately, a critical biography as well. Biographers invariably possess all sorts of information—and wisdom—not available to their subjects, who were after all caught up in the process of living, and some of them, smug and self-promoting, use this advantage to pass facile judgments upon their subjects; but Middlebrook is more concerned with understanding Sexton, and presenting a coherent "reading" of her, in that way allowing the reader to make his or her judgment. Given the flamboyant excesses of Sexton's life—her virtually countless love affairs, for instance, while still married to her long-suffering husband, Kayo—many observers will see the woman as exhibitionistic, promiscuous, deranged. Yet Sexton speaks for herself: ". . . ever since my mother died, I want to have the feeling someone's in love with me. . . . A fine narcotic, having people in love with me." As Sexton's closest friend and confidante, the gifted poet Maxine Kumin, said, "Anne always had the notion she was the most underloved person in the universe. There could never be enough proof that she was loved."

One measure of merit of contemporary biographies, in this age of word processors, taped interviews, and a penchant for delivering torrents of words without critical restraint, is the proportionality of the work; its formal presentation, pacing, presentation of materials, and analysis. After a decade of investigation, Diane Middlebrook surely had a staggering amount of material, but superfluities have largely been eliminated, and the poet's life arranged in chronological periods that seem reasonable, even logical. The work is informed by at least one guiding principle—that poetry was not Sexton's sickness, but her stay against sickness. Passages dealing with Sexton's poetry as poetry are very capable, and others' voices (Sexton knew many, many people, including the most prominent poets of her time) are artfully woven into the narrative. Yes, *Anne Sexton: A Biography* does contain material that might be regarded as scandalous, particularly those parts dealing with (real? fantasized?) incest in the Sexton family, including incestuous behavior on Sexton's part with her eldest daughter, Linda, but it will be a pity if this deflects attention away from the rest of the biography.

A final remark, which is rather more of a query: Is it ethical, under any circumstances, for a psychiatrist to release material involving one of his patients?—even if, in the case of Anne Sexton, it is probable that she would not have minded? (Yet, who can tell? With age, Sexton might have lost her desire for self-exhibitionism.) Therapy notes and hundreds of hours of audiotapes were made available to Diane Middlebrook by Sexton's psychiatrist of eight years, Dr. Martin T. Orne of the Institute of Pennsylvania Hospital, without which the biography as it stands could not have been written. Though Dr. Orne emerges as a model of compassion and insight, and though Anne Sexton herself adored him, one wonders—is this a dangerous precedent? Or is it merely another symptom of our era, in which the very nature of "privacy" seems to be undergoing a radical reassessment?

Bellow's Portraits

A Theft by Saul Bellow (Penguin)

Among contemporary American writers there are many stylists of distinction, for ours is an age of intense literary activity, much idiosyncratic virtuosity and invention. The general assumption may be that "realism" is not an experimental literary convention but simply "the way things are"; but practicing writers know that all genres, all visions, all artful employments of language are conventions, freely available to the virtuoso. Of presumed "realists" no contemporary of ours is more distinctive, more consistently inspired and defiantly risky than Saul Bellow, our genius of portraiture. What a gallery of outsized characters he has given us, more benign than Hogarth's but no less individual! What coruscating flights of language in his prose, what waterfalls of self-displaying energy! For one who has been reading Saul Bellow attentively since the early 1950s, the briefest passage of Bellow prose, a sentence fragment or quirky throwaway metaphor, is enough to sound the unmistakable Bellow note.

Saul Bellow's employment of the English language is in the service, however, of a larger agenda. He is not an experimental writer in the usual sense of the word, for the forms of his most characteristic fiction are conventional, and repeatedly used; nor does his elastic prose condense to opacity, forcing the reader to stop and admire it at the expense of the story. In Bellow, ideas too, "big" ideas, though obsessively aired, aria-like indeed, seem to us pretexts to enable the author to display, and to admire, and to analyze, the phenomena he loves best: the haunting contours and textures of the physical world, and the mystery of human personality in its extraordinary variety. Who but Saul Bellow would think to lyrically celebrate the "greatness of place," of Gary, Indiana (in *The Adventures of Augie March*); who could so brilliantly transpose the late Delmore Schwartz into "Von Humboldt Fleisher" (of *Humboldt's Gift*) that the mysterious charismic power of Schwartz is perfectly communicated to those who never knew him; who but Bellow might say of a character, Moses Herzog's rival Valentine Gersbach with his artificial leg, that the man resembled, walking, a Venetian gondolier, and, in repose, "Putzi Hanfstaengl, Hitler's own pianist"? Bellow's fiction provides us too with variations of the writer-self, the mesmerized, indeed besotted, deep thinker, like the young prodigy Zetland of the short story "Zetland: By a Character Witness," who ponders, in a fever: "What were we here for, of all strange beings and creatures the strangest? Clear colloid eyes to see with, for a while, and see so finely, and a palpitating universe to see, and so many human messages to give and to receive. And the bony box for thinking and for the storage of thoughts, and a cloudy heart for feelings. Ephemerids, grinding up other creatures, flavoring and heating their flesh, devouring this flesh. A kind of being filled with death-knowledge, and also with infinite longings." In *More Die of Heartbreak* (1987), the wily Ken notes that freaks have disappeared from the public world only to reappear in private life as "psychological types." These "types" are, of course, the novelist's prize specimens.

A Theft, Bellow's new novella and his thirteenth work of fiction, is both like and unlike previous work of his. All of Bellow's major characters bear an unmistakable family resemblance to one another, like the overheated, compulsively driven characters in Dostoyevsky; we recognize them instantly when they are described (Bellow's favorite adjective is "powerful"), and as soon as they begin to talk . . . and talk. Charley Citrine observes of his friend Von Humboldt Fleisher that he was "the very Mozart of conversation," and a similar observation might be made of Bellow's stand-up monologists with their flights of fanciful verbosity and seemingly inexhaustible energy. Clara Velde, the heroine of *A Theft*, is of Bellow's tribe, pitched directly at us in the novella's opening paragraph: "In a person of an inert character a head of [Clara's] size might have seemed a deformity; in Clara, because she had so much personal force, it came across as ruggedly handsome. She needed that head; a mind like hers demanded space. . . . Her forehead was powerful." But because Clara is a woman, and leading women have been conspicuously absent in Bellow's fiction, *A Theft* is something of a departure for its author, a venturous undertaking into the inner and outer lives of "a rawboned American woman." For Clara is not imagined by way of one of Bellow's articulate, ceaselessly analytic male protagonists, the way Herzog gives us his ex-wife, Madeleine, or Mr. Sammler his daughter; she is presented directly, head-on, and is indeed the pivotal consciousness of the novella.

Unlike previous Bellow heroines, Clara Velde is no mere object of masculine adoration or pejoration. She is strong-willed, with a "backcountry" spirit. We are told (though this is never entirely convincing) that she is a "corporate executive" in a journalistic agency specializing in high fashion for women. Her upbringing is Protestant, Midwestern, absurdly narrow; but she is passionate, even Amazonian in her appetites, and has been married, unhappily, four times. She is the "attentive" mother of three small girls, the exasperated wife of a lazy, unemployed husband (Wilder Velde appears only in the corner of our eye: He spends most of his time reading semi-trashy novels), the faithful and unfailingly devoted lover of a high-powered Washington consultant and international figure named Ithiel Regler, whom she loves, as she declares, with her "soul." It is the loss—the theft—of an emerald ring that Regler gave Clara, years ago, when they were considering marrying, that sets the somewhat attenuated plot of *A Theft* into motion, forcing Clara to more clearly define her relationship with the elusive Regler (he who knows "the big, *big* picture" and who once debriefed the shah of Iran on the subject of Henry Kissinger) and with her ten-year-old daughter, Lucy, by way of whom the ring is finally returned. But "story" in Bellow is always subordinated to portraiture, and *A Theft* is not the sum of its kinetic parts.

Though inspired in passages, and, over all, an intriguing possibility, the novella seems underimagined; its protagonist simply lacks the irresistibly interesting voice that would have made it come alive, in the way that Bellow's fiction generally comes alive—the triumph, indeed, of "voice"; of prose written for the ear. Clara Velde does not seem to us intelligent enough for her worldly position, nor even for her author's continued investment in her (how obvious that Bellow much prefers Regler); women readers will smile, or wince, when the mask slips and we are asked to admire Clara preparing an elaborate meal for her lover in the nude, wearing only clogs ("Whether she was dressed or nude, her movements were always energetic; she didn't know the meaning of slow-time"), and near the novella's conclusion, when Clara and her Austrian au pair girl, a Columbia University student, talk together ("How abnormal for two women, one of them young, to have such a mental conversation"; Frederic, the "arrogant" West Indian who steals the ring, is scarcely there on the page—as a personality he doesn't exist; and there is something melancholy in the coincidence that, only one person of color inhabiting Clara Velde's cartoon-glossy world, it is that person who turns out to be the thief. Clara's complaint to her psychiatrist, "The men I meet don't seem to be real persons. Nobody really is anybody" speaks to the sketchily imagined atmosphere of her narrative.

"You're a Surrealist in spite of yourself," the narrator of the story "Him with His Foot in His Mouth" is told by a friend; and this insight surely applies to Saul Bellow himself. Though he has been widely honored as a "realist" and a "novelist of ideas" (no more Establishment-rewarded American writer has ever lived: three National Book Awards, one Pulitzer Prize, the Nobel Prize in 1976), Bellow might be more accurately seen as a surrealist with an eye for the illuminatingly absurd; a writer whose deepest energies incline him, for all his public lamenting of our "fallen species," toward the sunlit spaces of comedy and away from the more subtle counterminings of tragedy. Bellow's works of fiction nearly always end on a strong, positive, "upbeat" note; his characters not only survive their snarled problems and pratfalls, but learn from their experiences, and are articulate about their learning. We are told clearly what they have learned and are not obliged to deduce it for ourselves. This is a fiction very different from, for instance, that of Kafka, or Faulkner, which forces us to participate in experience without defining it for us; Bellow's is a more socialized, accessible art, of accommodation, not terror.

John Updike's Rabbit

Rabbit at Rest by John Updike (Alfred A. Knopf)

With this elegiac volume, John Updike's much-acclaimed and, in retrospect, hugely ambitious Rabbit quartet—*Rabbit, Run* (1960), *Rabbit Redux* (1971), *Rabbit Is Rich* (1981), and, now, *Rabbit at Rest* (1990)—comes to an end. The final word of so many thousands is Rabbit's, and it is, singularly, "Enough." This is, in its context, in an intensive care unit in a Florida hospital, a judgment both blunt and touchingly modest; valedictory and yet enigmatic. As Rabbit's doctor has informed his wife, "Sometimes it's time." But in the nightmare efficiency of late twentieth-century medical technology, in which mere vegetative existence may be defined as "life," we are no longer granted such certainty.

Rabbit at Rest is certainly the most brooding, the most demanding, the most concentrated of John Updike's longer novels. Its courageous theme—the blossoming and fruition of the seed of death we all carry inside us—is struck in the first sentence, as Harry Angstrom, "Rabbit," now fifty-five years old, more than forty pounds overweight, waits for the plane that is bringing his son Nelson and Nelson's family to visit him and his wife in their semiretirement in Florida: He senses that it is his own death arriving, "shaped vaguely like an airplane." We are in the final year of Reagan's anesthetized rule— "Everything falling apart, airplanes, bridges, eight years . . . of nobody minding the store, making money out of nothing, running up debt, trusting in God."

This early note, so emphatically struck, reverberates through the length of the novel, and invests its domestic-crisis story with an unusual pathos. For where, in previous novels, most famously in *Couples* (1968), John Updike explored the human body as Eros, he now explores the body, in yet more detail, as Thanatos. One begins virtually to share, with the doomed Harry Angstrom, a panicky sense of the body's terrible finitude, and of its place in a world of other, competing bodies: "You fill a slot for a time and then move out; that's the decent thing to do: make room." Schopenhauer's definition of walking as "arrested falling" comes to mind as one navigates Rabbit's downward plunge: There is an angioplasty episode, recounted in John Updike's typically meticulous prose, that is likely to be quite a challenge for the hypochondriacs and physical cowards among us (I'm not sure I met the challenge—I shut my eyes a few times); there are candid and unself-pitying anecdotes of open-heart surgery; we come to know how it probably feels to suffer not one heart attack but two; how it feels to strain one's "frail heart" by unconsciously (i.e., deliberately) abusing one's flabby body. A good deal is made, in the Florida scenes, of the American retired-elderly; Rabbit thinks, with typical Rabbit crudeness, "You wonder if we haven't gone overboard in catering to cripples." A former mistress of Rabbit's named Thelma (see *Rabbit Is Rich*) reappears in these pages as a lupus sufferer, soon to die, not very gallantly described as smelling faintly of urine. There is an AIDS patient who exploits his disease as a way of eluding professional responsibility, and there is a cocaine addict—Rabbit's own son, Nelson—whose dependence upon the drug is pushing him toward a mental breakdown.

The engine that drives the plot in John Updike's work is nearly always domestic. Men and women who might be called "ordinary Americans" of their time and place are granted an almost incandescent allure by the mysteries they present to one another. Janice Angstrom to Harry, in *Rabbit Redux*, as an unrepentant adultress; a young woman, to Harry, as possibly his illegitimate daughter, in *Rabbit Is Rich*; and now Nelson, to Harry, as his so strangely behaving son, whose involvement with drugs brings the family to the very edge of financial and personal ruin. Thus, though characters like Janice, Nelson, and, from time to time, Rabbit himself are not very sympathetic, and, indeed, intended by their resolutely unsentimental creator not to be so, one is always curious to know their immediate fates.

John Updike's choice of Rabbit Angstrom, in *Rabbit, Run*, was an inspired one; one of those happy, instinctive accidents that so often shape a literary career. For Rabbit, though a contemporary of the young writer, born, like him, in 1933, and a product, so to speak, of the same world (the area around Reading, Pennsylvania), was a "beautiful brainless guy" whose career (as a high school basketball star in a provincial setting) peaked at age eighteen; in his own wife's view, he was, before their early, hasty marriage, "already drifting downhill." Needless to say, poor Rabbit is the very antithesis of the enormously promising class president of the Class of 1950 of Shillington High School, the young man who went to Harvard on a scholarship, moved away from his hometown forever, and became a world-renowned writer. This combination of cousinly propinquity and temperamental opposition has allowed John Updike a magisterial distance in both dramatizing Rabbit's life and dissecting him in the process. One thinks of Flaubert and his doomed fantasist Emma Bovary, for John Updike with his precisionist's prose and his intimately attentive yet cold eye is a master, like Flaubert, of mesmerizing us with his narrative voice even as he might repel us with the vanities of human desire his scalpel exposes.

Harry Angstrom, who tries to sate his sense of life's emptiness by devouring junk food—"the tang of poison he likes"—the very archetype of the American macho male whose fantasies dwell, not like Emma Bovary's, on romance, but on sports, appears as Uncle Sam in a Fourth of July parade in *Rabbit at Rest*, and the impersonation is a locally popular one. Rabbit, who knows little of any culture but his own, and that a culture severely circumscribed by television network shows, is passionately convinced that "all in all this is the happiest f—ing country the world has ever seen." As in *Rabbit Redux* he was solidly pro–Vietnam War, so, as his life becomes increasingly marginal to the United States of his time, in ironic balance to his wife's increasing involvement, he is as unthinkingly patriotic as ever—"a typical good-hearted imperialist racist." (*Rabbit Redux*)

Rabbit is not often good-hearted, however, living as he does so much inside his own skin. Surprised by his lover's concern for him, he thinks, funnily, of "that strange way women have, of really caring about somebody beyond themselves." From *Rabbit, Run* to *Rabbit at Rest* Rabbit's wife, Janice, is repeatedly referred to as "that mutt" and "that poor dumb mutt," though she seems to us easily Rabbit's intellectual equal. As a younger and less coarsened man, in the earlier novels, Rabbit generates sympathy for his domestic problems, but the reader is stopped dead by his unapologetic racism. ("Niggers, coolies, derelicts, morons." *Rabbit Redux*.) An extreme of sorts, even for Rabbit, is achieved when, at Thelma's very funeral, he tells the dead woman's grieving husband that she was a "fantastic lay." Near the end of the novel it is suggested that Rabbit's misogyny was caused by his mother! (Perhaps women should refrain from childbirth in order to prevent adversely influencing their sons?) It is a measure of John Updike's prescience in creating Rabbit Angstrom thirty years ago that, in the concluding pages of *Rabbit, Run*, Rabbit's ill-treated lover Ruth should speak of him in disgust as "Mr. Death." If "Mr. Death" is also, and enthusiastically, "Uncle Sam," the Rabbit quartet constitutes a powerful critique of America.

Of one aspect of America, in any case. For, behind the frenetic activity of the novels, as behind stage business, the "real" background of Rabbit's fictional Mt. Judge-Brewer, PA, remains. One comes to think that this background is the novels' soul, and the human actors but puppets or shadows caught up in the vanity of their lusts. So primary is homesickness as a motive for writing fiction, so powerful the yearning to memorialize what we've lived, inhabited, been hurt by, and loved, the impulse often goes unacknowledged. The being that most illuminates the Rabbit quartet is not finally Harry Angstrom himself but the world through which he moves in his slow downward slide, meticulously recorded by one of our most gifted American realists. Lengthy passages in *Rabbit at Rest* that take Rabbit back to his old neighborhoods—"hurting himself with the pieces of his old self that cling to almost every corner" (p. 181)—call up similar nostalgic passages in the autobiographical *The Centaur* and the memoir *Self-*

Consciousness as well as numerous short stories and poems tasked with memorializing such moments of enchantment. This, not the fallen adult world, the demoralizing morass of politics, sex, money, the ravaging of the land, is the true America, however rapidly fading. The Rabbit novels, for all their grittiness, constitute John Updike's surpassingly eloquent elegy for his country, as viewed from the unique perspective of a elegy for Pennsylvania.

After Rabbit's first heart attack, when he tells his wife of an extraordinary sight he has seen on one of his drives through the city, pear trees in blossom, Janice responds, "You've seen [before], it's just you see differently now." But John Updike has seen, from the first.

Henry Louis Gates, Jr.'s
Colored People

Colored People: A Memoir by Henry Louis Gates, Jr.
(Alfred A. Knopf)

As in one of those bizarre and thought-provoking visual paradoxes of the Dutch mathematician–graphic artist M. C. Escher,
where infinity opens up vertiginously within a single geometric figure, object and anti-object define each other, and "foreground" and
"background" are made to shift, depending upon one's perspective,
the highly combustible issue of race in America, and its consequences
in terms of the academic-literary canon, depends almost entirely
upon one's position. The much-publicized "culture wars" and the
serio-comic "battle of the books" of the American literary-academic
community—the bitter controversies over who will determine the
sacred "canon"—are less about putative standards of literature than
about what constitutes "worthy" life. Is the imprimatur of literature
to be bestowed exclusively upon a ruling class, Anglo-Saxon in origin, in any case European-descended, with a further emphasis upon
(heterosexual) male experience? Are the imaginative products of
other kinds of experience, i.e., other lives, by definition less significant, because those lives themselves are less significant? "Color is not
a human or personal reality," James Baldwin has said. "It is a political
reality." Substitute "gender," "ethnic identity," "class" for the word
"color," and you can see how far-ranging and how potentially anarchic the controversy is. And how far from being resolved, or even
fully articulated.

Henry Louis Gates, Jr., Professor of English and Chairman of Afro-American Studies at Harvard University, has been one of the most articulate commentators on the subject. His first scholarly interest was the recovery and editing of "lost" and ignored texts, primarily slave narratives; by way of his position as general editor of the Schomburg Library of Nineteenth-Century Black Women Writers, and what might be called a genius for academic entrepreneurism, he has ascended to academic stardom in the United States, the envy of his coevals of whatever color, gender, or -ism. Gates is the author of seminal works of cultural-literary-linguistic exegesis, the award-winning *The Signifying Monkey* and *Figures in Black*, as well as miscellaneous essays and reviews, some of them collected in the recent *Loose Canons: Notes on the Culture Wars*, a handbook of multiculturalism written with much zest, style, and sly good humor—characteristics of Gates's "academic" writing in general. *Loose Canons* is to the maze of *multi's* in the once monochromatic *culturalism* what Terry Eagleton's *Literary Theory: An Introduction* has been to academic literary criticism: an invaluable guide.

Overlapping with some of the more personal passages of *Loose Canons* is Gates's partial memoir *Colored People* (it ends in 1969, as the prodigious nineteen-year-old prepares to enter Yale). Presented as a document addressed to Gates's young daughters, to aid them in understanding the rapidly vanishing world of his boyhood, *Colored People* is "the story of a village, a family and its friends" as much as it is "Skip" Gates's personal account of his coming of age during one of the most tumultuous epochs in American history: the rise of the pacifist civil rights movement under the leadership of the Reverend Martin Luther King, Jr., in the mid-1950s. The account is artless, engaging, funny and moving and disturbing by turns; each chapter is thematically focused (religion, love/sex, politics, "playing hardball," family life, black/white styles of cooking, the ritual of "doing" hair), rich with fondly recalled detail, like home movies narrated by the brightest and most intriguing of friends. There is no *theory* here, no distracting subtext. Unlike the canonical works of black male autobiography that have surely shaped Gates's political thinking, Richard Wright's *Black Boy* and *American Hunger*, for instance, James

Baldwin's *The Fire Next Time* and *No Name in the Street*, and *The Auto-biography of Malcolm X, Colored People* is not an angry, still less an incendiary work; its predominate tone is nostalgic and affectionate. "Everybody worked *so* hard to integrate the thing in the mid-sixties, Aunt Marguerite mused, because that was what we were supposed to do then, what with Dr. King and everything. But by the time those crackers made us join them . . . we didn't want to go." Without glossing over painful episodes of racial discrimination and the overall "inconvenience" of segregation, Gates has written a black intellectual's valentine to his origins with which, in its emphasis upon familial attachments and pride of place, virtually any reader can identify.

Though he does not portray himself in such terms, for this is not a mythopoetic text, Gates does emerge as an archetypal "transitional figure": He is born into a seemingly ahistoric "colored" world of the 1950s, enters adolescence in a "Negro" world of the early 1960s, and comes to maturity in a politicized "black" world of the late 1960s—the shift in terms suggesting the rapidity of change, the increasing intrusion of the political into the private. (Beyond "black"—which many older colored people resisted using, for its historic negative connotations—lies the cumbersome "Afro-American," and beyond that the still more cumbersome "African-American." At the cutting edge of discourse at the present is the term "people [or persons] of color," but, as Gates predicts, the original "colored people" may well make a return—if coined in the correct quarters.) In any case, Gates introduces himself as *not* "Everynegro":

> I want to be black, to know black, to luxuriate in whatever I might be calling blackness at any particular time—but to do so in order to come out the other side, to experience a humanity that is neither colorless nor reducible to color. . . . What hurt me most about the late sixties and the early seventies is that we lost our sense of humor. Many of us thought that enlightened politics excluded it.

Piedmont, West Virginia, where Henry Louis Gates, Jr., was born in 1950, was a fairly prosperous mill town, in a culturally isolated valley, with a population of 2,565, of whom 350 were colored. The social topography of this thoroughly segregated world was as clearly defined as a map: Each ethnic group (Italian, Irish, WASP, colored, etc.) had its neighborhoods, and each ethnic group its prescribed work. (Colored men employed by the paper mill, for instance, like Gates's father, were allowed only one position regardless of their skill or intelligence: loading paper onto trucks.) White men and the occasional white woman on the prowl might venture into colored territory with impunity, but the obverse was not possible, nor even imaginable. A Norman Rockwell small-town landscape of the 1950s, where colored people knew their collective place. For most colored people, most white people were vague, shadowy-functional beings: "Mr. Mail Man, Mr. Insurance Man, Mr. Landlord Man, Mr. Po-lice Man . . . like allegorical figures in a mystery play." (This, ironically, in the light of surreptitious interracial affairs and unacknowledged births across racial boundaries—white genes fathered on black women, of course.) Segregation was perceived as a condition of existence, unquestioned. Everyone "got along pretty well," as Gates says, in a characteristic ironic riff:

> At least as long as colored people didn't try to sit down in the Cut-Rate or at the Rendezvous Bar, or eat pizza at Eddie's, or buy property, or move into the white neighborhoods, or dance with, date, or dilate upon white people. Not to mention to try to get a job in the craft unions at the paper mill. Or have a drink at the white VFW, or join the white American Legion, or get loans at the bank, or just generally get out of line. Other than that, colored and white got on pretty well.

That colored people in Piedmont were not allowed to buy their own houses and land was particularly infuriating to Gates's mother, a woman of strong convictions and extraordinary courage.

Initially, it was by way of television that the colored of Piedmont, West Virginia, were awakened to the civil rights movement, and to the glimpsed world of "property whites could own and blacks couldn't." Television became the "ritual arena for the drama of race." With civil rights legislation passed by Congress and the federal-enforced desegregation of public schools in Little Rock, Arkansas,

the state universities of Mississippi, Alabama, Georgia, and elsewhere, the seemingly ahistoric status quo abruptly changed: By
1956, the six-year-old Gates was attending an integrated school, apparently with no trouble from whites; by 1968, when he graduated
from high school, this clearly remarkable boy has been elected president of his class four times, and was valedictorian, on his way to a distinguished professional career of a kind unimaginable for colored
Piedmont students in previous generations. (Though Gates's father's
family, who lived elsewhere, included doctors, lawyers, dentists,
pharmacists, teachers; and his mother's family members were highly
respectable Christian men and women, "self-righteous" non-drinkers,
non-smokers, non-gamblers.) It is a point of Gates's memoir that despite national social upheaval in the 1960s, Piedmont colored did not
lose their identities and sense of worth; the boy Skip was made to feel
loved at all times, and knew himself "cloaked in the mantle of my
family." Compare this sepia-tinted portrait of familial/neighborhood
solicitude with the stark accounts of growing up black in urban areas
during those same approximate years published—remarkably, all in
1994—by the gifted black writers Brent Staples (*Parallel Time:
Growing Up in Black and White*) and John Edgar Wideman (*Fatheralong: A Meditation on Fathers and Sons, Race and Society*). One wonders:
What might have been Gates's fate if he had been born in a black
urban ghetto, and not in Piedmont, West Virginia? Among other
things, *Colored People* is a testament to the felicity of pure chance: the
helplessness of even the most gifted among us in the face of sheer
luck, whether good or bad.

Skip Gates's abrupt bad luck, which might well have determined
his entire life, occurred when he was fourteen years old, in 1964.
Having injured his knee playing football, he was carelessly misdiagnosed by a white surgeon; even more crudely accused of faking—
"There's not a thing wrong with that child," the doctor tells Mrs.
Gates, as her son lies writhing in agony on the floor; "the problem's
psychosomatic. Because I know the type, and the thing is, your son's
an over-achiever." It doesn't require much sagacity to deconstruct
"over-achiever": a Piedmont colored boy with straight A's in school
who hopes to be a doctor. Fortunately, the intrepid Mrs. Gates refused to believe the white authority and, in one of those impulsive ac-

tions that determine the course of a life, defied the doctor by checking her son out of the local hospital and driving him sixty miles to a university medical center—where he would endure, among other things, three operations in a single year. Eventually, Gates had to learn to walk again, since his leg muscles had atrophied and his hip had been permanently injured.

Though there are other trials (including an ugly near-lynching when Gates and high school friends try to integrate a local white tavern), fortune smiles on the protagonist of *Colored People*; if he is cast in the mold of an American archetype, it is that of a Horatio Alger boy-hero, whose meritorious character, clean living, and willingness to work hard bring him worldly success. *Colored People* is a gentle and eloquent document to set beside the grittier contemporary testimonies of black male urban memoirists; in essence a work of filial gratitude, paying homage to such virtues as courage, loyalty, integrity, kindness; a pleasure to read and, in the deepest sense, inspiring. And funny. Here is part of the "personal statement" the young Gates included with his application to Yale:

My grandfather was colored, my father was Negro, and I am black. . . . As always, whitey now sits in judgment of me, preparing to cast my fate. It is your decision either to let me blow with the wind as a non-entity or to encourage the development of self. Allow me to prove myself.

In 1929, in 1949, even in 1959, what would have been the fate of such brashness? But, fortunately for Henry Louis Gates, Jr., it was 1969, and a new America, and "they let me in."

John Edgar Wideman: Memoir and Fiction

The Cattle Killing by John Edgar Wideman
(Houghton Mifflin)

In a probate-office storage vault in Abbeville, South Carolina, an elderly, white ex–history professor is showing a black writer from Massachusetts whose slave ancestors lived in the Abbeville region itemized documents relating to the sale and possession of slaves. The black writer is grateful for the historian's generous assistance (though the historian has never met the writer before, he has volunteered to spend several days with him), and so it comes as a considerable shock to the writer that, as he gazes down at the back of the historian's head, he feels an "ice-cold wave of anger at him . . . at his thin, freckled bald skull" and an impulse to do injury.

It was Professor Lomax's skull I had envisioned shattering, spilling all its learning, its intimate knowledge of these deeds that transferred in the same "livestock" column as cows, horses, and mules, the bodies of my ancestors from one white owner to another. Hadn't the historian's career been one more mode of appropriation and exploitation of my father's bones. . . ? Didn't mastery of Abbeville's history, the power and privilege to tell my father's story, follow from the original sin of slavery that stole, then silenced, my father's voice . . .

I knew in that moment my anger flashed we had not severed ourselves from a version of history that had made the lives of my

black father and this white man so separate, so distant, yet so intimately intertwined.

(Fatheralong)

This isn't fiction, as we might wish, but a vividly delineated scene
from John Edgar Wideman's painfully frank memoir of 1994, which
records the author's search for a point of connection between himself
and his emotionally remote, elusive father. ("The first rule of my
father's world is that you stand alone. Alone, alone, alone. . . . My
mother's first rule was love. She refused to believe she was alone.")
Fatheralong is a sustained brooding upon mysteries of identity and
kinship; the title itself reflects Wideman's childhood mistaking of
the words in a hymn "Farther along we'll know more about you . . ."
For "Fatheralong." Though the memoir includes in its penultimate
chapter a celebratory rite of passage, a wedding attended by both
black and white family members (Wideman is married to a white
woman), its predominant tone is one of rage just barely contained by
finely honed language. Addressed to Wideman's incarcerated son
(who was sentenced to life in prison for the murder of a camp roommate when he was a young adolescent—information only alluded to
in the memoir), its departure point is Wideman's epiphany, gazing at
his newborn son in a hospital, of "the chill of the cloud passing . . .
between you and your boy. The cloud of *race*." In this context, the
documents shown to Wideman by Professor Lomax, who means only
to be helpful, and who may well have perceived his own generosity
as a token of reparation for his ancestors' crimes against Wideman's
ancestors, are an obscenity, confirming "how much the present, my
father's life, mine, yours [his son's], are still being determined by the
presumption of white over black inscribed in them."

Unsparing in its candor, *Fatheralong* is a fiercely compelling document no reader is likely to forget; a sequel of sorts to Wideman's
1984 memoir, *Brothers and Keepers,* which focuses upon the author's
younger brother Robby, who is serving a life sentence in Pennsylvania for felony murder. These are brilliant autobiographical works
to set beside such masterpieces of American memoir as Richard
Wright's *Black Boy (American Hunger)* (1945), James Baldwin's *The
Fire Next Time* (1962), and *The Autobiography of Malcolm X* (1964).[1]

* * *

Just as John Edgar Wideman's memoirs frequently read like fiction, so do his most characteristic works of fiction frequently read like memoirs. A transparently autobiographical "I"—variously named, or anonymous, or, as in Wideman's new novel *The Cattle Killing*, "Eye" ("Eye. Why are you called Eye. Eye short for something else someone named you. Who named you Isaiah.")—sifts through a fine-meshed, virtually Proustian consciousness the issues of race, identity, kinship, and the tragedy of history with which the memoirs deal. Since the boldly mythical title story of the collection *Damballah* (1981), and most ambitiously in the title story of the collection *Fever* (1989) and the novel *Philadelphia Fire* (1990), Wideman has been breaking down conventional narrative barriers between characters, places, and times. In Wideman's cosmology, it is quite natural for an African ancestor to inhabit the narrative space of, for instance, a young Philadelphia street-wise black; his frequent dissolution of language suggests the linguistic mysticism of James Joyce's *Finnegans Wake*, though Wideman's strategy is to restrict his range of associations to a single haunting and obsessive theme. A virtuoso of voice mimicry, Wideman is capable of leaping without warning from the measured cadences of an idealized eighteenth-century black speech ("Curled in the black hold of the ship he wonders why his life on solid green earth had to end, why the gods had chosen this new habitation for him, chained to other captives, no air, no light, the wooden walls shuddering, battered, as if some madman is determined to destroy even this last pitiful refuge . . . and Esu casts his fate, constant motion, tethered to an iron ring." {"Fever," in *Fever*}) to the voice of a contemporary Philadelphia black man working as a hospital attendant in a nightmare nursing home ("Yeah, I nurse these old funky motherfuckers, all right. White people, specially old white people, lemme tell you, boy, them peckerwoods stink. Stone dead fishy wet stink." {"Fever"}) Amid the dithyrambic lyricism of voices that tell the minutely interwoven tales of *The Cattle Killing* there abruptly emerges, at the novel's end, a distinctly contemporary American black voice, a vatic, incantatory voice of apocalypse arising from the nightly news tragedies of Pittsburgh and Chicago and Los Angeles and Detroit and New York and Dallas and Cleveland and Oakland

and Miami: "From the ashes of your sacrifice a new world of peace and plenty will arise, they say. The prophets of ghost dance, the prophets of the cattle killing, prophets of Kool-Aid, prophets of bend over and take it in your ear, your behind, prophets of off with your head, prophets of chains and prisons and love thy neighbor if and only if he's you, prophets of one skin more equal than others. . . ." This voice both is, and is not, that of John Edgar Wideman: It is the omniscient "Eye."

Though set for the most part in the eighteenth century in Philadelphia and vicinity, and in an earlier, mythic black Africa, *The Cattle Killing* is purposefully framed by contemporary American black voices. It begins with a prologue in which the mysterious "Eye" slips away from a literary conference apparently devoted in part to his own work ("You step out the hotel door and into another skin. . . . Is it Eye or I or Ay or Aye or Aie"); and travels to another part of the city to visit his aging father, and to read to him from a work-in-progress clearly resembling *The Cattle Killing*; it ends with an epilogue in which a young man named Dan, evidently Eye's son, has just completed reading the manuscript: "*Dear Dad.* Just finished *Cattle Killing*. Congrats. A fine book. Look forward to talking about it with you soon." A jarringly unlyrical voice, after all that has preceded it, yet it's crucial for Wideman to link generations of fathers and sons and to collapse the time gulf between them, and between the present and the past out of which the present has evolved; it happens that the young Dan has been doing his own research into the slave trade, and *The Cattle Killing* ends with a letter photocopied from the British Museum's African archives, from a nameless black African to his brother: "This note, the others I intend to write, may never reach you, yet I am sure a time will come when we shall be together again." As Wideman's "Eye" insists, these are "different stories over and over again that are the same story"—the exploitation of people of color by Caucasians, and their tragic, if inadvertent, complicity in some aspects of this exploitation.

Wideman has described his long, ambitious, hallucinatory story "Fever" (1989) as a meditation upon history, inspired by Absalom Jones and Richard Allen's *Narrative* (1794), as well as two recent accounts of the Philadelphia yellow fever epidemic of 1792–93, Gary

B. Nash's *Forging Freedom* (1988) and J. H. Powell's *Bring Out Your Dead* (1949). In "Fever," Negroes are not only blamed by influential white men like the bigoted Temperance leader Dr. Benjamin Rush for bringing "Barbedos fever" to Philadelphia; they are accused, against all evidence, of being immune to the disease themselves (" . . . a not so subtle device for wresting us from our homes, our loved ones, the afflicted among us, and sending us to aid strangers. . . . A dark skin was seen not only as a badge of shame for its wearer. Now we were evil incarnate, the mask of long agony and violent death." ["Fever"]) In the yet more ambitious and hallucinatory new novel *The Cattle Killing*, Wideman's most complex novel to date, the nightmare of the yellow fever epidemic is re-imagined, with many more characters, subplots, and settings (both Europe and Africa); though, oddly, for no reason that seems to make thematic sense, the re-imagined Dr. Rush, one "Benjamin Thrush," is credited with having never subscribed to the theory that Negroes from the West Indies brought the plague with them; even though, like the historic Rush, he himself is "part of the chorus insisting upon the Negroes' immunity, thereby denying them assistance until he witnessed with his own eyes how the deadly tide of fever had swept through [the] neighborhood . . . where the poorest folk, Negroes the poorest of these, are trapped."

The strategy of *The Cattle Killing* is set out explicitly for us at the start of the novel:

Certain passionate African spirits—kin to the ogbanji who hide in a bewitched woman's womb, dooming her infants one after another to an early death unless the curse is lifted—are so strong and willful they refuse to die. They are not gods but achieve a kind of immortality through serial inhabitation of mortal bodies, passing from one to another, using them up, discarding them, finding a new host.

Occasionally, as one of these powerful spirits roams the earth, bodiless, seeking a new home, an unlucky soul will encounter the spirit, fall in love with it, follow the spirit forever, finding it, losing it in the dance of the spirit's trail through other people's lives.

Souls transmigrate from body to body; the African ritual of cattle-killing among the Xhosa people, a desperate and futile attempt to ward off European domination, is evoked as a metaphor for the condition of contemporary American blacks: "The cattle are the people. The people are the cattle." Wideman doesn't suggest why such a bizarre and clearly self-destructive prophecy was ever preached in Africa; perhaps there is no historical explanation for what appears to have been a schism in the Xhosa people between an apocalyptic-visionary prophet and the more level-headed of the tribal elders, who understand that "to kill our cattle would be to kill ourselves." In a paroxysm of misguided purification, the tribe's cattle are slaughtered, with disastrous results.

The Cattle Killing juxtaposes lyric, parable-like tales with presumably authentic historic accounts and testimonies taken from the *Narrative* of Absalom Jones and Richard Allen; boldly, the author indicates little distinction between voices (which tend to the vatic), times, or settings. The result is a novel frequently difficult of access, reminiscent of Virginia Woolf's almost too determinedly lyric *The Waves*. In the foreground is a fairly straightforward story of a former slave who has become an itinerant Christian preacher, who is haunted by the memory of a Haitian woman he has glimpsed only once carrying a pale, apparently dead infant in her arms as she disappears into a lake; the preacher arrives in Philadelphia at the time of the mysterious yellow fever epidemic, and works for Bishop Allen of the African Church, while becoming involved with one Dr. Thrush (the historic Benjamin Rush), a madman/rapist in addition to being a dangerous racist who promotes the fiction, in defiance of self-evident fact, that Negroes are responsible for the epidemic. As the yellow fever rages, apocalyptic terrors and beliefs emerge, tempting the superstitious to interpret it in divine punitive terms: "God sent the fever to purge us. To cleanse. To humble us. . . ." Earlier, in Africa, the Xhosa people have fallen under the spell of a charismatic psychopath-prophet who convinces them that only the ritual destruction of their precious herds of cattle will save them from European domination: "Though the prophecy promises paradise, a terrible future lived in the words. They were a mouth eating the people. When we slaughtered our herds, we doomed our children." As *The Cattle Killing* moves to a muted conclusion, the loss of faith of the black preacher and his inability to speak without stuttering "in this language that's cost me far too much to learn"—that is, the white man's Christian tongue with its tradition of acquiescence in the face of tragedy—the narrative shifts abruptly back to "Eye," who has become a preacher of sorts on the subject of contemporary America and Africa—"One day I will tell you about Ramona Africa in her cell and Mandela in his cell and the names of the dead we lit candles for in Philadelphia, in Capetown, in Pittsburgh." The curse of "cattle-killing" is still operant.

That the experience of reading John Edgar Wideman's prose is radically different from any paraphrase of its subject matter and theme should be clear, as this brief discussion of *The Cattle Killing* suggests. With "Eye" as witness and omniscient narrator, we are constantly aware of the fiction being constructed, though Wideman is less intrusive in *The Cattle Killing* than in earlier works, like certain of the stories in *Damballah*. Still, no contemporary writer with the possible exception of John Barth is more riskily self-referential than Wideman. The dangers of such a preoccupation with self are obvious, yet there are rewards as well, for the gradual accretion of biographical fact establishes the reader as an intimate of the writer's, familiar with both the life and the work.[2] Or, at any rate, the "life" of Wideman as mediated by the work. In Wideman's metafictional imagination, it would seem that "life" and "work" are indistinguishable, so to interrupt a narrative to speak as himself or as the omniscient "Eye" is simply to be honest, authentic; to acknowledge the artificial nature of all language simultaneously with the acknowledgment of the driven personal quest that underlies it.

Though *The Cattle Killing* is a novel, it might be most helpfully read as a kind of music; an obsessive beat in the author's head from which he yearns, like Stephen Dedalus in a similar historic context, to be wakened; a work of operatic polyphony that strains to break free of linguistic constraints into theatrical spectacle. (In the heightened, surreal mode of, for instance, Suzan-Lori Parks's *Venus*, a recent play by this gifted young black playwright on the Victorian phenomenon of the Venus Hottentot.) Despite his tragic subject matter, John Edgar Wideman is frequently a celebrant of passion and intense subjectivity, as this passage from the penultimate section of *The Cattle Killing* suggests:

> Tell me, finally, what is a man. What is a woman. Aren't we lovers first, spirits sharing an uncharted space, a space our stories tell, a space chanted, written upon again and again, yet one story never quite erased by the next, each story saving the space, saving itself, saving us. If someone is listening.

Tempered with hesitation and even irony as these words are, they seem to us beautiful, tempting us to believe.

NOTES

1. The 1990s has been a time of exemplary black memoirs, suggesting the special appeal of the genre to those who perceive themselves, and may be perceived by others, as both inhabiting and being excluded from mainstream white America. Among these accounts of growing up black in America are Gerald Early's essays collected in *Tuxedo Junction* (1989), *The Culture of Bruising* (1994), and *Life with Daughters* (1995); Henry Louis Gates, Jr's. *Colored People* (1994); Brent Staples's *Parallel Time: Growing Up in Black and White* (1994), a memoir of the author's adolescence in Chester, Pennsylvania, which begins with the death of Staples's twenty-two-year-old younger brother, killed in a drug dispute ("I told myself to feel nothing. I had already mourned Blake and buried him and was determined not to suffer his death a second time"); and Veronica Chambers's *Mama's Girl* (1996), an account of the author's childhood and adolescence as the intellectually ambitious daughter of Caribbean-born parents, whose mother withheld, for a crucial period in Chambers's life, her love and support ("Black women are masters of emotional sleight of hand. The closer you get, the less you can see. It was true of my mother. It is also true of me.")

2. In the midst of the otherwise straightforward story "The Chinaman," from *Damballah*, Wideman interrupts to describe a private domestic scene involving himself and his family on a drive through Iowa; he refers casually to a woman named "Judy," of whom we know nothing except that she feels a migraine coming on. Some readers, familiar with Wideman's biography, will know that "Judy" is in fact Mrs. Wideman;

others will be mystified. And how startling, though thematically appropriate, for Wideman's memoir *Fatheralong* to abruptly shift course in its final chapter, addressed to an absent son who has not figured in the memoir so far, a boy who has caused, and has suffered, what the reader gathers has been a terrible fate: "I remember just a few days after hearing you were missing and a boy found dead in the room the two of you had been sharing. . . . I felt myself coming apart, the mask I'd been wearing, as much for myself as for the benefit of other people, was beginning to splinter." (p. 192) Again, readers familiar with Wideman's biography will know that he is addressing here the younger of his two sons, incarcerated in an Arizona prison for the murder of the son's roommate at camp some years before when the boy was a young teenager. Others will be mystified, at least until Wideman composes another of his extraordinary memoirs. As Wideman has said, "You had to be part of the whole thing to understand. . . ."

Exile and Homeland:
Brian Moore

The Magician's Wife by Brian Moore (Dutton)

For most novelists the art of writing might be defined as the use to which we put our homesickness. So powerful is the instinct to memorialize in prose—one's region, one's family, one's past—that many writers, shorn of such subjects, would be rendered paralyzed and mute. At the heart of even that compendium of virtuoso prose styles *Ulysses*, for instance, is the nostalgic desire, as James Joyce expressed it, to "record the speech of my father and his friends." Writers as disparate as Thomas Hardy, Marcel Proust, William Faulkner, and Edna O'Brien are so closely bound up with their regions as to be unimaginable without them; even the peripatetic Ernest Hemingway, Graham Greene, Paul Theroux, and Robert Stone tend to write from a fixed position of identity, the "Englishman," the "American" abroad. Of writers who set their fictions "nowhere" there are surely few, and these tend to be experimental, and minimalist; yet even Franz Kafka and Samuel Beckett might be said to have sprung from native soil, however transmogrified in their art.

In the company of fellow novelists, Brian Moore has become something of an anomaly. Born of an upper-middle-class Catholic family in Belfast in 1921, Moore saw duty with the British Ministry of War Transport, sent to North Africa, Italy, and France; in 1948, he emigrated to Canada, and became a Canadian citizen; for many years he has lived in Malibu, (southern) California, and Nova Scotia, Canada.

Clearly, judging from the evidence of his prose fiction, Moore has traveled widely, and has thought deeply about the relationship of individuals to their homelands and religious heritages, even as he has set his powerfully imagined novels in a remarkable variety of settings: Northern Ireland (*The Lonely Passion of Judith Hearne*, *The Feast of Lupercal*, *The Temptation of Eileen Hughes*, *Lies of Silence*); Canada (*The Luck of Ginger Coffey*); seventeenth-century "New France" in North America (*Black Robe*); a small French-speaking Caribbean island (*No Other Life*, based upon the history of Father Aristide, Haiti's only democratically elected president); New York City (*The Mangan Inheritance*, *An Answer from Limbo*); an unnamed East European country (*The Colour of Blood*); California (*Fergus*, *The Great Victorian Collection*, *Cold Heaven*); contemporary France (the controversial *The Statement*). The vividly rendered settings for Moore's new novel *The Magician's Wife* are France and Algeria in 1856, settings that suggest conflicting ideologies and traditions: the political power of imperialist Christian France vs. the political power of an intensely religious Northern African Muslim country.

Moore's nineteen very different novels range from a meticulously and lovingly rendered domestic/psychological realism in the mode of William Trevor to odd, unexpectedly surreal and not altogether convincing landscapes; *Cold Heaven*, for instance, opens as a suspense-mystery thriller but rapidly mutates to a mystical parable that reads like an unlikely collaboration between H. P. Lovecraft and Graham Greene at his most Catholic and sentimental. In virtually all of Moore's novels, there is a dramatic, vital connection between protagonist and place: Judith Hearne, the Catholic spinster drifting into alcoholism and isolation, is the lyric embodiment of repressed, claustrophobic Belfast, a descendant of the aging spinsters of James Joyce's *Dubliners*; the elderly Canadian missionary-narrator of *No Other Life*, a white man in a world of mulattos and *noirs* he has come to love, speaks eloquently of his inevitable expulsion from that world; the idealistic young Jesuit missionary Laforgue of *Black Robe*, whose quixotic task it is to "harvest souls" for Roman Catholicism out of the wilderness of Indian savages, is the very embodiment of civilized man confronted by the more intense passions of seemingly primitive lives; the fugitive Pierre Brossard of *The Statement*, based upon the career of the French Nazi collaborator and war criminal Paul Touvier, is characterized by a childlike, narcissistic love of the Roman Catholic Church and by a rabid French patriotism, preferring the possibility of death in France to exile elsewhere, in South America, for instance, with fellow war criminals, eating greasy *métèque* food—"I love France, it's my country, they're not going to drive me out of my country. I'm French, I'll die in France!" (*The Statement*)

Of Moore's novels, *The Statement* is the most boldly conceived. Breathless in execution, plotted like a cinematic thriller, *The Statement* provides hardly more than the exoskeleton of a conventional novel; though very different in form from Albert Camus's tour de force *The Fall*, it shares with that haranguing, obsessive work a desire to dissect our human stratagems of denial, concealment, and criminal hypocrisy by way of sheer "voice"—*The Fall* is a single monologue, and much of *The Statement*, its most powerful passages, is the monologue of the virulent and anti-Semitic murderer Brossard, who reveals himself to the reader, but rarely to himself. We identify with his pursuers, we want him to be hunted down as he deserves, and brought to justice—yet the crude "justice" at the novel's end is merely ironic, irresolute.

The more conventionally structured *The Magician's Wife*, narrated through the critical consciousness of a young French woman of no exceptional intelligence or passion, who happens to be married to the most acclaimed magician in Europe, would seem at the outset very different from *The Statement*, as from other recent works of Moore's. Indeed, the novel contains a number of ceremonial set pieces and lush, leisurely descriptions of court life at the Château of Compiègne in the reign of Emperor Napoleon III—where everything "runs like clockwork"—and of parallel social occasions in Algeria given by the French Governor-General and by prominent Arabs. Brian Moore's female characters are typically more sympathetic than his male characters, partly because, like the magician's wife, Emmeline, they have time to contemplate matters of morality and conscience of which their male counterparts, caught up in action, seem unaware. Through Emmeline's eyes we see the hypocrisy of French intentions to "civilize the Algerians and improve their lives" when the obvious motive is exploitation of the colony; we see the master magician Henri Lambert, for all his dedication to his craft and his idealization of French civilization, as "a man who made his living standing on a stage, smiling at strangers, hoping to deceive them." As husband, lover, would-be father, Lambert is a poor illusionist, but in front of an audience, especially credulous Arab audiences, in a country in which "sorcery" has a religious tradition, he can appear virtually godlike. Arrogantly he proclaims, as a vessel of French imperialism, "My powers are supernatural, granted to me by God." Through ingenious tricks, tirelessly rehearsed until they can be perfectly executed even under physical duress, Lambert succeeds in undermining faith in native Algerian magic, forcing Arab leaders to concede the superiority of the French, with tragic historical results for the Algerians.

Brian Moore's master magician is not a parodic form of the artist or novelist, a creator of illusory worlds, as Thomas Mann might be inclined to see him; he's a "charlatan" who defines his relationship to others in purely adversarial terms: "The audience is like an animal. If you fail to dominate it, it will turn on you." Given its suspenseful and spectacularly cinematic plot, *The Magician's Wife* would seem to be headed for a final catastrophe, yet when the catastrophe comes it isn't quite what one expects but rather more muted, more subtle, and perhaps more tragic.

In its contrast of opposing forms of belief, *The Magician's Wife* will remind readers of Moore's *Black Robe* with its examination of the tragic collision of European Catholic and North American Indian faiths, and of *The Statement*, in which the older, conservative anti-Semitic factions of the French Catholic church and the French government are pitted against their liberal, humanitarian adversaries. Like *Black Robe* and *The Statement*, and other recent work of Moore's, *The Magician's Wife* is a dramatization of historical events: The model for Henri Lambert is Jean Eugène Robert Houdin (1805–1871), the greatest of European magicians (whose renown must have inspired the novice magician Erik Weisz to rename himself Houdini), like Lambert sent by the French government to Algeria in 1856 to match his skills against dissident Arabs; Houdin's most successful trick, like Lambert's, was the theft of a man's strength through electromagnetism. As in Moore's other novels, however, the historical genesis is but the stimulus for a rich, absorbing, and thoughtful meditation upon the uses of "magic" and power, and the ways, sometimes with surprising effectiveness, individual human conscience can respond to such uses. The sympathetic figure of Emmeline gives to *The Magician's Wife* a measure of hope, if only the hope of an awakened European conscience.

Updike Toward
the End of Time

Toward the End of Time
by John Updike (Alfred A. Knopf)

Set in the near future in mythical Haskells Crossing, Massachusetts, an affluent and sequestered oceanfront suburb north of
Boston, John Updike's eighteenth novel and forty-eighth book,
Toward the End of Time, bears an oblique kinship with Updike's first
novel, *The Poorhouse Fair* (1959), similarly set in the near future, amid
the impoverished but articulate elderly. In *The Poorhouse Fair*, a com-
paratively pastoral fiction, American culture has become Hispani-
cized; much of the population seems to be institutionalized in
"swelling poorhouses" as part of the process of Settling:

> —an increasingly common term that covered the international
> stalemate, the general economic equality, the population shifts to
> the "vacuum states," and the well-publicized physical theory of
> entropia, the tendency of the universe toward eventual homogene-
> ity. . . . The end was inevitable, no new cause for heterogeneity
> being, without supernaturalism, conceivable.

At the conclusion of *Toward the End of Time*, a seemingly mystical
"heavenly circle," a torus, appears to the narrator, who links it to cy-
cles of human belief and nonbelief, or human delusion and intellectual freedom:

To generations its presence is evident and the source of omens, miracles, admonitions and reassurances. People live by its wan light, sing its praises while they work. . . . Then it gradually dims, succumbing to mockery and disproof. The generations grow bored with repeating the pieties of their fathers; a cry for human freedom and self-expression rises. . . . The altars are slighted; the temples fall into mossy ruin.

The contemporary world is this "fallen" world, yet "this world by itself is not enough; there must be another"—and, in time, like an elliptically orbiting comet, the torus reappears. Mankind can't endure without "supernaturalism" of some kind, however remote to their personal lives.

Toward the End of Time takes up such issues fairly lightly, for its narrator, Ben Turnbull, is rather more concerned with his waning sexual powers than with the waning of the universe. Like the aging retirees of Updike's recent short story collection *The Afterlife*, he's angry, frightened, resentful, embittered about his body's "accumulating failures" (*The Afterlife*) and his position in "a twilight of inconsequence." The morbidly narcissistic Ben, a retired investment counselor who can't look back upon his life with much pleasure or pride, nonetheless wants to leave something of himself behind by "scribbling these notes concerning an idle, precarious existence in the Earthly year 2020." Like Updike, Ben is gifted with 20/20 vision and sees things, including himself, with painful, pitiless clarity:

I had looked down once again into the dismal basement of life, where in ill-lit corners spiders brainlessly entrap segmented insects, chew them slowly, leave a fuzzy egg sac, and die. All those corpses . . . did they perish of starvation, having spun a web in vain, or of old age, in the natural course of things, after years of drawing upon Medicare and Social Security?

Like *The Poorhouse Fair*, Updike's new novel remains at heart a wholly realistic work, saturated in memory, emotion, meditation, and that staple of realist fiction, human relations. Its often inspired, and funny, "futurist" detail has the function of ectoplasmic daubs on a photograph: It isn't really integral to Ben Turnbull's experience as aging lecher, eventual cancer patient, a fantasist who compensates for his narrow life by drifting into what he calls "parallel universes." Cranky, maudlin, and nasty by turns, now poetic, now crude, yet continuously a rapt witness to what's about him, Ben seems rather more like eighty-six than sixty-six, and his preoccupation with his own aging highlights those prevailing Updike themes, the war between the sexes as James Thurber might have characterized it (Ben's younger, far more energetic wife, Gloria, eagerly anticipates widowhood, Ben thinks, awaiting his death like a "cheerful, soigné vulture"); and what the similarly obsessed Renaissance poets called mutability, the inexorable gravitational tug of death and dissolution ("[My] bed seems a slant surface from which I might fall into an abyss"). For all its strangeness, this is a familiar world in which time's arrow flies in the direction of "well-publicized" entropy and men rail against women who are no longer sexually attracted to them. This is hardly a tragic world, for tragedy implies grandeur and dignity, but a broken, twilit world in which even the art of fiction is dismissed: "that clacking, crudely carpentered old roller coaster, every up and down mocked by the triviality . . . of human experience, its Sisyphean repetitiveness."

If not tragedy, then comedy. A cheerily bleak, black comedy in which, as Ben laconically informs us, there have been catastrophic events that haven't, for reasons the novel doesn't make entirely clear, much affected him and his upper-middle-class Caucasian New England neighbors: a financial crash of 2000; a four-month Sino-American conflict that left millions of Chinese and Americans dead, and much of the United States a radioactive wasteland; the dissolution of the federal government. Oceans are exhausted of fish. Malevolent new mouse-sized animal species called "metallobioforms" ("oil-eaters" and "spark-eaters") have emerged. Earth's atmosphere is so polluted, the very stars have become "dull and hazy." With the weakening of governments, FedEx has gone into the protection racket, extorting money from anxious affluent homeowners like Ben. Yet, instead of nightmare, there's a reassuring grid of the comically banal in Haskells Crossing, where citizens read the *Boston Globe* and the *New York Times*, still delivered to their homes; they seem to have access to food, out of what undefined cornucopia we can't imagine, which they prepare in microwave ovens; they watch TV, mulch their fussy suburban gardens, fret over deer, marauding woodchucks, and occasional squatters on their property; they play golf and ski and, of course, bicker with their aging spouses like "The Honeymooners" seven decades later ("After a certain age marriage is mostly, in its bitter and tender moments both, a mental game of thrust and parry played on the edge of the grave"); Ben's "elderly proximity to death" drives him into fantasies of more passionate lives in which, variously, he's the robust lover of a doe-turned-female ("Deirdre") and of a thirteen-year-old Nabokovian nymphet ("Doreen"); perhaps less convincingly he's a cousin of Saint Paul, known to us as the author of the Biblical Gospel according to Saint Mark. (Clearly, John Updike's writerly ego is more modest than Norman Mailer's, for in Mailer's recent *Gospel of the Son*, it is Jesus Christ Himself whom the author impersonates. If the Virgin Mary is next, in a fiction of her own, my vote goes to Erica Jong as authoress.) Ben is also a tenth-century Irish monk slaughtered by pagan Norsemen, a sadistic Nazi pummeling a captive Jew (who resembles his own physician), and a lone human being in a mysterious primal-symbiotic relationship with an immense fungus. These are curious, wayward adventures that seem merely coincidental to A.D. 2020, as indeed the futurist setting seems merely coincidental to Ben's experience. (Compare, for instance, the classic dystopias Aldous Huxley's *Brave New World* and George Orwell's *1984*, in which radically altered "future" worlds have altered human consciousness, and the cult science-fiction novel *Do Androids Dream of Electric Sheep?* by Philip K. Dick, which was made into the film *Blade-Runner*; compare, too, the intensely imagined contemporary literary novels *The Handmaid's Tale* by Margaret Atwood and *Fiskadora* by Denis Johnson.) *Toward the End of Time* bears a coincidental kinship with Kurt Vonnegut's just-published *Timequake*, a valedictory "stew" of Vonnegut musings and satires whose specific "parallel-universe" premise is that a warp in space-time has caused everyone, for some inexplicable reason, to be propelled back a decade to relive their lives, as in a goofy nightmare of Nietzschean "Eternal Recurrence." Though there is a valedictory tone to Updike's novel as well, Updike's faith in the art of fiction is far firmer than Vonnegut's;

his prose, as always, is distinguished by passages of lyric beauty amid even the despairing rubble of Ben Turnbull's cobwebbed cellar. The prose-poem interludes in which, for instance, Ben recalls his impoverished rural childhood dominated by a passionate, aggrieved mother and a hapless father echo similar passages in other works of Updike's, from the early, gracefully elegiac short stories and the boldly Joycean nostalgia of *The Centaur* (1963) to the lapidary hauntedness of the memoir *Self-Consciousness* (1989) and "A Sandstone House" (in *The Afterlife*), so ubiquitous in his work as to seem the ground bass, the subtext, of virtually all of this enormously gifted writer's prose, and these passages ring with emotional urgency:

> At the kitchen table during a quarrel—and my parents' quarrels were always about the same thing, it seemed to me, about there not being *enough*—she would fold her arms and hide her grief-stricken face in them, terrifying me, for her face was the face of life to me, and I could not bear to have it hid. I witnessed so many tears of anger and frustration and pain on my mother's face, there in our bleak house . . . that I wonder if my heart was not permanently hardened, to save me from a lifelong paralysis of grief.

(Is this jokey old Ben or John Updike, in his perennial, supremely eloquent youth?) Elsewhere, by way of Ben, Updike lovingly describes a manmade and now abandoned second moon in the sky:

> This new moon, visible at night as a faintly luminous lariat slowly moving across the sharp sprinkle of stars, by daytime is imprinted on oxygen's overarching blue like the trace of a cocktail glass, a sometimes silvery ring of pallor.

Meeting such similes running wild in the deserts of Arabia, to paraphrase Coleridge on a poem of Wordsworth's, we should instantly cry, "Updike!"

Inside the Locked Room: P. D. James

A Certain Justice: An Adam Dalgliesh Mystery
by P. D. James (Alfred A. Knopf)

So it is here at last, the distinguished thing!
—Henry James, on his deathbed

Henry James's famous final words might be the epigraph for the literary genre we call mystery-detective. In these usually tightly plotted, formulaic novels a corpse is often discovered as soon as the reader opens the book:

> The corpse without hands lay in the bottom of a small sailing dinghy drifting just within sight of the Suffolk coast. It was the body of a middle-aged man, a dapper little cadaver, its shroud a dark pin-striped suit which fitted the narrow body as elegantly in death as it had in life. . . . He had dressed with careful orthodoxy for the town, this hapless voyager; not for this lonely sea; nor for this death.
>
> (P. D. James, *Unnatural Causes,* 1967)

> On the morning of Bernie Pryde's death—or it may have been the morning after, since Bernie died at his own convenience, nor did he think the estimated time of his departure worth recording—Cordelia was caught in a breakdown of the Bakerloo Line outside Lambeth North and was half an hour late at the office.
>
> (P. D. James, *An Unsuitable Job for a Woman,* 1972)

The bodies were discovered at eight forty-five on the morning of Wednesday 18 September by Miss Emily Wharton, a sixty-five-year-old spinster of the parish of St. Matthew's in Paddington, London, and Darren Wilkes, aged ten, of no particular parish as far as he knew or cared.

(P. D. James, *A Taste for Death*, 1986)

The Whistler's fourth victim was his youngest, Valerie Mitchell, aged fifteen years, eight months and four days, and she died because she missed the 9:40 bus from Easthaven to Cobb's Marsh.

(P. D. James, *Devices and Desires*, 1989)

In P. D. James's new, fourteenth novel, the formulaic opening is given a stylish aerial perspective that suggests something of the novel's sophisticated variant on the old form:

Murderers do not usually give their victims notice. This is one death which, however terrible that last second of appalled realization, comes mercifully unburdened with anticipatory terror. When, on the afternoon of Wednesday 11 September, Venetia Aldridge stood up to cross-examine the prosecution's chief witness in the case of *Regina vs. Ashe*, she had four weeks, four hours and fifty minutes left of life.

(*A Certain Justice*, 1997)

In this essentially conservative and conventional genre, in which form must mirror content, the principle of equilibrium that has been violated at the outset of the adventure must be restored, at least to the reader's satisfaction; that is, mystery must be "solved"—or dissolved. The chaos and general messiness of actual life with which the traditional novel contends can't be the subject of the mystery-detective, for its romantic premise is that mystery, the mysterious, that-which-is-not-known, can be caused to be known and its malevolent power dissolved. Of course, in superior examples of the genre, which would include most of P. D. James's novels, there are ironic qualifications: Murderers may be unmasked, for instance, yet not officially identified and not punished (as in *An Unsuitable Job for a*

Woman, which introduced the young private detective Cordelia Gray, as well as in *A Certain Justice*); the morally reprehensible and despicable, frequently accessories to crime, may prevail to inflict further damage upon their fellows.

P. D. James is expert at suggesting the complexity, often bureaucratic, that qualifies justice or renders it impotent; born in 1920 in Oxford, she was an administrator for the National Health Service from 1949 to 1968, and from 1968 to 1979 she worked consecutively in the forensic science and criminal policy services of the Police Department. There's a mordant zest in her presentation of bureaucratic claustrophobia and petty, and not-so-petty, hatreds among colleagues. Thematically, her novels are cris de coeur from solitary individuals like Cordelia Gray and the elder, melancholic widower Commander Adam Dalgliesh of New Scotland Yard, who find themselves immersed in narratives that resist satisfactory closure; for identifying the solution to murder isn't the same thing as having enough evidence to prove murder. One can recognize evil but lack the power to stop it. P. D. James's novels are known for their verbal density and near-static narrative movement, yet there are moments here and there of passionate lyricism in which the author herself seems to speak, as in this outburst at the conclusion of *The Skull Beneath the Skin* (1982):

Suddenly [Cordelia Gray] felt an immense and overpowering anger, almost cosmic in its intensity as if one fragile female body could hold all the concentrated outrage of the world's pitiable victims robbed of their unvalued lives.

The more disillusioned Adam Dalgliesh, learning he'd been misdiagnosed as suffering from a fatal leukemia when in fact he has a nonfatal mononucleosis, in the opening pages of *The Dark Tower* (1975), thinks pettishly that he'd reconciled himself to dying and surrendering the "trivial" concerns of his life, which include police detection. And now,

. . . He wasn't sure that he could reconcile himself to his job. Resigned as he had become to the role of spectator—and soon not

even to be that—he felt ill-equipped to return to the noisy playground of the world and, if it had to be, was minded to find for
himself a less violent corner of it. . . . The time had come to
change direction. Judges' Rules, rigor mortis, interrogation, the
contemplation of decomposing flesh and smashed bone, the whole
bloody business of man-hunting, he was finished with it.

(For "man-hunting" one might substitute "crime novel–writing.")
Less convincingly, Adam Dalgliesh is meant to be a poet of enigmatic
verse, tall, dark, austere, saturnine; a superlunary figure in the eyes of
such female admirers as Cordelia Gray and his romantic-minded colleague Detective Inspector Kate Miskin, yet strangely lacking in
spirit, intuition, and the sort of verbal virtuosity one might reasonably expect of a protagonist set up as not an ordinary policeman but a
literary man with a modicum of popular success. P. D. James wisely
refrains from offering us samples of Dalgliesh's work: "He didn't
overestimate his talent. . . . The poems, which reflected his detached,
ironic and fundamentally restless spirit, had happened to catch a
public mood. He did not believe that more than half a dozen would
live even in his own affections." (*A Mind to Murder*) Like any veteran
professional, Dalgliesh has anesthetized himself to shocks and has become in the process, as his creator surely can't have intended, something of a dour, condescending prig.

Tweedy Dalgliesh may be P. D. James's fantasy detective, but it's
her female characters with whom she most clearly identifies and in
whom the spark of exhilaration resides. Young Cordelia Gray on her
first case dares to commit perjury in order to protect a middle-aged
murderess with whom she sympathizes—an extraordinary violation
of law on the part of one whose profession is so involved with matters
of guilt and innocence; yet Cordelia gets away with it, clearly with
P. D. James's blessing. Detective Kate Miskin, who has made her way
up from a stifling, impoverished background, is both a competitive
policewoman who takes pride in bettering her male colleagues at the
shooting range and a covert admirer of sexually attractive officers;
she's energetic, adventurous, and willing to acknowledge the complicity of detective and murderer. While her superior officer Dalgliesh broods, Kate thinks:

They were on their way to a new job. As always she felt, along the veins, that fizz of exhilaration that came with every new case. She thought, as she often did, how fortunate she was. She had a job which she enjoyed and knew she did well, a boss [Dalgliesh] she liked and admired. And now there was this murder with all it promised of excitement, human interest, the challenge of the investigation, the satisfaction of ultimate success. Someone has to die before she could feel like this. And that . . . wasn't a comfortable thought.

This is the complicity, too, of the mystery writer and her subject: *Someone has to die before she can execute her art.*

It has been remarked that the genre of mystery-detective is as formal, or formulaic, as the sonnet, yet there's a crucial distinction among types of sonnets (Shakespearean, or English; Petrarchan, or Italian; Spenserian) and yet more distinction among individual, often idiosyncratic sonneteers. No American literary genre is more commercially profitable than the mystery, in which millions of hardcover novels are sold annually, and yet more millions in soft cover, in flourishing sections in bookstores and in one hundred eighty independent "mystery" stores, yet the genre itself contains subgenres of immense importance to practitioners and readers: If you're an admirer of American hard-boiled mystery (Raymond Chandler, Dashiell Hammett, James M. Cain, Jim Thompson, Ross Macdonald, James Ellroy, Robert Parker, James Lee Burke, Michael Connelly), you probably won't like American soft-boiled mystery (Ellery Queen, Rex Stout, Lawrence Block, Mary Higgins Clark, Sue Grafton, Jonathan Kellerman, Margaret Truman, Lilian Jackson Braun and her cat-sleuth series); if you favor espionage (Robert Ludlum, John Le Carré, Len Deighton, John Gardner), chances are you won't like historical mystery (Ellis Peters, Michael Clynes, Peter Ackroyd, Caleb Carr, Anne Perry, Joan Smith); though if you like legal thrillers (Erle Stanley Gardner, Melville Davisson Post, John Grisham, Richard North Patterson), you may well like police procedurals (P. D. James, Ed McBain, Ruth Rendell, Elizabeth George, Patricia Cornwell, Peter Turnbull, Thomas Harris). Overlapping with these subgenres are novels of suspense, or thrillers, a vast category that includes writers as diverse as Cornell Woolrich, Barbara Vine (pseudonym of Ruth Rendell), Robin Cook, Michael Crichton, Elmore Leonard, Dick Francis, Donald E. Westlake, Walter Mosley, Edna Buchanan, James Crumley, Michael Malone, S. J. Rozen, among others. In a separate category is "Sherlock Holmes"—the original sixty tales by A. Conan Doyle plus "sequels" by other writers, and commentary on the career and private life of this most famous of all private detectives; in an ancillary and increasingly quaint category is the traditional British mystery as practiced by Agatha Christie, Dorothy Sayers, Martha Grimes, Julian Symons, Margaret Yorke, R. D. Wingfield et al., characterized by genteel country-house settings, affably amateur detection, bloodless corpses, and tea. (The much-repeated query throughout P. D. James's novels, "Will you have some tea?" suggests the author's affinity with this tradition.)

As in a scientific experiment, the mystery-detective novel advances a number of plausible theories that are investigated by the agent of detection (in P. D. James this agent is a professional policeman, never an amateur), who discards them one by one as fresh disclosures come to light until, by the novel's end, yet ideally before the reader has caught on, only one solution remains. This solution should seem both inevitable and surprising—a daunting combination—though in actual fact, and this is true for P. D. James as well as her less celebrated colleagues, the murderer's identity is often anticlimactic, and as Edmund Wilson fumed in his classic grouse "Who Cares Who Killed Roger Ackroyd?", it isn't uncommon for even devoted readers of the genre to finish a novel without absorbing its ending or even to remember much of it shortly afterward. No literary genre (excepting perhaps women's romance) so lends itself to brainless addiction, for the reason that, while engrossing as it proceeds, at least in theory, the mystery-detective novel dissolves immediately at its conclusion. As Robert Frost said of the lyric poem, though the trope is more applicable to mystery-detective fiction than to most lyric poems, it rides on its own melting "like ice on a hot stove."

The classic structure of mystery-detective fiction is an artfully, sometimes a maddeningly withheld conclusion. The investigation proceeds by carefully plotted chapters, not directly toward its goal but horizontally and laterally, as in a maze. The chaotic open forms of Romanticism would be inappropriate for morality tales, in which a principle of disequilibrium is always specific and identifiable; there's an inevitable airlessness to the genre, an atmosphere of confinement most clearly represented by the locked-room mystery (for which P. D. James's most characteristic novels, including *A Certain Justice*, exhibit an unfortunate predilection). In these mysteries, as the term suggests, a murder, or murders, is committed in a very finite space, during a very finite period of time; there are X number of suspects, introduced to us at the start, whose comings and goings and alibis must be minutely calculated. This is the novel as crossword puzzle, hardly as simulated life. At its most excessive in the fussily choreographed Ellery Queen mysteries of the 1930s and 1940s, the locked-room mystery approaches self-parody; yet even in P. D. James's skilled hands, the conventions of the form can become unintentionally comic:

> Dalgliesh said: "So, if we're thinking at present of those people who had keys to Chambers, were there on Wednesday and knew where to lay hands on the wig and the blood, it brings us down to the Senior Clerk, Harold Naughton; the cleaner, Janet Carpenter; and four of the barristers: the Head of Chambers, Hubert St. John Langton; Drysdale Laud, Simon Costello and Desmond Ulrick. Your priority tomorrow is to check more closely on their movements after seven-thirty. And you'd better check what time the Savoy has its interval, how long it lasts and whether Drysdale Laud could get to Chambers, kill Aldridge and be back in his seat before the play started again. . . .

In actual police work, abrupt confession and informers play an enormous role in the solving of crimes; in fiction, rarely. The informer has no role in the storytelling process, for the object of the story is not to solve its mystery but to forestall it for some two hundred fifty or more pages. Obviously, the mystery writer's ingenuity determines the degree to which false leads seem natural to the reader and not transparently concocted. P. D. James is shrewd enough to both cook her data and appear rueful about it after the fact, by way of her hero Commander Dalgliesh. An associate remarks, at the conclusion of *A Mind to Murder*, a version of locked-room mystery set in a psychiatric outpatient clinic in London, that it was after all a perfectly straightforward case: the obvious suspect, the obvious motive.

"Too obvious for me, apparently," said Dalgliesh bitterly. "If this case doesn't cure me of conceit, nothing will. If I'd paid more attention to the obvious I might have questioned why [the murderer] didn't get back to Rettinger Street until after eleven. . . ."

Dalgliesh can't tell us that if he'd pursued the obvious, *A Mind to Murder* would have been tidily wrapped up in twenty pages.

In *A Certain Justice*, a variant of locked-room mystery set in minutely described chambers (lawyers' quarters in London close by the Bailey), P. D. James is so backed into a corner that she must resort to the narrative cliché of having the murderer boastfully confess to Dalgliesh ("What a pity for you that it is unprovable. There isn't a single piece of forensic evidence to link [me] with the crime"), knowing that Dalgliesh can't arrest him, and the novel ends with startling abruptness on the next page, as if both Dalgliesh and P. D. James were exhausted. This unsatisfactory ending blurs Dalgliesh's integrity as a police officer and makes us question James's motive in so presenting him, at this stage in his career, as lacking the energies of his younger colleagues like Kate Miskin. Unlike the sympathetic murderess of *An Unsuitable Job for a Woman*, who kills the man responsible for her son's death, the murderer of Venetia Aldridge is a rival who will benefit professionally from her death.

The art of mystery-detective fiction isn't an art of conclusions, however, but of suspension, and suspense. What appeals to readers in P. D. James's work is the balance between the pursuit of mystery (in fact, a fairly actionless pursuit by detectives among articulate and sharply drawn suspects) and what might be called her (P. D.) Jamesian sensibility, a fine-textured introspective prose that creates a powerful interior world at some odds with the exterior world presumably the focus of investigative mystery. Dalgliesh and certain of his colleagues perceive the world through the lens of discriminating, often skeptical intelligence; these are cultured police officers with often impressive vocabularies; even cleaning women, as in *A Certain Justice*, may reveal themselves as sharp-eyed observers of the scene, and a psychopathic killer like Garry Asche of that same novel will possess "an I.Q. well above the normal" and a sensibility to match.

P. D. James is wonderfully skilled at evoking atmosphere (especially one of nostalgic melancholy, in historic old churches); she's an indefatigable descriptive artist, sharing with her contemporary Iris Murdoch a passion for Balzacian inventory, whether of city- and landscapes, the London Underground, art works, architecture, interiors, clothing, or people; but her great gift is for the presentation of detailed information, like the inner workings of a psychiatric clinic, or a nuclear power station, or London's Middle Temple, in vividly rendered settings. One feels that, in P. D. James, a world exists complete and mysterious before the eruption of a crime exposes it to outsiders' eyes; this is often not the case in mystery-detective fiction, in which sets may have an air of being perfunctorily assembled, as characters may be hardly more than names on the page, mere puppets in the novelist's hands. In *An Unsuitable Job for a Woman*, an early novel suffused with intermittent rays of happiness, twenty-two-year-old Cordelia Gray undergoes a rite of passage as she begins to fall in love with the young man whose death, and whose desecrated corpse, she's been hired to investigate, while living in his rural cottage not far from Oxford; P. D. James doesn't merely trace the progress of Cordelia's emotional involvement, but allows the reader to participate in it, this "atmosphere of healing tranquility" so at odds with Cordelia's urban (London) life. In *Death of an Expert Witness* we're brought into the intricate, feuding hierarchy of a forensic science laboratory in Chevisham. In *A Mind to Murder*, it's The Steen Clinic for psychiatric outpatients; in *The Skull Beneath the Skin* it's a rich man's estate on an island off the Dorset shore, where an amateur production of Webster's *The Duchess of Malfi* is to be performed:

[Courcy Castle] made [Cordelia Gray] catch her breath with wonder. It stood on the edge of the sea, almost as if it had risen from the waves, a castle of rose-red brick, its only stonework the pale flush lines and the tall curved windows which now coruscated in the sun. To the west soared a slender round tower topped with a cupola, solid yet ethereal. Every detail of the mat-surfaced walls, the patterned buttresses, and the battlements was distinct, unfussy, confident. The whole was compact, even massive, yet the high, sloping roofs and the slender tower gave an impression of lightness and repose which she hadn't associated with High Victorian architecture. . . . The proportions of the castle seemed to her exactly right for its site. Larger and it would have looked pretentious; smaller and there would have been a suggestion of facile charm. But this building, compromise though it may be between castle and family house, seemed to her brilliantly successful. She almost laughed aloud with the pleasure of it.

In *Original Sin*, the most blackly comic, Murdochian novel in P. D. James's oeuvre, we learn more than we might wish to know of Britain's oldest, most distinguished publishing firm, the Peverell Press, founded 1792 with quarters in Innocent House—a Venetian-inspired Georgian building on the Thames, "four storeys of coloured marble and golden stone which, as the light changed, seemed subtly to alter colour." In the very long, intermittently engaging *A Taste for Death* we become posthumously acquainted with a baronet and a minister of the Crown who has had a mystical experience in a derelict church in Paddington; in *Devices and Desires*, we see the romantic Norfolk coast through Dalgliesh's eyes as he broods from the perspective of an inherited windmill, along with minutely following a tangled murder investigation and learning of the internecine power struggles of a nuclear power station.

A Certain Justice, set primarily in lawyers' chambers in London's Middle Temple, is quintessentially P. D. James. Here the unsparing focus is upon high-rank London lawyers in their public and private lives and the possibly "just" fate of an aggressive female criminal lawyer who has made a lucrative career out of successfully defending guilty clients. Who could be a more deserving victim than a coolly beautiful careerist feminist who's also a negligent mother to a troubled teenage girl, a demanding lover of a married politician, an abrasive colleague—and an unscrupulous defense lawyer to boot? Venetia

Aldridge, fated soon to die as a consequence of her very success, is typically unflinching in assessing herself:

> . . . It was only for the convicted clients that she felt even a trace of affection or pity. In her more analytical moments she wondered whether she might not be harbouring a subconscious guilt which after a victory, and particularly a victory against odds, transferred itself into resentment of the client. The thought interested but did not worry her. Other counsel might see it as part of their job to encourage, to support, to console. She saw her own in less ambiguous terms; it was simply to win.

Yet Venetia is thrilled by her own brilliantly manipulating theatrical performance in court, the more satisfying to her when she's defending a sadistic murderer like young Garry Asche, whose guilt she takes for granted.

Like predecessor corpses in *An Unsuitable Job for a Woman*, *A Mind to Murder*, and *Original Sin*, Venetia Aldridge's corpse is luridly "desecrated" after her death, as an expression of someone's (not necessarily the murderer's) sadistic loathing: She's found dead at her desk in Chambers, stabbed through the heart with a letter opener yet doused in blood not her own, a judge's horsehair wig placed mockingly on her head. (One of the complications of the plot has Venetia ambitious to become a judge, to the dismay of certain of her rivalous colleagues.) For all that there's a certain blame-the-victim subtext to *A Certain Justice*, Venetia is presented by P. D. James not only with irony but sympathy. Her passion for the law, her work-obsessed personality, her mordant intelligence identify her as a soul mate of Commander Dalgliesh (whom she never meets) and of P. D. James herself. A woman who has largely invented herself out of a loveless, deprived background (her father was a boys' school headmaster whose sadistic "disciplining" once drove a young boy to suicide), Venetia broods upon the past she should have left far behind; not knowing, as the reader won't know unless he or she cares to read the expertly plotted novel a second time, how this ignoble past, in no way Venetia's fault, will doom her to a brutal death and to the mocking desecration of her corpse by one who wanted "for her just once to pay the price of victory." Venetia's sensibility is thought-tormented, yet often lyric: In one of her reveries Venetia thinks how "memory [is] like a film of sharply focussed images, the set arranged and brightly lit, the characters formally disposed, the dialogue learnt and unchangeable, but with no linking passages." Yet like her murderer-to-be, she's in thrall to memory.

It's Venetia Aldridge, too, who recalls Henry James's admonition "Never believe that you know the last thing about any human heart"—

But he was a novelist. It was his job to find complexities, anomalies, unsuspected subtleties in all human nature. To [her], as she grew into middle age, it seemed that the men and women she defended, the colleagues she worked with became more, not less, predictable. Only rarely was she surprised by an action totally out of character. It was as if the instrument, the key, the melody were settled in the early years of life, and however ingenious and varied the subsequent cadenzas, the theme remained unalterably the same.

But Venetia is fatally complacent about knowing the characters of her own colleagues, among others.

If we leave aside the perfunctory ending, *A Certain Justice* is, in its economy, relative swiftness of pace, and character-driven drama, one of P. D. James's most accomplished recent novels; it even includes, a rarity in this cerebral writer's work, several chapters of thriller-type suspense. (There's a subplot involving Venetia's rebellious daughter, who has been seduced by the calculating killer Garry Asche, in a romantically wild setting on the North Sea coast.) If the primary— and primal—function of the mystery-detective novel is to suggest a restoration of equilibrium after murder's violent assault upon it, this fourteenth novel of P. D. James succeeds admirably, if ironically. P. D. James does not "transcend" genre; she refines, deepens, and amplifies it.

A Dream of Justice:
Dorothy L. Sayers

Thrones, Dominations by Dorothy L. Sayers and
Jill Paton Walsh (St. Martin's Press)

Lord Peter Death Bredon Wimsey burst upon the British mystery
novel scene in 1923, making his debut in *Whose Body?*, a prose
puzzle so contrived and chirrupy it resembles a filigree cuckoo clock.
The thirty-year-old first novelist Dorothy L. Sayers, whose previous publications had been slender books of verse, had clearly read
A. Conan Doyle's best-selling Sherlock Holmes tales, was an ardent
admirer of the wit and wisdom of Oscar Wilde, had a weakness for
West End comedies of manners and problems involving painstaking
feats of deduction; and knew how to write English prose with style
and zest. (Frequently, in her early novels, rather too much style and
zest. As a character says of Lord Peter, the reader might say of his creator: "Your narrative style . . . though racy, is a little elliptical.")
   Whose Body? reads as a virtual parody of a Sherlock Holmes mystery, positing a corpse wearing only gold pince-nez discovered in
a London bathtub: Who is the dead man, how and why has he
been murdered, and why placed with such ceremony in a stranger's
dwelling? The drawling, insufferably breezy aristocrat hero Lord
Peter winds his way unerringly through a snarl of a plot, a dilettante
detective of exceptional mental powers; a shrilly eccentric young nobleman with a "long, amiable face that looked as if it had generated
spontaneously out of his top hat, as white maggots breed from Gor-
gonzola." Dorothy L. Sayers's boldly fantastic British milieu in this

debut novel, as in the subsequent *The Unpleasantness at the Bellona Club*, *Murder Must Advertise*, and *Lord Peter Views the Body*, is populated by colorful caricatures with such names as Throgmorton, Thipps, Crimplesham, Swaffham, Murbles, Freke, Horrock, Griffin, Pyke, Gubbins, Frobisher-Pym, Dahlia Dallmeyer, and the comically inadequate Police Inspector Sugg. Lord Peter's faithful manservant is M. Bunter, a master of English circumlocution and improbable erudition who is far more proper than his showy lord, and an expert photographer and sleuth's assistant to boot.

Contemporary readers of mystery-detective fiction, which has evolved toward ever more realistic and graphic crime novels, like the police procedural, will find Lord Peter a taste acquired with some initial difficulty. If you persevere, however, Lord Peter becomes unexpectedly rewarding, and his very whimsy, so grating at the outset, like a tinny radio turned up too high, can be interpreted as the artful stratagem of a World War I veteran shell-shocked on the battlefield who has had to invent for himself a foppish persona to disguise his shrewd detective's cunning and his shot nerves. Lord Peter is a tour de force of character, superior to the tricky plots his creator has stuck him in; unlike most series detectives in what might be called the crossword-puzzle mode, of which Sayers is a master, Lord Peter actually matures, falls in love, and marries—appropriately, a plain-featured and strong-willed woman mystery writer named Harriet Vane, who has been wrongly charged with murder and whom he'll save from the gallows, in *Strong Poison* (1930).

With *The Nine Tailors* (1934), in which murder, Lord Peter's genius for amateur detection, and the ancient art of change-ringing (bell-ringing) are skillfully interwoven in the atmospheric fen country of East Anglia, Dorothy L. Sayers and her eccentric detective ascend to the Pantheon of Mystery: This scrupulously researched mystery is considered by admirers of the genre to be a masterpiece, and it has been an obvious influence upon the densely plotted, though rather less lighthearted police procedurals of P. D. James. The more romantic mystery *Gaudy Night* (1935), involving Harriet Vane and her devoted Lord Peter, set during a reunion at "Shrewsbury College," Oxford (Sayers graduated from Somerville College in 1915, one of the first women to earn an Oxford degree), became a best-seller in England and made Sayers famous. Along with Agatha Christie and John Dickson Carr, Sayers would be identified with the "golden age" of English mystery-writing: that ingenious but resolutely genteel art so scorned by American mystery writers like Raymond Chandler and Dashiell Hammett.

But the scholarly and devoutly Anglo-Catholic Sayers began to lose interest in Lord Peter and what she perceived to be the "frivolous" craft of mystery-writing she characterized as a "literature of escape" and not a "literature of expression," which by definition can't attain the highest level of literary achievement. In a letter of November 1938, she notes, "I have taken a dislike to [*Thrones, Dominations*], and have great difficulty in doing anything about it." This final Lord Peter mystery seems to have been abandoned at about that time, as Dorothy Sayers became increasingly involved in the writing of religious plays and theological essays, and was found among her papers when she died in 1957, at the age of sixty-four. Completed now by the British mystery writer Jill Paton Walsh in a remarkable collaborative tour de force, *Thrones, Dominations* has been published after sixty years and is an engrossing, intelligent, and provocative novel in the guise of a conventional "mystery": If it lacks the zest and flashy originality of the earlier Lord Peter novels, it seems fully in character with the later, more introspective novels, and its detailed portrait of a marriage, between the no-longer-young Lord Peter and the brooding Harriet Vane, set in well-to-do London society in 1936, is both convincing and moving.

Thrones, Dominations is not a very graceful title, and a few contemporary readers will recognize its source in Book II of John Milton's *Paradise Lost*, in which an unruly regiment of fallen angels, banished by God from heaven, are regrouping, and being addressed by their leader, Satan. Dorothy Sayers, who had a schoolgirl predilection through her life for prefacing many of her chapters with literary epigraphs, some more relevant than others, may have meant the title to indicate that Lord Peter and Harriet Vane, happily married as they are, inhabit a fallen world; it isn't just the murder of an acquaintance that distresses ("Murder is very different when one knew the victim," says a shaken Lord Peter) but the gathering agitation in Europe under Hitler's aggressive invasions, and the gloomy foreknowledge that another war, following so soon after the First World War, is inevitable.

In his now-classic essay of 1944, "The Simple Art of Murder," Raymond Chandler criticizes Dorothy Sayers, and by implication her colleagues in the "golden age" of British mystery, for writing formula fiction which was

> second-rate literature because it was not about the things that could make first-rate literature. If it started out to be about real people . . . they must very soon do unreal things in order to fit the artificial pattern required by the plot. When they did the unreal things, they ceased to be real themselves. . . . The only kind of writer who could be happy with these properties was the one who did not know what reality was.

Yet Chandler's own "realism" has become fantastical, set beside the crime novels and police procedurals now being written by writers as disparate as Ed McBain, Thomas Harris, James Ellroy, and Michael Connelly, in which murder is rarely an art, still less a genteel art to be solved by amateur detectives. While dismissive of the Sayers novels he read, Chandler might have found much to admire in *Thrones, Dominations*, for there is relatively little that is contrived in the tangled plot, and the psychological motives for the murder are respectfully explored, not merely glossed over, as in much mystery fiction. As Sayers's protagonist Harriet Vane thinks,

> [Her] new story was going to be a tragedy. Previous books, written while their author was struggling through a black slough of misery and frustration, had all been intellectual comedies. The immediate effect of physical and emotional satisfaction seemed to be to lift the lid off hell.

Though *Thrones, Dominations* deals with tragedy of a kind, sexual jealousy erupting into murder, it moves toward the celebratory communal ending we associate with comedy: The Wimseys learn they're going to have a baby, and, of all people, Bunter gets married. The novel takes a distinct feminist swerve in its concluding chapters, which we can assume were written by Jill Paton Walsh, and might not have met with the approval of the less optimistic Dorothy Sayers. *Thrones, Dominations* is a literary sport, and for the most part successful, wonderfully written in its descriptive passages (a trek through London sewers is vividly rendered) and provocative in its pointed discussion of detective fiction:

> "You seem not to appreciate the importance of your special form," [Lord Peter says to Harriet Vane]. "Detective stories contain a dream of justice. They project a world in which wrongs are righted, and villains are betrayed by clues that they did not know they were leaving. A world in which murderers are caught and hanged, and innocent victims are avenged, and future murder is deterred."

Has ever any fictional character spoken so forcefully to his own creator, as Lord Peter Wimsey?

Lost in Boxing

Dark Trade: Lost in Boxing
by Donald McRae (Mainstream)

More Than a Champion: The Style of Muhammad Ali
by Jan Philipp Reemtsma, translated from the
German by John E. Woods (Alfred A. Knopf)

In a fully civilized society, professional boxing would not exist. That it so profitably flourishes in the United States, where purses for highly publicized if unexceptional fights routinely involve millions of dollars, is a testament to both the flawed nature of our society and the dark fascination of this cruelest of sports.

These two very different books, both in the way of memoirs by men long involved with boxing, may help to illuminate some of this fascination with what Mike Tyson has eloquently called "the hurt business."

Of the two, Donald McRae's lengthy, ambitious *Dark Trade: Lost in Boxing* is the more engaging and sympathetically rendered. Where Jan Philipp Reemtsma is cerebral and analytical, McRae is emotionally direct; where the German Reemtsma's boxing experience seems, oddly, to be secondhand by way of television, tapes, and books, the South African–born McRae, in thrall to a thirty-year boxing addiction, has seen countless fights both minor and major in England and the United States, and is on friendly, even intimate terms with a number of boxers and their associates and families. *Dark Trade* bears comparison with Thomas Hauser's classic *The Black Lights: Inside the World of Professional Boxing* (1986), but while Hauser concentrated on the ascendant career of the promising but limited superlightweight Billy Costello, *Dark Trade* is more picaresque in form, taking the reader ringside to vividly rendered, in several cases graphically brutal, matches involving such well-known boxers as heavyweights Mike Tyson, Frank Bruno, and Evander Holyfield, middleweights Chris Eubank, Michael Watson (whose September 1991 match with Eubank ends in collapse and brain damage for him), Roy Jones, and James Toney (McRae's closest boxer friend); lightweights Oscar De La Hoya and Julio Cesar Chavez; featherweights "Prince" Naseem Hamed and Steve Robinson. McRae brings to the highly charged, obsessive world of professional boxing a novelist's eye and ear for revealing detail and convincingly recalled dialogue. This is an impassioned book, and something of a confession, for McRae fell under the spell of boxing in the 1960s, in the era of Cassius Clay/Muhammad Ali—a heroic figure whose worldwide celebrity helped forge a spiritual bond between the South African middle-class white boy and his black contemporaries, at that time politically disenfranchised by apartheid. Partly out of disgust with South African politics, McRae emigrated to England as a young man, where he became involved in boxing as an ardent observer and commentator. If "lost" in boxing, McRae also found his metier, or, as a typically fatalist boxer might say, his destiny.

Instead of the mordantly revealing title *Dark Trade*, McRae's original title for this book was the more ebullient *Showtime*:

> In the beginning I wanted to celebrate boxing. I planned to write about the bravest and the most skillful fighters, describing their big heart and sparkle. . . . I thought there was something beautiful and poetic in the solitary way they both prepared for a fight and then, afterwards, held each other in relief. . . . Yet these stories now touch as much on death. It was not meant to end up this way.

McRae questions the morality of his involvement in a sport that some of its own practitioners would not call a "sport" but a trade that deals in brutality and hurt. And while a famous boxer like Mike Tyson, though conspicuously past his prime, may earn as much as $140,000,000 for six undistinguished fights within sixteen months of his being released from an Indiana prison as a convicted rapist— a testament less to the connivance of boxing promoters than to the inexhaustible gullibility of the public—most boxers, including such great champions as Joe Louis and even Muhammad Ali, are victims, exploited by managers, promoters, and their own dreams of grandeur and immortality. ". . . Deep down, they know that they're fated to lose. They are not 'losers' in terms of their character but, rather, in the more overpowering sense of destiny being stacked against them. . . . In the end, no matter how hard they train or abstain, boxing gets them."

Defensive with outsiders, boxing admirers are often ambivalent about their admiration and may not entirely disagree with those who believe, on ethical and medical grounds, that boxing should be abolished by law. (Having witnessed "death bouts," McRae thoughtfully discusses this perennial issue.) Yet for all its brooding, *Dark Trade* is an immensely readable book that anyone with an interest in boxing will want to own. And it manages to conclude on an upbeat, if qualified, note: After the debacle of Mike Tyson, the first heavyweight in fifty years to be disqualified for unprofessional behavior in the ring (for twice biting the ear of his opponent Evander Holyfield in their championship match of June 1997), McRae focuses upon the admirable, "decent" Holyfield as a model for contemporary boxing, as Muhammad Ali was a model for his era. Boxing is finally about not the "lunacy" of a Tyson but the discipline and sportsmanship of a Holyfield. So long as boxers like Holyfield continue to fight, McRae will watch: "I can't help it. I, too, am yet to be released."

Is Joe Louis, who held the heavyweight title from 1937 to 1950, or Cassius Clay/Muhammad Ali, who won the title three times during his celebrated career from 1964 to 1980, the greatest heavyweight in history? A futile issue to debate, yet irresistible: for while Louis in his prime may well have knocked out Ali in his prime, Ali might well have outboxed (or outfoxed) the harder-hitting Louis, as he did the extraordinary puncher George Foreman. So boxing experts love to argue. Yet it's clear that Ali's magic transcended Louis's, as it transcended boxing itself, through his courageous refusal to be inducted into the U.S. army to fight in Vietnam in 1967, which resulted in the loss of his boxing license and his title for three years. Ali's celebrity was partly a phenomenon of contemporary mass media, which exported his handsome, charismatic image worldwide; he was, perhaps still is, along with Elvis Presley, the most universally identified "American" personality. Donald McRae's boxing memoir begins with Cassius Clay in the 1960s and ends with the recent film *When We Were Kings*, a documentary on the 1974 Ali/Foreman fight in Zaire, and the abrupt outburst:

> . . . The longer boxing existed without Ali, the crazier it became. The further Ali receded into memory, the more depraved boxing appeared. No fighter could match his genius either in or out of the ring. . . . But it is more the way in which Ali lived his life beyond the ropes which overwhelms all the fighters who have followed him. Ali transformed himself. He became a man far greater than a stark figure of violence or a cartoon character of hype.

In the slender, eccentric *More Than a Champion: The Style of Muhammad Ali*, Jan Philipp Reemtsma, a philologist by training and director of both the Hamburg Institute for Social Research and the Arno Schmidt Foundation, posits a provocative theory that Ali may be "the first postmodernist strategist"—presumably of boxing—because he cultivated so playfully ironic a persona with the press and with his opponents. Amid what he calls "anthropological speculation" that non-postmodernist readers may find baffling, Reemtsma argues that Ali is the prototype of a future human being "that we basically do not know at all, yet which for now is intimated only in its first traits, but to which the future probably belongs." Ali is a "cross between the Proteus-like dissociated individual and its antitype" who can be understood only if "one understands the connection between the *dissociated individual* and the *megalomaniac*, or put another way, between *variability* and *dominance*."

Impressed by Ali's renowned versatility in the ring, Reemtsma comes to the odd conclusion that such brilliance is sui generis; had he watched tapes of Ali's distinguished predecessors in lighter weights, where rapid footwork is the norm, notably of Sugar Ray Robinson, from whom Ali learned a good deal, he would have seen that "dissociation" and "Protean" are just another way of saying that the shrewd

boxer adapts to each new opponent and new situation with the intention not of displaying a dramatic ring style but more practicably of
winning the fight. And though Reemtsma remarks in passing that
Ali was a "second Jack Johnson" he fails to connect Ali's boxing persona with the legendary Johnson, the first black heavyweight title-
holder (1908–1915) whose calculatedly "outrageous" behavior—his
public arrogance and his relationships with white women—as well as
his remarkable boxing skills made him one of the most controversial
athletes in American sports history.

Much of *More Than a Champion* is taken up with a blow-by-
blow account of Ali/Frazier III (Manila, 1975), the fight that is generally considered Ali's (and Frazier's) greatest fight. Unfortunately,
Reemtsma's approach to this much-analyzed fight isn't very original
or interesting. Yet more belabored and tedious is his exhaustively
detailed summary of Sylvester Stallone's *Rocky* films—which are as
much about professional boxing as *E.T.* is about extraterrestrial life in
the universe. Though Reemtsma's admiration for Ali appears to be
genuine, if a bit hyped, he lacks the writerly ability of a Donald
McRae to communicate the passion (and ambivalence) of such admiration. No doubt the book is being published in the United States
because of its "intellectual" presumptions, but in fact it's a dubious,
sketchy, and at times unintentionally funny logomachy padded with
quotations from such estimable German sources as Christoph Martin
Wieland's *Sämtliche Werke* and Thomas Mann's *Felix Krull* and allu-
sions to Homer, Goethe, Freud, Kafka, and the Holocaust analyst Leo
Lowenthal; it's studded with questionable declarations ("We do not
learn anything from victories") and even these provocative declarations are awkwardly expressed:

> We do not grow from defeat. We are destroyed by defeat, and if
> not destroyed, then deformed; or we "change"—it is not easy, and
> perhaps it is not necessary, to differentiate all this very precisely.
> Defeat does not make us stronger, either. Weakness (whatever its
> basis) is the cause and effect of defeat.

But history is rich with wonder tales of boxers who learned from
defeat, among them Joe Louis (who lost his first title fight with Max

Schmeling in 1936, then won the rematch in 1938), Floyd Patterson (who lost ingloriously to the Swedish Ingemar Johansson in 1959 but won their next two fights to regain his title in 1960), and Ali himself in his rematches with Frazier and Leon Spinks, who'd beaten him in 1978. If anything dogmatic can be said about boxing, it's that the great boxer is precisely the man who learns from being defeated.

More Than a Champion may be more persuasive in the original German. As it is, something crucial seems to be lost in the translation. By exaggerating Muhammad Ali in an invented role as "Proteus *homo novus* and ruler of worlds," Reemtsma devalues Ali's humanity and his victimhood by boxing. With its self-conscious postmodernist theorizing and attenuated sense of boxing history, this document brings to mind the old boxing adage "Everybody's got a plan until they're hit."

The Miniaturist
Art of Grace Paley

The Collected Stories of Grace Paley (Virago Press)

How aptly named: Grace Paley. For "grace" is perhaps the most accurate, if somewhat poetic, term to employ in speaking of this gifted writer who has concentrated on short, spare fiction through her career of nearly five decades. First published in 1959 with the slender volume *The Little Disturbances of Man*, Grace Paley immediately drew an audience of readers who were not only admiring but loving. Her subsequent collections of stories—*Enormous Changes at the Last Minute* (1974) and *Later the Same Day* (1985)—confirmed Paley's reputation as a lyricist of the domestic life, a poet in prose whose ear for the Jewish-American vernacular suggests a kinship with her older contemporaries Isaac Bashevis Singer, Bernard Malamud, and Saul Bellow.

Like Flannery O'Connor, another American original who came of age in the 1950s, Grace Paley has concentrated upon short fiction, and her major work is assembled in a single, not extraordinarily hefty volume. (Paley began writing as a poet, but published no volume of poetry until *Begin Again*, 1993. Her miscellaneous essays, articles, reports, and public addresses have been collected in *Just As I Thought*, 1998.) Paley's reasons for not attempting longer, more ambitious and technically challenging forms of fiction include a defense of political activism: "Art is too long, and life is too short. There's a lot more to do in life than just writing." How much more there has been in Grace Paley's life, touched upon briefly, and often elliptically, in such stories as "Faith in a Tree," "The Expensive Moment," and "Listening," is suggested by Paley's self-portrait as a "member of an American movement, a tide really, that rose out of the civil-rights struggles of the fifties, rolling methods and energy into the antiwar, direct-action movements in the sixties, cresting, ebbing as tides do, returning bold again in the seventies and eighties in the second wave of the women's movement—and from quite early on splashed and salted by ecological education, connection, and at last action." (*Just As I Thought*)

Born in New York City in 1922, of Russian-Jewish immigrants who settled in the poor quarter of the Lower East Side, Paley emerged from the densely populated, fiercely individualistic Yiddish culture of which Anzia Yezierska (1885–1970) and Henry Roth (1906–1997) wrote in the 1920s and 1930s in such acclaimed novels as *Bread Givers* and *Call It Sleep* respectively; this vanished world of "heroic" elders Paley explores only by way of her father, who appears in her short fiction as an elderly gentleman of melancholy wisdom and much experience, unable to share in his writer-daughter's optimism. ("Tragedy!" cries the eighty-six-year-old invalid in "A Conversation with My Father." "When will you look it in the face?")

As the early stories record in vivid, attenuated detail, Paley married young, had her children young, and did not exactly enjoy a luxurious life while raising them in the 1940s. Though she would one day teach writing at Columbia, Syracuse, and Sarah Lawrence, she had little formal education. In the mid-1950s Paley became a political activist of more than ordinary idealism and commitment, rare for any American writer: She helped organize one of the first abortion "speak-outs" in the United States, in 1954; she helped found the Greenwich Village Peace Center, in 1961, and the Teachers & Writers Collaborative, in 1965–66; she was an early, and ardent, pacifist, and a protester of American military involvement in Vietnam; she was one of a small number of Americans invited to visit Hanoi, in 1969; she was an early member of Resist, an organization formed to aid grass-roots American organizations for ameliorative social change. In the 1970s, she helped demonstrate against the construction of nuclear power plants, and in the mid-1980s, she was involved in the support of Central American people in their struggle to free themselves of decades of American military intervention. It's no wonder that Grace Paley's fictional alter ego is named "Faith" and that she transcribes one of the dramatic turning points of her life in the story "Faith in a Tree," in the appropriately titled *Enormous Changes at the Last Minute*, the jolt into political wakefulness the young mother Faith experiences when she's confronted for the first time, graphically and unforgettably, by antiwar demonstrators in a neighborhood playground-park:

> A short parade appeared—four or five grownups . . . pushing little go-carts with babies in them, a couple of three-year-olds hanging on. . . . The grownups carried three posters. The first showed a prime-living, prime-earning, well-dressed man about thirty-five years old next to a small girl. A question was asked: would you burn a child? In the next poster he placed a burning cigarette on the child's arm. The cool answer was given: WHEN NECESSARY. The third poster carried no words, only a napalmed Vietnamese baby, seared, scarred, with twisted hands.
>
> We were very quiet. Kitty put her head down into the dark skirt of her lap. I trembled. I said, Oh!

(Significantly, this story occurs at about mid-point in *The Collected Stories*.) Into Faith's droll, child-centered world of small neighborhood adventures contemporary political history intrudes, ugly, stirring, in personal terms cataclysmic. There is a "before" and "after" in Faith's life, as in Paley's short fiction.

> And I think that is exactly when events turned me around, changing my hairdo, my job uptown, my style of living and telling. Then I met women and men in different lines of work, whose minds were made up and directed out of that sexy playground by my children's heartfelt brains. I thought more and more and every day about the world.

"Faith in a Tree" is a powerful story, yet in its blunt conclusion, which suggests rather more the directness of memoir than the indirection of fiction, it isn't characteristic of Paley's best work. To allude to "grace" in terms of prose is to suggest some of the strategies of poetry—primarily, in Paley's case, metonymy: the art of suggestion and association. Paley's quick sketches of seemingly ordinary domestic daily life—erotic, tenderly combative, irresolute—suggest the delicate, notoriously difficult art of watercolor. Her language is musical, pulsed to the rhythms of speech as heard by the ear, and not speech invented as prose, as subtly and beautifully cadenced as that of Bernard Malamud in his early, magical stories of urban Jewish lives. Like good poetry, a characteristic short story by Grace Paley can't be paraphrased. It is invariably more than the sum of its inspired moments, leaving in its wake an aura, an echo; this is prose meant to be read aloud, as an expression of "voice," not a resolution of plot. Paley's characterizations are by way of monologues we hear, not individuals we see. (We "see" virtually no one in these hundreds of pages of prose, have little idea what Faith looks like, unless we assume she bears some resemblance to the author, pictured on the dust jacket. It may come as a jolt to the reader to hear Faith addressed, in "The Long Distance Runner," as "fat mama" by an impudent adolescent boy.)

The first story in the volume, "Goodbye and Good Luck," begins, "I was popular in certain circles, says Aunt Rose": the monologue of an aging woman reminiscing fondly about her youth and the love of her life, a not-always-faithful actor in the Yiddish theater; it's a tale as well of "the rotten handwriting of time, scribbled up and down [my mother's] cheeks, across her forehead back and forth—a child could read." This is a story we expect will career to a predictable mordant ending; in fact, it has an unexpectedly blissful happy ending. In the beautifully condensed "The Pale Pink Roast," a man encounters his ex-wife, mother of his child, in a city park, returns with her to a new, attractive home, where, suddenly, they find themselves drawn powerfully to each other, though Anna is happily remarried:

"Shall we dance?" he asked softly, a family joke. With great care, a patient lover, he undid the sixteen tiny buttons of her pretty dress and in Judy's room on Judy's bed he took her at once without a word. Afterward, having established tenancy, he rewarded her

with kisses. But he dressed quickly because he was obligated by
the stories of his life to remind her of transience.

It is the ex-wife, Anna, who thinks cryptically: ". . . Cannibals, tasting
man, saw him thereafter as the great pig, the pale pink roast."

Another irresistibly readable story of the 1950s is the much-
anthologized "An Interest in Life," which was my personal introduction to Paley's miniaturist art. It begins,

> My husband gave me a broom one Christmas. This wasn't right.
> No one can tell me it was meant kindly.
>
> "I don't want you not to have anything for Christmas while I'm
> in the army," he said. . . .
>
> Still and all, in spite of the quality, it was a mean present to
> give a woman you planned on never seeing again, a person you had
> children with and got onto all the time, drunk or sober, even when
> everybody had to get up early in the morning.
>
> I asked him if he could wait and join the army in a half hour, as
> I had to get the groceries.

Virginia, the abandoned young wife and mother, acquires another, far
more reliable, sensitive, and loving suitor after her callow husband's
desertion; but the story ends in an unexpected erotic fantasy in which
the husband returns years later ("with his old key") and bumps the
amazed Virginia onto the kitchen floor:

> And before I can even make myself half comfortable on that polka-
> dotted linoleum, he got onto me right where we were, and the
> truth is, we were so happy, we forgot the precautions.

In "Wants," the opening story of *Enormous Changes at the Last Minute*,
an unnamed woman who sounds very like Virginia says,

> I saw my ex-husband in the street. I was sitting on the steps of the
> new library.
>
> Hello, my life, I said. We had once been married for twenty-
> seven years, so I felt justified.

He said, What? What life? No life of mine. I said O.K. . . .

Just as Grace Paley the pacifist and political activist is never polemical, preachy, or self-righteous in her fiction, so Grace Paley the feminist is unpredictable; an artist, and not a propagandist.

Of course, the predominant concerns of *The Collected Stories* are with women's issues. Virtually all of the stories are narrated from a woman's perspective, and men (and occasionally boys) are The Other: raffish, charming, verbose, irresponsible, and often absent. In her brief introduction to this volume, Paley defines herself as a woman writing at the historical moment at mid-century when "small drops of worried resentment and noble rage were secretly, slowly building into the second wave of the women's movement," but readers will discover that these emotions have been subsumed by an easygoing, forgiving, and humane sensibility in which foolish or self-serving behavior is observed with comic detachment, not savage indignation. What is refreshingly original about Grace Paley, apart from her gossamer way with words, is her disinclination to be judgmental; her refusal not to be funny, even at her own expense. Her female characters are founts of mock-sexist sagacity:

> Happiness isn't so bad for a woman. She gets fatter, she gets older, she could lie down, nuzzling a regiment of men and little kids, she could just die of the pleasure. But men are different, they have to own money, or they have to be famous, or everybody on the block has to look up at them from the cellar stairs. A woman counts her children and acts snotty, like she invented life, but men must do well in the world. I know that men are not fooled by being happy.
>
> ("An Interest in Life")

> Little boys need a recollection of Energy as a male resource.
>
> ("Faith in a Tree")

> . . . Do you notice that in time you love the children more and the man less?
>
> ("The Expensive Moment")

Children standing on the sidelines listening to Faith and her garrulous friends are likely to startle us with their commentary:

> What is this crap, Mother, this life is short and terrible. What is this metaphysical shit, what is this disease you intelligentsia are always talking about?

("Listening")

Grace Paley came of age at a time when literary irony, of the kind practiced by the virtuoso Vladimir Nabokov, was a high, prestigious value. Who but a woman, and among serious women writers who but Grace Paley, would write such unabashedly frank, emotional yet unsentimental stories about women's friendships and love, as "Friends" and "Ruthy and Edie"? Through the 1950s and 1960s, tessellated, self-conscious prose, symbolism and "experimentation" were in vogue, as well as the fey, relentlessly parodistic short fiction of Paley's neighbor and good friend Donald Barthelme. The gargantuan mock-epics of John Barth, *The Sot-Weed Factor* (1960) and *Giles Goat-Boy* (1966), now little read, were much praised at the time, and the "literature of exhaustion" was the literature of the future—if there was a future for humanist literature at all. Like a number of realist writers, however, Grace Paley continued to practice and to hone her less showy craft, focusing not upon technique but upon characters with the affect of "real people"; her stories evolved over the decades in terms of subject matter, settings, and form, but her vision of humanity remained unaltered, like her inimitable style, which would seem to have been perfected in the first stories she published. Paley's New Yorkers are the "soft-speaking tough souls of anarchy" who outlive literary fads and fashions and whose stories are as timely at the end of the tumultuous twentieth century as they would have been at the beginning.

In the poignant father-daughter story "A Conversation with My Father," the invalided father asks the narrator to please write a "simple story" of the kind Maupassant and Chekhov wrote—"Just recognizable people and then write down what happened to them next"; he's annoyed and confused by disjointed plots that seem to lead nowhere, people in trees "talking senselessly, voices from who knows where. . . ." And his daughter thinks:

> I *would* like to try to tell such a story, if he means the kind that begins: "There was a woman . . ." followed by a plot, the absolute line between two points which I've always despised. Not for literary reasons, but because it takes all hope away. Everyone, real or invented, deserves the open destiny of life.

It's this "open destiny" of life and of art that Grace Paley's *Collected Stories* celebrates and that has made of Paley one of the enduring talents of her epoch.

American Views:
Elizabeth Hardwick

I like a view but I like to sit with my back to it.
—Gertrude Stein

Criticism can talk," Northrop Frye provocatively remarked in his introduction to *Anatomy of Criticism* (1957), "and all the arts are dumb." Yet in the hands of some practitioners, among them Frye, criticism itself aspires to art; a profane sort of art, perhaps, in Auden's vocabulary ("The value of a profane thing lies in what it usefully does, the value of a sacred thing lies in what it *is*")—in that criticism must always be a reaction, never quite an action; a secondary creation, and not an original. Unlike the venturesome artist who creates something out of nothing, the critic can only "create" something out of something that already exists. In another, more cinematic distinction, "writing criticism is to writing fiction and poetry as hugging the shore is to sailing in the open sea"—this from the foreword to *Hugging the Shore* (1983), John Updike's masterly (and massive: nine hundred pages of Updikean prose) collection of essays and criticism. At sea, amid a beautiful blankness, we risk disaster and death; hugging the shore, we never lose our bearings and can return to land easily.

A modicum of respect for the subject, then, as the basis for the critic's project, would seem to be a primary element of serious criticism. A measure of judiciousness, tact, sympathy, and empathy; an awareness of historical and cultural context; an awareness of the "life and times"; an intimacy with the actual texts to be considered—these are perhaps not necessary for all intelligent and useful criticism, but their absence weakens the critic's effort and makes of it mere opinion-mongering—your word against mine. "Letting the mind play freely around a subject"—in Matthew Arnold's words—presupposes an interesting and informed mind. Add to such an ideal critic-portrait an accomplished prose style that would seem to mimic (and, in the reading, inspire in readers) the subtle modulations of a first-rate sensibility; and, not least, though rarely if ever acknowledged, the persuasive power of *graciousness*—that mysterious yet unmistakable quality of personality cherished in personal life yet ignored and undervalued in critical discourse.

These are qualities of high value in civilization, and criticism of such a kind might be said to be synonymous with civilization, though "art" may well predate civilization. For here we have the refined, reflective, idealized voice of the conscience of the race beside which, in fact, the arts are dumb, or mute; that is, presenting themselves directly without polemics or explanation. Without such criticism, we lose our cultural memory; all is a blooming, buzzing present, a vast tide of "entertainment." In reading literary criticism that qualifies as art, whether by Henry James, Virginia Woolf, V. S. Pritchett, John Updike or Gore Vidal or Elizabeth Hardwick—in their obviously very different ways—we confront a subject through the prism of a sensibility that "judges" in such a way as to expand the significance of the subject; to leave it, in a sense, altered from what it was. To read Edith Wharton, Henry James, Margaret Fuller, Gertrude Stein, Djuna Barnes, Katherine Anne Porter, Elizabeth Bishop, Nadine Gordimer, the "windy" prairie poets Carl Sandburg, Vachel Lindsey, and Edgar Lee Masters, among diverse others, in tandem with Elizabeth Hardwick's exemplary essays on these subjects, is, to use an irresistible critical cliché, apt in this context, illuminating. Hardwick's *Sight-Readings*, her fourth and perhaps strongest collection of essays, written between 1982 and the near-present, will provide for many readers a genuine enhancement of familiar works (Edith Wharton's *The House of Mirth*, Henry James's *Washington Square*, fiction by Katherine Anne Porter), and a way *in*, like the cracking of a code, to certain obscure or obdurate literary figures (Margaret Fuller, Gertrude Stein, Djuna Barnes); Hardwick's commentary on literary biographies (notably biographies of Edmund

Wilson, Katherine Anne Porter, Carl Sandburg, Norman Mailer, and the "crocodilian" celebrity-writer Truman Capote is, quite simply, brilliant, the most reasoned and responsible thinking on the subject the general reader is likely to encounter, and the more persuasive in that Hardwick herself is, characteristically without ostentation or polemics, a gifted miniaturist-biographer. (See also the sympathetic but not sentimental portraits of literary and fictional women in Hardwick's *Seduction and Betrayal*, 1974.) *Sight-Readings* is not lacking in literary close analysis and assessment of a more traditional nature, but for most readers it will shine as a gallery of memorably sketched portraits. Among twentieth-century literary essayists only Virginia Woolf has created comparable likenesses, in her own brilliant if slightly cranky prose. Yet Hardwick is never provincial, censorious, or frankly jealous, like Woolf; impossible to imagine her sniffing with bourgeois disdain at *Ulysses* as an "illiterate, underbred book . . . the book of a self-taught working man" or asserting that, for all his youthful reputation, Ernest Hemingway is "not an advanced writer." It was Virginia Woolf's secret conviction, though she did review contemporaries often, that "no creative writer can swallow another contemporary." Hardwick's essays refute that contention.

Sight-Readings consists of eighteen essays of mostly American writers (Nadine Gordimer, a sort of glittering caboose at the rear of the book, is the lone exception), female and male, exclusively Caucasian and predominantly middle-class, though within this territory there is much diversity of subject matter, genius, literary accomplishment, success, fame, and failure. *Sight-Readings*—the title—with its suggestion of quick-study mastery and facility, would seem to set the wrong, even a contrary tone for Hardwick's essays; how more appropriate a title would have been *Depth-Readings*. Each of the essays, even those on Mary McCarthy, Elizabeth Bishop, and Truman Capote the author designates as "Snapshots," is richly textured, contemplative, and wide-ranging: "Mrs. Wharton in New York" takes time to discuss William Dean Howells' *A Hazard of New Fortunes*, Henry James's *The American Scene* and *Washington Square*, with inspired references to Anton Chekhov, Stephen Crane, and Theodore Dreiser; "The Genius of Margaret Fuller" closes with a startling epilogue on "perfidious" Nathaniel Hawthorne, who seems to have bitterly resented Fuller's repudiation of a conventional female role and to have wished to slander Fuller after her death; "Gertrude Stein" refers expectedly to Hemingway, Picasso, and Joyce, and unexpectedly to Samuel Beckett and Philip Glass ("Gertrude Stein, all courage and will, is a soldier of minimalism"); "Cheever; or The Ambiguities," noting the "shadowy and troubled undergrowth of Cheever's stories," links the author with Melville's doomed *Pierre*; "Citizen Updike" posits the author as one of Augustine's "fair and fit" and includes a parenthetical aside on early Christian heresy ("Pelagius thought Adam's sin was his alone and we must commit our own sins. But no matter") "Into the Wasteland: Joan Didion" includes an apt quotation from Melville's first novel, *Typee*. The funniest—unless it's the saddest—essay, "Wind from the Prairie," primarily a review of a massive biography of Carl Sandburg by Penelope Niven ("a work of exhaustive, definitive coziness in the current American mode of entranced biographical research") considers the disastrous careers of Sandburg's prairie-coevals Vachel Lindsay and Edgar Lee Masters, and concludes with a gem of an aphorism by Franz Kafka. "Edmund Wilson," a review-essay of a biography of Wilson by Jeffrey Meyers, expands to consider biography as a genre, with references to Boswell's *Life of Johnson*, Johnson's *Life of Mr. Richard Savage*, James A. Froude's remarks on Thomas Carlyle, and Andrew Motion's recent biography of Philip Larkin, as well as discussing with admirable succinctness the idiosyncratic and interestingly kindred geniuses of Vladimir Nabokov and Charles Dickens. In the lyric and celebratory "snapshot" of Elizabeth Bishop we are cross-referenced to Thomas Hardy and D. H. Lawrence, Coleridge, Laforgue, Mayakovsky, and Pasternak, and learn in passing that "in the late 1930s, the fiction in the little magazines often struggled with the challenge of Kafka." We note, too, that the structure of Philip Roth's fiction is based often upon "identifying tirades rather than actions and counteractions" and that the "profligate imagination" of Richard Ford may have provided us with the first "full recognition of the totemic power in American life of the telephone and the message service." Along the way, we take down the titles of works to be read (assuming that, for most readers, these *are* unread): Margaret

Fuller's essay on Goethe ("a basic document in the history of intellectual freedom in the United States"), Nabokov's study of Gogol ("one of the most exhilarating, engaging, and original works ever written by one writer about another"), an early Wharton story, "Bunner Sisters" ("one of the author's most interesting works and an extraordinary wandering from the enclave").

Is it fair to judge a cover by its book? Though *Sight-Readings* contains vividly rendered portraits and pulses with kinetic energy, the book's jacket art is disappointingly blurred and inconsequential, a marsh seen through smudged glasses. How much more striking would have been a reproduction of a portrait in the American mode by James McNeill Whistler, John White Alexander, or George Bellows; or a work of abstract expressionism, to suggest Hardwick's virtuosity. And her wit: it's rare to laugh aloud reading literary criticism, but there is much in *Sight-Readings* to evoke such a response: of Edith Wharton's lover Morton Fullerton, Hardwick remarks, "In his love life, [Fullerton] is something like a telephone, always engaged, and even then with several on hold"; Gertrude Stein, whom Hardwick much admires, is "sturdy as a turnip . . . a tough root of some sort," her stubbornly eccentric art a matter of "insomniac rhythms and drummings" and her prose a "wondrous contraption, the Model T of her style." Clearly, Hardwick identifies with Stein in Stein's funny Wildean insights.

> I like a view but I like to sit with my back to it.
>
> What is the point of being a little boy if you are going to grow up to be a man?
>
> Before the flowers of friendship faded friendship faded.
>
> I am I because my little dog knows me.
>
> Ezra Pound is a village explainer, excellent if you were a village, but if not, not.

Edgar Lee Masters "has *ideas* as some have freckles"; the master work of Vachel Lindsay, *The Congo and Other Poems*, is an "infernal indiscretion," the result perhaps of the poet's "unanchored enthusiasm" for the American Midwest:

Tramping and reciting, forever in manic locomotion with note-book in hand to scribble whatever came into his head, head to be laid down at night on YMCA pillow, leaving little time for ro-mantic life.

Djuna Barnes is noted to have "a crippling facility for inspired verbal cartooning"; Truman Capote's notorious "La Côte Basque" is "a story or something," and Capote himself, following the debacle of *Answered Prayers* with its cruel, assaultive portraits of friends, is envisioned by Hardwick as a "leper with a bell announcing his presence . . . marked with a leper's visible deformities, a creature arousing fear of infection."

What was Capote thinking of? At times one is led to imagine him afflicted with Tourette's syndrome, a disease [that] brings on fa-cial tics, not unusual in other physical misfortunes; the true pecu-liarity of the symptoms is echolalia, endless talking characterized by an uncontrollable flow of obscenities.

Because they showcase Elizabeth Hardwick's gifts for both portrai-ture and a subtle form of polemics, the essays on biography may linger longest in the reader's mind. Indeed, these should be required reading for anyone undertaking the difficult art, or craft, of biography—"the quick in pursuit of the dead," as Hardwick wittily describes the genre. The pitfalls of contemporary biographical "entrancement" are isolated in Penelope Nivens's exhaustive life of Sandburg, in which the biogra-pher is primarily a collector of unedited and unanalyzed data, unwill-ing to, or perhaps incapable of, aesthetic judgment:

Having gone through the heap [the vast Sandburg archives], settled into the poet and each member of his family, reliving their nights and days with an intrusive intimacy, the biographer wants to record each scrap. The index cards or data sheets come to have a claim of their own, and the affirmation, the yes, yes, of Sandburg's scurry through life is her own affirming journey. The book is te-dious and sentimental and long, long, long. . . . The scholar of the papers, of *the life of*, knows, like some celestial Xerox machine, de-tails that consciousness erases overnight.

Even less edited, less analyzed, and less structured than the Sandburg biography, *Mailer: His Life and Times* by Peter Manso is advertised as a "major biography" though in fact the massive book is little more than an assemblage of interview transcripts, originally totalling 20,000 pages; the testament of a "hippodrome of garrulity" that seems to suggest a radically new definition of what it is to be a writer: "You, and in this case your times, are what people have to say about you." Literary accomplishment seems to be beside the point, for perhaps the biographer hasn't had time to read the subject's oeuvre:

> The absence of a [biographer], of a signature of responsibility, the conception of ideas as shadows of comment, vague and undefended, in a like way absorbs the activity of the commentator, the critic. What can be said about more than six hundred pages of anecdote?

Of course, Hardwick finds a good deal to say about this new, techno-logical-driven "oral tradition," and about Mailer's kindred "nonfiction novel" *The Executioner's Song*, which was similarly created out of staggering quantities of interview transcripts (beyond 16,000 pages): a "compositional blur" shaped and given a putative Western plain-ness and anonymity by Mailer, into a novel that would win, perhaps perversely, the Pulitzer Prize for fiction that had been denied to those novels of Mailer so much more clearly his "own." On the process of creating something like a book out of such material, Hardwick notes:

> A bit of neatening, of course, and punctuation, the period, the comma. The taped text is always a great, gluey blob, and what is needed are sentences dry and separate as kernels of corn. A close reading of taped books suggests that the invisible hand is less busy than might be imagined. Punctuation, laying it out, pasting it up. The real labor of the books returns to the source, the wretched bulk of the testimony, the horror of its vast, stuttering scale.

So, too, and perhaps more appropriately, since the last phase of his life was so frequently "party-going, forever receiving and producing banter about feckless stumblings and torrid indiscretions," Truman Capote is the subject of another tape-recorded oral biography assem-

bled by George Plimpton that consists of "lumps of monologue pil-
ing up one after another like wood stacked for the winter" and virtually no authorial commentary or critical assessment of Capote's work.
Perhaps—though Hardwick doesn't so indicate, and may not have
felt that this is a valid conclusion—these massive transcript-books
are an inevitable consequence of the information glut of our time,
electronically inspired and, as it were, subsidized; not substitutes for
more authentic books, but meta-books, handbooks of undigested
data, clippings, and reviews, anecdotes and gossip and trivia possessing the value to subsequent writers and scholars that unpublished
archival materials have always possessed.

There are other, more traditional ways in which a biographer is
unequal to his or her subject, and these, too, Hardwick thoughtfully
examines. In passing, in her essay on James's *Washington Square* (the introduction to the Library of America paperback edition), she alludes
critically to Leon Edel's dogged psychologizing of his subject in the five-
volume life of James, finding fault with Edel's claim that Catherine
Sloper is "the image of himself [James] as victim of his brother's—and
America's—failure to understand his feelings"; in Edel's myopic reading
of James the creative artist, it is "sibling rivalry" that is the stimulus, to
be located virtually anywhere in James's work. Hardwick's reading
of *Washington Square* is, unsurprisingly, far freer, focusing upon the
young woman protagonist Catherine as a vessel of "classic recognition
and the power of enlightenment." It would seem to be Elizabeth Hardwick's natural, and admirable, instinct to defend the writer against the
biographer/critic, for who otherwise will speak for the writer, now deceased? The heavy hand of Freudian literary theory would reduce to ster-
ile and tedious formulae the free play of the writer's imagination, as well
as restrict his or her more conscious strategies of form and structure; the
writer becomes, in so claustrophobic a determinist drama, merely a conduit for the expression of the usual repressed, largely infantile fantasies.

In "The Fate of the Gifted," Hardwick considers Djuna Barnes, "a
writer of wild and original gifts," who would seem also to have eluded
her biographer; in this case Andrew Field, whose awkwardly titled
Djuna: The Formidable Miss Barnes lacks a "vivacity" commensurate
with its subject: the biography "is under considerable strain in all its
parts and can only chatter along desperately about one who was noted

for her silences." More reprehensible, because both critically inadequate and morally suspect, is Joan Givner's biography of Katherine Anne Porter, which pursues its hapless subject, ninety years old at the time of her death following the ravages of old age, with "root biographical facts [that] have the effect of a crushing army." Givner's "smug provincialism" would make of Porter's exquisitely rendered fiction the mere repository of "problems of life," inevitably traced back to a deprived childhood, resentments and fabrications, a "longing for love." Hardwick's more discerning and appreciative eye sees in the celebrated "Miranda" stories of Porter and in the extraordinary short novel "Noon Wine" the artist at work, not the neurotic; in art, detail is "transfigured," not merely recalled and recorded.

> How certain human beings are able to create works of art is a mystery, and why they should wish to do so, at great cost to themselves usually, is another mystery. Works are not created by one's life; every life is rich in *material*. By the nature of the enterprise, the contemporary biographer with his surf of Xerox papers is doing something smaller and yet strikingly more detailed than the great Victorian laborers in the form. Our power of documentation has a monstrous life of its own. . . . It creates out of paper a heavy, obdurate permanency.

Yet the artist may be hounded by the biographer for inconsistencies and foibles in the life ("Garrulousness and a certain untidiness in 1932 are excavated and rebuked in 1982, showing at least one of the dangers of living"); the biographer, like Givner, may take on the moral rectitude and ill-disguised malice of an independent public prosecutor, as if to demean another is to enhance oneself; as if the biographer, scavenging the life, isn't exploiting that life, and wholly dependent upon it for the completion of a professional project. "It is not always clear that [Givner] understands the elegance of [Porter's] prose," Hardwick mildly remarks. Add to which deficiency the biographer's outrage that her subject has turned out to be human, and flawed, not a figure of fantasy; and her conviction, an occupational hazard of many biographers of writers, that there is, must be, an "umbilical attachment" of the life and the work. Biography as *pathog-*

raphy; and as *ressentiment*, in Nietzsche's notable phrase, in *Toward a Genealogy of Morals*: the revenge of the weak against the strong by way of the tyranny of a restrictive "morality," but also, perhaps, the revenge of the unimaginative against the imaginative. Biographies written out of such motives cast a chill over the last years of many lives, in inevitably recording the "demeaning moments of malice and decline [with] the effect of imprinting them upon the ninety years. In the biographies of today, all things are equal except that the ill winds tend in interest to be—well, more interesting." We feel this to be true, generally; but of course there have been any number of meritorious biographies published in recent decades in which respect for the subject is balanced by documentation and analysis. Simply for the record, Hardwick might have mentioned these.

Is biographical truth possible, in any case? Unless the subject is a fanatic diarist, the greater part of his or her inner life will be lost, not simply to the biographer but to the very subject. In Hardwick's acute observation, quoted above, the "scholar of the papers" may retain details that "consciousness erases overnight," but no one, including even the subject, can retain the ephemera of consciousness that, like a sky of rapidly moving clouds, is ever-shifting and cannot be tracked; hardly is it *there* before it's *gone*. The sum of a man, says Emerson, is what he is thinking all day long. This *is*ness is both the only true reality of our lives and, paradoxically, inaccessible to another, and only fleetingly comprehended by ourselves. Yet in this phantasmagoria, not in factual detail, and certainly not in anecdotal recollections, sometimes genial, sometimes malicious, does the mysterious personality reside. Fastening upon what can be perceived (by someone) and has been documented (by someone), biography is susceptible to the retaining of a spurious "history": the single occasion when you wear a pink-striped shirt, not the several dozen occasions when you wear a white shirt, is likely to end up in the biography. Metonymy gone wrong. Freud remarked, "Anyone who writes a biography is committed to lies, concealments, hypocrisy, flattery and even to hiding his own lack of understanding, for biographical truth does not exist, and if it did we could not use it."

In raising such timely issues, Elizabeth Hardwick's *Sight-Readings* is an important as well as an immensely readable and instructive gathering of essays by one of our most esteemed writers.

Three American Gothics

Jeffrey Dahmer, November 1994

Sooner murder an infant in its cradle than nurse unacted desires, the English visionary poet William Blake counsels in *The Marriage of Heaven and Hell*. Jeffrey Dahmer was no pedophile, however: His seventeen acknowledged victims were young men between the ages of fourteen and thirty-three. He cruised bars, bus stations, "adult" bookstores seeking prey. He was Caucasian, his victims mainly black, Hispanic, and Asian—by sexual preference, or chance? Or did he shrewdly reason that, perceived as "marginal" human beings, his victims, should they have survived to testify against him, would not appear so convincing to police or in a courtroom as he? In an extraordinary and now notorious confirmation of Dahmer's racist assumptions, two Milwaukee police officers, in May 1991, actually returned to Dahmer a fourteen-year-old Laotian boy when the boy was found dazed and bleeding in a city street. (After the case broke months later, this incident stirred a good deal of public outrage, since it exposed the racist attitudes of the Milwaukee Police Department; even under fire, police officials were reluctant to censure, or even to criticize, the officers.) Dahmer was finally arrested a few months later, following the flight of another abused victim into the street, tried, and convicted of fifteen counts of homicide; at the time of his bludgeoning death on November 28 at the Columbia Correctional Institute in Portage, Wisconsin, Dahmer was serving fifteen consecutive life terms.

The "serial killer" with no apparent motive for his monstrous crimes except the gratification of desire has become, in the 1990s, an icon of pop culture. The most difficult of criminals to trace, since his connections with his victims are almost always wholly imagined, such a killer is a romantic figure in reverse: sexually obsessed, isolated by his compulsions, the very portrait of demonic possession; one whose entire outward life has been constructed as a means to satisfy the forbidden.

When Dahmer sighted a potential victim, a young man or boy who aroused him, his first thought was "How can I get him?" His second thought was "How can I keep him?" Dahmer lured his victims to his apartment with promises of drugs, alcohol, and money; he then trapped them, killed, and dismembered them, storing body parts on the premises (not all of them refrigerated: Dahmer's neighbors in his apartment building complained of the stench, but no investigation was ever made). Though Dahmer had a history of sexual misbehavior, and was in fact reporting to a Milwaukee parole officer at the time of most of his killings, he seems to have operated, like so many serial killers, in a dreamlike suspension of ordinary logic and common sense; the remarkable thing in such cases is the blindness or indifference of authorities, the purposeful lack of curiosity, or denial, of family and relatives. (What did Long Island serial killer Joel Rifkin's mother and sister, with whom he lived, imagine he was doing on his nights out, with his accumulating mementos of female victims, and an occasional decomposing body in his truck?) So long as the serial killer chooses his victims from the ever-shifting population of drifters, prostitutes, the disenfranchised of contemporary America, those seemingly lacking identity, he can operate with impunity for a very long time. He will only be caught through some blunder of his own, not through police investigation.

Media fascination with lurid crimes feeds a seemingly insatiable sensation-hungry public, yet such treatments generally focus upon the criminal as freak, as monster; a "stranger" in the midst of the presumably normal. What is less known, or acknowledged, are the odd, disturbing, yet surely significant connections between extremes of psychopathic behavior and behavior considered "normal," if not enlightened. The notorious fetishism of the serial killer, for instance, is simply a heightening, to a point beyond parody, of the lover's obsession with some aspect, or part, of the beloved—"part," in some quarters, taken literally. (Dahmer's most cherished love objects were not young men, nor even the bodies of young men, but parts of their bodies.) There is the impulse, too, to memorialize an "erotic" interlude by way of mementos or souvenirs, or even art; the grotesque exaggeration of the lover's mock-wish to "devour" the beloved that manifests itself in actual acts of cannibalism. Dahmer, for instance, seems to have had artistic impulses of a kind, painting the skulls of some of his victims, taking Polaroid shots of their dismembered bodies arranged as "still lifes." So too Dahmer's necrophagy, or cannibalism: He explained that he wanted to keep his victims with him, and there was no other way except to kill and eat them. (At least in theory. Dahmer in fact seems to have been fairly abstemious.) We know that acts of cannibalism defined as "ritual cannibalism," thus not in violation of taboo, have been a feature of peoples and religions considered "primitive" by contemporary Western standards of civilization (and sanitation), but, in metaphor at least, they are a staple of most religions, including Christianity. *Take of my body and eat.* The communal incorporation of the divine being, or life force, into one's own (mortal) body by way of the mouth; the mystic conjoining of lover and loved (or worshipped) object; the "transcendence" of the merely physical, finite, and ephemeral. Mere sexual gratification, so quickly achieved, is hardly the point of such willfully, riskily extended "perverted" behavior; that it is of enormous significance to the killer explains why he keeps such evidence close at hand, in fact enshrining it, instead of disposing of it.

What an enigma, the "serial killer"—he who murders not for monetary gain, which we might understand, but for passion's capricious sake! This is the stuff of poetry, even if bad poetry; of art, even if repellent art. The serial killer is not even a savage beast, but an anomaly in nature itself, for if, in Darwinian terms, nature is compulsively concerned with the propagation of the very best genes of a species, it is impossible to read the serial killer as "natural" in any way; even in the disagreeable, politically incorrect way in which some sociobiologists see rape (of female by male) as "natural." So the serial killer like Jeffrey Dahmer remains a riddle, a koan, not simply in human terms but in biological terms as well. We understand him, finally, no better than we understand ourselves.

Timothy James McVeigh, May 1995

Timothy James McVeigh, the chief suspect in the nation's worst terrorist bombing, grew up in the northwestern corner of New York State, in Pendleton, a rural community of small farms and suburban homes twenty miles north of Buffalo and five miles southwest of Lockport. Pendleton is not even a village, lacking its own post office, a commercial center, public schools, and a coherent identity. It's more a region than a community, farmland interspersed with American-ubiquitous ranch houses of modest dimensions, often with flagpoles in the front yards (like the McVeigh family's home). Here and there are the remains of old, weatherworn farmhouses, perhaps an old rotted barn, coop, or silo—relics of an era so seemingly remote in 1995 that they might be from another century. Pendleton, like nearby Millersport, Rapids, Wrights Corners, and Cambria Center, is a place of such minimal visual identity that one suspects that lives here are intensely inward—in the way, that is, of contemporary "inwardness," a function not of the inner self, or soul, but of the media. If you seek identity in such places, you will take it from stylized, generic, actor-oriented television or film images, not from the community. There is no community. By tradition, western New York State has been a region of hunters, fishermen, "sportsmen." Now that wildlife has been severely depleted, and hunting strictly regulated, gun lovers are obliged to travel some distance to use their guns.

Timothy McVeigh, a lover of guns and explosion fantasies since adolescence, grew up in Pendleton, and was bused into Lockport to attend public school. He would have been identified as "from the country"—the vague, just slightly pejorative designation given such boys and girls, as if identity might be a matter of geography and distance.

In the mythos of the surrounding countryside, Lockport, with its twenty-five thousand inhabitants, is *the* city. Until last week, its arguably most notable citizens were the late William Miller (Barry Goldwater's vice-presidential running mate in the 1964 election), the late William Morgan, inventor of volleyball, and lately Michael Cuzzacrea, world record-holder for marathon running while flipping a pancake. It's a city of vertiginously steep hills built on the banks of the Erie Barge Canal, Lockport's predominant feature, cutting through it in a deep swath and dividing it approximately in two. (The well-to-do sector is generally south of the canal, sloping upward; Lowertown, steeply downhill, has been working-class, semi-industrial, relatively undeveloped.) Uptown, as it's called, are elegant mansions and walled "estates" dating as far back as the 1850s. Indeed, within its city limits, Lockport has changed very little since the 1950s, a decade of local prosperity. As soon as you cross the city limits, however, you're in Lockport Mall/fast-food/gas station Hell, U.S.A.

Shabby not only at its edges, Lockport still exudes an air of romance. It might have been imagined in a more innocent time by Thornton Wilder or Edward Hopper, appropriated now by David Lynch. In the canal area, it seems to possess on even the sunniest days a faint sepia cast, as in an old photograph. Downtown Main Street has a look of malnourished "urban renewal"—reasonably new buildings juxtaposed with aged buildings, structures under perennial renovation, For Sale/For Lease signs, vacant lots in what would seem to be prime real estate territory. It is the Erie Barge Canal that draws one's attention, though. To walk along the canal's high banks, amid cracked and littered pavement, gazing down at the foaming black water fifty feet below, is mesmerizing.

In Lockport, at Star Point Central High School, Timothy McVeigh is said to have had an undistinguished, virtually anonymous career. The iconographic image of the fanatic, the madman, the coolly plotting terrorist, is difficult to derive from such a modest, homogeneous American background. D. H. Lawrence described the essential American soul as "hard, isolate, stoic and a killer," but this seems a romantic exaggeration in our media-processed time. To grow up in Pendleton, New York, to be bused to school into Lockport, is to know oneself distinctly marginal; wherever the fountainheads of significance, let alone power, they are surely not here, nor are they even within easy driving distance. The way of the marginal personality, like Timothy McVeigh, must be through identification with power. When not isolates, such men (yes, they are nearly always men) join paramilitary groups or para-religious cults, for which they are often willing to die.

To visit such wholly American places as Pendleton and Lockport is to be granted a revelation: How little where we have lived, with whom we have lived, and of whom we are born has any longer to do, in the public sense, with who we are. What connection is there between place of origin and destiny? Where Timothy McVeigh came from is of relatively little significance set beside where, as a young man, he went: into the United States army and the Gulf War, to a semirural paramilitary organization called the Michigan Militia, and, finally, to Oklahoma City and the Federal Building, destroyed by a crude homemade bomb on April 19, 1995. Where we come from in America no longer signifies—it's where we go, and what we do when we get there, that tells us who we are.

Mike Tyson, July 1997

The American poet William Carlos Williams said it most succinctly and provocatively: "The perfect man of action is the suicide."

That boxers are men of action for whom language, articulated motives, and that mode of behavior we consider rational are not primary qualities is self-evident. The boxer, more than any other athlete, is a phenomenon of lightning-quick reflexes and instantaneous judgment guided by conditioned, repetitive training. In an unexceptional fight, a well-trained boxer can operate almost by rote. It's in exceptional situations that boxers exhibit their unique talents, or lack of talent. On its highest level, boxing is both an art and a craft; a remarkable display of human imagination, inventiveness, and what can only be called by the old-fashioned term "character." (The classic fights of Marciano–Walcott, Ali–Frazier, Hagler–Hearns, Leonard–Hearns are of this caliber.) Controlled ferocity is the ideal. Where control is wanting, we are left with mere ferocity, inchoate rage. An aggrieved boxer or desperate boxer, sensing defeat, or wishing to be defeated, may strike out with fouls. As the notorious welterweight Fritzie Zivic once said, "You're boxing, you're not playing the piano." Even a great champion like Roberto Duran has been known to thumb an opponent's eye, and certain classic fights of Basilio, La Motta, Grazier, Zale, Pep, and Saddler, not to mention Jack Dempsey and Harry Greb, are notable for shameless low blows, rabbit punches, and other outlawed tactics. Savagely biting an opponent, Mike Tyson's widely condemned act of aggression against his dominating opponent Evander Holyfield in their debacle of a heavyweight title fight, is less common but hardly unknown. It would seem to be a more primitive, crueler, and more destructive act than most fouls, a gesture of last resort; the sort of behavior that presages the end of a career. When, in his desperate apology for this desperate act, Tyson says he doesn't know why he did it, his only explanation is that he "snapped," we can take him at his word: If there's any explanation, he doesn't know it.

Yet how much more rational was Tyson's boast of his motives after a 1989 fight with Carl Williams—"I want to fight, fight, fight, and destruct the world." If Tyson had caused no scandal at the time, it was because he'd won the fight and retained his title. He hadn't yet been put to the test. (That would come in the following year, when he lost ignominiously to a boxer of the second rank, Buster Douglas, and began the vertiginous downward spiral that has become his career.) The madness of boxing, most dramatically exhibited by boxers who publicly "snap," is always there, like one of those underground fires that smolder for years undetected. In no sport more than boxing is the terrifying aphorism of Nietzsche appropriate: "What someone *is*, begins to be revealed when his talent abates, when he stops showing us what he can *do*."

Like Jack Dempsey, whom Tyson in many ways resembles (including the early deterioration of his talent after winning the heavyweight title), Tyson has always generated that pre-fight anticipation we feel, as he approaches the ring, as "electricity"—a banal term for

an ineffable sensation. Like Dempsey, Tyson has always seemed to ir-
radiate a powerful, vengeful rage barely contained by the discipline
of the sport; an air, embodied in the very flesh, particularly in their
masklike facial scowls, of mysterious hurt and the wish to do spectacular hurt to others. The athlete as bearer of the crowd's collective
frenzy. Yet also, in time, and with equal "electricity," the athlete
whom crowds love to hate. What an iconic moment Tyson has provided us, to take its place alongside such images as that of Dempsey
being knocked ingloriously out of the ring, legs flailing, in the notorious Dempsey–Firpo fight of 1923 (which Dempsey, who should
have been disqualified by the referee, forged on to win) and the young
Muhammad Ali snarling at his "knocked-out" opponent Sonny Lis-
ton in their second, absurdly truncated heavyweight title match of
1965—"Get up and fight!" Here in 1997 we have the image of Mike
Tyson spitting out his mouthpiece and with the calm of a pit bull
leaning to his opponent's neck, in a clinch, to seize the man's ear in
his teeth and try to tear it off. (To call the injury a "bite" is to mini-
malize it. It was more than a bite, it was an assault. If you didn't see
the fight you may have thought that Tyson "snapped" in some visible
way, overcome by fury at having been butted above the eye, from
which he was bleeding profusely; in fact, this assault, no less than the
second bite that followed five minutes later, was clearly premeditated. And Tyson chose not the most natural form of retaliation for a
head butt, another butt, but biting, which sends a very different signal.) Boxing's taboo secret—that the boxers are upright animals, restrained by "regulations" and by the third man in the ring, and that
we, as spectators, are embodied in their mad struggle—has found its
most vivid, poetic image.

How thin and fragile the veneer of civilization is in such iconic
moments. "Boxing" is civilized, mere "fighting" belongs to an earlier, atavistic world that predates civilization as it predates what we
call rational, responsible behavior. Acts are always prior to motives.
Acts are always prior to theories. There is a horrific thrill in the spectacle of a man tearing at another man with his teeth—what a forbidden image. As any display, or hint, of cannibalism is forbidden. The
symbolic use of one's teeth is far more primitive-seeming than the

boxer's artful employment of the "boxing glove" (not the bare knuckles, as in the past—to spare not the boxer's chin but his knuckles, which break easily) and arouses shock, revulsion. One commentator for "Showtime," which broadcast the bout, spoke of Tyson's behavior as "despicable" and did in fact looked stunned by it. Yet is there, upon reflection, any significant moral difference between the boxer intent upon slamming his opponent's head with his fists to knock him out (i.e., to induce a brain concussion) and biting him? As a young, immensely popular ascendant heavyweight contender in the mid-1980s, Mike Tyson spoke of trying to catch his opponent on the tip of his nose to "drive his nose into his brain." To have done so would be to have performed within the legal parameters of the sport; to have bitten the nose would have been in violation of the sport. Yet surely a brain injury is more serious than a facial laceration? Boxing is a blood sport whose very existence in our society isn't in violation of our society but an expression of its fundamental ruthlessness and hypocrisy, its unnamed, because unspeakable, atavistic rage.

Mike Tyson has been universally condemned for his behavior, and will be suitably punished. Since the rapid, to some observers tragic, deterioration of his talent in the early 1990s, his loss of those defensive skills and quicksilver aggressive tactics that had made him as promising, at the outset, as the very different Cassius Clay at the outset of his career, Tyson has been a lost individual, seemingly lacking, in both life as visibly in the ring, a coherent core of being. Far from being the outcast he has been rendered by the media, a freaky being on the margins of our collective coherence, Tyson is in fact a more accurate mirror of our time than his stalwart opponent Evander Holyfield. This is certainly not to defend Tyson, whose behavior is indefensible, but consider: Holyfield has so cultivated a persona of pious rectitude, that of a self-proclaimed "warrior" for Jesus, the gospel-singing heavyweight to set beside Mike Tyson (who prefers rap music, like "Public Enemy"), most commentators take him at his own estimate. Yet head-butting would appear to be a strategy of Holyfield's, no less despicable in terms of its potential for outlaw injury than biting. If you watch the fight carefully you will see how Holyfield, moving in for a body punch, lowers his head for an "unintentional" butt to the vulnerable bridge of the eye. In the heat of the fight, to Tyson, as to any boxer, the difference between "unintentional" and "intentional" may be a subtle one. Of course Tyson was justified in wanting to retaliate; he wouldn't have been a champion fighter if he wasn't fueled by such emotions. The best retaliation would have been winning the fight: The greatest boxers are those who, when hurt badly, bleeding profusely from the face like Marvin Hagler (in his brief, brilliant fight with Tommy Hearns) and Rocky Marciano (in his protracted, blood-drenched agony of a fight with Ezzard Charles), are inspired to fight bravely and more dangerously than before. Tyson, it's now clear, has no such resources, of either a physical or psychological nature; he has no "character" once his rote-strategy of nondefensive aggression is thwarted, as it would be thwarted by any shrewd opponent like Holyfield. Where Tyson erred was in fouling, not fighting better; he'd believed that he was going to lose because of the gash above his eye, and he may have been correct, but, lacking the character, or "heart," of a true champion, who will fight even when he knows he might lose, he didn't try. A boxer disqualifies himself in a fight for which he is being paid a good deal of money, under contract ($30 million for Tyson's exhibition), because he has no self-respect, and thus no respect for others. Tyson says, "Don't be surprised if I behave like a savage. I am a savage."

Most boxers' sense of themselves is shaky, undefined, and inchoate, as that of actors. (Boxers are actors, in fact. Boxing is "entertainment" depending for its existence upon the fickle, wayward will of a crowd.) Since early childhood, Tyson's sense of himself has always been low, if not damaged, as biographers like Montieth Illingworth have noted (*Mike Tyson: Money, Myth and Betrayal*). No amount of money and celebrity, even, apparently, such outward signs of grace as a world heavyweight title, can atone for such a deficiency. Tyson's mother (whom he recently denounced in interviews as an "alcoholic"—as if any mother, bringing up children in desperate poverty in Brownsville, Brooklyn, abused by the fathers of her children, would not be more than merely an "alcoholic") is said to have passively accepted abuse from men, but then to have flared up in violence herself, upon one occasion boiling water to throw at a lover. This model of the long-abused, passive victim suddenly turned violent aggressor would seem to be imprinted upon Tyson's psyche, for he speaks repeatedly of having been "abused" and "exploited" through his life—an odd notion for one who has earned more than $100 million in a little more than a decade. (Of which two years were spent in prison.) Tyson is, in the ring, a curious amalgam of the passive, or impassive, and the demonically active; his "snapping" is in response to real or imagined wrongs committed against him, which allow for excessive, even savage retaliations. Most people, unfamiliar with boxing, assume that it's an aggressive, sadistic sport; in fact, it's deeply masochistic, and all fighters, with no exceptions of which I can think (including even Marciano, who retired undefeated), are injured in the ring. To dole out hurt, you must be willing to absorb hurt; even to train for doling out hurt, you must be willing to absorb hurt from sparring partners. The best fighters fight brilliantly when they've been hurt, and so it's hurt they must seek. As a young child, Tyson was routinely beaten and mocked for his high, girl-like voice; he was said to have been strangely passive despite his large size. Only after he learned to erupt, and lose control, at about the age of ten, did he begin to assert himself against bullies. The profile of his life has been one of "losing control" at climactic moments, a curious form of self-punishment.

The scandal of Holyfield–Tyson II forces admirers of boxing to consider: Why is biting any more demonic than fighting itself? Its demonism isn't conventional, that's all. This dissolution of the veneer of civilization, the calling into question of publicly sanctioned and rigidly maintained divisions between what is "moral" and what is "legal" is a taboo subject, painful to consider and too emotional for most of us to discuss. Where taboo is violated, reason itself is fractured. We fear and dread the violation of taboo and yet, as Mike Tyson once said, "Outside of boxing, everything is so boring."

"I Had No Other Thrill or Happiness": The Literature of Serial Killers

Serial Killers by Joel Norris (Anchor Books)

Probing the Mind of a Serial Killer
by Jack A. Apsche (International Associates)

Death Benefit by David Heilbroner (Harmony Books)

The Stranger Beside Me: Ted Bundy by Anne Rule (Signet)

Aileen Wuornos: The Selling of a Serial Killer,
directed by Nick Broomfield (Lafayette Films)

*Killing for Company: The Story of a Man Addicted to
Murder* by Brian Masters (Random House)

*The Man Who Could Not Kill Enough:
The Secret Murders of Milwaukee's Jeffrey Dahmer*
by Anne E. Schwartz (Birch Lane Press)

A Father's Story by Lionel Dahmer
(William Morrow)

Hunting Humans: The Encyclopedia of Serial Killers,
vols. 1 and 2, by Michael Newton (Avon)

True Crime: Serial Killers and Mass Murderers, vol. 2,
by Valarie Jones and Peggy Collier (Eclipse)

The heart has its reasons, which reason does not know.

—Pascal, *Pensées*

I'm in charge of entertainment.   —Ted Bundy[1]

It was shortly after the New Year of 1976, in the affluent Detroit suburbs of Oakland County—Birmingham, Royal Oak, Franklin Village, Berkley—that the nude, violated corpses of abducted boys and girls began to be found, like nightmare art works, by roadsides or in parking lots or snowy fields. The children, objects of intensive local searches, had been taken in daylight close by their homes or schools; they ranged in ages from ten to sixteen. By March 23, despite highly publicized police vigilance, there were to be at least seven victims. Most of the children had been sexually assaulted and then killed, by diverse means—shooting (handgun, shotgun), strangulation, suffocation, carbon monoxide poisoning, bludgeoning. What linked the murders and gave to them their particular signature was their mock-ritualistic nature: The killer had taken time to meticulously wash and scrub several of the children, either before or after their deaths; their bodies had been laid out for public discovery in funeral positions; in several cases, their freshly laundered clothes had been neatly folded and placed nearby. Because the murderer's scrupulosity suggested a cruel parody of solicitude, local media baptized him "The Babysitter."

To live in a narrowly bounded area in which a serial killer is operating, with seeming impunity, is an experience virtually impossible to explain, or to forget. If there is any personal connection with the victims, it alters permanently one's sense of the world. In 1976, though the "hippie" Manson family had been execrated in the press, the very term "serial killer" was relatively unknown: Yet to burst upon America's consciousness, though already in rehearsal, were "Son of Sam" (first murder, July 1976), Ted Bundy (first national notoriety, late 1970s), Henry Lee Lucas (first national notoriety, early 1980s), "The Green River Killer" (first known killing, 1982). I was not acquainted with the families of any of the murdered children, but among my Birmingham, Michigan, friends were several who were and I remember the atmosphere of those days, and weeks: the talk, the emotion, the visceral dread; the horror and astonishment that such acts should happen *there*, in a suburban world so attractive, so affluent, so exclusive, so "policed." Detroit, its inner core still bearing the war-zone look of the race-motivated riot of 1967, was the region of "senseless" violence, not its white suburbs.

I remember, en route to a luncheon at a friend's house, driving out of my way into an adjoining residential neighborhood to pass the home of one of the murdered children—how typical the street of handsome, primarily colonial houses, how typical the house where tragedy had struck, motiveless as a shaft of lightning. *If we are not safe here, then where?* To live in an area in which a serial killer is stalking his victims is to feel oneself trapped within another's mad, malevolent dream, for the serial killer behaves with the logic of dreams—his madness yields a distinct pattern, yet is unpredictable, and seemingly unpreventable.

After March 23, 1976, the chain of murders ceased. "The Babysitter" was never apprehended and the case, in theory, remains open.[2]

Somehow it has happened that the "serial killer" has become our debased, condemned, yet eerily glorified Noble Savage, the vestiges of the frontier spirit, the American *isolato* cruising interstate highways in van or pickup truck that will yield, should police have the opportunity to investigate, a shotgun, a semiautomatic rifle, quantities of ammunition and six-packs and junk food, possibly a decomposing female corpse in the rear. Serial murder has emerged as the "crime of the 1990s"[3] and our collective fascination is matched by a flood of luridly packaged paperback books on a vertiginous assortment of killers from "Adorno, George" to "Zon, Hans Van." (See *Hunting Humans*, vols. 1 and 2.) The enormous critical and popular success of the Hollywood film *The Silence of the Lambs*, an entertainingly improbable re-imagining of some of the crimes of the psychotic Ed Gein,[4] both heralded the phenomenon and contributed to it. Even the San Francisco poet Thom Gunn has written oddly sentimental verse apparently celebrating, if not Jeffrey Dahmer's murders and cannibalizations, Jeffrey Dahmer's imagined passion:

I beg from memory each limb,
Each body-part that spoiled with time:
The sidelong hungry look of him,
From him a stammer, from another
A single bicep blue with Mother,
From one a scalp, with hair's regalia,
From one large hands and lazy grin,
From someone reddened genitalia,
And last, the image of the chest
From my original conquest,
The cage once tented in its skin,
Now great free-standing ribs that I'm
Leaving as bare bone rather than
Refleshing, best part of the best,
　　Only love, Iron Man.
　　　　　　—from *Troubadour, Songs for Jeffrey Dahmer*[5]

If statistics are reliable, they are certainly alarming: From 1970 to the present, there have been more serial murders reported than in all previous American history.[6] In the years since World War II, the annual solution rate for homicides has dropped from 90 percent to 76 percent—that is, one in every four murders remains unsolved.[7] (It is believed that 50 percent of all violent crimes in the United States go *unreported*.) Of these unsolved murders, the FBI estimates that at least 3,500 are committed by serial killers who will kill again, and again, and again, so long as they are capable, since these are individuals whose self-definition, whose sole *happiness*, is bound up with killing. The FBI also estimates that there are at least five hundred serial killers currently at large and unidentified in the United States and that, with only 5 percent of the world's population, the United States produces an astounding 75 percent of the world's serial killers.[8] "These people are the crème de la crème, the ultimate challenge to society and law enforcement," says an FBI Special Agent, adding, with no apparent awareness of the irony of his remark, "We're not interested in causes, and we're not interested in cures. We're interested in identification, apprehension, incarceration and prosecution."[9]

Of the diverse materials considered here—hardcover and paperback books, newly published and reprinted; a low-budget English documentary film on America's "first female serial killer"; a facsimile of "the controversial trading cards they couldn't ban" (i.e., *True Crime: Serial Killers and Mass Murderers*, vol. 2)—all warrant interest, if only clinical interest. *Milwaukee Journal* crime reporter Anne E. Schwartz's study of the necrophiliac-necrophagist Jeffrey Dahmer, psychologist Jack A. Apsche's study of Philadelphia "Bishop" Gary Heidnik, and former Manhattan prosecutor David Heilbroner's account of the one-man crusade by Louisville lawyer Steven Kenney to expose the serial killer "practical nurse" Virginia McGinnis make for compelling if painful reading: Lionel Dahmer's self-lacerating memoir of his failed relationship with his son Jeffrey, written with the assistance of the mystery novelist Thomas H. Cook, is a melancholy, unnerving document; likely to become a classic of its rarefied genre, Brian Masters's revoltingly detailed account of the homosexual necrophiliac English killer Dennis Nilsen, a best-seller in England when first published in 1985, is reminiscent of the hybrid prurient-speculative work of Colin Wilson (*Order of Assassins, The Encyclopedia of Murder*)—depravity examined through the lens of a serious intelligence. Ann Rule's memoirist account of the life and career of the infamous Ted Bundy, whom Rule had known as a friend and colleague at Seattle's Crisis Center, has gone through thirty printings since its original publication in 1980 and has attained the status of a genre classic, like Joel Norris's more recent *Serial Killers*, part textbook and part psychobiological polemics. *Hunting Humans* is the *Who's Who* of the genre—first published in 1990, and many times reprinted.

In the burgeoning literature of serial murder, Norris's work is considered a milestone. Cerebral yet passionate, judiciously if doggedly argued, based upon a medical-psychological model, *Serial Killers* contains detailed case studies of, among others, Henry Lee Lucas, Bobby Joel Long, and Charles Manson, whom Norris interviewed at San Quentin. Norris makes the point that serial killers, the overwhelming majority Caucasian males between the ages of twenty and forty, are physically and psychologically damaged individuals; most of them have suffered brain injuries from childhood beatings, and most of them are visibly scarred; nearly all are chronic alcoholics and drug users. (Manson, for example, was an unwanted, battered child, already pathologically brutalized by the age of twelve.) None of them is "sane" if to be "sane" is to exercise volitional control over one's actions. For all of us, but tragically for the abused, heredity, biology, and environment are fate, and there is no escape from severe childhood trauma. According to Norris, the compulsive killings of serial killers constitute "morality plays" in which, repeatedly, with different victims, the same tale is enacted; committing and recommitting murder may be interpreted as "a sum total of the perceived childhood horrors and [the killer's] chronic damaged physical condition . . . the survival pattern of a person who has never developed the channels for emotions such as fear, lust, and rage and is driven by them as if . . . within a primordial neurological soup, an unstructured conscious dream world in which there is no logic and no social order." The killer employs ritual as a kind of "behavioral skeleton—much like an insect" to provide an architecture for his fantasies. In this harshly determinist cosmology, as brainlessly mechanical as any state of nature envisioned by Thomas Hobbes, the serial killer has no free will, no free intelligence, no "self" apart from the psychopathological predicament of his fate. Though Norris does not venture quite so far, what the serial killer seems to be is an active pathogen in the organism of society; serial killing is a "disease," indeed an "epidemic," in urgent need of diagnosis and treatment by professionals. Predictions involving potential serial killers should be the result of "interdisciplinary projects" in the fields of biochemistry, neurology, genetics, social psychology, and criminal justice. (Norris is of this professional class—a psychologist and consultant on criminal cases in Georgia and Florida.)

Because, in Norris's scheme, the serial killer is a tropism and not a rationally functioning human being, his actions can be codified and predicted. There are seven "key phases" of serial killing: the aura phase (compulsive fantasizing, withdrawal from reality—"the killer is simply a biological engine driven by a primal instinct to satisfy a compelling lust"); the trolling phase (active search for prey, a series of "compulsive, frenzied, and paranoic behavior patterns" in which the killer becomes hyper-alert and focused; an obsessive "weaving" as if laying out a net as "neurons deep in the primitive brain begin to fire and cause a turbulence of early memories and primal emotions to mingle with live sensory data") wooing (disarming victims by winning their confidence, luring them into a trap); capture; murder (often bringing orgasmic relief; sometimes "an insight so intense that it is like an emotional quasar, blinding in its revelation of truth"); the totem phase (the killer takes photographs of the victim, and/or ritualistically dismembers him or her, possibly eating parts of the body; often he preserves parts, or buries them in "sacred" places); depression (post-murder, the killer's sense of power fades; the symbolic murder has not altered his life).

Here is a bizarre species of romantic love, the project of a ghoulish Don Juan whom no quantity of bodies—or body parts—will satisfy. Yet a mechanistic model can't account for the obvious fact that, though battered children are unfortunately not uncommon, serial killers are; in fact, they constitute a statistical rarity among murderers. Why do some "damaged" individuals grow into active psychopaths and others, the great majority, do not? (Conversely, why would "Son of Sam" David Berkowitz, Ted Bundy, Dennis Nilsen, and Jeffrey Dahmer, among others, who had in fact not been brutalized as children, become murderers?) And should these "damaged" individuals be detected by way of an "interdisciplinary project" and their condition diagnosed before they kill, how exactly would they be treated? Continuous therapy? Detention? Every commentator I have ever read on the subject of serial killers, including Norris himself, makes the point that the serial killer is virtually impossible to "reform"; he is often highly manipulative and "charming"; he tells psychiatrists, parole boards, judges, and interviewers what they want to hear. Short of locking these "damaged" people up permanently, or implanting electrodes in their brains, it is difficult to imagine what can be done to prevent them from killing, in a democratic society in which civil liberties are honored. Can, and should, *the potential for violence* be, in effect, punished?

And then, what faith have we in psychiatry, psychology, social work, parole, and probation officers? Even when not cruelly overburdened with clients, these professionals are often gullible and self-serving. Jeffrey Dahmer, for instance, was already a convicted sex offender on supervised probation at the time he killed fifteen men and stored parts of their (partially cannibalized) bodies in his apartment; in theory, he was under the jurisdiction of the Wisconsin Department of Correction, but his female probation officer never visited his residence and clearly knew nothing essential about him. (Several of Dahmer's murders were within hours of visits to his probation officer.) Equally ironically, numerous hospitalizations and "therapies" failed to prevent the delusional racist Gary Heidnik from abducting, raping, chaining, impregnating, in some cases killing and cannibalizing a number of women in the basement of his Philadelphia home; in his account of Heidnik's career, *Probing the Mind of a Serial Killer*, Apsche notes a psychiatrist's report that "with continued psychotherapy, Mr. Heidnik's prognosis is good." The date of this report happens to be March 18, 1987—the very date that Heidnik killed one of his female victims, carved, cooked, and stored parts of her body in a freezer for appalled Philadelphia police to discover a week later. Typically, when convicted murderer Henry Lee Lucas—convicted for the brutal slaying of his *mother*—found himself recommended for parole in 1970 from Michigan State Penitentiary, he warned prison officials that he would kill again if he was released—but the parole board released him anyway. Lucas retaliated by killing a woman only a few miles from the prison shortly after he was freed; as a witty rejoinder, he dumped her body within walking distance of the prison gate. Then he took off on a spree of sadistic killings that would not end until 1983, thirteen years later. (Lucas, neurologically impaired, now on Death Row in Texas, is suspected of between one hundred and five hundred murders committed from 1951 to 1983, and was convicted of nine.) Apsche quotes serial killer-torturer John Wesley Dodd, whose specialty was young boys: "I can't say that I've discovered much about myself. The biggest thing is that everything could have been prevented. . . . I've had so many contacts with police and confessed to so many crimes and never been charged, or the charges were dropped and I was never prosecuted for one reason or another."[10] Dodd was repeatedly freed because the law required that only part of his extensive record be available for review during his trials and because, as a Caucasian male of some intelligence, he made a "good appearance" in court.

Clearly, there are serial killers quite distinct from the protoplasmic/clockwork model Norris presents. Virginia McGinnis of Heilbroner's

Death Benefit is, in fact, the antithesis of the fantasy-driven murderer: The Ice Lady, as she was called, methodically planned her crimes, which were essentially insurance frauds, with herself as beneficiary. Her motive?—"She was obsessed with having beautiful things." In the course of her twenty-year career, McGinnis was the beneficiary of life insurance policies on, among others, her husband, her mother, her three-year-old daughter. Poisonings, thefts, fires, even a ludicrous "accidental hanging" (of the daughter) ran through her life—yet authorities, including insurance company investigators, made no effort to apprehend her. McGinnis even tried to buy her baby granddaughter (for $500) from her impoverished daughter-in-law so that she could insure the child, and presumably murder her. Were it not for the zeal and courage of Steven Kenney, a Louisville lawyer who abandoned his lucrative corporate law practice to pursue McGinnis, in the face of outrageous prosecutorial indifference, McGinnis would be free today, enjoying the "death benefit" from her last victim—a mildly retarded young woman whom McGinnis insured the day before she pushed her off a cliff in Big Sur. (At McGinnis's trial, the State Farm officer who issued the policy admitted that McGinnis's many prior claims for insurance worried him and that he feared, if he issued the new policy, twenty-year-old Deana Roberts would be killed. But he issued it anyway—business is business.) Heilbroner's book, richly detailed, is a model of unobtrusive investigative reportage. Rare in this genre, it moves to an uplifting conclusion: Virginia McGinnis may be the very image of evil's banality but her nemesis Steven Kenney emerges as the image of the stubborn curiosity, skeptical intelligence, and idiosyncratic altruism we wish for in ourselves. A lawyer who jeopardizes his own career and private life in a quest for an elusive, possibly quixotic justice—*and he succeeds*. (McGinnis is serving out a life sentence without possibility of parole in a California prison.)

The luckless Aileen Wuornos, crudely (and inaccurately) touted as "the first female serial killer," is another who resists classification in Norris's scheme. Since confessing to the murders of seven men in Florida, in 1992, with the explanation that she killed in each instance in "self-defense," this Michigan-born prostitute has been the subject of much media attention. (A feature film is planned on her life and career, with consultants the Florida police who arrested her and the very woman who'd been Wuornos's accomplice—now turned state's evidence in exchange for immunity from prosecution. A True Crime trading card in Wuornos's honor is forthcoming, as is a True Crime Comic.) In the well-intentioned but maddeningly protracted and repetitious film *Aileen Wuornos: The Selling of a Serial Killer*, one of those hand-held-camera documentaries that make of their own limitations and rebuffs a theme of the narrative, and which can only be viewed by VCR, with one's thumb firmly on the fast-forward button of the remote control, Wuornos emerges as a pathetic, delusional, doomed figure who may well have killed her first victim, an abusive customer, in self-defense but who thereafter killed for money and property. (Typically, Wuornos and her female accomplice, who was also her lesbian lover, were driving a stolen car belonging to one of the dead men when they were arrested.) Abused as a child, alcoholic and adrift as an adult, Wuornos is overweight, poorly groomed, and uninspired as a prostitute; a born loser who is betrayed with dismaying alacrity by her lesbian lover, whom she still adores; betrayed by the absurd "born-again" Christian woman who adopted her with the transparent intention of exploiting her notoriety (for instance, by charging extravagant fees for interviews); and by the inept, obese public defender who cynically advised her to plead no contest to charges of first-degree murder, with the result that Wuornos has been sentenced to death in the electric chair—several times over. (The public defender too accepted cash for an interview; the film shows him taking $10,000 from the film director Nick Broomfield to share with Wuornos's adoptive "mother.") Wuornos is so little in control of herself that, when things go badly for her in court, she shouts at male officials, "I hope your wives and daughters are raped!" Exiting, she makes an obscene gesture at the judge. She insists in interviews that she is *not* a serial killer "like Jeff Bundy" (*sic*). By the film's end, Wuornos is beginning at last to realize that her only friends are eagerly selling her out—it's to their advantage that she die as the "first woman to be executed in Florida." Taken back into custody, however, she smiles and waves at the camera under the delusion that, through the filmmaker's efforts, she will avoid the death penalty. (In fact, Wuornos's case is being appealed. But, with seven confessions to capital crimes, her prospects are grim as her prison-issue clothes.)

As Ann Rule presents him in her lengthy, indeed exhaustive and exhausting *The Stranger Beside Me*, Ted Bundy is far more complex than any schematized "serial killer" profile can suggest. This most infamous of contemporary sex murderers, America's own Jack the Ripper, Bundy remains an enigma: handsome, charismatic, much-admired by women to the very end;[11] a graduate of the University of Washington with a 3.51 average; a law student active in Washington Republican politics for whom Governor Daniel Evans wrote a glow-ing letter of recommendation in 1973; blessed with the sociopath's boundless faith in himself and the ability to make others share that faith. It was said of Bundy that he could have had a career in Repub-lican politics. It was said of Bundy that he was simply too *normal* to be the serial killer responsible for a growing number of rape-murders in Washington in the early 1970s and then (after Bundy moved to Utah) in Utah in the mid-1970s. (When Bundy was tried for first-degree murder in the deaths of two young women in Florida, he would claim "insanity"—"diminished responsibility"—as a defense.) In short, Bundy was the exact antithesis of the stereotypical sex-fiend loser, the man who wreaks revenge on women because, like "Son of Sam" Berkowitz or Joel Rifkin, he was ignored or scorned by women, the proverbial outcast at life's feast; nor had he any reason to be vio-lently angry at society for having brutalized and marginalized him, like, for instance, the Satanists Richard Ramirez (the "Night Stalker" of Los Angeles in the 1980s) and Charles Manson.

Bundy's first probable killing, according to Rule, was the murder of a little girl in 1961, when he was fifteen, for which he was never suspected. His last victim, in Florida, in 1978, was a twelve-year-old girl. Exalting in his courtroom performances, in which he intermit-tently acted as his own lawyer, Bundy successfully appealed his Florida convictions for an astounding ten years, costing the state be-tween $6 million and $7 million in legal fees. As the date of his exe-cution neared in early 1989, Bundy began suddenly to confess to his murders as a way of negotiating another stay of execution, a shrewd maneuver that yet did not succeed. Now blaming the baleful influ-ence of pornography for his crimes, Bundy confessed to twenty-eight murders; experts believe he probably killed as many as one hun-dred young women. Though clearly, by his own admission, under the sway of the sexual compulsion "to do great bodily harm to females," Bundy was a clever petty thief and con man who planned his savage murders rather like theatrical adventures. (He often wore disguises, including a plaster cast on his leg.) He was not a multiple personality in whom memory is fractured and inaccessible. Above all, Bundy took enormous pleasure in media attention, both before and after his arrests. As Rule notes,

> It was only after the killings that Ted realized just how newsworthy he was. He began to exalt in the thrill of the chase, and it became a part of the ritual, a part even more satisfying than the murders themselves. His power over the dead girls lasted such a short time, but his power over the police investigators went on and on. . . . How often he would talk to me of being in the limelight, being the Golden Boy.

How proud Bundy would be to consider the numerous books written in his honor, the most abidingly popular being Ann Rule's admirable if distressing work. One can imagine him smiling as he reads, on the back of the paperback, that a reviewer for the *New York Times* has called him "the most fascinating killer in modern American history."

*   *   *

> The death . . . of a beautiful woman is, unquestionably, the most poetic topic in the world—and equally is it beyond doubt that the lips best suited for such topic are those of a bereaved lover?
>
> —Edgar Allan Poe, "The Philosophy of Composition"

> I wished I could stop but I could not. I had no other thrill or happiness.
>
> —Dennis Nilsen

The serial killer has come to seem the very emblem of evil, for his crimes are flagrant and self-delighting violations of taboo, so excessive as to beggar any measure of punishment. Merely "an eye for an eye, a tooth for a tooth" is inadequate here. The burgeoning chronicles of serial killing make for unnerving illumination and invite the proposition that beneath a mask of civility, as Voltaire argued against the naive idealism of Rousseau, the nature of man is that of a beast of prey; indeed, of madness itself. Yet to examine the mind of the serial killer is to examine the human mind in extremis, and should anything "human" be alien to use? Where the "human" crosses over into the "monstrous" is after all a matter of law, theology, or aesthetic taste. (Or politics. Recall that U.S. army lieutenant William Calley, who led his platoon in a slaughter of between three and four hundred unarmed civilians, including children, in My Lai, Vietnam, on March 16, 1968, was court-martialed and sentenced to life imprisonment as a first-degree murderer—but pardoned by President Richard Nixon in 1969, presumably because mass murder committed in U.S. army uniform is something other than mass murder.)[12]

Our fascination and revulsion for the "monstrous" among us has to do with our uneasy sense that such persons are forms of ourselves, derailed and gone terribly wrong, as the autistic personality is oneself deprived, by a fatal trick of brain chemistry, of the ability to relate to others through language, eye contact, touch; as the schizophrenic is a mirror of oneself trapped in a dream life endured in consciousness. The psychopathic serial killer is a deep fantasist of the imagination, his fixations cruel parodies of romantic love and his bizarre, brutal acts frequently related to cruel parodies of "art." The serial killer's immersion in fantasy; his apparent helplessness in the face of his compulsion—in some cases, like "Son of Sam," the killer claims to hear demonic voices; the ritualistic and totemic elements of his grotesque "art"; the seemingly insatiable need to orchestrate, and reorchestrate, a drama of hallucinated control; the mystical-erotic "high" released by the consummation, after a lengthy period of premeditation—all suggest a kinship, however distorted, with the artist. It is as if the novelist, playwright, visual artist were incapable of translating his fantasy into words or images but was compelled, by powerful unconscious urges, to locate living individuals to perform for him, at his bequest.

And there is the actual "art"—the totemic rituals that led an anonymous ax murderer in 1985, in New York, to arrange his victims' skull fragments in identical patterns, or "The Babysitter" of

Oakland County, Michigan, in 1976, to bathe and scrub his child-victims and lay their bodies in formal funeral positions to be discovered. Among Ed Gein's numerous macabre ornaments were skulls on bedposts and a belt of female nipples. John Wayne Gacy,[13] now on Death Row in Illinois, has painted hundreds of Fauvist-Primitive images of his clown alter ego Pogo, a gigantic, malevolent smiling figure—"A clown can get away with murder," Gacy has said. And there is Dennis Nilsen's self-pitying verse, written in homage to the sixteen young men he'd drugged, strangled, fondled, masturbated over, and at last dismembered—"I try to smile / Despite the vengeance looking at me, / Covered in your tomato paste, / A man of many parts / I try to forget. / Even the perfume of your passing / Lingers on. / More problems now / With all your bits and pieces . . . / I try to smile / But you're not smiling now. / In April death is dead / And all the new life lives / Upon our garbled inquest." *Killing for Company* includes as much as any reader will want of Nilsen's verse, stream-of-consciousness prose ramblings, and "Sad Sketches," romantic line drawings of the naked, mutilated bodies of his young male victims, which he frequently covered in body makeup and photographed as well, afterward boasting to Masters, "I did it all for me. Purely selfishly. . . . I worshipped the art and the act of death, over and over." The banal rimes of a typical Ted Bundy poem, addressed to one of many woman friends, suggests the shallowness of the man's soul: "I send you this kiss / deliver this body to hold. / I sleep with you tonight / with words of love untold. / I would love you, if I might / with words that unfold / these arms to press you tight." Even Joel Rifkin, Long Island's most recent tabloid killer, turns out to be an impassioned, prolific scribbler of verse as an adolescent: "A siren temptress calls me near / a stranger beyond darkness haze / pleading from within the shadows / and though I be helpless to help her / help her I must. . . ." (See *New York Post*, October 8, 1993, for more of the same.) As Nabokov's Humbert Humbert dryly observed in *Lolita*, "You can always count on a murderer for a fancy style."

Yet not, it seems, female murderers, who, constituting an estimated 8 percent of American murderers, are rarely sentimental, still less morbid. Sexual fetishes, the great passion of the male psychopath, seem not to engage them at all. They kill for money, or because they are in positions where killing is easy (baby-sitting, nursing) and they have a grudge against the world. Most often, they are merely the distaff half of a murderous couple whose brainpower is supplied by a man; often, like the slavish females of Charles Manson's harem, they are willing disciples of a cult leader, sexually and emotionally bound.

The most famous, or infamous, necrophile in American literary history is, of course, and unfairly, a woman—the redoubtable Emily of William Faulkner's Gothic tall tale–parable, "A Rose for Emily," who sleeps in secret for decades with the mummified remains of the Yankee seducer who meant to betray her, and whom she poisoned before he could escape. Here are the elegiac cadences of Edgar Allan Poe put to a use more subtle than ever in Poe:

> For a long while we just stood there, looking down at the profound and fleshless grin. The body had apparently once lain in the attitude of an embrace, but now the long sleep that outlasts love, that conquers even the grimace of love, had cuckolded him. What was left of him, rotted beneath what was left of the nightshirt, had become inextricable from the bed in which he lay; and upon him and upon the pillow beside him lay that even coating of the patient and abiding dust.

(Contrast Poe's characteristic death-intoxicated erotic work— "Lenore," "Annabel Lee," "The Sleeper," "The Fall of the House of Usher," "Ligeia," "Berenice," among others—in which the deceased beloved is imagined in abstract, melodramatic language so lacking in specificity as to seem hardly more than Poe's fevered fantasy.)

Necrophilia in actual women, however, certainly in women serial killers of record, would seem to be virtually nonexistent. Even heterosexual necrophilia is a rarity. (How most accurately to characterize the California "Co-Ed Killer" Edmund Kemper, who murdered numerous young women, dissected their bodies, and raped various organs; who killed two of his grandparents and his mother, whose decapitated head he preserved as both a masturbatory object and a dart board?) Homosexual necrophiliacs demonstrate a curious, compulsive, surely self-defeating habit of storing or burying the remains of their victims in their residences, beneath floorboards (like Dennis Nilsen), or in closets and deep freezers (like Jeffrey Dahmer). The horrific crawl space beneath John Wayne Gacy's house was so packed with decaying bodies that the stench pervaded his property, yet Gacy began dumping bodies into the Des Plaines River only as a last resort—he would rather have kept them at home. "It may be that when I was killing those men I was killing myself," Dennis Nilsen observed. Naturally, one would not want to physically abandon oneself.

Necrophilia is a cure, for some, for (male) impotence; at any rate, an imaginative attempt at a cure. The necrophiliac exerts control over the dead body as, he believes, he could never exert control over the living. (In Dahmer's case, as it came out at his trial, the necrophiliac's preference was to have sex with the viscera of his victims, as if the "whole" were too intimidating. Cannibalizing of the parts came next.) Or it may be, as Brian Masters quotes Erich Fromm, that necrophiliacs are deeply narcissistic individuals whose aim "is to transform all that is alive into dead matter; they want to destroy everything and everybody, often even themselves; their enemy is life itself." Why necrophiliacs tend to be homosexual is not explored in these books, but the narcissistic "mirroring" of the living murderer-lover in the dead victim would seem to be the motive.

I knotted the string because I heard somewhere that this was what the *thuggi* did in India for a quick kill. I . . . looked at Stephen. I thought to myself, "All that potential, all that beauty, and all that pain that is his life. I have to stop him. It will soon be over . . ."

His heart was stopped. He was very dead. I picked up his limp body into my arms and carried it into the bathroom. . . . I washed the body. . . . I threw him over my shoulder and took him into the back room. I sat him on . . . the chair. I sat down, took a cigarette and a drink and looked at him. . . . "Stephen," I thought, "you're another problem for me. What am I going to do with you?" . . . I laid him on top of the double bed. . . . I lay beside him and placed the mirror at the end of the bed. I stripped . . . and lay there staring at both our naked bodies in the mirror. He looked paler than I did. . . . I put talcum powder on myself and lay down again. We looked similar now. I spoke to him as if he were still alive. I was telling him how lucky he was to be out of it. I thought how beautiful he looked now and how beautiful I looked. He looked sexy but I had no erection. He just looked fabulous.

This is Dennis Nilsen, quoted at exhaustive length in Brian Masters's cogently titled *Killing for Company*. The hallucinatory identification of murderer with victim, "I" with "him," the mad hope of "vivifying" another by killing him—these are motives that underlay Nilsen's acts, suggesting a profound incomprehension of the *otherness* of others. When his killings were over, Nilsen spoke of feeling "intense fulfillment and mutual release for us both. . . . I cared enough about them to kill them . . . I was engaged primarily in self-destruction . . . I was killing myself only but it was always the bystander who died." The excessive attention Brian Masters lavishes upon this serial killer begins to pall fairly early on in *Killing for Company*, despite the unfailingly intelligent nature of the author's prose and the obvious sincerity of his involvement with his subject. By far the most illuminating chapter in the book is the final one, "Answers," in which Masters, the author of literary studies of Molière, Sartre, Rabelais, Marie Corelli, among others, breaks out of his claustrophobic reportage and considers a vast range of thinkers on the subject of murder, perversion, punishment—Dostoyevsky, James Hoggs's *The Private Memoirs and Confessions of a Justified Sinner*, psychological theories of aggression and nihilism advanced by Anthony Storrs, Ernest Jones, Colin Wilson, and others. By the time Masters reaches an epiphany of sorts vis-à-vis his garrulous subject, the reader may feel he or she has anticipated him.

It is not *why* [Nilsen] dismembered bodies that bewilders, but *how* he could face himself having done so. . . . How is it possible to wake up in the morning to a man's head in a pot on the gas stove? How can one place pieces of people in suitcases and leave them for months at a time . . . ? How was he able to tell me, with quasi-scientific curiosity, that the weight of a severed head, when you pick it up by the hair, is far greater than you would imagine? . . . It is Nilsen's inhuman detachment, his invulnerability to the squalor of human remains, that makes him finally unrecognizable.

One can sympathize with the exasperation here without sharing in
the conviction that it is a serial killer's demeanor that should most
distress us.[14]

*   *   *

> Nothing can exist in a natural state which can be called good or
> bad by common consent, since every man who is in a natural
> state consults only his own advantage, and determines what is
> good or bad according to his own fancy and in so far as he has
> regard for himself alone . . . ; therefore sin cannot be conceived
> in a natural state, but only in a civil state. . . . The law and ordi-
> nance of nature under which all men are born, and for the most
> part live, forbids nothing . . . that appetite suggests.
>
> —Spinoza

> I really screwed up this time.
>
> —Jeffrey Dahmer, to his father

Central to the meaning of the "human" is the concept of taboo. In
a state of nature, apart from social communities and their religious
and tribal traditions, does taboo exist? And what exactly *is* taboo?
Why are some cultures hospitable to acts (ritual cannibalism, for instance) while others abhor the very thought of them? Why is the "sacred" in one culture the "obscene" in another? Our lives in the civil
state of which Spinoza speaks are densely yet invisibly codified with
taboos we would never consider violating—or would we?

Clearly, specific taboos are not genetically inherited, but must be
taught, one generation's legacy to another. One must hypothesize a
genetic disposition for the idea or form of "taboo," which is inherited, yet there are human beings whom we call, for lack of a better
term, "psychopaths," who do not inherit; or repudiate the inheritance
under the compulsion of a greater appetite. These atavistic strangers
among us excite our fear and our revulsion but also our fascination
and, in some, our admiration. "Jack the Ripper" of London's White-
chapel district of 1888 was a historic figure who has long since ascended to the plane of myth, a caricature of male misogyny and
physical revulsion for women; there can be no mythopoetizing of the

merely human without a collective unconscious hunger fueling it. The individual who violates taboo is *undefined*, unlike those of us who know ourselves *defined*, and so it is a temptation to project extraordinary powers—romantic, dark, "Satanic"—upon him. But this is a naive and mistaken assumption, as these materials, and others, suggest. Most criminals are losers, in crime as in life. The romance of crime is merely that—a romance, a fiction.

Of serial-killer losers, none is more pathetic than Jeffrey Dahmer. The dullest sort of light plays about the workmanlike pages of Anne E. Schwartz's *The Man Who Could Not Kill Enough*, which covers the Dahmer case from the evening of his arrest in July 1991 through his "sensational" trial and sentencing in early 1992. Schwartz is the *Milwaukee Journal* reporter who broke the Dahmer story when a police source woke her with an excited telephone message: "Rauth and Mueller found a human head in a refrigerator at 924 North 25th Street, apartment 213. There are other body parts in the place, too. You aren't gonna believe what-all's in this goof's apartment. He was cutting up black guys and saving their body parts. . . ." The book's tone is of this quality, suggesting the antic breeziness of a television cop program in which a clever, feisty female reporter is featured; it is informative as a daily newspaper is informative in an easy-access, quantitative way, with a good deal of ephemeral Milwaukee political gossip thrown in. There is little engagement with Dahmer as a subject, or with the phenomenon of the necrophiliac serial killer as anything but a celebrity-freak to be gawked at. Schwartz remains steadfastly on the outside, as if to align herself with the most ingenuous of readers:

> Many people came to court to see if they could sense any underlying evil in Jeffrey Dahmer by looking at him. I remember being filled with a strange sense of anticipation as I waited in the courtroom to see what a serial killer looked like. I was shocked to see that he looked just like an ordinary fellow. I had thought the pupils of his eyes might do spirals. What he had done was awful, but I could not get over how ordinary he looked. The times I saw him up close, I saw nothing there. He did not appear crazed, like

mass murderer Charles Manson, nor did he exude the charm of serial killer Ted Bundy. There was just nothing to him.

And so on.

The particular poignancy of Lionel Dahmer's *A Father's Story* is
that it is so clumsily groping and questioning a document; so much a
cry from the heart, a sequence of anguished questions that yield no
answers. Lionel Dahmer tries to deal with the fact that he is the father
of Jeffrey Dahmer and that, somehow, father and son are meaning-
fully linked; the book's epigraph is from William Wordsworth—"In
deep and awful channel runs / This sympathy for Sire and Sons." As
the psychopath feels not the slightest gram of guilt for the cruelest of
crimes, so often those close to him take on the burden of guilt, trying
to locate, in themselves, possible causes, motives, the wellsprings of
horror. When, in 1988, Jeffrey Dahmer was first convicted of a sexual
felony, Lionel Dahmer thought, "In the eyes of parents . . . children
always seem just a blink away from redemption. No matter to what
depth we watch them sink, we believe they need only grasp the life-
line, and we can pull them safely to shore. . . ." Lionel's belief in his
ability to make any difference in his disturbed son's life, still less to
"save" him, was defeated at that juncture, as Jeffrey was taken away
to serve a year's sentence in the Milwaukee County House of Correc-
tions. (As in a television situation comedy, Jeffrey is always assuring
his anxious father that he's sorry for his behavior—"I'll never do anything like that again, Dad." Ironically, unknown to Lionel Dahmer as
to the numerous mental health counselors, therapists, defense attor-
neys, and probation officers who would touch his life, Jeffrey had already killed four young men in 1988. He'd been only eighteen at the
time of the first killing, in Ohio.)

Despite its stated intention of confronting "every error of judgment, every miscalculation, every instance of obliviousness" that
might have contributed to Jeffrey Dahmer's derangement, *A Father's
Story* is a testament to the futility of such an effort. Not that it is not
passionately argued, or insincere in its language; not that it draws
back squeamishly from its modest revelations. (Though Lionel Dahmer does not enumerate the details of his son's crimes, and no one
reading only *A Father's Story* would have a clear idea of the charges

brought against Jeffrey Dahmer.) In chapters interspersed with family snapshots, Lionel meticulously scrutinizes his own lonely, introverted childhood in the hope of comprehending his son's; he recalls his need for fantasizing "control" in relationship to Jeffrey's pathological need; he analyzes his adolescent predilections (for magic tricks, fires, making explosive chemical mixtures—the other boys called him "Dahmer the Bomber") in relationship to what he knows of Jeffrey's (who, as a boy, was fascinated with dead animals—skinning and dissecting them in secret). Lionel Dahmer wonders if perhaps the extraordinary amount of powerful medications Jeffrey's mother took through her difficult pregnancy might not have contributed to the boy's dull-normal, affectless personality and his alcoholic dependency. (Like the majority of serial killers, including Dennis Nilsen, Jeffrey was an alcoholic who became violent and dissociated when he drank. He already had a drinking problem by seventh grade.) Lionel rereads letters he'd written to Jeffrey years ago and is ashamed of the "utter emptiness" they express—the awkward, affable banalities of a parent with little to say to an estranged, troubled son with nothing at all to say to him. By the memoir's conclusion, Lionel wonders if he is responsible for having passed on to Jeffrey a defective gene, and if the "Dahmer line" should be allowed to die out.

That Thomas H. Cook should be involved in the preparation of *A Father's Story* is appropriate, for Cook is a gifted mystery novelist (*The City When It Rains, Mortal Memory, Sacrificial Ground*) whose predominant themes are dysfunctional families and whose plots frequently involve the search of a father for his child—a search for knowledge that may be an actual search, a spiritual adventure. *A Father's Story* limns a similar quest, in intelligent and compassionate terms, but without a resolution. For, finally, Lionel Dahmer's "confession" and his stringent self-censure are so disproportionate to his son's pathology as to seem bleakly and unintentionally comic, like blaming oneself for having slammed a door and precipitating an earthquake. To what extent can, or should, any reasonable parent assume responsibility for an adult child's life?—his or her accomplishments, as well as failures? Had Lionel Dahmer done a survey of the literature of serial killers, he would have learned that Jeffrey's middle-class, generally nurturing background is exemplary compared to the backgrounds of 99 percent of such killers: no child abuse, no head injuries, no alcoholic prostitute for a mother, no nightmare foster homes or institutions. (For an education in how parents can make of a seemingly normal child a full-fledged psychotic killer, see Flora Rheta Schreiber's *The Shoemaker*, another classic in this gory genre.)

The unexamined egoism of the principle underlying such a document—the masculine line of descent of which Wordsworth speaks in "this sympathy for Sire and Sons"—takes no one else into consideration, including of course the mother. But how can one deal with a budding Jeffrey Dahmer, laconic, deeply secretive, a chronic liar as a teenager? How does one even begin to comprehend a son who steals a full-sized department store mannikin—"a male figure, fully dressed in t-shirt and shorts"—and hides it in his bedroom closet, with the vague mumbled excuse that he'd taken the mannikin "only to demonstrate that he could do it"? (If you want to know what young Jeffrey was doing with the mannikin, which Lionel seems not to have guessed, see Schwartz's *The Man Who Could Not Kill Enough* with its catalogue of Jeffrey Dahmer's myriad perversions, including his "paraphilia" episodes.) How does one confront a zombie-son with no interest in educating or training himself, no friends, no future? *Is* it a defective gene? Or simply bad luck? The blunt fact of Jeffrey Dahmer, as it would appear to be the defining fact for male serial killers in their adolescence, is that, while their coevals are establishing friendships that may last for decades, while they are "dating" and fantasizing romantic and sexual relations of the kind presumed "normal," the serial killer-to-be is fantasizing violent sadistic acts that empower him sexually and yearning for the day when he has the opportunity to make them real. *I had no other thrill or happiness.*

NOTES

1. Quoted in Ann Rule, *The Stranger Beside Me*, p. 400.
2. *Hunting Humans*, vol. 1, p. 21.
3. Ibid., p. 2
4. Ed Gein (1906–1984). Gein, obsessed with the thought of "turn-

ing female" in some way, at first raided local cemeteries to bring back body parts to his home in Plainfield, Wisconsin, where he lived alone as a recluse. Eventually Gein began creating his own corpses, in the mid-1950s. When he was apprehended, police found in his cluttered house skulls, noses, lips, labia, many decorative displays of human bones; human skin used for lamp shades, wastebaskets, chair upholstery. For ceremonial occasions such as dancing beneath a full moon, Gein wore a human's scalp and face, a skinned-out "vest" complete with breasts, and female genitalia strapped above his own. His name virtually unknown, Gein has nonetheless passed into American mythology as the model for *Psycho* and, less directly, *The Texas Chainsaw Massacre*, as well as *The Silence of the Lambs*. (*Hunting Humans*, vol. 1, p. 133)

5. *Threepenny Review*, Fall 1993.

6. Jack A. Apsche, *Probing the Mind of a Serial Killer*, p. 6.

7. *Hunting Humans*, vol. 1, p. 1.

8. Joel Norris, *Serial Killers*, p. 19. (But since American methods of police investigation, including highly sophisticated forensics, are far superior to methods in nearly all foreign countries, it may simply be the case that serial killers, notoriously difficult to trace, are more readily identified in this country than elsewhere. Similarly, "murder" itself may be underreported in other countries.)

9. "Serial Murder and Sexual Repression," by David Heilbroner, *Playboy*, p. 147.

10. Apsche, p. 19. *Probing the Mind of a Serial Killer*, with its transcripts of interviews of the "God-directed" Gary Heidnik, is a bleakly instructive text. Apsche, a professional in the mental health ministry, is uncharacteristically frank: "There is at this time no cure for serial murderers. In treatment they will revert to their helpful, eager to please, manipulative and affable selves. They are uncontrollably sadistic. . . . It should be kept in mind that whenever these people are paroled they will murder again." (p. 29)

11. Throughout his trials, and well after Ted Bundy was sentenced to death for several savage sex slayings, attractive young women—"Ted groupies," as they were known—continued to claim undying love for their hero. Rule notes, at one of the trials:

The front row—just behind Ted and the defense team—was jammed with pretty young women, as it would be each day. Did they *know* how much they resembled the defendant's purported victims? Their eyes never left Ted, and they blushed and giggled with delight when he turned to flash a blinding smile at them. . . . It is a common syn-

drome, this fascination that an alleged mass murderer has for some
women, as if he was the ultimate macho figure. (p. 354)

(The most credulous of all Ted groupies, a woman named Carole Boone,
married Bundy and bore his child.) The equally savage sex killer Richard
Ramirez (one of his rape-murder victims was a nine-year-old girl) also acquired a devoted female following. If this is indeed a common syndrome,
how to account, in evolutionary terms, for the deep, abiding, brainless
masochism of the female sex? *Is* the mass murderer the "ultimate macho
figure," the bearer of the most precious genes?

12. In his dress uniform cap, his upraised hand smeared with a simulation of blood, Lt. William Calley is represented in *True Crime* trading
cards. The body count of between three and four hundred victims makes
him second only to James Warren Jones (of Jonestown), with a body
count of 916 cultist victims of "imposed suicide."

13. John Wayne Gacy, homosexual torturer-murderer of at least
thirty-three young men and boys, was a successful Chicago building con-
tractor, involved in Catholic parish activities, Jaycees good works, and
Democratic politics (his proudest photograph shows the portly Gacy
with Rosalynn Carter in 1978). Gacy killed and buried twenty-nine of
his victims in the crawlspace beneath his suburban house. Several times
young men managed to escape him after having been raped and tortured,
but because they were homosexuals, and because Gacy was so highly regarded in the community, police declined to press charges. Gacy was finally caught when he killed a fifteen-year-old neighborhood boy—a
"good" boy. (See *True Crime: Serial Killers*, Time-Life Books, 1991.)

14. Nilsen was found guilty of six counts of murder at his trial of
October–November 1983 and sentenced to life imprisonment with the
recommendation that he serve a minimum of twenty-five years. Since
Nilsen was thirty-eight when he became incarcerated, he will be only
sixty-three when he is released. Contrast Jeffrey Dahmer's sentence of
957 years on fifteen counts of murder, handed down by a Milwaukee,
Wisconsin, judge in February 1992.

III

"THE MADNESS OF ART": ESSAYS AND INTRODUCTIONS

"Then All Collapsed": Tragic Melville

> To produce a mighty book, you must choose a mighty theme.
> —Herman Melville, *Moby-Dick*, "The Fossil Whale"

Among the classic American writers of the nineteenth century who were his approximate contemporaries—Ralph Waldo Emerson, Edgar Allan Poe, Nathaniel Hawthorne, Henry David Thoreau, Harriet Beecher Stowe, Henry Wadsworth Longfellow, Walt Whitman, and Emily Dickinson (though Dickinson's poems would not be assembled and published until 1890, years after her death)—it is Herman Melville who has emerged as our tragic visionary. Author of one of the great novels in the English language, *Moby-Dick* (1851), published when Melville was only thirty-two, he strikes contemporary readers as uncannily prophetic in his dramatization of the (blind, adversarial, self-doomed) position of mankind in nature. *Moby-Dick* is a work of the writerly imagination at the very height of its powers, boldly exuberant, "rising and swelling" with its subject, a chronicle of nineteenth-century New England whaling, a compendium of wonder tales of the sea, an adventure story, a Shakespearean tragedy of heroic courage and blindness, a brilliantly lyric meditation upon the vicissitudes of life as seen by the young sailor Ishmael, who alone escapes the devastation wreaked upon the *Pequod* by the Great White Whale—bringing us, after the bountiful chapters that precede, to the stark, inevitable conclusion:

Now small fowls flew screaming over the yet yawning gulf; a sullen white surf beat against its steep sides; then all collapsed, and the great shroud of the sea rolled on as it rolled five thousand years ago.

"Then all collapsed"—this succinct and ominous phrase might be kept in mind as a ground bass to Melville's writings post–*Moby-Dick*.

Though not of so high an achievement as *Moby-Dick*, several of Melville's shorter prose works—"Bartleby the Scrivener," "Benito Cereno," "The Encantadas, or The Enchanted Isles," "The Paradise of Bachelors and the Tartarus of Maids," and the posthumously published novella *Billy Budd* (written 1888–91, published 1924)—have become classics in their own right. With the notable exception of *Billy Budd*, these tales were written between the years 1852 and 1856, for magazine publication, and were gathered together as *The Piazza Tales* (1856), a misleading and inadequate title meant perhaps to suggest a writerly kinship with Nathaniel Hawthorne's exemplary *Mosses from an Old Manse* (1846), which had made a powerful impression upon Melville. (Hawthorne's influence upon Melville is incalculable. It was the younger writer's initial reading of Hawthorne that inspired him to recast his jovial "romance of the whale fisheries" *Moby-Dick* as a deeper, more meditative and tragic-prophetic work, and Hawthorne's characteristic mode of allegory is everywhere prevalent in Melville's writings after 1850.) In the shorter tales, as in his long, more ambitious, and increasingly difficult novels, Melville's themes are stark and intransigent: the helplessness of even the most assertive and defiant of human beings in confronting an unknowable, uncontrollable Nature ("The Encantadas," that rhapsodic prose poem of beauty and desolation in the Pacific); the inevitable sacrifice demanded by civilization of the Adam-like individual to the tyranny of the "strict adherence to usage" and "forms" ("With mankind, forms, measured forms, are everything," as Captain Vere declares in *Billy Budd*); the thwarting of individual (always male, and sometimes homoerotic) desire ("Bartleby the Scrivener," "Benito Cereno," "The Bell-Tower," *Billy Budd*); a deep and abiding, not very American distrust of mechanical/scientific progress ("The Bell-Tower," A Hawthornian parable of the risks of egoism; "The Lightning-Rod

Man," a parable in a lighter vein, warning against those confidence men who would "drive a brave trade with the fears of man" by selling credulous Americans such pseudoscientific inventions as lightning rods). A predominant theme in Melville, so pervasive through his work as to be practically unnoted, is the curious isolation of his characters, who seem rootless, family-less, and itinerant, such as the brooding, sharp-eyed adventurer of "The Encantadas" (whose query "What outlandish beings are those?" speaks for Melville's essential vision) and the bold, doomed "great mechanician" Bannadonna, whose fate, perhaps presaging the age of invention itself, is to be bludgeoned to death by his own "magic metal," a kind of robot: "So the blind slave obeyed its blinder lord, but, in obedience, slew him. So the creator was killed by the creature. So the bell was too heavy for the tower. So the bell's main weakness was where man's blood had flawed it. And so pride went before the fall." ("The Bell-Tower") The most isolated of Melville's characters is mysterious Bartleby, who appears out of nowhere, has no family, no identity apart from his "copying" in a Wall Street law office, which he repudiates with the statement, maddening in its simplicity and stubbornness: "I would prefer not to." Is Bartleby a precursor of the cipher figures of Kafka, Beckett, Ionesco, undifferentiated as ants in a depersonalized, dehumanized twentieth-century urban civilization? Is Bartleby kin to the equally mysterious and unexplained *isolatos* of Hawthorne's parables—"Wakefield," "The Man of Adamant"? Is he afflicted with the instinct to self-injury and defeat explored by Poe in "The Imp of the Perverse"? Is he, perhaps, an alter ego of the narrator's, as of Melville himself, refusing to participate in the fixed, dull, routine, if inevitable rituals of a money-making society in which all are "copyists" and originality is discouraged? Even the symbolism of "Wall Street" suggests a tragic division between human beings who are walled in their own ego selves and walled out of the lives of others.

Yet, though imbued with a tragic vision as elevated as that of Sophocles and Shakespeare, Herman Melville was paradoxically a writer of romance, and not "realism," as the nineteenth-century sensibility would have comprehended it. (Note Melville's defensive disavowal of "romance" in the second chapter of *Billy Budd* on the basis of his having given the Handsome Sailor one small imperfection—an inclination to stutter in times of stress.) The romantic-Gothic sensibility, coupled with the habit of a somewhat didactic and discursive allegorizing, has made Melville difficult of access to many contemporary readers. ("Benito Cereno" and *Billy Budd* in particular might be helpfully read in the light of Hawthorne's remarks on romance in his famous preface to *The House of the Seven Gables* [1851].)

That air of the strange, the uncanny, the dreamlike "not-real" in Melville, even as the author goes to great pains to set down historical facts and dates (a technique carried to daunting extremes in *Moby-Dick*, with its elaborately detailed "whale" chapters), is purposeful; for Melville's imagination is always fixed to universals, and not particulars. The Handsome Sailor, Billy Budd, is a type, not an individual; the rebellious "slaves" of Benito Cereno's drifting ship *San Dominick* are granted virtually no humanity, still less sympathy from their white oppressors, but crudely designated as "negro"; the carousing bachelors and exploited virgins of "The Paradise of Bachelors and the Tartarus of Maids" have no identities apart from the biologically determined sexual; Bartleby the Scrivener is more idea than man, though an inspired idea, whose abrupt elevation at the conclusion of that tale seems appropriate: "Ah, Bartleby! Ah, humanity!"

Herman Melville was born in 1819 at a time of westward expansion and a spirit of pioneer adventure in the United States; he died in 1891, after decades of writerly silence, at a time of enormous industrial growth, concentrated wealth, and increasing Populist unrest. He would seem to have been, in the rapidly ascending, and rapidly descending, trajectory of his career, a child of the earlier era at odds with and estranged from the later: a writer of romance in a world in which realism was more valued. His career is considered among the most tragic of classic American writers, nearly as plagued by disappointment as that of Poe, our martyred genius.

Like the career, Melville's personal life divides into two seemingly antipathetic and unequal parts, as if lived by different individuals. His youth was nomadic, adventuresome, and "masculine" in the most elemental sense of the word; his maturity and middle and old age were sedentary, burdened by family and financial responsibilities ("Dollars damn me," Melville famously lamented to his friend Hawthorne), and increasingly isolated and embittered. As a young voyager/writer he struck it rich with his first books, the best-sellers *Typee: A Peep at Polynesian Life* (1846) and *Omoo* (1847), swiftly though passionately written following his discharge from the U.S. Navy in 1844; as a mature writer, realizing his idiosyncratic, uncompromising genius in such difficult works as *Mardi* (1849), *White-Jacket* (1850), *Moby-Dick* (1851), *Pierre* (1852), and *The Confidence-Man* (1857), he suffered the indignity of both critical censure and crushing commercial failure. Like the stricken Captain Vere of *Billy Budd*, having lost the love and vigor of his youth, Melville seems to us "[a] spirit that spite its philosophic austerity may yet have indulged in the most secret of all passions, ambition, never attained to the fullness of fame." As a writer and thinker, Melville was an iconoclast of whom it might have been said, as he'd said so admiringly of Hawthorne:

There is the grand truth about Nathaniel Hawthorne. He says No! in thunder; but the Devil himself cannot make him say *yes*. For all men who say *yes* lie; and all men who say *no*—why, they are in the happy condition of judicious, unencumbered travelers in Europe; they cross the frontiers into Eternity with nothing but a carpetbag—that is to say, the Ego.

How strange to us, living a century and a half following the publication of *Moby-Dick*, the greatest American novel of the nineteenth century, to realize that its author died in such obscurity that his few obituaries identified him as the author of *Typee* and *Omoo*, a man who'd lived among cannibals, and that the literary world took virtually no notice of his passing; that his career as a writer of prose fiction ended with the publication of *The Confidence-Man*, when Melville was only thirty-eight years old. His fate would seem to have been eerily prefigured in the figure of Bartleby, a former clerk in the Dead Letter Office in Washington, whose defeated nature confounds the pity of the most sympathetic observer; Bartleby dies of inanition in the Tombs (the New York "Halls of Justice"): "Strangely huddled at the base of the wall, his knees drawn up and lying on his side, his head touching the cold stones, [lay] the wasted Bartleby."

Melville's failure has numerous explanations. His sedentary, house-bound life in New England allowed him no replenishment of the rich, exciting adventures of his young manhood; he seems to have had few firsthand experiences after the approximate age of twenty-five that could stimulate his imagination. Yet, ironically, it was only after this period that Melville believed his deeper life had begun:

> Until I was 25 I had no development at all. From my 25th year I date my life. Three weeks have scarcely passed, at any time between now [1850] and then, that I have not unfolded within myself.

Perhaps the most self-evident explanation for Melville's failure with his contemporaries is the unremitting bleakness of his vision, which was certainly at odds with the predominant Christianity of the time and with the extroverted American faith in "progress" of all kinds. And there is Melville's notorious stylistic difficulty, his lengthy and frequently graceless sentences and his predilection for asides that impede narrative momentum (as in "The *Town-Ho's* Story," in which continuous interruptions and confusing flash-forwards mar the suspenseful tale of Steelkilt and Radney; and *Billy Budd*, in which all action, even the climactic, is subordinated to analysis, summary, and philosophical rhetoric). These aesthetic problems arise, at least in part, from Melville's conception of the art of fiction as primarily moralizing allegory, in which the author (or the author's conversational persona, unnamed) tells the reader what to think, as a father might explain a parable to a child. After the early seafaring and adventure novels, Melville seems to have had no intention of conveying experience to his readers, still less of allowing them to participate in experience, and to make their own discoveries about his characters; he is very different from, for instance, Edgar Allan Poe, whose Gothic romances are usually constructed along lines of suspense, and whose most famous tales ("The Tell-Tale Heart," "The Black Cat," "The Fall of the House of Usher") strike us, for all their archaic diction, as unnervingly modern in effect. Melville, by contrast, is basically an essayist for whom drama is not an end in itself, but the mere pretext for speculation. The terms of his allegories are generally free of ambiguity, "good" and "evil" explicitly assigned (as in *Billy Budd*, in which the Christly Billy is traduced by the Luciferian Claggart, and sacrificed by his "starry" father Captain Vere to death by hanging); contemporary readers may be puzzled by the apparent lack of inner lives of such characters as Billy, who are described minutely from without. Only once did Melville attempt anything resembling a novel (in which psychologically motivated men and women interact in a purportedly realistic social setting), in *Pierre, or The Ambiguities* (1852), an emotional autobiography charting the author's hurt and disillusionment after the critical and commercial failure of his masterpiece *Moby-Dick*: *Pierre* is an ambitious, angrily pessimistic work fatally marred by a prose style that, for all its sporadic brilliance, chokes on its own venom. It, too, met with a dismal reception from both reviewers and the public, and Melville's reputation, within the space of only a few years, was, in effect, destroyed for the remainder of his lifetime.

Interest in Melville was revived in the 1920s, following the publication of *The Collected Works of Herman Melville*, edited by Raymond Weaver, an edition that included the previously unpublished novella *Billy Budd*. It would have confirmed Melville's cosmic pessimism and ironic humor to learn that, decades after he'd poured his heart and soul into his writing, only to be repeatedly rebuffed, he was now to be enshrined, posthumously of course, as a major American writer. By the 1950s, with the publication of numerous critical studies by such Melville scholars as Richard Chase, Lawrence Thompson, Milton R. Stern, and the poet Charles Olson, Melville's reputation had become unassailable, as secure as that of Nathaniel Hawthorne, whom he'd so admired.

To enter Herman Melville's unique world, we must recognize it as difficult of access to readers shaped by contemporary expectations. Though Melville writes in our language, it is a significantly altered language: elevated, ponderous, didactic, at times rather static, as if disdaining the very principles of "storytelling." With the exception of Melville's deliberately light, whimsical pieces (represented in this volume by "The Piazza" and "The Lightning-Rod Man") and the wonderfully narrated "Bartleby the Scrivener," a tour de force of bleak Hawthornian parable in an affable Melvillian voice, his prose pieces are most helpfully approached as constructs of language, not awkward replications of the "real" world. We should interpret his characters not as flat, two-dimensional, and occasionally stereotypical, but as representations of ideas. It was Melville's assumption that he was writing for an audience of reasonably educated, affluent Caucasian males like himself, not an audience of women (though he'd hoped to seduce female readers, for whom he had contempt, with his "rural bowl of milk" *Pierre*), still less persons of color, whose eventual participation in American democracy and culture would have astonished the creator of Benito Cereno's Babo. The direction of Melville's imagination after the debacle of *The Confidence-Man* lay in verse journals and verse narratives (*Battle-Pieces and Aspects of the War*, 1866; *Clarel: A Poem and a Pilgrimage in the Holy Land*, 1876), and poetry of a formal, nostalgic nature (*John Marr and Other Sailors*, 1888), so perhaps it is as a poet rather than a dramatist that Melville is most helpfully approached, a maker of language and images.

Of Melville's shorter tales "Benito Cereno" is the most haunting and mysterious. Contemporary readers may well find it the most controversial. Drawn directly from a historical source, Captain Amasa Delano's *Voyages*, and packed with documentary detail, including a court deposition said to have been almost literally transcribed into the manuscript by Melville, the novella begins as a Gothic romance set aboard ship: The role of the virginal female confronted by erotic mystery is played by the young, excessively naive American Captain Delano, of the sealer *Bachelor's Delight*, confronted with the enigma of the exotic, elegantly attired but strangely sickly young Spanish gentleman Captain Benito Cereno, of the slave-bearing, storm-battered old European vessel *San Dominick*. Delano is fascinated as much by the mysterious young Captain Cereno as he is by the drifting ruin of the ship, where virtually no whites remain (where are the rest of the ship's officers? where, in particular, its "police force"?) but, oddly, black Africans move freely about. Sphinx-like elder Negroes are contemplating Delano and his men as they board the ship to offer aid; others are briskly sharpening rusty hatchets; Cereno's attentive manservant, the "dog-like" Babo, never leaves his master's side, inspiring the myopic Delano to exclaim: "Faithful fellow! . . . Don Benito, I envy you such a friend; slave I cannot call him." The irony of the remark is unintended by Delano: Babo is in fact not a "slave" but a Negro in revolt against his white captors.

The *San Dominick* is a place of "enchantment"—"enthrallment." A form of the haunted or accursed castle of Gothic legend, seemingly controlled by the nobleman-heir, the fated Benito Cereno, the ship is in fact in the control of "primitive" (that is, non-Caucasian) forces; not a mere commercial vessel hauling kidnapped African "slaves" to the New World but the very image of decadent, impotent Europe. "The ship seems unreal; these strange costumes, gestures, and faces are but a shadowy tableau just emerged from the deep, which directly must receive back what it gave." Melville dwells obsessively upon the imagery of Gothic nightmare-romance, which accounts for the novella's slow and repetitive narrative movement, for the theme of "Benito Cereno" is enchantment itself: the not-knowing and not-naming of Delano's erotic attraction for Cereno, with its analogue in the not-knowing and not-naming of Captain Vere's attraction for the Handsome Sailor Billy Budd. Cereno is a Gothic doomed hero, heir to a ship, or a castle, he is no longer able to command, like Poe's Roderick Usher, whom he physically resembles; so intense is Delano's interest in him, so heightened his fascination, that "Benito Cereno" is fueled by a subtext paradoxically at odds with its surface story, of a failed Negro revolt on the high sea and its judicial aftermath. This is why we wait in vain for Melville to suggest that the revolt of the enslaved Africans might be in some way fully justified: Are these kidnapped human beings not fighting for their lives? Is not "rebellion" against tyranny, seizing one's rights by force and violence, in a distinctly American tradition? Readers of color will react with particular revulsion against a text that so casually aligns the "negro" with evil, in this famous exchange at the tale's conclusion:

> "You are saved," cried Captain Delano, more and more astonished and pained; "you are saved; what has cast such a shadow upon you?"
> "The negro."

There was silence, while the moody [Benito Cereno] sat, slowly
and unconsciously gathering his mantle about him, as if it were
a pall.

Yet, subtextually, "Benito Cereno" is thematically resolved, in the
tender, even intimate conversation between the American and the
Spaniard, who each credit the other with having saved his life; how
poignant it is that Cereno, after his ordeal, should speak of Captain
Delano as "my best friend." If we see "Benito Cereno" as moving
toward this moment of recognition, however fleeting, we see the
solution to the mystery Melville has laid before us in such poetic,
incantatory detail, perhaps unacknowledged, even unrecognized, by
the author himself.

   Billy Budd (*An Inside Narrative*) was not published until 1924. The
text we have is teasingly incomplete, very likely interlarded with in-
accuracies, since the manuscript found among Melville's papers was
written in Melville's difficult hand, with many emendations and in-
sertions, and not successively paginated. It is a writer's nightmare to
contemplate the publication of a work not only unrevised, but unfinished; there is evidence that Melville worked on the tragedy for years,
from 1888 until the very spring of his death in 1891, seeking but
failing to find, in his own estimation, its ideal "symmetrical" form.
The prose style of *Billy Budd* is ponderous and arthritic, burdened by
excessive analysis; depictions of crucial dramatic scenes, particularly
the scene in which Billy with a single unintended blow of his hand
kills Claggart, are sketchy and underwritten; parts of early chapters
containing overly explicit descriptions of Billy, Claggart, and Vere
suggest the notes an author writes to himself in a work-in-progress,
to be judiciously excised when his manuscript is revised and polished. Yet the wish to make of *Billy Budd* a great work to set beside
Moby-Dick, the valedictory gesture of an American genius so ill
served by America, is totally comprehensible. And we can see, in the
text at hand, the glimmerings of a brilliant and heart-stopping work:
the sacrifice of a heroic, Christ-like young man to assure the "strict
adherence to usage" demanded by the military. (Benjamin Britten's
opera *Billy Budd* may in fact be this work, the most aesthetically
powerful realization of the material.) Even in its incomplete state,

this dreamlike, mythic work has been recognized as central to an understanding of Melville's tragic vision, and compared to such classics of sacrifice as Sophocles' *Antigone* and Shakespeare's *The Winter's Tale*. The poignancy of its subtextual romance, in which Billy Budd ("The Handsome Sailor"—"Baby Budd"—"Beauty"—"all but feminine in purity"—"a sort of upright barbarian, much such perhaps as Adam presumably might have been ere the urbane Serpent wriggled into his company") is the unacknowledged beloved of both Captain Vere and the monomaniacal Master-of-Arms Claggart, adds to the novella's emotional power, as if, for once, allegory's bland, generalized face bore the face of a living individual: the aging, infirm, yet starry-minded Herman Melville himself.

The Essential
Emily Dickinson

Between them, our great visionary poets of the American nineteenth century, Emily Dickinson (1830–1886) and Walt Whitman (1819–1892), have come to represent the extreme, idiosyncratic
poles of the American psyche: the intensely inward, private, elliptical, and "mystical" (Dickinson); and the robustly outward-looking,
public, rhapsodic, and "mystical" (Whitman). One declared: "I'm
Nobody! Who are you?" The other declared: "Walt Whitman, an
American, one of the roughs, a kosmos. . . ." Both were poets whose
commitment to poetry was absolute and uncompromising, and
whose unconventional lives were so arranged that poetry, the "Soul *at
the White Heat*" (Dickinson, 365, c. 1862), took primacy over all else.
(Neither married, for instance, and though Whitman may have
boasted of progeny, there are no Whitman children on record. Emily
Dickinson was surely celibate through her sequestered life.) When
Dickinson died at the age of fifty-five, of Bright's disease, she had
lived almost exclusively in her father's house (as she spoke of it) near a
busy thoroughfare in the rural town of Amherst, Massachusetts, as a
perpetual daughter of the well-to-do household who did not chafe at,
but on the contrary celebrated, what Dickinson called "the Infinite
Power of Home." If it seems almost too symbolically apt that the one
great visionary is a woman and the other a man, and that each seems
to have wished to promulgate an exaggeration of gender type (the

virgin, the "rough"), it should be emphasized that Dickinson frequently employs a seemingly masculine persona, and most of her poems transcend gender; Whitman is proudly "masculine"—yet his most subtle poems are suffused with an androgynous, even "feminine" sensibility. Dickinson and Whitman can be said to embrace the American cosmos, and their luminous poetry, misunderstood and even repudiated in the poets' lifetimes, possess a remarkable contemporaneity in our own.

Though it was known among her family and friends that Emily Dickinson had written poems much of her life, the size of the cache discovered by her sister Vinnie after Dickinson's death astonished everyone: 1,775 poems of varying degrees of completeness and legibility, some of them scribbled on the backs of bills. (It was Dickinson's practice to write on scraps of paper that accumulated in her apron pockets during the course of a day, to be artfully assembled at night in the privacy of her room.) So considerable is the poet's posthumous fame that it comes as a revelation to many readers that Dickinson published fewer than twenty poems during her lifetime. Her obscurity as a poet at the time of her death surpassed even that of William Blake, the enigmatic purity of whose *Songs of Innocence* and *Songs of Experience* suggests a kinship with Dickinson's work. Like the visionary Blake, long considered an eccentric, if not a madman, in the world's eyes, Dickinson was fascinated with the seductive interiority of the imagination: "Within is so wild a place," Dickinson declares. And, in language and imagery Blake would have understood:

Much Madness is divinest Sense—
To a discerning Eye—
Much sense—the starkest Madness . . .
'Tis the Majority
In this, as All, prevail—

(435, c. 1862)

Contrary to popular legend, Emily Dickinson was by no means an absolute recluse; she frequently saw a number of Amherst friends and neighbors, participated in a busy household, and maintained friendly relations with several distinguished literary men of the day, two of whom were associated with the Springfield *Daily Republican*, a newspaper of national reputation. The third, T. W. Higginson, a writer for *The Atlantic Monthly*, has had the misfortune to enter literary history as the man who failed to recognize Dickinson's genius, but in fact, after Dickinson's death, at the urging of her editor Mabel Loomis Todd, Higginson was instrumental in getting Dickinson's "verse" (as it was condescendingly called) into print. At the time of their primarily epistolary relationship, however, through the 1860s, when Dickinson sent him more than one hundred poems for commentary, Higginson was simply not discerning enough to rise above the conventional poetics of the day: He criticized Dickinson's metrics as "spasmodic" and attempted, with the good intentions of many an obtuse editor confounded by genius, to "correct" her experimental rhyming and syntax. Dickinson dealt with this disappointment by retreating from any active hope of seeing her poetry published, let alone appreciated; her refuge, and her strength, would lie in the subversive strategies of anonymity, invisibility, self-reliance. The poet is indeed, and ideally, "Nobody." Rejection is transposed into defiance: "I'm ceded—I've stopped being Theirs—" (508, c. 1862). And, in images that conflate poet and female: "They shut me up in Prose— / As when a Little Girl / They put me in the Closet— / Because they liked me 'still'—" (613, c. 1862).

The poet goes farther, to suggest a radical distinction between two sorts of consciousness, two species of human being:

> Best Witchcraft is Geometry
> To the magician's mind—
> His ordinary acts are feats
> To thinking of mankind.
>
> —(1158, c. 1870)

The witch-poet is the magician of words; ironically, another of her guises is that of a woman of her time, place, and social class. Look for her and she is—where?

> I hide myself within my flower
> That fading from your Vase,

You, unsuspecting, feel for me—
Almost a loneliness.

(903, c. 1864)

In characteristically bold imagery, the poet defines her repressed imagination: "My Life had stood—a Loaded Gun— / In Corners— till a Day / The Owner passed—identified— / And carried Me away—" (754, c. 1863).

It is believed that Dickinson wrote as many letters as poems, of which approximately a thousand remain. The letters are as elliptical, rich in imagery, and teasingly coy as the poems; here is part of a letter of 1862 to her literary friend Samuel Bowles, of the *Daily Republican*, at the time suffering from ill health:

Dear friend.
Are you willing? I am so far from Land—to offer *you* the cup—it might some Sabbath come *my* turn— Of wine how solemn—full!
   . . . While you are sick—we—are homesick— Do you look out tonight? The Moon rides like a Girl—through a Topaz Town—I don't think we shall ever be merry again—you are ill so long—
   When did the Dark happen?

Dickinson discovered, in adolescence, her distinctive voice, and the energies out of which she writes both poetry and prose are inclined to be romantically adolescent and rebellious; at once self-effacing and self-declaring. The air of deprivation that typifies the angrier of the poems is really self-deprivation, though attributed to other sources. Hunger—literal? sexual? a hunger for the manly attributes of freedom and power?—is a familiar motif of the poetry, set forth in brilliantly compact images:

It would have starved a Gnat
To live so small as I—
And yet I was a living Child—
With Food's necessity

Upon me—like a Claw—
I could no more remove
Than I could coax a Leech away—
Or make a Dragon—move

(612, c. 1862)

"Gnat"—"Claw"—"Leech"—"Dragon": a child's inventory of monstrous forces to be exorcised; by way of the poet's witchcraft-art,
brought into control. For the poet is the "spider" as well, working at
night in the secrecy of her room, unwinding a "Yarn of Pearl" unper-
ceived by others and plying "from Nought to Nought / In unsub-
stantial Trade—"

Dare you see a Soul *at the White Heat?*
Then crouch within the door—
Red—is the Fire's common tint—
But when the vivid Ore
Has vanquished Flame's conditions,
It quivers from the Forge
Without a color, but the light
Of unanointed Blaze.

(365, c. 1862)

Literary fame is perhaps not the goal, but it seems to have been a subject to which the poet has given some thought: "Some—Work for
Immortality— / the Chiefer part, for Time—" (406, c. 1862). And in
a flight of speculative discretion:

Fame of Myself, to justify,
All other Plaudit be
Superfluous—An Incense
Beyond Necessity—

Fame of Myself to lack—Although
My Name be else Supreme—
This were an Honor honorless—
A futile Diadem—

(713, c. 1863)

Yet more wryly in this late, undated poem that might have been written by a poet who had in fact enjoyed public acclaim:

> Fame is a bee.
> It has a song—
> It has a sting—
> Ah, too, it has a
> wing.

(1763)

And what mysterious eloquence in this similarly late, undated poem, with its powerful Shakespearean resonance:

> Fame is a fickle food
> Upon a shifting plate
> Whose table once a
> Guest but not
> The second time is set.
>
> Whose crumbs the crows inspect
> And with ironic caw
> Flap past it to the
> Farmer's Corn—
> Men eat of it and die.

(1659)

As Mabel Loomis Todd remarked, "Emily was more interested in her poems than in any man."

The poet's willed anonymity/invisibility in her art requires an ascetic paring-back of all that is superfluous and distracting and merely "historical" (as opposed to "eternal"). Consequently, much of the external world, the "real" world one might say, is excluded from Dickinson's art; the national disgrace of slavery, the very fact of the Civil War, for instance, are not once named in her poetry though she was writing no less than a poem a day during the terrible years 1862–63. The very antithesis of the public-minded, war-conscious, rhapsodically grieving Walt Whitman! Dickinson never shied away from the great subjects of human suffering, loss, death, even madness, but her perspective was intensely private; like Rainer Maria Rilke and Gerard Manley Hopkins, she is the great poet of inwardness, of that indefinable region of the soul in which we are, in a sense, all one. This is an archetypal world in which "Great streets of silence [lead] away / To Neighborhoods of Pause—" (1159, c. 1891)

Measured against verse characteristic of her era, Emily Dickinson's poems constitute a kind of counter-poetry. Her miniaturist work is as radical and jarring as Cézanne's landscapes would have seemed to nineteenth-century eyes enamored of the enormous, sublime landscapes of Frederic Edwin Church, Albert Bierstadt, and the Hudson Valley School. Just as the adolescent Emily Dickinson dared to reject Christianity and, in a church-centered village society, declined to attend church services, so too in her art, though she was exceedingly well read in poetry (Shakespeare, Milton, Byron, Shelley, Goethe, the Brownings, Tennyson, Longfellow, Bryant, Emerson, for instance, as well as lesser, popular poets of her day), she rejected any semblance of orthodoxy. The very look of many of Dickinson's poems on the page is revolutionary: Her seemingly breathless pauses and dashes, her odd, Blakean capitalizations, her disjointed phrases and radical variants of rhyme, rhythm, cadence—all point to a poet of unique, unnerving gifts. The signature Dickinson strategy of inverting syntax to call attention to perversities of meaning ("The most obliging Trap / Its tendency to snap / Cannot resist"; 1340, c. 1875) has been traced by scholars to the poet's artful, sometimes playful, adaptation of the rules of Latin grammar for her own purposes. At times, Dickinson seems to anticipate the bold mimicry of childish speech and schizophrenic dream babble that fascinated James Joyce in the latter part of *Ulysses* and *Finnegans Wake*:

This dirty—little—Heart
Is freely mine.
I won it with a Bun—
A Freckled shrine—

But eligibly fair
To him who sees

The Visage of the Soul
And not the knees.

(1311, ca. 1874)

Another "modernist" technique in Dickinson is the mimicry of quicksilver moments in which images, thoughts, sensations seem to fly through the poet's mind, recorded in the very instant of their manifestation: "The Red—Blaze—is the Morning— / The Violet— is Noon— / The Yellow—Day—is falling— / And after that—is none—" (468, c. 1862). And, in its entirety, this koan-like little gem: "The competitions of the sky / Corrodeless ply." (1494, ca. 1880) Even in the finely chiseled, much-revised longer poems there is a trompe l'oeil quality, a brilliant mimesis of the ephemera of thought passing through a mind of surpassing discrimination.

Despite the transparency of Dickinson's poetry, in which the "personal" casts but the palest shadow, as in the finely crafted prose of Henry David Thoreau, one has a vivid sense of turbulent emotions, passion, loss. If this is a species of confessional poetry—and what intensely felt poetry is *not* confessional?—it has been purged of all pettiness and self-pity; the poem becomes a vehicle of exorcism through the very precision of its language, as in the much-debated poem whose first stanza is "Wild Nights!—Wild Nights! / Were I with thee / Wild Nights should be / Our luxury!" (249, c. 1861) but whose conclusion is wholly unexpected. Until fairly recent times in America, as elsewhere, premature death was not uncommon. Nor was it, one supposes, invariably perceived as "premature." Dickinson was literally surrounded by death from childhood onward—the deaths of family members, relatives, friends, and Amherst neighbors; many of them, like her father's, unexpected, and never satisfactorily diagnosed ("apoplexy," the doctor decided). Then there was the slow sinkings-into-death endured by chronic invalids like Dickinson's mother, nursed by her daughter until her death in 1881, when Dickinson was fifty-one years old. Many of Dickinson's most austere, accomplished poems can be considered deathbed or graveside elegies, responses to individual deaths that make no references to the specific; the imagery of death's ceremonial inevitability is never far distant from her imagination: "I felt a Funeral, in my Brain, / And Mourners to and fro" (280, c. 1861); "Because I could not stop for Death— / He kindly stopped for me—" (712, c. 1863); "I heard a Fly buzz—when I died" (341, c. 1862); "After great pain, a formal feeling comes—" (341, c. 1862); "What care the Dead, for Chanticleer— / What care the Dead for Day?" (592, c. 1862); "I've seen a Dying Eye / Run round and round a Room—" (547, c. 1862). The poet is both observer and participant; death is the greatest of riddles, the most profound of ironies:

> To eyelids in the Sepulchre—
> How dumb the Dancer lies—
> While Color's Revelations break—
> And blaze—the Butterflies!
>
> (496, c. 1862)

Dickinson has written as frankly of despair and the terror of spiritual collapse as any poet who has ever written, but the poet's cri de coeur transcends personal anguish to forge convictions, or hypotheses, regarding the general fate of mankind; as in the extraordinary poems of her most fertile, prolific decade, the 1860s: "The Brain, within its Groove" (556, c. 1862); "There is a pain—so utter— / It swallows substance up—" (599, c. 1862); "I felt a Cleaving in my Mind— / As if my Brain had split—" (937, c. 1864); and, most terrifying of all, in the very grace of its utterance, "The first Day's Night had come—" (410, c. 1862). And what tranquility of resignation, beyond tragedy, in this poem of two packed lines:

> To Whom the Mornings stand for Nights,
> What must the Midnights—be!
>
> (1095, c. 1866)

And this heartrending aside, in the midst of an elegy:

> Oh Life, begun in fluent Blood,
> And consummated dull!
>
> (1130, c. 1868)

Yet there is a side of Emily Dickinson that is not elegiac, nor even stoic and "profound"; her temperament was as much subversively playful as solemn, and even rather wicked, as in a number of her frankly funny asides on persons, customs, reigning orthodoxies she has observed. The first poem in this anthology, written when Dickinson was nineteen years old, suggests both her precocious skill as a young poet and her mordant sense of humor ("The *worm* doth woo the *mortal*, death claims a living bride"); it demonstrates how confidently she could craft "verse" in swinging couplets. And how wise she was, to abandon the genre forever. I include it here, along with other of Dickinson's genial parodies and comic takes ("A Charm invests a face / Imperfectly beheld—"; 421, c. 1862) and corrosive theological aphorisms (". . . The Maker's cordial visage, / However good to see, / Is shunned, we must admit it, / Like an adversity"; 1718, c. ?) to give the reader a sense of Dickinson's generally unacknowledged variation of voice; and, of course, because the poems merit attention. It seems instructive to know that in the year of miracles in which so many of her great elegiac poems were composed, 1862, Dickinson was capable of a Wildean sly good humor:

What Soft—Cherubic Creatures—
These Gentlewomen are—
One would as soon assault a Plush—
Or violate a Star—

(401, c. 1862)

(How intriguing to note that, in these lines, the poet distinguishes herself from "gentlewomen" as from another species; and fantasizes, as from a male perspective, their "violation"!)

At the last, on her very deathbed, it was the droll miniaturist Dickinson who contemplated her fate, composing a final letter that reads as a perfect little poem, a gesture of the gentlest irony:

Little Cousins—
Called back—
Emily.

(May 1885)

Called Back was the title of a popular sentimental religious novel of the time, but it was, more significantly, a printer's term: Printed material would be "called back" if typographical errors had been discovered.

There is no poet, and particularly no American poet, who has not been touched by Emily Dickinson. Like the flamboyant Dylan Thomas, though she is a far greater poet than Thomas, Dickinson is immensely seductive to young poets; one can admire her passionately, one can have virtually memorized any number of her poems, yet to be "influenced" by her is simply not possible. She is sui generis. To be influenced by Dickinson, as by Dylan Thomas, is a fatal error. (Unless, of course, one is a poet of genius oneself, like William Carlos Williams. Or, in her own mordant way, Sylvia Plath.)

I began reading Emily Dickinson as an adolescent, and have continued through my life; her work retains, for me, the drama and "white-hot" intensity of adolescence, like the work of Henry David Thoreau. Certain of Dickinson's poems are very likely more deeply imprinted in my soul than they were ever imprinted in the poet's, and inevitably they reside more deeply, and more mysteriously, than much of my own work. For the writer is, as Dickinson's poet-persona suggests, a creature forever in motion, calculating and breathless at once; casting out demons, joy, gems, "profundity" in skeins of language, then moving restlessly on. Her work, if it endures at all, can only endure, in Auden's striking phrase, "in the guts of the living."

The *Essential Dickinson* is, I suppose, a personal selection—yet not a private one. It includes the poems generally considered great—and they are many. It contains the much-anthologized; but it also contains the virtually-never-anthologized. Dickinson is one of very few poets whose work repays countless readings, through a lifetime. I am continually discovering poems I'd believed I knew, seeing them in a different light, from a different perspective. We return to Dickinson for that magical experience so famously described by Dickinson herself, in a letter to her would-be mentor T. W. Higginson:

If I read a book [and] it makes my whole body so cold no fire can ever warm me I know that is poetry. If I feel physically as if the top of my head were taken off, I know *that* is poetry. These are the only way [*sic*] I know it. Is there any other way.

"The Madness of Art": Henry James's "The Middle Years"

This strange, parable-like tale of 1893, written in James's fiftieth year, belongs to that species of fiction by James that suggests dream or myth; fiction on the brink of dissolving into abstraction. It can hardly be read in "realistic" terms except as the dreamily fractured landscapes of Cézanne can be read against the "real" landscapes of Aix-en-Provence that evoked them.

Clearly, "The Middle Years" is a confession of the artist's anxiety over the worth of his art and the terrifying aloneness to which the demands of his art have brought him. James's own lament over the "essential loneliness of my life," in a letter of 1900, echoes here: "This aloneness—what is it still but the deepest thing about one? Deeper, about *me*, at any rate, than anything else; deeper than my 'genius,' deeper than my 'discipline,' deeper than my pride, deeper, above all, than the deep counterminings of art." The novelist-protagonist of "The Middle Years" yearns for a second chance at his art; yet more passionately for an audience, the "sympathy of the community." Not commercial success and a wide readership so much as someone who will understand, somebody to *care*.

The setting is Bournemouth "as a health resort." The time is an April day of softness and brightness. Poor Dencombe, as James speaks of him, mysteriously ill, fatigued by a brief walk from his hotel to a sea cliff bench, sits and opens, with no eagerness, a copy of his new, just-published novel, *The Middle Years*. Dencombe is a writer of difficult, exquisite texts, never commercially successful, prone to an eloquent melancholy. "The infinite of life was gone . . ." he thinks, contemplating the sea. "It was the abyss of human illusion that was the real, the tideless deep." Exhausted, burnt-out, Dencombe awaits redemption passively, like so many of James's male, middle-aged artists or "sensitive" men; unless perhaps it is already too late? He dare not speculate into the future, out of a terror of what he might envision. "It was indeed general views that were terrible; short ones . . . were the remedy."

Henry James presents as mordant comedy the predicament of a distinctly Jamesian novelist so exhausted by the effort of his art—"It had taken too much of his life to produce too little"—that, confronted with his latest and perhaps last novel, not only is he incapable of feeling the mildest tinge of enthusiasm for it, but he seems to have forgotten it entirely. "Utter blankness" has intervened. Not a single page, not a single sentence comes to him. Yet, as he reads, sitting on his bench above the sea cliff, he finds that *The Middle Years* is, even by the harsh measure of its author's judgment, "extraordinarily good." Note the powerful, even mystical language in which James describes this awakening of the author by way of becoming his own reader: "He dived once more into his story and was drawn down, as by a siren's hand, to where, in the dim underworld of fiction, the great glazed tank of art, strange silent subjects float." This analogue of fiction with the boundless and unchartable imagination at the point at which it is identical with the unconscious might strike the casual reader of Henry James as radically antithetical to the "Jamesian style"—the "Jamesian" mode of a finely calibrated and inexhaustibly contemplated fiction. It suggests, on the contrary, the tremendous pressure of the unconscious; its unknowability. The processes of art yield, and in a way are lost in, the product of the artist's effort—the aesthetic object. We can infer the mysterious potency of the former by the evidence of the latter, but this is a mere inference, a glimmering of something vast, rich, deep, unchartable. Excited by the discovery that his novel is so much finer than he'd expected, Dencombe wonders if he might have a second life, after all. "Ah for another go, ah for a better chance!"

As if this murmured wish were a command, Dencombe is immediately met by the young, attractive, vibrantly alive Doctor Hugh—first glimpsed, in fact, with a book in hand from which he is reading aloud to two female companions; by chance, Doctor Hugh has Dencombe's very novel, with its "alluringly red" cover. This is the artist's "aesthetic object" glorified, and the fantastical "Doctor Hugh"—his very name an echo of "you"—is the artist's yearned-for audience: Dencombe's "greatest admirer in the new generation."

James's usually tactful scrim of admiration for women is here abruptly jettisoned: Doctor Hugh's patient-patroness, the Countess, is a large, indeed obese lady who wears a hat shaped like a mushroom; her companion is a young woman with vitreous eyes, like a figure in a play or a novel, "some sinister governess or tragic old maid." (In other tales of James's of this general period, "The Wheel of Time," for instance, and the renowned "The Beast in the Jungle," it is women who are deep, brooding, and faithful; women who sacrifice themselves at the altar of masculine self-absorption. *Intensities of fidelity*, in James's words, are identified with the feminine.) "The Middle Years" is, among other things, a gently homoerotic fantasy; the passionate bond is between men—the mysteriously moribund elder and the life-giving, ardent younger. How touching is Dencombe in his plea to Doctor Hugh, in this almost comical Jamesian circumlocution, "I want to what they call 'live.' "

Only in fantasy, hardly in realistic fiction of the type and quality, for instance, of James's great novels *The Wings of the Dove* and *The Golden Bowl*, could such a denouement occur: By a melodramatic complication of plot the handsome young doctor is forced to choose between the wealthy neuresthenic Countess and poor Dencombe, and chooses Dencombe.

". . . I gave her up for *you*. I had to choose . . ."

"You chose to let a fortune go?"

"I chose to accept, whatever they might be, the consequences of my infatuation," smiled Doctor Hugh. . . . "The fortune be hanged! It's your own fault if I can't get your things out of my mind."

On his deathbed, Dencombe is tempted to think that the entire experience has been a delusion, but Doctor Hugh assures him it has not—"Not your glory." Dencombe responds rhapsodically, "It *is* glory—to have been tested, to have had our little quality and cast our little spell. The thing is to have made somebody care." Doctor Hugh insists that Dencombe's life has been a success, "putting into his young voice the ring of a marriage bell." In this brief tale in which James includes so few metaphors and rhetorical flights of the kind characteristic of his mature style, this unexpected simile strikes the ear as deliberate, pointed: *the ring of a marriage bell*.

The buried theme of "The Middle Years" is this strange marriage of artist and "greatest admirer"; if we consider it in mythic terms, we might hypothesize a ritual of the (bloodless) sacrifice of the moribund elder, and the passing of potency to the younger. The "aesthetic object" is a literal prop in this ritual, the printed book *The Middle Years* with its "alluringly red" cover, a symbolic representation, perhaps, of male sexual potency, the very gift of life. In this homoerotic/mythic vision, the female is bypassed entirely; all physicality banished, or denied. Doctor Hugh is, not very plausibly, a physician of a purely disembodied sort; he may touch poor Dencombe's life, but he does not touch poor Dencombe's body, even to examine him. He is a physician in a higher, spiritual sense, the artist's personal redeemer, come at the end of Dencombe's life to assure him that, yes, contrary to Dencombe's fears, he *has* had glory, he *has* fulfilled his destiny. "The Middle Years" is as allegorical as a tale by Hawthorne or Melville; its minimal outwardly "realistic" details hardly disguise its deeper, abstract purpose, that of providing the mythic rite to assure the artist's "immortality" in the newer, younger generation. The entire dreamlike story reads like one of those extended passages in Henry James's journal in which the writer plumbs the depths of his own soul. Its moment of epiphany would seem, in the surpassing beauty of its language, to have generated the diaphanous fiction that surrounds it. In Dencombe's words:

"A second chance—*that's* the delusion. There never was to be but one. We work in the dark—we do what we can—we give what we have. Our doubt is our passion, and our passion is our task. The rest is the madness of art."

How significant that even the great artist's redemption can only be by way of his communion with a real, palpable, emotionally engaged audience; a reaching-out to, a touching of this "new generation"— the mysterious "Doctor Hugh"—*you.*

The Riddle of Christina Rossetti's "Goblin Market"

Pleasure past and anguish past,
Is it death or is it life?

—"Goblin Market"

Nothing in the life and career of Christina Rossetti (1830–1894) quite prepares us for the astonishing balladlike narrative poem "Goblin Market." A younger sister of the celebrated Pre-Raphaelite painter and poet Dante Gabriel Rossetti, known for her Christian Anglican piety and admired by her contemporaries for such exquisitely wrought but conventional poems as the sonnets "After Death," "The World," "Dead Before Death," and "Cobwebs," Rossetti fashioned in "Goblin Market" an exotic, gorgeously written poem that shimmers with meanings like a dream of uncommon subtlety. The poem is 567 lines long, Rossetti's longest and most formally ambitious piece of writing; its rhymes are startling, original, rather childlike in affect, with the disturbing, disingenuous musical cadences of the nursery rime throughout. Stresses are emphatic, even harsh:

Mórniňg aňd evéniňg
Maíds héard the góblǐns cŕy:
"Coḿe búy oǔr orćhaȓd fruíts,
Coḿe búy, coḿe búy:

When rhymes and stresses are purely symmetrical, the tone is teasing, even taunting:

Píneăpp̆lĕs, bláckbĕrrĭes,
Áprĭcŏts, stráwbĕrrĭes;—
Áll rípe t̆ŏgéthĕr
Ĭn súmmĕr wéathĕr,—

For this is the Goblin Men's special language, mock-lyric, meant to taunt, tease, disconcert, and seduce.

"Goblin Market" is as much a riddle as a poem of artful ambiguities. It will remind readers of such dreamlike predecessors as Samuel Coleridge's "Christabel" (with the snaky-seductive vampire Geraldine) and John Keats's "La Belle Dame Sans Merci" (a ballad of the tragic meeting of a young knight and a "faery" seductress) and "The Eve of Saint Agnes" (an elaborately composed narrative poem of Spenserian stanzas greatly admired by the Pre-Raphaelite Brotherhood, to which by propinquity and temperament Christina Rossetti was attached)—works that, for all their genius, fail to communicate the immediacy of erotic (or frankly sexual) yearning evoked in certain stanzas of "Goblin Market." The Romantic poets imagine seduction from a masculine perspective, but Rossetti's perspective is distinctly female, achingly specific. The vulnerable sister, Laura, she who is seduced by the Goblin Men, is imagined as "a vessel at the launch / When its last restraint is gone." Laura's complicity in a violation that will be both physical and spiritual is expressed in language of uncommon directness, startling in a poem of its time:

She sucked and sucked and sucked the more
Fruits which that unknown orchard bore,
She sucked until her lips were sore;
Then flung the emptied rinds away . . .

Goblin Market and Other Poems, with illustrations by Dante Gabriel Rossetti, was published in 1862 to critical acclaim, establishing Christina Rossetti's reputation in London literary circles. The title poem's immediate appeal for Victorian readers would have been for its sensuous, suspenseful story, with its balladlike unfolding; the literary ballad being a popular verse form usually involving relatively unsophisticated "simple" characters. Its moral appeal, a Victorian necessity, is clearly, perhaps too clearly for contemporary tastes, stated in the concluding stanza:

> For there is no friend like a sister
> In calm or stormy weather;
> To cheer one on the tedious way,
> To fetch one if one goes astray,
> To lift one if one totters down,
> To strengthen whilst one stands.

(The very voice of "wise, upbraiding" Lizzie, who speaks for Victorian morality, conscience, and rectitude of the kind satirized by Lewis Carroll in *Alice's Adventures in Wonderland* and *Through the Looking Glass*, 1865, 1872.)

For contemporary readers, it is the elusive subtext of "Goblin Market" that seizes our imaginations, provoking us to wonder at the poem's more subtle and possibly more subversive meanings. As sympathetic feminist critics[1] have noted, "Goblin Market" is an inspired, original female reworking of the old misogynist myth of the biblical Garden of Eden, Eve's weakness, temptation, and fall, the subsequent loss of paradise, the sacrifice of a personal savior, and redemption. (Where the old myth enters its final phase, there is no redemption.) The poem bears an obvious thematic relationship with such myths as the tale of Pandora's box (in which yet another curious, imprudent female unleashes horrors upon herself and the world by an act of impulsive disobedience) and the European fairy tale of Bluebeard (in which numberless curious, imprudent brides of Count Bluebeard meet their grisly fate by opening a door in his castle he has forbidden them to open). There is no suggestion in "Goblin Market," however, that Laura has, in the end, lost anything of value. Rossetti doesn't imagine a Miltonic "fortunate fall" but simply a fall, and a miraculous redemption; and a return to the idyll of sisterhood from which Laura temporarily strayed.

As a reading experience, "Goblin Market" is irresistible. Its quickened, breathless rhythms and eccentric rhymes with their air of improvisation draw in the reader at once. Here is an urgent, accelerated, fevered pace:

All ripe together
In summer weather,—
Morns that pass by,
Fair eyes that fly;
Come buy, come buy:
Our grapes fresh from the vine,
Pomegranates full and fine . . .
Taste them and try . . .
Come buy, come buy.

Like her contemporary Emily Dickinson, with whom she shares a number of thematic obsessions, Christina Rossetti evokes states of being through domestic, seemingly ordinary images; in this case fruits—the familiar (apples, cherries) mixed with the exotic ("rare pears and greengages," "Citrons from the South"). Where Dickinson's poetry is elliptical and spare, calculatedly riddlesome, Rossetti's is more conventionally developed and explicated, but both poets achieve striking effects by juxtaposing (domestic, ordinary) images and actions with (exotic, transcendent) meanings. Dickinson's poems, too, are generated around images of fruits, foods, drinks—"I taste a liquor never brewed" (of 1861), for instance, in which the "liquor" is both poetic and passionate (female) yearning, with an air of the forbidden yet irresistible. Rossetti's more punitive, perhaps because more Christian, sensibility, presents the forbidden fruits as temptations from a debased species of male; if not resisted, as Laura seems incapable of resisting, these temptations will result in deterioration and death. And what wonderfully bizarre tempters the Goblin Men are: No hallucinatory visions out of Carroll's Alice books are more comic-grotesque and chilling:

One had a cat's face,
One whisked a tail,
One tramped at a rat's pace,
One crawled like a snail,
One like a wombat prowled obtuse and furry,
One like a ratel tumbled hurry skurry.

She heard a voice like voice of doves
Cooing all together . . .

(How particularly uncanny that, though the Goblin Men are plural, their seductive voice is singular.)

"Sweet-tooth Laura" eagerly exchanges a "precious golden lock" from her head (her priceless virginity?) for the Goblin Men's forbidden fruit, which she devours, in fact "sucks," more greedily than any other female in literary history, including even the mythic mother of all our sorrows, the biblical Eve. Lizzie, Laura's "good" twin, full of "wise upbraidings," awaits her at home, seeming to know beforehand what Laura has done, and the danger that lies in store for her. For Laura has been seduced not only by the Goblin Men's exquisite fruits but by her own repressed, unacknowledged sexual appetite as well, which mesmerizes her:

I ate and ate my fill,
Yet my mouth waters still . . .
You cannot think what figs
My teeth have met in . . .

Soon, Laura is "longing for the night" while Lizzie, uncontaminated by the taste of the Goblin Men's fruit, is content, even oblivious of the night; Laura is "like a leaping flame" while the prudent Lizzie is "most placid in her look." Repudiated by the Goblin Men who have seduced her, as, in Victorian terms, a "good" woman, once "fallen," was likely to be repudiated by the very man who had seduced her, Laura begins to pine away: "Her tree of life dropped from the root." She endures the night "in a passionate yearning. / And gnashed her teeth for balked desire, and wept / As if her heart would break." Except in frankly pornographic work, no one of Christina Rossetti's time whether male or female could have written directly of sexual desire; women were generally believed, in fact, to have no sexual or erotic desire. But Laura of "Goblin Market" finds herself trapped in the throes of such desire, taking no solace any longer in the domestic idyll in which she and her sister have lived like innocent children. Only when Lizzie ventures out into the "haunted glen" to purchase fruits for Laura at the price, nearly, of being violated herself, is Laura revived, and saved. Lizzie's fierce virginity confronts the Goblin Men's primitive rapacity in an astonishing scene that must have been disturbing to Victorian readers:

> Their tones waxed loud,
> Their looks were evil.
> Lashing their tails
> They trod and hustled her,
> Elbowed and jostled her,
> Clawed with their nails,
> Barking, mewing, hissing, mocking,
> Tore her gown and soiled her stocking,
> Twitched her hair out by the roots,
> Stamped upon her tender feet,
> Held her hands and squeezed their fruits
> Against her mouth to make her eat.

But, "like a royal virgin town" (an apt metaphor for the Age of Queen Victoria, the dowager-virgin), Lizzie holds fast; Lizzie cannot be violated by male force. An exemplary feminist heroine,

> Lizzie uttered not a word;
> would not open lip from lip
> Lest they cram a mouthful in:
> But laughed in heart to feel the drip
> Of juice that syruped all her face,
> And lodged in dimples of her chin,
> And streaked her neck which quaked like curd . . .
> In a smart, ache, tingle,
> Lizzie went her way;
> Knew not was it night or day . . .

Lizzie returns to the languishing Laura, her beloved sister, whom she invites to "Eat me, drink me, love me; / Laura, make much of me." The denouement of the poem has a fairy-tale logic, however implausible and unconvincing its narrative terms: Laura "kissed and kissed and kissed [Lizzie] with a hungry mouth" and sucks the Goblin Men's juices from her, experiencing an exorcism of the juices' power over her. The redeeming life Lizzie brings to Laura is an antidote to the original poison, as, perhaps, in Rossetti's Christian imagination, the sacrifice of Jesus Christ is an antidote to mankind's "original" sin, the eating of the forbidden apple and the disobeying of God the Father. The exorcism as Rossetti describes it is richly erotic; sensual and intimate, wringing "Life out of death." And the poem ends in a coda of rejoicing in a future time "when both were wives / With children of their own" and the perils of the "wicked quaint fruit-merchant men" have long been vanquished. The terrible "poison in the blood" of ungovernable sexual desire is but a memory, a familiar tale the sisters tell their children. (Of the sisters' presumed husbands we see and hear nothing: Lizzie and Laura would seem to be virgin mothers.)

This is a somewhat forced, very Victorian-moral conclusion to a teasing, provocative riddle of a poem. For "Goblin Market" evokes questions it does not answer. Who are the Goblin Men? Why precisely are their fruits delicious, yet dangerous and forbidden? And why are there no human men in the sisters' world? Why is Laura susceptible while Lizzie, her virtual twin, is not? Why, after Laura's seduction, do the Goblin Men immediately withdraw from her? Why isn't it possible for Laura to repeat her sensual experience? (Is Rossetti implying that a woman's "fall" from chastity and her initial experience of intense sexual pleasure would preclude her from reexperiencing it? But why? However ostracized a "fallen" woman might be from proper Victorian society, she could surely have had lovers. And the degree of ostracism would be relative: As a chaste middle-class Victorian spinster, Christina Rossetti herself became a volunteer worker at Saint Mary Magdalen Home for Fallen Women on Highgate Hill—a final, ironic footnote to "Goblin Market.") Is the relationship between male and female little more than a cruel game on the part of the male, who would appear to risk nothing in the transaction except a loss of sperm? Or are the Goblin Men not meant to suggest men at all but merely beasts, their appeal exclusively to bestial/sexual desire? How seriously is the reader to take Rossetti's final vision of a matrilineal and matriarchal world in which the highest value is "sisterhood"? It is difficult to believe that the sisters' original state, in which they sleep "Cheek to cheek and breast to breast / Locked together in one nest," is a more desirable state than that of mature sexual experience; but, given the peculiarly limited terms of Rossetti's world in this poem, what can possibly constitute female maturity?

Like most powerful poetry, "Goblin Market" eludes absolute meanings. It remains a haunting aesthetic creation very like the lush, dreamlike, technically accomplished and ornamental romantic-mystic art of the Pre-Raphaelite Brotherhood, with which Christina Rossetti was associated; the poem is enhanced by the vivid, sensuous images by Dante Gabriel Rossetti that express so poignantly the soul's urgent and unspeakable yearnings.

NOTES

1. Among these are Sandra Gilbert and Susan Gubar, who in *The Madwoman in the Attic* (1979) discuss "Goblin Market" in terms of "the aesthetics of renunciation"; and Alicia Suskin Ostriker, who in *Feminist Revision and the Bible* (1988), discusses "Goblin Market" as a subversive revision of the biblical myths of the Garden of Eden and the sacrifice of Jesus.

Rediscovering
Harold Frederic's The
Damnation of Theron Ware

What a wonderful novel, Harold Frederic's once-acclaimed and now virtually forgotten *The Damnation of Theron Ware* (1896)! I first discovered it in the mid-sixties when I was teaching courses in American literature at the University of Windsor; it had been newly discovered at that time, and reprinted as a "classic of American realism," with an introduction by Van Wyck Brooks. Frederic's novel provided an odd, unexpected link between the crude naturalism of the young Stephen Crane (whose first novel, *Maggie: A Girl of the Streets*, was published in 1893) and the elegant dissections of wealthy New York society of Edith Wharton (whose first novel, *The House of Mirth*, was published in 1905). The theme of a young minister's "damnation" would seem to reverberate with echoes of Nathaniel Hawthorne, but the barest glimmer of Hawthornian obsession with sin and mankind's relationship to God prevails in *The Damnation of Theron Ware*; it has more in common with Oscar Wilde's *The Picture of Dorian Gray* (1891), in which a young, ingenuous hero is "poisoned" by a book of amoral hedonism, and by his friendship with a mentor whose disregard for convention unhinges him utterly. I had not read *Theron Ware* in more than twenty years, and taking it up again, with only a blurred memory of the tragicomic odyssey of its feckless hero, I wasn't quite prepared for the novel's warm, intelligent good humor, its complex and ambiguous story, its shrewd, disturbing insights into the human psyche. And what an inspired ending: perfect in its irony, and with a special significance for the present time when "Talk is what tells"—in our national politics as in the more manipulative quarters of populist religion.

Theron Ware is a cautionary tale of sorts, of a young, attractive, good-hearted, and not very well-educated Methodist Episcopal minister from rural upstate New York who loses his hitherto unexamined faith in the course of a vertiginous six months, plummeting from "saint" to "degenerate" as a result of his encounter with ideas and people simply too overwhelming for him to absorb. In its admixture of sharp social observation and melodramatic storytelling, above all in its sympathetic yet detached, and at times cruel, portrait of the Reverend Theron Ware, the novel is clearly the inspiration for both Sinclair Lewis's *Main Street* (1920) and *Elmer Gantry* (1927). Like Lewis, Harold Frederic turns a seemingly unjudging, thus pitiless, lens upon small-town America and its pretensions and anxieties; his Theron Ware is a precursor of the intrepid Carol Kennicott of *Main Street* ("Had she really bound herself to live, inescapably, in this town called Gopher Prairie [Minnesota]?") and, in his phase as religious hypocrite and charlatan, whose sermons increase in power as their sincerity decreases, a precursor of the evangelical preacher Elmer Gantry. On the whole, Frederic's touch is less heavy-handed than Lewis's; his characters less caricatured; his authorial voice subtler and more expansive. Intellectual discussions among the improbable sophisticates of Octavius, New York (there are three of them: a Roman Catholic priest, an agnostic doctor-scientist, a young Irish Catholic woman of unusual independence), are unfailingly engrossing, like similar exchanges in *The Picture of Dorian Gray*; they are far from parodies. Like Sinclair Lewis, however, Frederic clearly knows his American landscape, and his depiction of life in Octavius (very likely a fictitious analogue of Frederic's hometown, Utica) is American literary "realism" at its most accomplished.

It is unsurprising that *The Damnation of Theron Ware* created a scandal when it was published; considering its merciless exposure of religious bigotry and self-delusion, it's a wonder that it was published at all. Or that, published, it did not provoke violent hostility, including the refusal of numerous libraries and bookstores to carry it, of the kind that greeted Kate Chopin's equally daring *The Awakening* (1898). (Of course, Kate Chopin was a woman—a woman writing boldly and sensuously about a wife and mother who commits adultery. That made all the difference.) Far from being reviled or banned, however, *Theron Ware* became a best-seller, alone among Frederic's several novels, and made its forty-year-old author famous. In his time, Frederic was favorably compared to William Dean Howells, Stephen Crane, Frank Norris, Hamlin Garland, Theodore Dreiser. He will strike a contemporary reader as "modern" in ways that these writers, with the exception of Crane, do not. *Theron Ware*'s passionate debate of theories of Darwinian evolution, biblical piety and scholarship, women's rights, and what in fact defines integrity is presented by Frederic as both intellectually engaging and funny; the author's sensibility is more forgiving than damning. Pervading all is the writer's fascination with the world he evokes. In a sense, the novel refuses to take sides in any debate. "Truth is relative," says the worldly Father Forbes, as, with patrician disdain, he shuts the yearning Reverend Theron Ware out of his life forever. Frederic's satiric vision is that of a Henry Fielding and not the savage indignation of a Jonathan Swift.

Like a number of successful novelists of his era, Harold Frederic was trained as a journalist; he began his career working for newspapers in Utica and Albany, then moved on to become London correspondent for the *New York Times*, which prominent post he held for fourteen years. His journalist's sharp eye and ear for revealing detail and instinct for the symbolic juxtaposition of the private and the public are everywhere evident in *Theron Ware*: The meticulous attention to Methodist and Roman Catholic religious ceremonies and customs, the eyewitness drama of meeting-camp conversions, descriptions of houses and interiors, conversations—all ring wonderfully true, and convincing. Here is the welcoming speech of a trustee of Theron Ware's church, at his first meeting with the new minister: "We walk here . . . in a meek an' humble spirit, in the straight an' narrow way which leadeth unto life. We ain't gone traipsin' after strange gods, like some people that call themselves Methodists in other places. We stick by the Discipline an' the ways of our fathers in

Israel. No newfangled notions can go down here. Your wife'd better take them flowers out of her bunnit afore next Sunday."

At the opening of *Theron Ware* we find ourselves looking into a sea of uplifted, expectant faces, as of individuals awaiting a mystical salvation. Instead, it is the final session of the annual conference of the Methodist Episcopal Church, at which an elderly, mildly senile bishop reads out the lists of ministerial appointments for the coming year. Handsome young Theron Ware is this year's star—yet, unaccountably, he is assigned not to the well-to-do congregation that has lobbied for him, but to provincial Octavius, New York, for which he and his young wife are clearly unsuited. This is the first of Theron Ware's disappointments, but he accepts it with Christian forbearance. The occasion allows Frederic to deftly sketch several generations of Methodist ministers, presenting in miniature a quick history of Caucasian Protestant America: the very aged, survivors of "heroic" times who lived in frontier poverty and disdain for earthly goods, wholly dedicated to their mission; the robust middle-aged who resemble prosperous farmers, tending toward "self-complacency rather than learning or mental astuteness"; and the newly ordained, who are the least impressive—"Zeal and moral worth seemed to diminish by regular gradations as one passed to younger faces." The novel bears out Frederic's implicit theme: that the religious spirit in America reverses the myth of progress as it takes on the features of the materialist society whose mission it is to "convert."

One of *Theron Ware*'s motifs is the casual, unexamined bigotry of the young minister's congregation. Not a love for Jesus Christ but a deep suspicion of all who think differently is their fundamental bond. Roman Catholics are particularly despised and feared; anti-Semitism has become assimilated into their very vocabulary. ("Don't you let them jew you down a solitary cent . . ." rolls off Alice Ware's tongue with an ease that strikes us, at the present time, as obscene.) Frederic's portrayal of right-wing Christian sentiment strikes a disturbingly contemporary note, for this is paranoia as religion; or religion as paranoia; an essentially militant spirit that ironically languishes in times of peace. Its spirit is best displayed in opposition, combat. As the disillusioned Father Forbes tells Theron Ware, though there would seem to be great advances in knowledge and civilization over the course of millennia, "where religions are concerned, the human race are still very like savages in a dangerous wood in the dark, telling one another ghost stories around a camp-fire. . . . The most powerful forces in human nature are self-protection and inertia."

It is the exoticism of Roman Catholicism—its ritualized Latin prayers, its music, statues, stained glass windows, the mysterious sacrament of extreme unction, the apparent passivity and unquestioning obedience of its worshipers—that first attracts the young Methodist minister to it, in defiance of all he has been taught to believe. Theron Ware falls under the enchantment of Octavius's Father Forbes and the beautiful red-haired young Irish-American woman, Celia Madden, who is the organist at Forbes's church, and whom he mistakes at first for a devout Catholic. How ironic that it is Father Forbes who, in a casual dinner conversation, plants the seeds of fatal doubt in Theron Ware's mind by speaking of the archetype of the "divine intermediary"—"this Christ-myth of ours." The effect upon Theron Ware is electric:

> Theron Ware sat upright at the fall of these words, and flung a swift, startled look about the room,—the instinctive glance of a man unexpectedly confronted with peril, and casting desperately about for means of defense and escape. For the instant his mind was aflame with this vivid impression,—that he was among sinister enemies, at the mercy of criminals. . . . Then, quite as suddenly, the sense of shock was gone; and it was as if nothing at all had happened.

From this point, however, Theron Ware's "damnation" progresses by steady degrees.

Celia Madden is a remarkable fictional creation for her time, or any other: a thoroughly self-defined woman presented without irony, and without punishment. She calls herself a "Greek"—a "pagan"— who remains a Roman Catholic only because its symbolism is "pleasant" to her. Her father's extreme wealth allows her a freedom unknown to most women, and so she need never marry; to her, marriage is an anachronism—"that women must belong to somebody, as if they

were curios, or statues, or race horses." Celia confides in the infatuated Reverend Ware that repudiating marriage does not mean repudiating love, which he takes to mean a statement of some application
to him. Celia Madden's boldness—"I am myself, and I belong to myself, exactly as much as any man"—and a perfunctory farewell kiss
provoke a fatal misinterpretation by Theron Ware, like earlier conversations with Father Forbes and Dr. Ledsmar, and the novel's denouement is catalyzed. What Theron Ware had believed to be a
"metamorphosis" of the self, an acquiring of a "new skin" of intellectual and moral enlightenment, his new acquaintances see as "degen-
eration"; ironically, and cruelly, it seems to have been his very naïveté
that initially attracted them: "We thought you were going to be a
real acquisition," Celia Madden says. And so Theron Ware is rejected,
turned away as a "bore." And promptly goes on the first drinking
binge of his life, with church funds.

Where Kate Chopin's *The Awakening* is an American tragedy in
the mode of Flaubert's *Madame Bovary*, Frederic's *Theron Ware* is a
comedy; its protagonist approaches suicide, but is never quite so desperate. He collapses; he is ill; he recovers. (There are women to help
him—of course.) Frederic allows him a generous measure of insight:
"Everything about me was a lie. I wouldn't be telling the truth, even
now, if—if I hadn't come to the end of my rope." His unquestioned
religious faith is lost forever, and he will live from now on without illusion, in an altered landscape in which there is no God "but
only men who live and die like animals." This is the most extreme
fin-de-siècle despair, the dark obverse of the bright Walter Pa-
teresque aestheticism that is Celia Madden's "pagan" religion, and an
apt description of the worlds explored by Frederic's contemporaries
Stephen Crane, Frank Norris, Jack London, and Theodore Dreiser.
But even this insight is comically undercut in *The Damnation of
Theron Ware*, for by the novel's end Theron Ware, no longer a minister, has entered the far more promising world of business; through
a friend's intervention, he will be superintendent of a real estate
company in Portland, Oregon. His very shallowness allows him confidence and resilience; he is no conscience-stricken Reverend Dim-
mesdale, brooding upon his past, but an American of the upcoming
century. In a final delicious irony, Frederic allows Theron Ware a

vision of the future in which he sees, in mimicry of the novel's opening scene, "a great concourse of uplifted countenances, crowded close together as far as the eye could reach. They were attentive faces all, rapt, eager, credulous to a degree. Their eyes were admiringly bent upon a common object of excited interest. They were looking at *him*. . . ." In Theron Ware's reverie, a mighty roar of applause follows, and suddenly he knows his destiny. "I can speak, you know, if I can't do anything else. Talk is what tells, these days. Who knows? I may turn up in Washington, a full-blown senator before I'm forty. Stranger things have happened than that, out West!"

In mock-Darwinian terms, Theron Ware adjusted to altered circumstances and a new environment; he will not only survive, but succeed. Of nineteenth-century idealism, he is the new century's inheritance.

It is certainly a loss to American literature that Harold Frederic died only two years after the publication of his most ambitious novel, at the age of forty-two. And what irony in his death: Despite Frederic's skepticism regarding religious beliefs, he seems to have acquiesced in his Christian Scientist wife's refusal to provide medical care for him when he became gravely ill; she was tried for, and acquitted of, manslaughter after his death.

Tragic Conrad:
Heart of Darkness
and The Secret Sharer

My task which I am trying to achieve is, by the power of the written word, to make you hear, to make you feel—it is, before all, to make you *see*.

—Joseph Conrad, Preface,
The Nigger of the "Narcissus," 1897

Like those other masterworks of the English fin-de-siècle, Robert Louis Stevenson's *Dr. Jekyll and Mr. Hyde* (1886), Oscar Wilde's *The Picture of Dorian Gray* (1890–91), and Henry James's *The Turn of the Screw* (1898), to which it bears a subtle thematic kinship, Joseph Conrad's *Heart of Darkness* (1902) is a work of the imagination that has transcended its late-Victorian era to acquire the stature, with the passing of time, of one of the great visionary self-examinations of Western civilization. Based, like most of Conrad's fiction, upon personal experience, *Heart of Darkness* is a rare Symbolist work with roots in historic authenticity; its theme is nothing less than the acknowledgment of a tragic darkness—the ethic of the "brute"—in the heart of late-nineteenth-century Christian-capitalist Europe. Out of his outraged witnessing of what he called "the vilest scramble for loot that ever disfigured the history of human consciousness"—the plunder of Africa by Europe—Conrad created a universal parable of man's fallen nature in the guise of an adventure/mystery tale.

In *Dr. Jekyll and Mr. Hyde*, Robert Louis Stevenson created a vivid, iconic metaphor for civilized man's divided nature: There is the "good" if passionless Dr. Jekyll, and there is his suppressed brother-self, the stunted, impassioned, "evil" Hyde, who dwells within Jekyll and can be released—fatally—by a magic elixir. In Oscar Wilde's *The Picture of Dorian Gray*, the seductively beautiful youth Dorian

commits sins against humanity that are engraved not on his unblem-
ished, never-aging face but on the face of his portrait, which has been
hidden away: what more striking metaphor for the hypocritical nature of privileged Caucasian bourgeois society? In Henry James's
enigmatic *The Turn of the Screw*, that most elegantly constructed of
ghost stories, the reader is confronted by a seemingly good Christian
governess who may herself be the catalyst of the destruction of her
young charges: Does this zealous, well-intentioned young woman
discover perversity and evil surrounding her, or is she luridly imagining it? Joseph Conrad's *Heart of Darkness*, though elaborately composed of oscillating images of light and dark, order and chaos, is by
far the most realistic of these unusual works of fiction; yet here, too, is
a powerful mythic portrait of a "good" man, Kurtz (the chief of the
inner station of the trading company, "an emissary of pity, and science, and progress, and devil knows what else"), who is simultaneously an "evil" man (a vicious, unscrupulous trader in ivory who ends
up tyrannizing African natives, his jungle sanctuary surrounded by
the grisly emblems of his madness, the decapitated heads of native
"enemies"). Kurtz, whom Marlow had sought avidly, risking his own
life in a treacherous and foolhardy adventure that comes close to destroying him, is both Dr. Jekyll and Mr. Hyde; the elixir that fatally
releases his primitive, evil self is simply distance from home, the
freedom of a white man's power over those whom he considers
his racial "inferiors" and whose influence over him is subliminal and
unacknowledged:

> I tried to break the spell [Marlow says]—the heavy, mute spell of
> the wilderness—that seemed to draw him to its pitiless breast by
> the awakening of forgotten and brutal instincts, by the memory of
> gratified and monstrous passions. This alone, I was convinced, had
> driven him out to the edge of the forest, to the bush, toward the
> gleam of fires, the throb of drums, the drone of weird incanta-
> tions. . . . There was nothing either above or below him, and I
> knew it. He had kicked himself loose of the earth. . . . His soul was
> mad. Being alone in the wilderness, it had looked within itself,
> and, by heavens! I tell you, it had gone mad.

It is Marlow's compelling argument, and, through Marlow, Conrad's, that the mind of man is capable of anything "because everything is in it, all the past as well as all the future." Marlow's (and Conrad's) journey up the Congo is, in one sense, a journey back into time; beginning with Marlow's apprehension that England, too, was once "one of the dark places of the earth" and moving to a consideration of the "fascination of the abomination"—the fascination of civilized man for his primitive, atavistic roots. What romance in Conrad's prose, in his celebration of such truths: "The voice of the surf heard now and then was a positive pleasure, like the speech of a brother." And in the memorable passage in which Marlow describes his excitement at setting out, at last, to meet the mysterious chief of the inner station, Kurtz:

> Going up that river was like traveling back to the earliest beginnings of the world, when vegetation rioted on the earth and the big trees were kings. An empty stream, a great silence, an impenetrable forest. The air was warm, thick, heavy, sluggish. There was no joy in the brilliance of sunshine. . . . You lost your way on that river as you would in a desert . . . till you thought yourself bewitched and cut off forever from everything you had known once—somewhere—far away—in another existence perhaps.

The anxieties aroused by Charles Darwin's controversial, bitterly contested theory of evolution by way of natural selection, first promulgated in *Origin of Species* (1859) and subsequently in *Descent of Man* (1871), are given tragic dramatic form in the tale of Kurtz's deterioration in the jungle; the much-acclaimed Kurtz of whom it is said, by Marlow, that "all of Europe had gone into [his] making." Conrad's irony is a constant throughout the narrative, like a haunting vibration beyond the sounds of words normally uttered. And what intransigent irony in Kurtz's final words, as if Shakespeare's unregenerate Edmund or Iago, and not Lear or Othello, were the touchstones of moral truth. Kurtz's famous pronouncement of his own spiritual condition—"The horror! The horror!"—is a judgment upon man's universal propensity for evil. What is this mysterious kinship that Marlow feels with the doomed man he has traveled hundreds of miles to meet, only to discover him moribund, hideous?—"It was as if an animated image of death carved out of old ivory had been shaking its hand with menaces at a motionless crowd of men made of dark and glittering bronze." (Compare Marlow's subterranean connection with Kurtz to the idealized and romanticized connection between the immature young captain of *The Secret Sharer* and his double, the fugitive Leggatt.) Yet, in his symbolic role as chief of the coveted inner station, Kurtz is indeed, as Marlow claims, a remarkable man:

> His stare . . . was wide enough to embrace the whole universe, piercing enough to penetrate all the hearts that beat in the darkness. He had summed up—he had judged. "The horror!" . . . It was an affirmation, a moral victory paid for by innumerable defeats, by abominable terrors, by abominable satisfactions. But it was a victory! That is why I have remained loyal to Kurtz to the last. . . .

(Kurtz's real-life model was a man named Georges Antoine Klein, an employee of the Brussels-based trading company Société Anonyme Belge pour le Commerce du Haut-Congo, whom Conrad met shortly before Klein's death. His body was buried at Tchumbiri on the Congo.)

Through the prism of shimmering, musical language that is the essence of Conrad's achievement in *Heart of Darkness*, the author has hoped to elevate Kurtz, a white racist murderer whose actions have parodied the idealism of his speech, to the stature of tragedy; he is one whose degradation, at the end of his life, can't be the sole measure of his moral worth.

Like Herman Melville, who also went to sea as a very young man, Joseph Conrad acquired in his early, impressionistic years a rich store of material to be transformed into tales and novels of exoticism, danger, and rites of passage. Born Józef Teodor Konrad Korzeniowski at Berdichev in Podolia, Poland, on December 3, 1857, Conrad lost his parents at a young age, attended school in Cracow, and first went to sea, on a French merchant marine vessel, at the age of seventeen. He is said to have attempted suicide at the age of twenty-one, but recovered quickly and signed on with the British Merchant marine, for whom he would serve, at various ranks, for the next sixteen years. He became a naturalized British subject in 1886 and changed his name to Joseph Conrad; in that year he wrote his first short story, "The Black Mate." His numerous voyages took him virtually everywhere—to the West Indies, to Constantinople, to Sumatra, India, Java, Australia, Singapore; most famously, and almost fatally, to the Belgian Congo in 1890. Though desperate to earn a living, the youthful Conrad was clearly a romantic for whom sailing was an emotional, perhaps even a spiritual vocation. Surely this is Conrad speaking in the voice of Marlow, confiding in his fellow seafarers at the outset of *Heart of Darkness*:

> Now when I was a little chap I had a passion for maps. I would look for hours at South America, or Africa, or Australia, and lose myself in the glories of exploration. At that time there were many blank spaces on the earth, and when I saw one that looked particularly inviting on a map (but they all look that) I would put my finger on it and say, "When I grow up, I will go there."

By the time Marlow has grown up, however, Africa had "ceased to be a blank space of delightful mystery. . . . It had become a place of darkness. But there was in it one river especially . . . resembling an immense snake uncoiled, with its head in the sea, its body at rest curving afar over a vast country, and its tail lost in the depths of the land." This great river, the Congo, fascinates Marlow "as a snake would a bird."

In June 1890, Conrad was appointed captain of a river steamer on the Congo; ominously, his predecessor had been butchered by native Africans and his body left to rot unburied in the jungle. Conrad's difficult four-month adventure, recorded more or less faithfully in *Heart of Darkness*, left him near death; devastated with dysentery and fever, his health was broken for the remainder of his life. Conrad's predilection for extreme pessimism, depression, and anxiety would seem to have been exacerbated by his physical condition. In May 1891, for instance, following his return to Europe, he confided in a letter to a friend, "I am still plunged in deepest night, and my dreams are only nightmares." (See *Conrad,* by Norman Sherry, Thames and Hudson, 1972.) Yet the experience was transforming to Conrad, comparable to the experience of writers who have seen armed combat firsthand, or have been wounded in battle, for Conrad would one day claim that "before the Congo, I was just an animal." By the end of 1894, Conrad had retired from seafaring; his first novel, *Almayer's Folly,* was published and well received in 1895. His remarkable career had begun.

Though always a controversial figure, criticized in some quarters for his intensely poetic, frequently rhetorical prose, and for the unremitting pessimism of certain of his works, Conrad is generally acclaimed as one of the progenitors, along with his mentors Gustave Flaubert and Henry James, of the Modernist novel; he has been called a master of the psychological novel, the political novel, and the "intellectual mystery" novel; the fastidiously rendered prose of such works as *The Nigger of the "Narcissus," Heart of Darkness,* and *Nostromo,* among others, identifies him as a writer for whom language is a kind of music, rendered with a poet's ear. Following Henry James's example in his essay "The Art of Fiction" (1888), Conrad set out, in his Preface to *The Nigger of the "Narcissus"* (1897), to establish his belief in the alliance in prose fiction of the moral and the aesthetic; his elevation of the writing life is extreme, suggesting almost a religious, or mystical, vocation; the artist is one who snatches "in a moment of courage . . . a passing phase of life" in the effort of showing life's "vibration, its color, its form; and through its movement, its form, and its color, reveal the substance of its truth."

By the time of Conrad's death in 1924, in Canterbury, England, this Polish-born emigrant for whom English was not his first, nor even his second, language, would be celebrated as one of the greatest of English novelists, revered as a classic in his own time.

Since its initial publication in 1902, in the volume *Youth,* Conrad's most meticulously poetic work of fiction, *Heart of Darkness,* has acquired an extraordinary reputation. Nine decades after its publication it remains one of the most read, and debated, of English works of fiction; it was the model, in spirit, of the flawed but enormously ambitious film by Francis Ford Coppola *Apocalypse Now* (1979); it has easily become the surpassing masterwork of Conrad's distinguished career, displacing even *The Nigger of the "Narcissus,"* *Lord Jim* (1900), *Nostromo* (1904), *The Secret Agent* (1907), *Victory* (1915), and such brilliantly realized tales as *The Secret Sharer* and "An Outpost of Progress." Part of this is due, of course, to the novella's brevity; like Henry James's *The Turn of the Screw*, it is a feat of dramatic compression in which virtually every passage, if not every sentence, moves us ineluctably toward our moment of revelation: the unmasking of Kurtz, and his twin, terrible pronouncements "Exterminate all the brutes!" and "The horror! The horror!" (The latter has achieved a kind of transcultural autonomy, very like Edvard Munch's 1895 woodcut *The Scream*—a bleakly comic shorthand for twentieth-century angst.) Unlike other, longer works of Conrad's that provide the reader with imbricated layers of exposition, history, psychology, and description, *Heart of Darkness* moves swiftly forward as Marlow's journey moves him, by starts and stops, forward; this is an adventure/mystery story, set in the most exotic of locales and fueled by a nightmare logic. The reader is meant to replicate Marlow's voyage as he journeys up the Congo in a snakelike passage into the depths of a formerly blank, unmapped territory: the human soul.

In recent years, Joseph Conrad's work, or, more specifically, ideas of gender, race, class, and hegemony implicit in his work, have been severely criticized. The assumptions of Caucasian male privilege are no longer taken for granted among many readers. It should be acknowledged by Conrad's admirers that the audience for whom he imagined his work was almost exclusively male, and assuredly Caucasian. To readers not in this category, the occasionally dogmatic and even derisive nature of certain of Marlow's remarks will strike a discordant note:

It's queer how out of touch with truth women are. They live in a world of their own, and there never has been anything like it, and never can be. It is too beautiful altogether, and if they were to set it up it would go to pieces before the first sunset. Some confounded fact we men have been living contentedly with ever since the day of creation would start up and knock the whole thing over.

Leaving aside for the moment the improbability of an entire sex, and that the child-bearing sex, being permanently "out of touch with truth," we might assume, for argument's sake, that Marlow is speaking critically of a financially well-off, minimally educated class of women who, being denied the possibility of careers and any measure of autonomy apart from fathers, husbands, brothers, or sons, was kept in a perpetual state of childish dependence upon men—the "fact"-bearing sex. In the Gothic-melodramatic final scene of Marlow's tale, in which he visits Kurtz's fiancée, the very emblem of Victorian moral hypocrisy and delusion, Conrad's misogyny is disguised by an air of pity and condescension; a full year after Kurtz's ignoble death, his Intended is still in mourning, a neurasthenic apparition in black with "a pale head, floating towards me in the dusk . . . she carried her sorrowful head as if she were proud of that sorrow." The valiant Marlow, who detests lies, for lies are "tainted with death," nonetheless "laid the ghosts of [Kurtz's] gifts at last with a lie" by telling Kurtz's Intended that, at the end of Kurtz's life, it was her name he uttered. (In fact, ironically, Kurtz's last words were "The horror! The horror!") Men must lie to women, Conrad argues, to preserve women's child-like state of delusion. In Conrad's ranked moral universe, men of a certain class are custodians of truth, facts, ideas, and the respect for tradition outlined in the British Navy handbook *An Inquiry into Some Points of Seamanship*; women are associated with lies, subterfuge, hypocrisy. (Caucasian women, that is. For a portrait of a black woman, consider Marlow's description of Kurtz's native mistress, of whom Marlow speaks awkwardly as "barbarous"—"savage and superb, wild-eyed and magnificent"—with a face that communicates a "tragic and fierce aspect of wild sorrow and of dumb pain mingled with the fear of some struggling, half-shaped resolve"—"like the wilderness itself, with an air of brooding over an inscrutable purpose." Words piled upon words: suggesting a generalized allegorical figure, a carved wooden sculpture symbolizing African Woman, and not a living, breathing individual woman who is supposed to be passionately in love with the dying Kurtz.)

Conrad has been criticized more sharply for his presentations of men and women of color. Consider Marlow's astonishment and amusement when a black African emulates "white" behavior:

. . . I had to look after the savage who was fireman. He was an improved specimen; he could fire up a vertical boiler. . . . To look at him was as edifying a sight as seeing a dog in a parody of breeches and a feather hat, walking on his hind-legs. . . . He had filed teeth, too, the poor devil, and the wool of his pate shaved into queer patterns, and three ornamental scars on each of his cheeks. He ought to have been clapping his hands and stamping his feet on the bank, instead of which he was hard at work, a thrall to strange witchcraft.

Elsewhere, African natives are "dusty niggers," "surly niggers," "cannibals." Conrad, the moralist, the artist for whom prose fiction is a vocation like the priesthood, painfully reveals himself in such passages, and numerous others, as an unquestioning heir of centuries of Caucasian bigotry. Yet it might be argued that Marlow, for all his condescension, represents a degree of humanity not found in the other Caucasian Europeans who are intent upon wresting from black Africa all they can get. Marlow isn't in the Congo for ivory, or money, or to advance his career; he takes on the captaincy of the steamboat for adventure's sake, and becomes fascinated with the demonic figure of Kurtz, the very embodiment of European civilization. Marlow's sharp, cinematic eye brings alive for us these suffering black men, whose plight is meant to move the hearts of Conrad's educated, well-to-do English readers:

Six black men advanced in a file, toiling up the path. . . . I could see every rib, the joints of their limbs were like knots in a rope; each had an iron collar on his neck, and all were connected together with a chain whose bights swung between them, rhythmically clinking. . . . These men could by no stretch of imagination be called enemies. They were called criminals. . . . They passed me within six inches, without a glance, with that complete, deathlike indifference of unhappy savages.

Other black men, enslaved and driven like animals until they are of no further use, are allowed to crawl off and die. Marlow is horrified by these "moribund shapes"—"phantoms"—dying of exhaustion

and malnutrition "as in some picture of a massacre or a pestilence."
Yet we wait in vain for Marlow to protest to anyone, though he soon
encounters the chief accountant of the station, an impeccably dressed
and groomed Englishman. There is the suggestion in *Heart of Darkness*, as elsewhere in Conrad's work, of a pessimism so deeply en-
trenched as to be identical with a self-serving political conservatism
that conveniently renders any form of activism, even protest, ineffec-
tive. For if all men harbor darkness in their hearts, why try to save
them? Why even pity them?

The famous tale *The Secret Sharer*, from Conrad's collection *'Twixt
Land and Sea* (1912), similarly reflects the narrowness of its creator's
perspective. Here, it is class, not sex or race, that determines a man's
worth: An immature young captain, uneasy in his responsibility,
mysteriously protects a fugitive named Leggatt who has fled another
ship after having killed a man; the young captain goes to extraordinary, foolhardy risks to allow Leggatt to escape being brought back to
England to be tried; by the end of the suspense story, with the flight
of Leggatt, the equation between the two men, forged out of their
similar backgrounds and temperaments, has been many times reiterated: Leggatt swims clear of the ship "as though he were my second
self . . . a free man, a proud swimmer striking out for a new destiny."
The difficulty for contemporary readers of *The Secret Sharer*, which
was one of Conrad's favorites among his own stories, is that the bond
immediately forged between the young captain and the young fugitive is class-ordained and narcissistic: Leggatt has even attended the
captain's school, Conway ("You're a Conway boy?"). Leggatt's act of
violence is portrayed as a virtuous act by an upstanding if hot-headed
first mate; the man he has killed is of a lower social rank, one of the
common sailors: "He wouldn't do his duty and wouldn't let anybody
else do theirs. . . . You know well the sort of ill-conditioned snarling
cur. . . ." Why does the young captain so eagerly take Leggatt at his
own word, and make no attempt to verify the story?

He appealed to me as if our experiences had been as identical as
our clothes. And I knew well enough the pestiferous danger of
such a character where there are no means of legal repression. And
I knew well enough also that my double there was no homicidal

ruffian. I did not think of asking him for details, and he told me the story roughly in brusque, disconnected sentences. I needed no more. I saw it all going on as though I were myself inside that other sleeping suit.

Where the doppelgänger ("double") relationship between Marlow and Kurtz is mysterious, subtle, and ever-shifting in its meanings, the relationship between the captain and Leggatt is superficial and far too heavily underscored. But *The Secret Sharer* remains one of Conrad's most characteristic stories, and it contains passages of language as beautifully evocative as the most celebrated passages in *Heart of Darkness*. The opening is particularly effective, setting the tone for a tale of solitary risk and initiation:

On my right hand there were lines of fishing stakes resembling a mysterious system of half-submerged bamboo fences, incomprehensible in its division of the domain of tropical fishes, and crazy of aspect as if abandoned forever by some nomad tribe . . . for there was no sign of human habitation as far as the eye could reach.

The silent approach of Leggatt, like a phantom in a dream:

The side of the ship made an opaque belt of shadow on the darkling glassy shimmer of the sea. But I saw at once something elongated and pale floating very close to the ladder. Before I could form a guess a faint flash of phosphorescent light, which seemed to issue suddenly from the naked body of a man, flickered in the sleeping water with the elusive, silent play of summer lightning in a night sky. With a gasp I saw revealed to my stare a pair of feet, the long legs, a broad livid back immersed right up to the neck in a greenish cadaverous glow. One hand, awash, clutched the bottom rung of the ladder. He was complete except for the head. A headless corpse!

As if the young captain is the "head," the consciousness; and the romantic fugitive Leggatt the "body," the physical being and "secret sharer."

If Conrad's ideal in writing is to make us *see*, *The Secret Sharer*, as brilliantly as *Heart of Darkness*, frequently fulfills that ideal.

All enduring works of art—whether Homer's *Iliad* and *Odyssey*, the tragedies of William Shakespeare, the popular novels of Honoré de Balzac, Charles Dickens, Mark Twain, as well as the more literary, esoteric novels of Joseph Conrad, Virginia Woolf, and James Joyce— bear the imprint of their time, place, and social perspective. All art is selective and therefore, from some perspective, unfair; no art can be universal, for no artist is universal; we are all local individuals, shaped by the customs of our tribes. The enduring artist is not the creator of perfect works but of works that transcend the circumstances of their creations and contribute to the aesthetic development of their craft. One need not identify with a writer's cultural perspective to recognize that he or she may be possessed of unique, valuable gifts; like Joseph Conrad, an artist whose fiction repays close and repeated readings, and whose unsparing tragic vision has a particular resonance for the twentieth century with its blood-tide of history— the devastation of two world wars and countless near-continuous smaller wars, the unspeakable horror of the Holocaust, the slaughter of hundreds of millions of men, women, and children in the service of deranged totalitarian "ideals." Joseph Conrad is one of the great visionaries bearing witness to the predicament of civilized man: How to match the "technique" and "method" so ironically celebrated in *Heart of Darkness* with a corresponding humanity that acknowledges, but does not succumb to, man's flawed and treacherous soul.

Arthur Miller's Death of a Salesman: *A Celebration*

> "He's a man way out there in the blue, riding on a smile and a shoeshine. And when they start not smiling back—that's an earthquake. And then you get yourself a couple of spots on your hat, and you're finished. Nobody dast blame this man. A salesman is got to dream, boy. It comes with the territory."
>
> —*Death of a Salesman*

Was it our comforting belief that Willy Loman was "only" a salesman? That *Death of a Salesman* was about—well, an American salesman? And not about all of us?

When I first read this play at the age of fourteen or fifteen, I may have thought that Willy Loman was sufficiently "other"—"old." He hardly resembled the men in my family, my father or grandfathers, for he was "in sales" and not a factory worker or small-time farmer, he wasn't a manual laborer but a man of words, speech—what his son Biff bluntly calls "hot air." His occupation, for all its adversities, was "white collar," and his class not the one into which I'd been born; I could not recognize anyone I knew intimately in him, and certainly I could not have recognized myself, nor foreseen a time decades later when it would strike me forcibly that, for all his delusions and intellectual limitations, about which Arthur Miller is unromantically clear-eyed, Willy Loman is all of us. Or, rather, we are Willy Loman, particularly those of us who are writers, poets, dreamers; the yearning soul "way out there in the blue." Dreaming is required of us, even if our dreams are very possibly self-willed delusions. And we recognize our desperate child's voice assuring us, like Willy Loman pep-talking himself at the edge of a lighted stage as at the edge of eternity—"God Almighty, [I'll] be great yet! A star like that, magnificent, can never really fade away!"

Except of course, it can.

*   *   *

It would have been in the early 1950s that I first read *Death of a Salesman*, a few years after its Broadway premiere and enormous critical and popular success. I would have read it in an anthology of *Best Plays of the Year*. As a young teenager I'd begun avidly devouring drama; apart from Shakespeare, no plays were taught in the schools I attended in upstate New York (in the small city of Lockport and the Village of Williamsville, a suburb of Buffalo), and so I read plays with no sense of chronology, in no historic context, no doubt often without much comprehension. Reading late at night when the rest of the household was asleep was an intense activity for me, imbued with mystery, and reading drama was far more enigmatic than reading prose fiction. It seemed to me a challenge that so little was explained in the stage directions; there was no helpful narrative voice; you were obliged to visualize, to "see" the stage in your imagination, the play's characters always in present tense, vividly alive. In drama, people presented themselves primarily in speech, as they do in life. Yet there was an eerie, dreamlike melding of past and present in Arthur Miller's *Death of a Salesman*, Willy Loman's "present-action" dialogue and his conversations with the ghosts of his past like his revered brother Ben; there was a melting of the barriers between inner and outer worlds that gave to the play its disturbing, poetic quality. (Years later I would learn that Arthur Miller had originally conceived of the play as a monodrama with the title *The Inside of His Head*.)

In the intervening years, Willy Loman has become our quintessential American tragic hero, our domestic Lear, spiraling toward suicide as toward an act of selfless grace, his mad scene on the heath a frantic seed-planting episode by flashlight in the midst of which the once-proud, now disintegrating man confesses, "I've got nobody to talk to." His salesmanship, his family relations, his very life—all have been talk, optimistic and inflated sales rhetoric; yet, suddenly, in this powerful scene, Willy Loman realizes he has nobody to talk *to*; nobody to *listen*. Perhaps the most memorable single remark in the play is the quiet observation that Willy Loman is "liked . . . but not well-liked." In America, this is not enough.

*   *   *

Nearly fifty years after its composition, *Death of a Salesman* strikes us as the most achingly contemporary of our classic American plays. It has proved to have been a brilliant strategy on the part of the thirty-four-year-old playwright to temper his gifts for social realism with the Expressionistic techniques of experimental drama like Eugene O'Neill's *Strange Interlude* and *The Hairy Ape*, Elmer Rice's *The Adding Machine*, Thornton Wilder's *Our Town*, work by Chekhov, the later Ibsen, Strindberg, and Pirandello, for by these methods Willy Loman is raised from the parameters of regionalism and ethnic specificity to the level of the more purely, symbolically "American." Even the claustrophobia of his private familial and sexual obsessions has a universal quality, in the plaintive-poetic language Miller has chosen for him. As we near the twenty-first century, it seems evident that America has become an ever more frantic, self-mesmerized world of salesmanship, image without substance, empty advertising rhetoric, and that peculiar product of our consumer culture "public relations"—a synonym for hypocrisy, deceit, fraud. Where Willy Loman is a salesman, his son Biff is a thief. Yet these are fellow Americans to whom "attention must be paid." Arthur Miller has written the tragedy that illuminates the dark side of American success—which is to say, the dark side of us.

Killer Kids

The Bad Seed by William March (Ecco Press)

First published in 1954, when it was an immediate and much-discussed best-seller, *The Bad Seed* has long been out of print, and its eccentric author, William March, author of five previous novels and three short story collections, long forgotten. Popular culture swallows the creations of individuals and excretes them, so to speak, as autogenetic-mythopoetic figures: Of those worldwide millions familiar with Frankenstein (that is, Dr. Frankenstein's unnamed creature) and Dracula, for instance, presumably only a small fraction know that these are literary creations, still fewer the names and identities of their authors. Popular culture has no memory or sense of chronology; "history" is a matter of costuming, not a complex matrix of forces yielding complex meanings. To the degree to which horror fiction is successful, it tends to be detached from a specific author and from the vehicle of language itself. So with the "bad seed" that germinated a mass-market harvest of evil, murderous children where none had previously existed; or, if they'd existed, had been too nuanced and ambiguous in their meanings, thus too difficult of access, to have emerged as mythopoetic.

"As flies to wanton boys are we to th' gods, / They kill us for their sport"—Gloucester's remark in *King Lear* indicates a general acknowledgment of childish cruelty. Yet there are remarkably few child-monsters in folklore, fairy tales, popular myths and legends, still fewer in literature. Where a child or young person would seem to be evil, he or she is likely under the spell of another, or of the very Devil. The ethereal, childlike Carmilla of Sheridan Le Fanu's dreamy Gothic tale "Carmilla" (1872) is revealed to be a vampire, deadly even to those who adore her; but Carmilla is a descendant of an accursed Austrian family of aristocrats, "long extinct," and presumably not to blame for being a blood-sucking monster. Henry James's subtly imagined *The Turn of the Screw* (1898) presents us with not one but two haunted children ("If [one] child gives the effect another turn of the screw, what do you say to *two* children?") in the angelic Miles and Flora, whose innocence, or corruption, is the focus of their new governess's excited concern. More boldly than in any other work of his fiction, perhaps because the genre is Gothic, a tale of apparent ghosts, thus not "real," James approaches Victorian taboo subjects of sexual perversity and sadism in *The Turn of the Screw*; most daringly, he explores the mystery of child sexuality. Since the art of the novella is elliptical and suggestive, and we observe the children exclusively from the perspective of their new governess, we are never able to know with certainty to what degree the children have been corrupted by the now deceased Peter Quint and their former governess Miss Jessel, or whether in fact they're quite innocent, victims of their new governess's zeal to save their souls at any cost. Perhaps the predominant theme of this relentlessly analyzed classic is our inability to know, let alone guide or control, the inner lives of others; our tragedy is to pursue, as the obsessed governess has done, an elusive "truth" to the point at which the pursuit becomes pathological and destructive. Are little Miles and Flora under an evil enchantment, from which they must be saved, or are they simply secretive children who prefer fantasy worlds, and fantasy adults, to the "real" that surrounds them? The only weakness of Benjamin Britten's powerful opera adaptation of *The Turn of the Screw* is that the ghosts Peter Quint and Miss Jessel are portrayed as unmistakably present, while James's novella retains its ambiguity to the very end; little Miles dies of fright in the governess's arms, his secret (if he has had a secret) intact. We are not even allowed to know if the boy has been expelled from school for having told boys he "liked" secrets of (homo)sexual love learned from Peter Quint, nor do we know whether Flora's hysteria and her outbursts of "shocking" language are a consequence of her having been thwarted in her alliance with Miss Jessel, or the result of her new governess's exaggerated vigilance. The fated children are not monsters, however, but victims; one or another adult has destroyed them.

Altogether different "evil" children figure in Richard Hughes's *A High Wind in Jamaica*, or *The Innocent Voyage* (1929) and William Golding's *Lord of the Flies* (1954). In Hughes's lyric, macabre tragi-comedy ten-year-old Emily, daughter of an English family residing in the West Indies, commits an act of murder for no apparent reason, stabbing to death a defenseless man; she pursues another small child with the intention of killing her, but tires and loses interest; her court testimony condemns to death an innocent man for the very murder she herself had committed. "It is a fact that it takes experience before one can realize what is a catastrophe and what not"— Hughes explores the nuances of such an observation from a number of angles in this eerie, magical, and now unfortunately little-known tale of middle-class English children on a ship, bound for England, that has been captured by a motley crew of modern-day pirates. *A High Wind in Jamaica* is part fairy tale, part horror parable, a gripping portrayal of the ways in which Emily and her companions are affected by their bizarre outlaw experience on the sea, and in turn affect their pirate abductors. What Hughes sees as the natural amorality of children, their feckless "innocence," contrasts with the troubled, conscience-stricken responses of adults. For here is a further turn of the screw: the little girl as heartless murderer, though not lacking in emotion and even childish sentimentality. As in James's novella, the child's private world is inaccessible to even sympathetic, attentive adults; Emily's father, reunited with her in England, though knowing nothing of her savagery, instinctively shrinks from her. And the omniscient, unnamed narrator whose consciousness has floated deftly in and about *A High Wind in Jamaica* like the very sea breeze itself draws back at last from the enigmatic little girl in her new school in England:

In another room, Emily with the other new girls was making friends with the older pupils. Looking at that gentle, happy throng of clean innocent faces and soft graceful limbs, listening to the ceaseless, artless babble of chatter arising, perhaps God could have picked out from among them which was Emily: but I am sure that I could not.

Is Hughes suggesting that all little girls, all children, are potential Emilys? Is their, or our, savagery primed to be released in the right "outlaw" circumstances? Or is Emily an anomaly, as she seems to have been among her child companions, none of whom has behaved as she did? *A High Wind in Jamaica* is too poetic and subtle a work of art to make explicit its meanings, unlike the self-consciously high-concept *Lord of the Flies*, in which, as the author described his didactic intentions, "the defects of society [are traced back] to the defects of human nature." Golding's allegory would seem to have been influenced by readings in popular anthropology as well as by both *A High Wind in Jamaica* and Joseph Conrad's Symbolist masterpiece *Heart of Darkness* (1902), in marooning representative British schoolboys on a desert island and tracking their gradual reversion to savagery. A voguish novel of the conservative 1950s and early 1960s, *Lord of the Flies* was taught in high school and college English classes for its readily explicated symbols and its value as a stimulus for "discussion." Though much of the novel is in fact sparely and elegantly written, like Golding's later much-praised allegorical work (*The Inheritors, Pincher Martin, Free Fall, The Spire*), there does seem to be a paint-by-numbers quality to its structure and periodically articulated epiphanies. The schoolboys—Ralph, the natural "civilized" leader; Piggy, the myopic, good-hearted, fattish, and bumbling intellectual; Jack, the demonic tribal chieftain; Roger, the sadist, torturer, executioner, and right-hand man of the chief; Simon, the mystic—are types rather than characters, like masked performers in a ritualistic play. Predictably, the novel brings us from the boys' initial hope of maintaining their civilized inheritance—

"We've got to have rules and obey them. After all, we're not savages. We're English; and the English are the best at everything. So we've got to do the right things."

—through a gradual breakdown marked by incursions of primitive dream-visions, paranoia, and violent outbursts to the final debacle, the murder of Piggy and the triumph of madness. Ironically, the last sane boy, Ralph, is being pursued by a gang of boys intent upon killing him and mounting his head on a spear, when as in a cinematic flourish British naval officers arrive on the island to rescue everyone. These bemused adults see not the vicious creatures we know them to be but merely "little boys, their bodies streaked with colored clay, sharp sticks in their hands," the psychopathic Jack, painted like a savage, the remains of Piggy's spectacles at his waist. Comments the naval officer, "Fun and games."

The "Lord of the Flies" is a hallucinatory beast the boys have come to worship out of terror at their predicament, a projection of their demonic selves. It's given symbolic visual form as the decapitated head of a butchered sow they've mounted on a stake. The mystic Simon seems to hear this fly-buzzing horror speak:

> "Fancy thinking the Beast was something you could hunt and kill!" said the head. For a moment or two the forest and all the other dimly appreciated places echoed with the parody of laughter. "You knew, didn't you? I'm part of you? Close, close, close! I'm the reason why it's no go? Why things are what they are?"

This is an unlikely "vision" for a boy, as heavy-handed as Ralph's epiphany at the novel's end with its self-conscious echo of Conrad:

> He gave himself up to [tears] now for the first time on the island; great, shuddering spasms of grief that seemed to wrench his whole body. His voice rose under the black smoke before the burning wreckage of the island; and, infected by that emotion, the other little boys began to shake and sob too. And in the middle of them, with filthy body, matted hair, and unwiped nose, Ralph wept for the end of innocence, the darkness of man's heart, and the fall through the air of the true, wise friend called Piggy.

It's doubtful that Golding can have had actual children in mind in this allegory, for he describes twelve-year-old as "little boys"; *Lord of the Flies* is a grim anti-pastoral in which adults disguised as children replicate the worst of their elders' heritage of ignorance, violence, and warfare. The novel's final image is that of a British naval cruiser on the horizon. Golding's interest is not in children but in re-creating, in a stark and suspenseful drama, a demonstration of mankind's curse of "original sin"—in post-Conradian cliché, mankind's "heart of darkness."

By contrast, the child-murderer Rhoda of William March's *The Bad Seed* is not representative of other children, nor even of adult wickedness. She's sui generis, a freak of nature masquerading as an angelic little girl of eight; surrounded by well-intentioned but foolish adults who react to her outward, innocently beguiling behavior in mawkish, stereotypical ways that must have given March, allegedly a hater of children (he was one of eleven siblings, and might be said to have been an intimate observer of the genre *child*), a grim pleasure to record. Pigtailed, always immaculately dressed, and doll-like Rhoda is "quaint"—"modest"—"old-fashioned"—a "remarkable little creature"—though in fact (as we come gradually to learn) she's a machine for murder, having inherited the "seed," or gene, for such behavior from her mother's mother, who'd killed, among numerous others, all but one of her own children. Speaking of this grand-mother-psychopath, and unwittingly of the child Rhoda, an avid collector of lurid true-crime tales says:

> The thing that made these people what they were wasn't a positive quality, but a negative one. It was a *lack* of something in them from the beginning, not something they'd *acquired*. Now, color blindness and baldness and hemophilia [are] all caused by a lack of something . . . and nobody [denies] that they [are] transmitted. Feeble-mindedness [is] a lack of something, too; and certainly it [is] passed from generation to generation. . . .

Bad seed, bad blood, bad gene: Here is a grim genetic determin-ism that, if true, and it's a debate that has probably endured through millennia, renders every environmental factor, including education, moral instruction, religion, law, psychiatry, the model deportment of others and their love, civilization itself, quite useless to effect change in the allegedly afflicted individual.[1] It would seem to be the case, as experts in the pathology of serial killers might argue, that such socio-pathic behavior can't be prevented except forcibly by imprisonment, and this extreme view is March's, who may well have identified with both Rhoda, the "bad seed," and her stricken mother, Christine. (March's unhappy private life, his apparently miserable childhood, and his adulthood plagued by mysterious breakdowns, phobias, and neuroses, is illuminatingly discussed by Elaine Showalter in her in-troduction.) "The essential and terrifying pattern" of a life deter-mined at the instant of conception is the stuff of tragedy, but March's treatment is rather more melodrama, and, unexpectedly, in some of the lulls when the monstrous Rhoda is offstage, Wildean drawing room satire, in which pseudo-intellectuals prattle at length about such topics as Freudian psychoanalysis ("My incestuous fixation on [my brother] is so obvious that it doesn't need elaboration . . . incest being so *trite*. What was more interesting in the eyes of my analyst was [my] latent penis hostility and penis envy [and] my impulse to mar and castrate men and women both"), the rapid decline of America (". . . the age we live in is an age of violence. It looks to me like violence is in everybody's mind these days. It looks like we're just going to keep on until there's nothing left to ruin"), and re-pressed, or "larvated," homosexuality:

"What does 'larvated' mean?" asked Emory. "That's one I hadn't heard so far."

"It means covered, as with a mask," said Mrs. Breedlove. "It means concealed."

"It means something that hasn't come to the surface yet," said Kenneth Penmark.

Most of the characters of *The Bad Seed* are "larvated." These in-clude a voyeurist janitor, whose demotic stream of consciousness may have been the author's attempt to simulate debased "lower-class" speech, and whom the vengeful Rhoda will burn alive; Rhoda's hap-less mother, Christine, who comes to the belated recognition that she is both a daughter and mother of psychopathic killers; and, of course, little Rhoda herself, March's parody of the good little pigtailed girl-child of Victorian sentiment. So unmitigatingly wicked is Rhoda, it would be a rare reader, however opposed in principle to the death penalty, who would not wish for her demise; the Warner Brothers film of 1956, starring the child-actress Patty McCormack in a much-lauded performance, hoped to placate audiences by having Rhoda struck by a rather stagey lightning bolt at the film's end—a comic-grotesque "moral" ending to an otherwise excruciating fable.[2] The ironic ending provided by William March, in which Rhoda survives her mother's suicide without a backward glance, is far more plausible.

Reissued with a chic-tacky cover of a little blond girl-mannikin in a generic 1950s living room, and with a cogent, funny introduction by the feminist cultural critic Elaine Showalter, *The Bad Seed* is not an accomplished work of imaginative fiction like *A High Wind in Jamaica*, nor has it the ambition of the schematic *Lord of the Flies*. But it remains an inspired "suspense thriller" of more than ordinary intellectual pretensions that gains momentum as it proceeds, away from Wildean comedy and in the direction of tragedy; focusing upon the crisis of conscience in Christine Penmark, the only fully realized character in the novel and the only character for whom March seems to have felt any sympathy. For how does a parent deal, after all, with a child who is a monster? Wholly sociopathic, soulless, undisturbed, and certainly unrepentant of her crimes, which to her are not "crimes" at all? In Doris Lessing's *The Fifth Child* (1988) a similar crisis occurs, focusing upon the mother of the "evil" Ben, with more circumstantial detail and a more realistic examination of what we would call "family dynamics,"[3] but Christine Penmark is the mother of only this single child and bears the brunt of recognition: "I alone am responsible. It was I who carried the bad seed that made [Rhoda] what she is." Like March, Christine even embarks upon the composition of a novel about a woman who comes to the gradual recognition that her child is a monster, in the hope that, imagining how the novel might end, she might imagine how her and Rhoda's story might end. (Christine does work out an ending, but it's not the ending of *The Bad Seed*.)

If, forty-three years after its original publication, *The Bad Seed* retains little literary interest (though March was called a "neglected genius" by his friend Alistair Cooke), it retains a considerable cultural significance. For *The Bad Seed*, a fantasy of child-hatred by a bachelor with a misogynist streak, struck a chord of recognition in millions and became a watershed of sorts: Following its popular success in 1954, the metaphor "bad seed" would not only become permanently assimilated into our common American vocabulary, but March's bold image of the deceptively innocent "evil" child would be the inspiration for a flood of novels and films about psychopathic, demonically possessed and/or simply murderous children. Among these titles, of widely varying degrees of worth and popular success, are *The Exorcist, The Other, The Omen, The Changeling, Children of the Corn, Kill Baby Kill, Child's Play, The Midwich Cuckoos* (film version, *Village of the Damned*), *The Good Son, Mikey, Bloody Birthday, The Reflecting Skin. Unman, Wittering and Zigo* is about slightly older, boys' school demons; Stephen King's first, enormously successful novel, *Carrie* (1974), made into an equally successful horror film, is the vengeful fairy tale of a just-pubescent girl-child with telekinetic powers. Classic short stories of the genre are Ray Bradbury's "Small Assassin," "The Veldt," and "The Playground"; Jerome Bixby's "It's a *Good* Life"; Richard Matheson's "Born of Man and Woman." *Rosemary's Baby* ends with an inspired cradle scene in which not a demonically possessed infant is enshrined but the very Devil himself in human-cherubic form. How can any normal mother resist loving her baby? The surreal cult film *The Brood*, written and directed by David Cronenberg, features a "brood"—or litter—of murderous suckling tots engendered out of their beautiful mother's ferocious hatred; they have no existence apart from her hatred, a lethal psychic force of which she herself is unconscious. The subgenre of "possessed" or alien children overlaps thematically with the popular fifties science fiction subgenre of invasion novels and films, the most famous of which is *The Invasion of the Body Snatchers* (1956), that touchstone of American paranoia. (The alien pod people are conspicuously non-suburban-American, dangerous as Communists. This is the film of the McCarthy era that ends with its hero in the middle of an expressway screaming, "They're coming! They're coming!" as cars zoom indifferently past.) Most of these titles are generic horror, unlike *The Bad Seed*, which contains no supernatural elements (and is therefore a suspense thriller), but all that feature children have in common the phenomenon of the "evil" child who must be exorcised or destroyed by forces of (adult) "good." We can isolate 1954, two years after Dwight Eisenhower's crushing defeat of Adlai Stevenson for the presidency, as this curious watershed year before which, in popular culture, children were invariably portrayed as angelic, and after which children might be as demonic as adults.[4] There came to be a zestful communal repudiation of the taboo against acknowledging distrust, hatred, even loathing of children. Traditional piety surrounding children, even infants, was suddenly suspect: To have fallen for Rhoda Penmark's phony innocence, or that of these other demons, was to be exposed as a fool. For perhaps these children, and by extension all children, aren't really children but malicious adults in disguise. They are as capable of deceit and violence as their elders, yet they are more reprehensible than adults because after all they *are* children, and meant to be "good"; that is, meant not to violate our stereotypical expectations. William March is especially chilling in dramatizing Rhoda's single-mindedness of purpose, her alarming insect rapacity, the very antithesis of the scattered concentration and emotions we know to be characteristic of actual children: the lurking adult monomaniac in pigtailed disguise. Rhoda even arouses in the voyeurist janitor a perverse love, though March doesn't develop this aspect of his theme; the girl-child as nymphet, not only inspiring lust in adult men but participating to a degree in this lust herself, would remain a fantasy for Vladimir Nabokov to celebrate in his *Lolita, or The Confessions of a White Widowed Male* (1955). Here, famously, the old taboo against acknowledging sexual desire for children, and acting to consummate that desire, was broken for the first time in "high" art (though hardly in child pornography).

More and more it has come to be revealed that the fifties, that decade of apparent conformity and somnolence under the publicly benign, endearingly smiling Eisenhower, with shadowed Nixon crouching in the wings, was in fact an era of spirited, righteous hatreds. There are after all "good" hatreds. There was the Red Menace to draw patriotic hatred from all quarters. There was the psychoanalytically inspired backlash against the Victorian tradition of mother love most rabidly espoused by Philip Wylie in his runaway best-seller *Generation of Vipers* (originally published in 1942 and reissued as a "classic" in 1955, with copious annotations by the author, on the occasion of its twentieth reprinting), a misogynist's *Mein Kampf* that enriched our American vocabulary with "mom" and "momism" as virulent pejoratives to set beside "kike," "nigger," "fairy," "dyke," "commie," "pinko." There were violent grassroots and nationally organized reactions, including lynchings of blacks, against the succession of liberal Supreme Court rulings declaring racial segregation unconstitutional; it was a fruitful time for Ku Klux Klan recruiting and "demonstrations." Jews, blacks, even "Krauts" and "Japs" could no longer be demonized in popular culture, but children and women were fair game. By demonizing the child, American pop-consciousness could overlook the abuses of actual children, surely as prevalent then as now, though yet to be named and categorized. ("Battered children," "battered women," and shelters and medical facilities to treat them had yet to be invented.) Why, when a taboo is repudiated, is there such a rush of communal relief and excitement? Do we secretly yearn to hate that which we have been obliged to love? Is there a perverse thrill in believing the very worst about what had seemed to us only yesterday the very best? Is the profane simply more viscerally stimulating than the sacred? Does writing eloquently of a hitherto pornographic subject, the exploitation of an eleven-year-old girl by an adult male, instead of crudely, void the moral issue? (As John Berryman speculates in his prologue to *Berryman's Sonnets*: "The original fault was whether wickedness / was soluble in art.") Does demonizing a vulnerable segment of our society absolve us from guilt over our involvement, or lack of involvement, with these individuals?

And what is the curious consolation of "bad-seed" politics—the belief that genetic inheritance determines entire lives? Does it comfort us to be told that our efforts at social amelioration are worthless? That the "selfish gene" is unredeemable, so why bother? That the "darkness of man's heart"—"original sin"—has sullied us all, but some more than others? Is it a comfort to believe that the wicked are, in the bad-seed sense, like the child Rhoda, not to blame for their wickedness, but that they deserve to be punished anyway? And to

punish them, if we're good people, is in fact "good"? Precisely because it lacks the complexity, subtlety, and ambiguity of what we call
art, American popular culture, like American politics (which is a
branch of popular culture), is a mirror that tells us more about our
collective soul than we might sometimes wish to know.

NOTES

1. Theories of the genetic inheritance of criminal characteristics and
tendencies have always been controversial, for obvious reasons. If there is
a murderous "X chromosome" that might be detected in fetuses, what
then? Present-day genetic research seems to be ever more specifically
pinpointing genes for various kinds of behavior that, in earlier eras,
would have been considered volitional, a consequence of "free will." This
discussion of dyslexia by the biologist Richard Dawkins parallels William
March's amateur theorizing:

> Reading is a learned skill of prodigious complexity, but this provides
> no reason in itself for scepticism about the existence of a gene for read-
> ing. All we would need in order to establish the existence of a gene for
> reading would be to discover a gene for not reading, say a gene which
> induced a brain lesion causing specific dyslexia. Such a person might
> be normal and intelligent in all respects except that he could not read.
> (*The Extended Phenotype: The Gene as the Unit of Selection*)

2. The film, oddly, is far less cinematic and sensational than the novel,
being a too-faithful adaptation of the Broadway stage production by
the workmanlike Maxwell Anderson. Potentially grueling, dramatically
spectacular scenes like the one in which, in the novel, poor Leroy the
janitor runs as a human torch, burning alive, while Rhoda looks on
smirking and licking her ice-cream cone, are not visualized, nor are the
"recovered memories" of Christine's ax-wielding mother, which Alfred
Hitchcock would have brilliantly exploited. There is even an absurd,
mood-shattering postscript in which an exasperated stage mother, Nancy
Kelly, puts her naughty stage daughter, Patty McCormack, over her knee
and spanks her—as if frustrated audiences had been lusting for such a reaction through the film. (A good old-fashioned American spanking as
punishment for three murders.) And Patty McCormack looks gigantic
for an alleged eight-year-old. In effect, *The Bad Seed* awaits its full realization in film.

' 3. Of *The Fifth Child*, which reads like a nightmare parable, Doris Lessing remarked that the child Ben "isn't evil at all. He's just out of the right place. If he is in fact the result of a gene which has come down through many centuries, all he is, is a different race of being that's landed up in our . . . complicated society." In *Conversations with Doris Lessing*.

4. In Lillian Hellman's *The Children's Hour* (1934) and Arthur Miller's *The Crucible* (1953), "demonic" (but not demon-possessed, and not murderous) adolescent girls conspire to bring down essentially good, decent, independent-minded adults. Hellman's play explores issues of female sexuality (lesbianism) in a conservative, conformist private-school community; Miller's play, set in seventeenth-century Salem, Massachusetts, during the era of the Puritan witch trials, was a powerful critique of the anti-Communist/Red Menace hysteria that was the dominant political issue of the 1950s. It is interesting to note that both playwrights chose spiteful adolescent girls as deceitful informers bent upon destroying exemplary adults. (Miller's play drew upon historical documents, but the real-life accuser of the martyred John Proctor was a child, not a sexually precocious adolescent.) Where the "invasion" novels and films of the 1950s imagined demonic forces from other planets (i.e., overseas), these more complex and realistic works of drama imagined demonic forces in the very phenomenon of "accusing" and "informing."

5. In his Afterword to the Berkley paperback edition of *Lolita*, Nabokov speaks of having completed the handwritten manuscript of the novel in spring 1954, coincidentally the season of *Bad Seed* publication and controversy. Though Nabokov the aesthete would have wished to distance himself from March, his novel bears a significant cultural relationship to March's. Humbert Humbert fantasizes the child Lolita (with whom he has just had sex for the first time) as possessing a body "of some immortal daemon disguised as a female child."

Workings of Grace:
Flannery O'Connor's
"The Artificial Nigger"

> I see from the standpoint of Christian orthodoxy. . . . For me
> the meaning of life is centered in our Redemption by Christ
> and what I see in the world I see in relation to that.
> —Flannery O'Connor,
> "The Fiction Writer and His Country"

This graceful, parable-like short story, with its precise, weighted language and its comically sympathetic rural Georgians Mr. Head and his ten-year-old grandson Nelson, is virtually unique in Flannery O'Connor's oeuvre, ending not in violent death, nor even in devastating irony, but with tenderness.

O'Connor's more characteristic prose fiction bristles with cruel and sometimes savagely funny observations; "The Artificial Nigger" is comedy of another order. Because they are an old man (Mr. Head at sixty behaves rather more like a man in his mid-seventies) and a young boy (though Nelson is a "miniature old man"), the grandfather and grandson are presented as sinners of a mild, entirely human sort. Mr. Head is foolishly proud and vain ("Mr. Head could have said . . . that age was a choice blessing and that only with years does a man enter into the calm understanding of life that makes him a suitable guide for the young"), and Nelson is impudent, vain, and quarrelsome (". . . the boy's look was ancient, as if he knew everything already and would be pleased to forget it"). These are genial cartoonish figures, country bumpkins to be subjected to O'Connor's typical ritual of humbling, unmasking, and redemption. On its surface, "The Artificial Nigger" is a straightforward story, hardly more than an amusing anecdote: A back-country grandfather takes his grandson to Atlanta for a day visit with the secret intention of showing the child that "he had no cause for pride merely because he had been born in a city. . . . [Nelson would] see everything there was to see in a city so that he would be content to stay at home for the rest of his life." In Atlanta, the two become lost; quarrel; Mr. Head frightens Nelson by hiding from him, and then denying that Nelson is his grandson, when the child desperately needs him; Nelson is furious with Mr. Head and refuses to speak to him; at last, exhausted by their adventure, and having no one but each other, the two are reconciled; they return to their rural home, with Nelson determined never to journey to Atlanta again. There is a situation-comedy slickness to this resolution, which would seem to undercut the boy's discovery of blacks and his attraction to them; he seems to have reverted to his grandfather's ways, unilluminated by his grandfather's religious vision. Beneath the anecdotal surface, however, the story moves toward what O'Connor calls "an action of mercy"—the mysterious operation of grace in the characters' lives, intersecting as they do with both "real" and "artificial" Negroes, bringing Mr. Head to an eloquent epiphany that presumably changes his life and his subsequent attitude toward his grandson, himself, and God:

> He saw that no sin was too monstrous for him to claim as his own, and since God loved in proportion as He forgave, he felt ready at that instant to enter Paradise.

Since there has been little to prepare us for Mr. Head's vision, little to suggest that he is a man deeply immersed in Christian orthodoxy and the Bible, this turn of mind is not very convincing; but "The Artificial Nigger" like O'Connor's fiction generally is not meant to be realistic.

Suffused with Catholic ideology, or in any case a passionate wish to believe in Christ and salvation by way of the Catholic Church, Flannery O'Connor is the most visual and relentlessly "symbolic" of writers. Her dreamlike rural landscapes are alive with that intense, primitive power of the inwardly focused imagination we find in the seventeenth-century New England Puritans and in other deeply religious individuals for whom nothing can be accidental, contingent, or without meaning; on the contrary, everything is charged with significance; as the Jesuit poet Gerard Manley Hopkins has said, "The world is charged with the grandeur of God." When such believers are gifted with imagination (and what is imagination but, in part, a mysterious metaphor-making capacity), the "natural" world scarcely exists except as a supernatural manifestation; surfaces are masks through which an underlying, far more significant reality asserts itself in ways that may be startling and original and sometimes grotesque. In Catholic orthodoxy, for instance, the Communion wafer, or Host, is not a symbol of Christ's bodily sacrifice, it *is*— literally—Christ's body. As O'Connor has said in "The Grotesque in Southern Fiction," what she sees on the surface of the world is of interest to her only as she might penetrate "through it into an experience of mystery itself." In O'Connor's fiction, a bird-shaped water-stain on a bedroom ceiling is a manifestation of the Holy Ghost emblazoned in ice instead of fire ("The Enduring Chill"); the setting sun is "a huge red ball like an elevated Host drenched in blood ("A Temple of the Holy Ghost"); a fire started in a woods by vandals is a revisiting of the ordeal of Old Testament prophets in a fiery furnace ("A Circle in the Fire"). There are lyric passages in O'Connor that call to mind the luminous beauty of paintings by the astonishing seventeenth-century artist Georges de La Tour that portray ordinary domestic life (a woman placidly picking fleas off her body, for instance) in such vivid chiaroscuro as to imply a supernatural symbolic meaning. There are broadly comic passages that suggest the stylized caricatures of the American regionalist painter Thomas Hart Benton. O'Connor spoke of herself as a "realist of distances" for whom the grotesque—the violent, comic, and caricatured—was of primary interest; the "ordinary aspects of daily life" were of little fictional interest. The "realist of distances" looks for a single image that will connect or combine or embody two points: One is a point in the concrete, the other a point not visible to the naked eye "but believed in by him firmly, just as real to him, really, as the one that everybody sees."[1]

Consequently, "The Artificial Nigger" is a highly artificial, self-consciously wrought story in the mode of 1950s symbolic prose. O'Connor's models may well have been Joseph Conrad (particularly *Heart of Darkness* and *The Secret Sharer*, which were available in 1950

in a popular mass-market paperback with an introduction by the distinguished critic Albert J. Guerard) and James Joyce (particularly
"Dubliners"), prose stylists notable for their reiterated patterns of
imagery and their penchant for carefully phrased, musically cadenced
final-paragraph epiphanies. The story's opening is ornamental and
static as an altarpiece, with an elaborate description of moonlight in
the room Mr. Head and Nelson share, in which "the color of silver"—
"dignifying light"—"miraculous moonlight"—"snow-white in the
moonlight" point emphatically away from the merely naturalistic;
Mr. Head's trousers exude "an almost noble air, like the garment
some great man had just flung to his servant"; the invisible narrator
informs us, with startling erudition, that Mr. Head "might have been
Vergil summoned in the middle of the night to go to Dante, or, better, Raphael, awakened by a blast of God's light to fly to the side of
Tobias." Really? the reader thinks. Who is telling us this? And in
what tone—mocking, whimsical, deadly serious?

Once past this tessellated opening, which seems to have been written for academic New Critics of the era, primed on Robert Penn Warren and Cleanth Brooks, to decode, the story begins to breathe on its
own, and O'Connor trusts to her characters, through dialogue, to engage and move us. Their wide-eyed adventures in Atlanta, which involve wandering into a Negro neighborhood, where they soon get
lost, are reminiscent of the cruder, bawdier adventures of Virgil and
Fonzo Snopes in Memphis in William Faulkner's *Sanctuary* (1931),
which end with the country bumpkin Snopeses being brought to a
Negro brothel by a Snopes cousin. Mr. Head and Nelson are both fascinated by and fearful of Negroes; their reconciliation is by way of
their awed contemplation of an "artificial nigger"—a vulgar lawn or-
nament they discover in a white Atlanta neighborhood:

> It was not possible to tell if the artificial Negro were meant to be
> young or old; he looked too miserable to be either. . . . [Mr. Head
> and Nelson] stood gazing at [him] as if they were faced with some
> great mystery, some monument to another's victory that brought
> them together in their common defeat. They could both feel it
> dissolving their differences like an action of mercy.

The "artificial nigger" is a mysterious agent of grace, perhaps like the crucified Christ. In *Mystery and Manners*, the collection of essays and letters published in 1969, five years after her premature death at the age of thirty-nine, the author speaks straightforwardly of "The Artificial Nigger" in Catholic terms, stating that the "artificial nigger"[2] reunites Mr. Head and Nelson in a way not to be explained except as a "working of grace."

Does "The Artificial Nigger" succeed as a story if the reader is unaware of, or unsympathetic with, its Christian subtext? Here, as elsewhere in O'Connor's most accomplished short fiction, the story moves with its own dramatic momentum; the Christian imagery is sensed rather than made explicit; for the skeleton beneath the story is not nearly so engaging as the story itself. Amid O'Connor's work, "The Artificial Nigger" is memorable for its portrayal of comic yet sympathetic characters and for the unexpected "mercy" of its conclusion.

NOTES

1. *Mystery and Manners* by Flannery O'Connor, eds. Sally and Robert Fitzgerald (Farrar, Straus & Giroux, 1969), p. 42.

2. *Mystery and Manners*, p. 116. Here, the word "nigger" is used by Flannery O'Connor herself; it would appear to have been a usage common to her, as to her fellow Caucasian Georgians. Forty years after the composition of "The Artificial Nigger," the very word "nigger" has become so highly charged with political significance that any work of art containing it, especially by a white Southerner, is unwittingly abrasive, even provocative. O'Connor could not have foreseen how the word "nigger" would come to seem, in some quarters of America, an actual obscenity of the nature of those sexual obscenities she would not have wished to include in her fiction. (There is at least one distinguished American university in which a large-enrollment literature class petitioned successfully to have "The Artificial Nigger" removed from its syllabus as a racist text.)

Edward Hopper's "Nighthawks, 1942": Poem and Painting

EDWARD HOPPER'S *NIGHTHAWKS, 1942*

The three men are fully clothed, long sleeves,
even hats, though it's indoors, and brightly lit,
and there's a woman. The woman is wearing
a short-sleeved red dress cut to expose her arms,
a curve of her creamy chest; she's contemplating
a cigarette in her right hand, thinking that
her companion has finally left his wife but
can she trust him? Her heavy-lidded eyes,
pouty lipsticked mouth, she has the redhead's
true pallor like skim milk, damned good-looking
and she guesses she knows it but what exactly
has it gotten her so far, and where?——he'll start
to feel guilty in a few days, she knows
the signs, an actual smell, sweaty, rancid, like
dirty socks; he'll slip away to make telephone calls
and she swears she isn't going to go through that
again, isn't going to break down crying or begging
nor is she going to scream at him, she's finished
with all that. And he's silent beside her,
not the kind to talk much but he's thinking
thank God he made the right move at last,
he's a little dazed like a man in a dream——
is this a dream?——so much that's wide, still

mute, horizontal, and the counterman in white,
stooped as he is and unmoving, and the man
on the other stool unmoving except to sip
his coffee; but he's feeling pretty good,
it's primarily relief, this time he's sure
as hell going to make it work, he owes it to her
and to himself, Christ's sake. And she's thinking
the light in this place is too bright, probably
not very flattering, she hates it when her lipstick
wears off and her makeup gets caked, she'd like
to use a ladies' room but there isn't one here
and Jesus how long before a gas station opens?—
it's the middle of the night and she has a feeling
time is never going to budge. This time
though she isn't going to demean herself—
he starts in about his wife, his kids, how
he let them down, they trusted him and he let
them down, she'll slam out of the goddamned room
and if he calls her *Sugar* or *Baby* in that voice,
running his hands over her like he has the right,
she'll slap his face hard, *You know I hate that: Stop!*
And he'll stop. He'd better. The angrier
she gets the stiller she is, hasn't said a word
for the past ten minutes, not a strand
of her hair stirs, and it smells a little like ashes
or like the henna she uses to brighten it, but
the smell is faint or anyway, crazy for her
like he is, he doesn't notice, or mind—
burying his hot face in her neck, between her cool
breasts, or her legs—wherever she'll have him,
and whenever. She's still contemplating
the cigarette burning in her hand,
the counterman is still stooped gaping
at her, and he doesn't mind that, why not,
as long as she doesn't look back, in fact
he's thinking he's the luckiest man in the world
so why isn't he happier?

*T*he attempt to give concrete expression to a very amorphous impression is
   the insurmountable difficulty in painting.

These words of Edward Hopper's apply to all forms of art, of
course. Certainly to poetry. How to evoke, in mere words, the powerful, inchoate flood of emotions that constitute "real life"? How to
take the reader into the poet's innermost self, where the poet's language becomes the reader's, if only for a quicksilver moment? This is
the great challenge of art, which even to fail in requires faith.

Insomniac nights began for me when I was a young teenager.
Those long, lonely stretches of time when no one else in the house
was awake (so far as I knew); the romance of solitude and self-
sufficiency in which time seems not to pass or passes so slowly it will
never bring dawn.

Always there was an air of mystery in the insomniac night. What
profound thoughts and visions came to me! How strangely detached
from the day-self I became! Dawn brought the familiar world, and
the familiar self; a "self" that was obliged to accommodate others' expectations, and was, indeed, defined by others, predominantly adults.
Yes but you don't know me, I would think by day, in adolescent secrecy
and defiance. *You don't really know me!*

Many of Edward Hopper's paintings evoke the insomniac's uncanny vision, none more forcefully than "Nighthawks," which both
portrays insomniacs and evokes their solitude in the viewer. In this
famous painting, "reality" has undergone some sort of subtle yet
drastic alteration. The immense field of detail that would strike the
eye has been reduced to smooth, streamlined surfaces; people and objects are enhanced, as on a lighted stage; not life but a nostalgia for
life, a memory of life, is the true subject. Men and women in Hopper's paintings are somnambulists, if not mannequins, stiffly posed,
with faces of the kind that populate our dreams, at which we dare not
look too closely for fear of seeing the faces dissolve.

Here is, not the world, but a memory of it. For all dreams are
memory: cobbled-together sights, sounds, impressions, snatches of
previous experience. The dream-vision is the perpetual present, yet
its contents relate only to the past.

There is little of Eros in Hopper's puritanical vision, "Nighthawks" being the rare exception. The poem enters the painting as a

way of animating what cannot be animated; a way of delving into the painting's mystery. *Who are these people, what has brought them together, are they in fact together?* At the time of writing the poem I hadn't read Gail Levin's definitive biography of Hopper, and did not know how Hopper had made himself into the most methodical and premeditated of artists, continuously seeking, with his wife Jo (who would have posed for the redheaded nighthawk), scenes and tableaux to paint. Many of Hopper's canvases are elaborately posed, and their suggestion of movie stills is not accidental. This is a visual art purposefully evoking narrative, or at least the opening strategies of narrative, in which a scene is "set," "characters" are presented, often in ambiguous relationships.

"Nighthawks" is a work of silence. Here is an Eros of stasis, and of melancholy. It is an uncommonly beautiful painting of stark, separate, sculpted forms, in heightened juxtapositions, brightly lit and yet infinitely mysterious. The poem slips into it with no transition, as we "wake" in a dream, yearning to make the frozen narrative come alive; but finally thwarted by the painting's measured void of a world, in which silence outweighs the human voice, and the barriers between human beings are impenetrable. So the poem ends as it begins, circling upon its lovers' obsessions, achieving no crisis, no confrontation, no epiphany, no release, time forever frozen in the insomniac night.

The Artist Looks at Nature:
Some Works of Charles Sheeler (1883–1965)

Charles Sheeler's *The Artist Looks at Nature* (1943), an oil painting in a mode significantly different from this underrated American artist's characteristic work, is also his most pointedly symbolic creation. In its disturbing juxtaposition of a seemingly exterior landscape and a mysteriously related (or unrelated) reproduction of that landscape, it reminds us of those several canvases of the Belgian Surrealist René Magritte (1898–1967) that present the viewer with a similar displacement and questioning of expectation, notably *The Signs of Evening* (1926) and *The Alarm Clock* (1957). (Among other works of Magritte that present art works or reproductions in dreamlike relationships to "reality" are *The Human Condition* [1933], *Free to Roam* [1933], *The Fair Captive I* [1931], *The Fair Captive II* [1965], *The Call of the Peaks* [1942], *Evening Falls* [1964], *The Domain of Arnheim* [1949], *The Field-glass* [1963]. As a self-consciously experimental post-Duchampian artist, perhaps more intellectual than artist, Magritte was inevitably concerned in all his art with fundamental metaphysical questions, or doubts, of the artist "looking at nature.") Sheeler's painting is distinguished by its inclusion of a self-portrait of the artist while Magritte's paintings are empty of all human presence, as if the curious art works were anonymous creations.

In Sheeler's gently magic-realist painting, "Charles Sheeler" himself is seen from the back at a projected distance of about fifteen feet from the viewer; in Magritte's *The Signs of Evening* and *The Alarm Clock*, a scene from nature and a still life containing apples are positioned before undefined landscapes. In Sheeler, the art work the artist is creating, whether a painting or a drawing, is one of his most luminous, successful drawings, *Interior with Stove* (1932), that clearly had a profound symbolic meaning for the artist despite its ordinary domestic nature. In Magritte, typically, the scene from nature and the still life are impersonal, generic, perhaps purposefully banal. In Sheeler, the art work is a small, unobtrusive rectangle in a rectangle, the painting itself, that measures twenty-one by eighteen inches; in Magritte, the art works are much larger, centrally positioned and so obtrusive as to block out the landscape beyond. Sheeler's art work, the interior, domestic scene, in its own way generic and perhaps banal, makes no demand upon the viewer; Magritte suggests in his coolly executed paintings that the artist's vision of nature is not wholly subjective, unreliable, and inauthentic in the most basic sense, but a conspicuous repudiation of nature—as Picasso has famously said, "Art doesn't reproduce what we see. It makes us see." As in Magritte's several paintings of pipes, each bearing the handwritten caption (or warning) *Ceci n'est pas une pipe* ("This is not a pipe"), the viewer is meant to interpret the painting as a self-conscious artifact, not an attempt to reproduce "reality." Though the background landscapes in both Sheeler and Magritte are wholly unrelated to the foreground art works, the background in Sheeler clearly suggests someone's vision, or experience, of reality, while in Magritte the backgrounds (a silhouette of mountains, a landscape with a clouded sky) are arbitrary and of no inherent significance. At a time of doubt and personal unhappiness, following the protracted illness and death of his beloved wife in 1932–33, Charles Sheeler seems to have reacted against his own art, at least temporarily, saying he had been working "from the head rather than the heart." This statement is more applicable to Magritte, as to the Surrealists generally, for whom, if emotion exists in art, it is unconscious, subversive, or parodistic. The "head" and the "heart" are at war—and the "head" is triumphant. In art at least, if not in life.

In Charles Sheeler's *The Artist Looks at Nature*, the most distinctive feature isn't the artist, a mild, even inconsequential middle-aged figure in the lower right corner, seated turned from us, in a casual posture, but a maze-like composition of stone or cement walls, fences, smooth-surfaced grass, and, apparently, a view of Boulder Dam. In this "assembly of elements . . . association of irrelevancies" as Sheeler describes the work, the only color is the pale, undramatic green of the grass, with a small, almost indistinguishable rectangle of dark red in the upper left corner, the roof of a house (the artist's house?). Shadows are muted and undramatic as well; the time is nearly noon, but there is no brightness, only a kind of generalized illumination. Perspective is subtly askew; distances are foreshortened, distorted. At first glance the view looks almost "real" but is in fact wholly surreal, for aspects of Boulder Dam have been imposed upon a rural landscape with no evident logic. Perhaps the most unnerving aspect of the painting is the fact that the faceless artist who we are to assume is "Charles Sheeler" is concentrating on a scene nowhere in front of him. Why is he painting his interior scene out of doors? What relationship is there between what he sees and what he paints? We must conclude that his subject is a scene out of memory, a kind of haunting. The artist appears to be dressed neither for the outdoors nor for work: he's wearing a white shirt and a vest, a necktie, and formal shoes. The unemphatic gray of his clothing matches the gray of his thinning hair and the gray of the maze-like walls. Here is a portrait of the artist as conventional in outward respects—hardly a rebel or a revolutionary. Is this an ironic vision? Self-abnegation, self-parody? Sheeler was the most meticulous of craftsmen, working on a single painting or drawing for as long as nine months, his typical workday rarely less than eight hours; what he would seem to have lacked in inspiration, or in passion, he compensated for with the energies of technique. In an interview published in *Life* (August 8, 1938), Sheeler says of himself that he works "like any day laborer"— the very antithesis of the romantic artist. Magritte's paintings are populated with images of bourgeois men, in bowler hats; Magritte seems to have thought of himself as a parody of a bourgeois, for whom art, at crucial times in his career, came with startling swiftness— driven by concepts, and not by a desire to replicate reality or to evoke emotion in his viewers; Magritte was sometimes capable of producing a painting a day. The one so diligent and self-effacing, the other so defiantly hurried and boastful: our American Modernist, Charles Sheeler, our European Surrealist, René Magritte.

Sheeler's is the work that repays a closer, more psychologically sympathetic analysis. In *The Artist Looks at Nature*, the nature of the art work that haunts the artist is obviously significant. This conté crayon drawing, *Interior with Stove*, is one of Sheeler's most compelling works. It suggests the more formalist work of Sheeler's American contemporary Rockwell Kent and the more narrative-driven work of his American contemporary Edward Hopper. A drawing in which precisely rendered geometric shapes are predominant, and the central image is the flattened, depthless silhouette of a wood-burning stove, this is a composition in which formal elements are more important than an air of verisimilitude. The drawing is modeled upon a photograph of the identical scene taken in 1917 in a Doylestown, Pennsylvania, house in which, evidently, a bright lamp was substituted for an actual stove fire. Already, in the original photograph, Sheeler chose not to record "reality"—the motive for most photography—but the altering and heightening of it, for dramatic purposes. Where in the photograph details are illuminated by the intense light, in the drawing of many years later, the effect is that of an overexposed print in which most details are erased from the walls and floor: dust, grime, nicks, and imperfections, the incursions of time. Sheeler's brilliant drawing, like similarly powerful and dreamlike works by Rockwell Kent and Edward Hopper, is therefore not a representation of an actual experience but an abstraction from experience—a stylized interpretation of experience. The old stove, the floor, walls, window, latch door, beamed ceiling—all of which would be rendered with Durer-like exactitude by a "realist" like Andrew Wyeth—evoke an air of Symbolist meaning, the plumbing of mysterious, unarticulated emotion.

What is one to make of Charles Sheeler's atypical *The Artist Looks at Nature* in the context of the artist's other, more characteristic work? Clearly, it lacks the formalist beauty of Sheeler's *Bucks County Barn* of the same year (1932) and the earlier masterpiece *Bucks County Barn* of 1923 with its eerie, floating image of buildings floating in a timeless haze of pale, uniform beige, as of memory. Is Sheeler suggesting that he, the artist, an individual who happens to be an artist, or an artist who happens to be an individual with a unique and ineradicable personal history, is so trapped in his interior obsession that he can't "see" the world? Or, if he can see it, can't paint it? Sheeler suggests a homespun surrealist vision in the making of art out of the chance arrangements of private life: "The world is in one's back yard, [if one has] the eyes to see it." Yet, ironically, in *The Artist Looks at Nature*, it isn't the world in his back yard but an unnerving arrangement of ominous walls and anemic greenery that seems to have sprung, not out of nature, but out of the artist's own walled, self-tormented mind.

Sheeler's stylized, modernist employment of geometric figures—the Platonic essences beneath surfaces—has been much commented upon by art historians. Technically proficient, both as a photographer and an artist, he has been identified as a "Precisianist" in the numerous ambitious works of industrial structures, skyscrapers, and machinery which brought him considerable renown in the twenties and thirties as a poet-chronicler of the Age of Industry and with which he remains most identified. (The critic Michael Kimmelman called Sheeler "an iconographer for the religion of technology" in 1988, in assessing his Precisianist oeuvre; more wittily, a critic for the *New York Daily Worker*, in 1949, dubbed him the "Raphael of the Fords." What is one to make of Sheeler's deadpan, seemingly unironic studies of massive hydroelectric turbines, high-rise transmission towers, the driving mechanism of a locomotive, and the stilled propeller of a 1,600-horsepower airplane? These canvases, commissioned by *Fortune* in the late thirties, possibly as a celebration of American mechanical genius in the face of tottering capitalism, are deservedly little known today; Sheeler's literalness fails to raise them above the level of brilliant illustrative advertising.)

No less technically proficient and "precisianist" but more emotionally accessible are Sheeler's numerous studies of southeast Pennsylvania barns and eighteenth-century farmhouses. *Barn Abstraction* (1917, 1946) bravely repudiates the aesthetics of nostalgia that would have surely brought so gifted an artist popular, commercial success; in related works, through the decades, Sheeler flattens structures to two dimensions, banishes human figures, even barnyard cows, horses, sheep, the comforting icons of many another rural memoirist. (A few of Sheeler's photographs contain chickens. Probably because chickens happened to be there.) The artist went on record as disdaining the "quaint" and the "historical": "My paintings have nothing to do with history or the record—[they are] purely my response to intrinsic realities of forms and environment." Sheeler's elegant barn exteriors (never interiors) and farmhouse interiors are never so reduced to geometric or cubist structures that they become unrecognizable; there is a strong, unconscious memoirist subtext underlying even the most flattened and abstract of subjects, though no sense of history comes through—or time. These are dauntingly static surfaces, like enormous still lives, in which no human figures intrude to provide scale and emotional color. (Compare the stylized, dreamlike canvases of Edward Hopper in which solitary figures appear, or coexist in immobility and silence like mannequins under a spell: *Western Motel*, *Office at Night*, *Sunlight in a Cafeteria*, *New York Movie*, *Room in New York*, and, among numerous others, Hopper's most famous, frequently reproduced *Nighthawks*.) Sheeler may have declined to use the human figure in his work for philosophical reasons—his distrust of the quaint and the sentimental. He may have realized that he wasn't comfortable with the human figure, and couldn't render it in a way that satisfied his formalist eye. There is an aesthetic safety in static, non-living shapes, even as these lock the artist into a kind of isolation. In the striking oil painting *The Upstairs* (1938), based upon an earlier photograph of a Doylestown farmhouse interior, classically simple geometric figures are so arranged to suggest stairs leading up from a well-lighted room into the darkness of an unseen upstairs—an ominous, unknowable future. The oil *Staircase, Doylestown* (1925) is saved by its rich earthen colors and lack of shadows from suggesting the twisting, convoluted, repetitive self-torment of the trapped artist—but only just saved. Like the almost too vivid *Interior with Stove* that haunts the artist in the mock outdoors of *The Artist Looks at Nature*, these paintings exude an air of obsessive memory. All is still, silent, utterly mysterious. One seems to be gazing upon one's own posthumous future.

Perhaps the only human figure fully presented in Sheeler's austere art is that of his wife, Katherine (*Portrait,* 1932), a conté crayon drawing executed during his wife's terminal illness. In this poignant likeness, which is beautifully, meticulously rendered out of an infinity of minuscule dots like atoms, Sheeler's wife, who appears to be of youngish middle age, is studied, motionless, almost waxen. Her expression is calm, resigned; she betrays no emotion, nor does the artist suggest any emotion beyond that of a melancholy dignity. Though living, Katherine Sheeler resembles a person recollected in memory. *Portrait* is the very poetry of loss.

Thirty years after his death, Charles Sheeler is due for reassessment. Despite the narrowness of his subject matter and the austerity of his aesthetics, he created a considerable number of striking, even haunting works of art in diverse modes—photographs, drawings, oil paintings, watercolors. William Carlos Williams, his friend and admirer, speaks for both poet and painter in his spirited manifesto of 1925, *In the American Grain*: "He wants to have the feet of his understanding on the ground, his ground, the ground, *the* only ground that he knows, that which *is* under his feet." Sheeler belongs to a generation of innovative, brilliantly and variously talented American artists whose work, often hung together in museums and galleries, constitutes a kind of extended family: Marsden Hartley, Georgia O'Keeffe, Arthur Dove, Charles Demuth, Edward Hopper. (George Bellows [1882–1925] is of this generation, but died at so young an age, forty-two, as to seem of another era.) His strongest work, though impeccably modernist, emptied of narrative and psychological content, succeeds in evoking a profound meditative emotion. These Bucks County barns already passing into extinction, these heraldic industrial compositions, such highly charged private works as *Interior with Stove*, *The Upstairs*, *Portrait*, and *The Artist Looks at Nature*, are luminous achievements—the epitome of Sheeler's passionate formalism.

IV

WHERE I'VE BEEN, AND WHERE I'M GOING: PREFACES, AFTERWORDS

Where Are You Going, Where Have You Been? Selected Early Short Stories: *Afterword*

What does it mean to "love" an art or a craft, like writing? And to "love" the primary materials (people, landscapes, events) that the effort of writing evokes? Is this a "love" that can be measured ethically?—in any way practicably? How strange to claim that the artist's love for his or her work is so passionately bound up with the artist's life in its deepest, most mysterious sense that this "love" *is* the life; and the means by which the artist expresses his or her gratitude to the world for having been born into it.

My lifelong love of writing is underlaid by a lifelong love of reading, itself rooted in childhood. So to me any act of the imagination, no matter how coolly calibrated or layered in that uniquely adult vision we call irony, is first of all an act of childlike adventure and wonder.

Over a period of three decades I seem to have published somewhere beyond four hundred short stories—a number as daunting, or more daunting, to me, as to any other. The motives have nearly always to do with memorializing people, or a landscape, or an event, or a profound and riddlesome experience that can only be contemplated in the solitude of art. There is the hope too of "bearing

Author's note:
These prefaces and afterwords were written for reprint editions of several books of mine; the pieces on short stories were written for editions of *Prize Stories: The O. Henry Awards* and *The Best American Short Stories*.

witness" for those who can't speak for themselves; the hope of recording mysteries whose very contours I can scarcely define, except
through transforming them into structures that lay claim to some
sort of communal permanence. For what links us are elemental experiences—emotions—forces—that have no intrinsic language and
must be imagined as art if they are to be contemplated at all.

It's instructive for me, in assembling these early stories, to see
how, from the first, such motives underlay my fiction. My earliest
publications, "In the Old World" (not included here; written when I
was nineteen, and collected in *By the North Gate*) and "The Fine
White Mist of Winter" (the oldest story in this volume, originally
published in 1962) dramatize white-black (or, in the idiom of those
days, white-"Negro" relations); my current novel-in-progress, *What I
Lived For*, begun in June 1992, also dramatizes, in very different
form, such relations. And what I perceive to be the subterranean
philosophical query of much, perhaps all, of my writing, is there
from the first, leaping to my eye at a casual rereading as if no time at
all had passed between 1962 and 1993—

> Murray stared out at the great banks of white, toppled and slanted
> in the dark. Beyond his surface paralysis, he felt something else,
> something peculiar—a sense, maybe, of the familiarity of the
> landscape. He had watched such scenes as this almost every night
> in the winters of his childhood farther north, when he used to
> crouch at his bedroom window in the dark and peer out at the
> night, at the snow falling or the fine whirling mist, which held no
> strangeness, he felt, except what people thought strange in it—
> the chaos of something not yet formed. . . . The earth seemed to
> roll out of sight, like something too gigantic to conceive of.
>
> ("The Fine White Mist of Winter")

This is autobiography in the guise of fiction, for the protagonist is
not only my young, yearning, questing self (who so often crouched at
the single window of my bedroom at home in Millersport, New
York, peering out into the night at the "chaos of something not yet
formed") but my self of this very day, this hour. The harsher tonalities
of such stories as "At the Seminary" (a pre-feminist work, indeed!),

"Unmailed, Unwritten Letters," and "How I Contemplated the World from the Detroit House of Correction, and Began My Life Over Again," as well as the sexual tensions of other stories, are also qualities of my present work, though subjects, landscapes, types of characters, and modes of telling have changed.

Like tributaries flowing into a single river, and that river into the ocean, a writer's individual works come to seem, from the impersonal perspective of time, a single effort; as the individual personality, undergoing its inevitable modulations through time, is first and last unique.

My earliest collections of short stories, *By the North Gate* (1963) and *Upon the Sweeping Flood* (1966), contained all, or nearly all, the stories I had written and published up to that time. With *The Wheel of Love* (1970), having more short stories in reserve, and being in a position to shape my collections more deliberately, I included only stories that were thematically related. From that point onward, my books of stories were not assemblages of disparate material but wholes, with unifying strategies of organization; so I was forced to omit more and more stories I might otherwise have wished to preserve.

And now, this further "selection" of the "selected"—yet another opportunity for abridgment, an opportunity and a challenge. The frequently anthologized ("Where Are You Going, Where Have You Been?" is by far the title of mine most reprinted in anthologies) have been included with a story virtually no one could know, "Silkie," which never found its way into any hardcover collection of mine; experimental fictions like "The Turn of the Screw" (imagined as a further turn of the screw beyond Henry James's—the secret inspiration for the great Gothic novella itself) and "Daisy" (a rhapsody, playing with the ecstatic loss of control that is madness, involving the tragic relationship between James Joyce and his schizophrenic daughter Lucia), included with the seemingly straightforward and naturalistic "Small Avalanches" (a story of which I remain peculiarly fond, perhaps for its unimpeded forward motion—so different from the prose of my current work). "The Molesters," never reprinted in any story collection, is a part of my novel of 1968, *Expensive People*, where it was presented as the work of a fictional alter ego, a doomed woman writer; yet I may as well acknowledge it as my own, especially since its setting, its "Eden County"/western New York landscape, is so clearly my own.

All writers are time travelers to whom no time is merely "present" or "past," for memory is a transcendental function. These stories of the 1960s and 1970s remain so close to my heart as to constitute not just a part of my career as a writer but much of my private identity as a person. I think of them as, somehow, concentric; unfolding in time, thus seemingly linear and chronological, yet, in their essence, forming rings upon one another, rings that emerge out of rings, with *By the North Gate*, my first book, at the core.

Expensive People:
The Confessions of a "Minor Character"

Expensive People, originally published in 1968, was imagined as the second of an informal, thematically (but not literally) integrated trilogy of novels written in the 1960s, the first and third being *A Garden of Earthly Delights* (1966) and *them* (1969). These novels, differing considerably in subject matter, language, and tone, have in common the use of a youthful protagonist in his or her quintessentially American adventures; they were conceived by the author as critiques of America—American culture, American values, American dreams—as well as narratives in which romantic ambitions are confronted by what must be called "reality."

Appearing in the fall of 1968, *Expensive People*, with its climactic episode of self-destructive violence, was perceived as an expression of the radical discontent, the despair, the bewilderment and outrage of a generation of young and idealistic Americans confronted by an America of their elders so steeped in political hypocrisy and cynicism as to seem virtually irremediable except by the most extreme means. What is assassination but a gesture of political impotence?—what are most "crimes of passion" except gestures of self-destruction, self-annihilation? When the child-murderer of *Expensive People* realizes that he has become, or has been, in fact, all along a mere "Minor Character" in his mother's life, he is made to realize absolute impotence; inconsequence; despair. He has slipped forever "out of focus."

A desperate act of (premeditated) matricide will not restore his soul to him but will at least remove the living object of his love and grief.

A complex, multi-tiered novel can be an exercise in architectural design and it can be, in the writing, true labor; a novel like *Expensive People*, with its relaxed first-person narration, its characteristically succinct and chatty chapters, and its direct guidance of the reader's reading experience, can ride upon the ease of its own melting, as Robert Frost said of the lyric poem. Of my numerous novels *Expensive People* glimmers in my memory as the most fluidly written in its first-draft version; my precise memories of writing it, giving voice to the doomed Richard Everett in long unbroken mildly fevered sessions, are tied to the upstairs, rear study of the first of the several houses of my married life, a brick colonial, modest, with four bedrooms, at 2500 Woodstock Drive, Detroit, Michigan. (What happy days: At the time I was an instructor in English at the University of Detroit, where I taught, with unflagging enthusiasm and a boundless energy that perplexes me today, four courses, including two generously populated sections of "Expository Writing"—freshman composition.)

The "I" of my protagonist Richard became so readily the "eye" of the novelist that, at times, the barrier between us dissolved completely and the voice in which I wrote was, if not strictly speaking my own, an only slightly exaggerated approximation of my own. (The most immediate model for the novel's peculiar tone was evidently Thomas Nashe's *The Unfortunate Traveler: or, The Life of Jack Wilton*, 1594, often called "the first novel in English"; my narrator alludes to "*that other unfortunate traveler* from whom I have stolen so much" in Part I, Chapter 23, but in rereading the ebullient sixteenth-century work I can see only occasional and glancing similarities.) The fluid writing experience of *Expensive People* would have been impossible if I had not worked from an earlier first-person "confession," also narrated by a disturbed and self-destructive adolescent boy, in a more subdued, naturalistic key; this was a completed novel of about two hundred fifty pages with which I was dissatisfied, as an unworthy successor to *A Garden of Earthly Delights*, which yet had its hooks in my soul and could not be discarded. (With the completion of *Expensive People*, however, the manuscript was quickly and unsentimentally tossed away: No more than self-conscious Richard Everett would I have wished to keep any evidence of early botched and faltering versions of my more "eloquent" self.)

What a powerful hold the world of "expensive people" had upon me in those years! The short story collections *The Wheel of Love* (1970) and *Marriages & Infidelities* (1972) focus upon similar themes, frequently from the perspective of estranged and hyperesthetic adolescents like the protagonists of "Boy and Girl," "How I Contemplated the World from the Detroit House of Correction, and Began My Life Over Again," "Stalking," "Stray Children," "Problems of Adjustment in Survivors of Natural/Unnatural Disasters," and "Where Are You Going, Where Have You Been?" The novella *Cybele* (1979) most clearly resembles *Expensive People*—it is set in precisely the identical suburban Detroit world—but its tone is far more pitiless and unyielding than Richard Everett's; the voice is that of the ancient goddess Cybele mockingly recounting the rake's-progress misadventures of one of her doomed mortal lovers.

Normal men and women—by whom I mean, I suppose, non-novelists—may be surprised to learn that novelists are haunted by a quickened sense of mortality when they are writing novels; the terror of dying before the work is completed, the interior vision made exterior, holds us in its grip. Once the work is completed, however, once transformed into a book, an object, to be held in the hand, the novelist does permit himself or herself to feel a modicum of accomplishment: not pride so much as simple relief. *Here it is. Now I* can *die.* Rereading a novel after many years is thus a disorienting experience. For while there does remain the original, however unmerited satisfaction of the achievement in itself, there now arises, unexpectedly, a sense of profound and irrevocable loss.

The novel has become, in the intervening years, a species of "lookback" time, to use the poetic astrophysical term; it has, for all its immediacy to others' eyes, a fossil-image glimmer for the writer. Behind many of the proper names of *Expensive People* ("Fernwood," "Johns Behemoth," "Epping Way," "Bébé's Hofstadter," "Mr. Body," even "Spark," et al.), as behind a scrim, there exist authentic names, and authentic entities; the descriptive scenes bear witness to a greedily appropriated authentic landscape, that of Birmingham/Bloomfield Hills, Michigan; at every interstice, in virtually every turn of phrase, use of metaphor, literary allusion (to, for instance, Nada's note to herself, to revise "Death and the Maiden" and change its title—which title, changed, will be "Where Are You Going, Where Have You Been?"), literary parody, and aside, I am forcibly reminded not only of my old long-forgotten sources but of my former, now lost self in the act of writing: inventing. Yet more painfully I am reminded of the losses of dear friends and acquaintances of that crowded era of my life more than two decades ago; and of the era itself, so tumultuous in our American history and so crucial in our fractured sense of our national identity. My romance with Detroit, I've characterized this phase of my life. My romance with novel-writing itself.

So the vertigo of memory haunts me in rereading *Expensive People*. Did expensive houses sell for as little as $80,500 in those years? Comedy ends abruptly with death and since so many of my "expensive people" have indeed died, including the exemplary woman to whom *Expensive People* was dedicated, isn't the jocular tone of the narrator inappropriate? Isn't it . . . too unknowing? too *young*? Even the novel's thinly codified secret (having to do with the execution of an ambitious woman writer as fit punishment for having gone beyond the "limits of her world"—upstate New York) strikes me as sobering and not, as I'd surely intended, blackly comic. I recall too that the shooting of a woman by her son was based upon an actual incident of that era, but I can't recall any of the details of that case, nor even if I made any effort to seek them out. For the writer, emblematic material is most highly charged when it is only glancingly and obliquely suggested; once the idea presents itself, our instinct is to turn discreetly away. Sometimes even to shade our eyes.

Most of *Expensive People* is fiction, of course. An invented tapestry of "observed" data stretched upon a structure of parable-like simplicity. I saw myself then, as I see myself now, as a perennially romantic traveler, an "eye" enraptured by the very jumble and clamor of America. Richard Everett is speaking of his parents but he may well be speaking of all the inhabitants of his world when he confesses, "Yes, I loved them."

Wonderland *Revisited*

So much of a novelist's writing takes place in the unconscious; in those depths the last word is written before the first word appears on paper. We remember the details of our story, we do not invent them.

—Graham Greene

We are led to value highest that which has cost us the most. Of my early novels, *Wonderland*, the fifth to be published, obviously the most bizarre and obsessive, stands out in my memory as having been the most painful to write. The most painful in conception and in execution. The most painful even in retrospect. For it was evidently so mesmerizing, so haunting, so exhausting an effort, I must have willed it to be completed before, in that regulatory limbo of the unconscious to which we have no direct access, it was ready to be completed. As Graham Greene so eloquently says, we remember the details of our story, we do not invent them. When I reread *Wonderland* after its hardcover publication I knew that the ending I'd written was not the true ending; in the months between finishing the manuscript and seeing it published, I had continued to be haunted by it, "dreaming" its truer trajectory. I knew then that I had to recast the ending, at least for the paperback edition and subsequent reprints. The original ending and a brief hallucinatory prologue that framed the thirty years of the novel were jettisoned, and the "true" ending supplied. *Wonderland* could not end with a small boat drifting out helplessly to sea (specifically, Lake Ontario); it had to end with a gesture of demonic-paternal control. This was the tragedy of America in the 1960s, the story of a man who becomes the very figure he has

been fleeing since boyhood: a son of the devouring Cronus who, un-
knowingly, becomes Cronus himself.

My practice as a novelist up to and including the composition of
the similarly obsessive *Son of the Morning*, published in 1978, was to
write a complete first draft in one long head-on plunge; by which,
though this was perhaps not my conscious choice, I would be nearly
as immersed in my characters' experiences as they themselves were.
The first draft completed, I would be exhausted; often, overcome by a
sense of psychic derailment; my graphic vision of the runaway Shelley, wasted and ungendered and sickly yellow with jaundice at *Wonderland*'s end, is an exaggerated self-portrait, meant perhaps to exert
authorial control over the torrential experience of novel-writing—
which is the formal, daylight discipline of which novel-imagining is
the passion. Once the first draft was completed, I would put it away
for some weeks or months, and, after an interregnum during which I
took on more finite projects, including, for who knows what restoration of the soul, the intensive reading and writing of poetry, I would
systematically rewrite the entire manuscript, first word to last. And
this was the triumph of art, it seemed to me: the re-writing, the recasting, the re-imagining of what had been a sustained ecstatic
plunge. A novel is prose artfully structured, structure imposed upon
prose. Control imposed upon passion. *Wonderland*'s theme of a protagonist who seems without identity ("You do not exist," Dr. Peder-
sen tells Jesse) unless deeply involved in meaningful experience (who
is more qualified than a neurologist to determine where brain and
spirit fuse?) is an oblique portrait of the novelist as well.

This book is for all of us who pursue the phantasmagoria of personality—
how boldly, how trustingly, *Wonderland*'s dedication exposes its secret
heart! In the broadest terms, literature is of two distinct types: that
which offers us a distillation of experience, and that which offers us
experience itself. My method of composition in those years was ideally suited for my goal—that of offering, so far as literature may be
said to offer anything palpable, tangible, "real," at all, not a cool, in-
tellectualized distillation of fictitious characters' experiences, but experience itself, mediated by language and form. Instead of exploring
the "phantasmagoria of personality" (the mystery of our *selfness*
within our *species-hood*) obliquely, which is the more navigable way,

Wonderland, from its first sentence to its last, plunges us into the vortex of being: We begin with a terrified fourteen-year-old boy who "knows" something terrible is going to happen to him, or has indeed already happened and is awaiting him at home; and we continue with him as an adult, adding on, as if in psychic replication, his wife and younger daughter, all of them caught up in this vortex of being as it confronts non-being—for that is the secret horror inside the costly microscope Dr. Cady has given his son-in-law Jesse. *Do we exist? What is "personality"? Is it permanent, it is ephemeral?*—can it be destroyed as easily as Dr. Perrault boasts, "with a tiny pin in my fingers?"

Because such questions are the novel's heart, its deep verticality and inwardness are driven by convulsive narrative leaps: months and even years pass, but only those actions possessing psychic significance are dramatized. Opening with an act of despair that seems to us so tragically American—the slaughter of a family by its "head," who then kills himself—*Wonderland* moves from the Depression through World War II through the Korean War and the "Cold War" and the Vietnam War and the turbulent years of that decade (approximately 1963–73: from the assassination of President John F. Kennedy to the end of the Vietnam War) known as the sixties. Background is foreground, in a sense, only in terms of the Depression, which has devastated Jesse Harte's father; the assassination of Kennedy, which is experienced by the Vogel family at a crucial time in their lives; and the grimly self-destructive yet intermittently radiant visions of the sixties, to which both Jesse's mock-brother Trick Monk and his daughter Shelley fall victim. Like virtually all of my novels, *Wonderland* is political in genesis, however individualized its characters and settings. It could not have been conceived, still less written, at any other time than in post-1967 America, when divisive hatreds between the generations, over the war in Vietnam, and what was called, perhaps optimistically, the "counter-culture," raged daily. (So too *them*, the novel immediately preceding *Wonderland*, could not have been written before the "long, hot summer" of urban race riots of 1967.) How specifically rooted in time and place *Wonderland* is, from the meticulously observed view of the Erie Canal, its cascading waterfalls and locks seen by Jesse from the perspective of a certain

bridge in Lockport, to the demoralized street scene in Toronto, thirty
years later, where the drug-addicted young, moribund, unsexed, affectless, begging from strangers, have "the appearance of victims of
war, photographed to illustrate the anonymity of war." (Yes, that was
Yonge Street, Toronto, in those days. A "street of the young" in any
large North American city, in those days.)

For *Wonderland*, as a title, refers to both America, as a region of
wonders, and the human brain, as a region of wonders. And "wonders" can be both dream and nightmare.

After rewriting the ending of *Wonderland* for its paperback
reprinting in 1972, I ceased thinking about it; I did not want to
think about it; of my early novels, it was the one of which readers
sometimes spoke in odd, rapturous-accusatory terms—"I was eighteen years old, my roommate at college gave it to me to read, I was up
all night, I couldn't put it down. *Why don't you write novels like that
any longer?*" I did not want to write novels quite like that any longer,
nor even to reread this specific one, the very thought of which made
me feel faint, as if in recollection of some close call, some old, survived danger. (Perhaps I should mention parenthetically that my interest in neurology, so evident in *Wonderland*'s long speculative
middle section, was the consequence of an apparent medical condition, which necessitated one or more trips to a neurologist in Windsor, Ontario, where my husband and I lived at the time: But the
"condition" turned out to be not physical, or in any case not seriously
physical, but a temporary confluence of symptoms caused by what is
now called, so commonly, "stress.") Approaching the novel now, a
cavernous twenty-two years after its composition, I am probably
most struck by what might be called its kinetic exuberance. I mean it
as a purely neural expression—neither laudatory nor condemnatory—
to say that, both in its epic conception and its execution, *Wonderland*
leaves me a bit breathless: as the narrative itself seems breathless,
caught up in that vortex of being that is our human predicament, yet
not, or not commonly, the province of the novelist. Indeed, so fueled
by energy was *Wonderland*, it spilled over into a play, *Ontological Proof
of My Existence*, a dramatization and expansion of Jesse's visit to
Toronto, to win, or buy, his daughter back from her drug-dispenser

lover; and into such short stories of that time as "How I Contemplated the World from the Detroit House of Correction, and Began My Life Over Again," an analogue of Shelley's experience as a runaway to Toledo. (In retrospect, it seems that Shelley Vogel was crying out for a novel of her own, a story that was not a mere appendage of her father's; but this was a novel that I could not, or would not, write. The material was simply too devastating.)

Much in *Wonderland* has to do with memory. The escape from memory, the surrender to memory. Theories of memory. The "invention" of memory. Of all art forms, the novel is the most indigenously equipped to take its populace through a delimited space of time, shoring up memory in both characters and readers; at a certain point, as if by magic, the memory of the novel is shared by both characters and readers. So, in *Wonderland*, when the adult Jesse remembers, or fails to remember, the attentive reader is a part of his consciousness; we sense the onset of his breakdown when isolated figures and memory shards out of his deeply suppressed past begin to intrude into his rigidly controlled present. No other art form so builds upon memory so *necessarily*, as the novel: In this it mimics, as Dr. Cady suggests, personality itself. (For there can be no *person* without memory.) And no other art form is so dependent upon and so infatuated with memory, as the novel: The novelist might be defined as one who, in the guise of fiction, is involved in a ceaseless memorialization of the past. (*Wonderland* includes a Postmodernist snapshot of a kind, when, in the concluding pages of the first section, the beleaguered Jesse, pausing in his desperate drive from Lockport to Buffalo, spies upon a young family in a green swing behind a farmhouse—Carolina and Frederic Oates and their three-year-old daughter Joyce.) The uses we make of our homesickness!

For the melancholy we feel when completing a novel is akin to the melancholy we feel when, by the inexorable process of time, we are expelled forever from home.

"American, Abroad"

"American, Abroad" is a fiction constructed out of a myriad of small authentic details, of the kind that impress us, as travelers, with an almost hallucinatory vividness. All its observable reality *is* real, and many of its conversations. There really was, in the late 1980s, in the European country where I had gone on a lecture/reading tour, an Iranian terrorist team that had "targeted" one of our ambassadors; there really was an ambassador's daughter, a yipping terrier, a false alarm at the palatial embassy residence where, one evening, I was being honored much as my character Caroline Carmichael is being honored. Of course, the fact that "American, Abroad" is cast in a certain mode of language makes it fiction, not memoir. Caroline Carmichael is not me, except as we overlap. Much of what she sees, I saw; much of what I saw, she sees. Sometimes we feel exactly the same way about what we see; in other, perhaps more crucial, ways, we don't.

Without intending it, I have written, over the years, a small gathering of European-set stories, and these stories are all "real"—as a composite is real. The stories have a distinct family resemblance and are altogether different in tone, theme, and characterization from my more characteristic American-set stories, which are, despite authentic settings, much more fictional. When I travel, my imagination recedes; to use Emerson's surreal metaphor, I become an eyeball, a pure consciousness, avid to register all I can see, hear, smell, taste, absorb. The external world is a forest of signs and symbols, inviting, but always eluding, interpretation.

In "American, Abroad," even fellow Americans become mysterious, elusive. I must have imagined Caroline Carmichael into being in order to give a coherent dramatic shape to my sense of unease and vulnerability, yet my sense of wonderment too, a kind of generic American spirit that possesses us, sometimes, in foreign countries where we are both ourselves—private, solitary—and citizens of a rich, vast, legendary country into which, by sheer good fortune, we were born. This is precisely the kind of fiction an American writer can't write at home.

What I've liked about "American, Abroad" is the fact that it might have turned tragic, but did not. It might have ended in a wounding, devastating epiphany for its heroine, but did not. For sometimes, vulnerable and exposed as we are, we do triumph—to a degree.

"Why Don't You Come
Live with Me It's Time"

Sometimes, out of a mirror, a face not quite my own rises to me—I see my grandmother's face, as it is captured in certain snapshots, and, less consistently, in my memory. This phenomenon—and the fact that I loved my grandmother, my father's mother, very much, and have never been able to write about her—underlies the composition of "Why Don't You Come Live with Me It's Time."

And, too, the phenomenon of insomnia: the complex, even philosophical relationship the insomniac comes to have with both sleep and wakefulness, as a consequence of thinking about these states of consciousness so obsessively. If you are an insomniac, you know what I mean; if you are not—lucky you! An insomniac, by definition, is one who thinks too much, and perhaps over-finely.

And there was the romance, when I was a teenager, of slipping quietly out of the house in the early morning hours, to stare at the night sky, the surrounding darkness, the highway (not a city street, as in my story: but Transit Road, a two-lane country highway)—to contemplate the few cars that rushed past, with a fervid romantic wonder, *Who are these people?* What would have interested me only minimally by day was fascinating by night.

Hammond, N.Y., the fictitious setting of my story, is also the setting of my novel *Because It Is Bitter, and Because It Is My Heart*. It bears a dreamlike resemblance to Lockport, N.Y., where I was born, and where my Grandmother Woodside lived.

As a young girl, I was fascinated by questions I did not know were archetypal philosophical questions—clichés of the intellect, one might call them. The night sky greatly interested me; the "Universe"; vast concepts of space, time; the mystery of human personality. Such questions, which even cosmologists falter in addressing, are most intense in us in early adolescence; afterward, we are supposed to grow up and forget them. Perhaps the writer—this writer, at least—is simply one who, so long as a question remains unanswered, cannot forget it, thus cannot repudiate the romance of adolescence.

As a child, living close to water (the Tonawanda Creek flows at the edge of my parents' property in Millersport; the Erie Canal runs through Lockport, dividing the city dramatically in two), I was forced to contemplate bridges a good deal. Especially those old, single-lane, rattling bridges that are the bridges of nightmare—yet, somehow, we *do* cross them. Again and again.

When I am in a realist phase—in which most of my novels are written—how I yearn for the freedom, the mythopoetics, of the sur/real!—the kind of art that is not really to be categorized as "fantasy"—"dark fantasy"—"horror"—"the Gothic"—yet assuredly is not *realistic*. "Why Don't You Come Live with Me It's Time" is so close to my heart, and memory, it becomes, finally, impossible to define it as anything other than itself: an extended riddle, perhaps, in the form of a story.

Foxfire:
Confessions of a Girl Gang

Looking into the depths of the sky, we are looking into Time: The stars of distant galaxies that seem to us so beautiful, so fraught with meaning beyond our human ability to comprehend, are in fact not *there*, but long extinct; even our own sun is eight minutes into what astronomers call *look-back time*. Maddy Wirtz, the chronicler of the *Foxfire* confessions, in adulthood an astronomer's assistant, is able to tell her story only through the prism of *look-back time*— "Undertaken now because I have the proper telescopic instrument." Which is to say, the perspective of Time.

My secret title for *Foxfire: Confessions of a Girl Gang* during the months of its composition was "my *Huck Finn*." Never before had I written a novel so romantically adventurous and head-on in its narrative; never before a novel that reproduces the chronology of a story in a diary-like way, nor one in which adolescents speak so candidly, so comically, and, to my ear at least, poetically. Maddy Wirtz, "Maddy-Monkey," my young alter ego, is a straightforward and reliable narrator. Like Huckleberry Finn, telling his story, Maddy is to be trusted utterly by the reader—she tells the truth, and she is as unsparing of herself as of others. Here is the voice of adolescence—distrustful of most adults, and of all institutions, for very good reasons. Under the spell of their gang leader, Legs Sadovsky, Maddy and her sisters in *Foxfire* may resemble Huckleberry Finn too in their early, unexamined optimism—their "Americanness." The quality of childlike zest and curiosity, the sense that the past does not throw a shadow over the future, is a quality Europeans, steeped in far more history than we, envy us for, and it is a quality I find in myself, hardly less now than when I was Maddy's age and in many ways not so very different from her. For to be "American" is to feel that your life can be changed by your own actions—you have only to *act*.

Of course, I dare not push the analogy with Mark Twain's great classic too far, for obvious reasons. *Huckleberry Finn* occupies a singular place in our American literature, like nothing before or since; nothing that Twain himself wrote approaches it in depth, or in energy and inspiration. *Foxfire: Confessions of a Girl Gang* is very much a *girls'* story, and, as such, defines itself in sometimes playful but more often uneasy opposition to a male- and adult-dominated world. We sense that this opposition is not so easily maintained as the gang girls imagine it might be. We sense that neither sex can live without the other; that the dream of a Foxfire Homestead, a Utopian sisterhood in the midst of a heterogeneous working-class world, is doomed. We sense that Legs Sadovsky, for all her intelligence, cunning, and idealism, is finally too reckless—too blinded by her own "Americanness" to succeed. The qualities for which Maddy loves Legs are the very qualities that blind her. For almost without being conscious of the transition, as Maddy notes, the *Foxfire* girls pass from childlike innocence to precocious criminality; at first victimized by adults, and terrifyingly vulnerable to the cruel whims of adults (like the lie Legs's father tells a juvenile court judge, that his fiercely virginal daughter is "promiscuous"), they become calculated victimizers themselves. The ante is constantly being raised—their exploitation of sex. And finally, in a mad scheme to get $1 million, they go too far—too far for Maddy Wirtz to follow.

Can there be a pure "sisterhood" separate from, still less hostile to, men? Is Foxfire doomed because, fundamentally, spiritually as well as physically, the female can't live without the male?—or in ideological isolation?

Foxfire: Confessions of a Girl Gang, like my earlier novels *Marya: A Life, You Must Remember This*, and *Because It Is Bitter, and Because It Is My Heart*, had its emotional genesis in powerful memories of a girlhood in upstate New York. It is set in Hammond, a fictitious city that is also the setting of *Because It Is Bitter*, and nearly identical to Port Oriskany, of *You Must Remember This*: a composite of Lockport (pop. 25,000) and Buffalo (pop. 339,000). My family's rural home, in a crossroads called Millersport, is between these cities, but Lockport was the closer, and it was in Lockport that many of our relatives lived and where in the 1950s I was bussed to school. The steep hills of Lockport, the excitement of even its shabbiest streets, parks, stores, and bus stations, above all the dominating and somehow luminous presence of the Erie Barge Canal cutting through the heart of the city—what more romantic setting for a dramatic testing of the dreams of adolescence as they collide with reality? For me, as for Maddy, the prism of *look-back time* allowed me to confront memories of the early 1950s in a way inconceivable when I'd lived them. Not that the novel is autobiographical, or "confessional"—except in emotional terms.

For, as Legs tells Maddy, even if our souls are not immortal, but evanescent as flames, aren't they, like flames, *real* enough at the time of their existence? So too, this romance of a novel, a piece of my heart.

"You Petted Me,
and I Followed You Home"

"You Petted Me, and I Followed You Home" is one of a number of stories of mine that evolved over a period of time, discontinuous and unpredictable. The little lost dog is "real"—the image, the memory, of a dog like this dog, following us one day in the street, in a now-forgotten city, continues to haunt. And the strange title—these words, partly reproachful, with an undercurrent of passion and possessiveness, were once spoken to me, and have haunted me through the years. *You petted me, and I followed you home*—the refrain runs through my mind at odd, unexpected times, apparently lodged deep in my memory. A virtual incantation, a curse, a prophecy!—I must have believed that writing this story would erase the phrase from my interior life.

The story itself was written swiftly, in longhand, on a number of sheets of paper, my usual not very practical method. Scenes were then reordered, and some were excised, in the rewriting and revising, which, for me, is the more pleasurable aspect of writing. In the first phase, there is anxiety and tension and a sense that however swiftly I write, I won't get everything down, much will be lost; in the second, much longer phase, there is a sense of slow-growing but usually reliable satisfaction, as the chaos of "feeling" is subordinated to an aesthetic structure. When I reread early versions of a story, I sometimes wonder if I haven't pared too much back; I think perhaps

"You Petted Me, and I Followed You Home" in its final published form is rather too pared back, more "minimalist" than it might have been. I knew the woman and the man much more intimately than I'd indicated, the woman especially—but there seemed not enough space, given the restrictions I'd set for myself, to accommodate this knowledge.

In any case, the dog completes the story, obliterates the human beings, in an action terrifying to me, as I'd understood from the outset it would.

"Mark of Satan"

"Mark of Satan" began with a vision of a rural setting—the forlorn house, shimmering heat waves, bamboo growing wild and ragged in a marshy backyard. There's that eerie rustling sound of dried bamboo in the wind. Bamboo is a softwood tree like willow, or you might call it a marsh weed like cattails, that, though seemingly stationary to the human eye, is always on the prowl. Bamboo will "march" in all directions, vigorous, brash, unstoppable—or almost. I was thinking of grace "marching" through our lives mostly unseen by us. I was thinking of that diminishment of the soul we've all felt, and will surely feel again: the soul at that terrible, tender point at which it veers toward extinction; and I wondered if we generate, out of our own desperation and terror of spiritual death, some sign of "grace" to lead us back to life. (The elliptical thought came to me, perhaps not relevant to this story, that Jean-Paul Sartre defined genius as "not a gift, but the way a person invents in desperate circumstances.") In this story, the bearer of grace is an actual person, the unconsciously beautiful, seductive, and innocent Thelma McCord, with her angelic child Magdalena. To experience grace we must surrender our customary irony; but—is it possible for us to surrender irony, our "mark of Satan," entirely? For many of us, what would take its place?

Out of a mixture of these elements, "Mark of Satan" came more quickly to be born than any story of mine in recent years.

Will You Always Love Me?

It had been an accident, of that he was convinced.

This thing that happened to them, . . . it was like nothing that'd ever happened to them before.

How the subject came up no one would recall afterward.

Is a foot male or female? they were asking.

A woman had come to save his soul, and he wasn't sure he was ready.

Each of the stories in this volume springs directly from its initial sentence, and has been written, in a sense recorded, to move as swiftly as possible, granted the complexities of the story, to its final sentence. Each of the titles—"American, Abroad," "Life After High School," "Is Laughter Contagious?", "The Revenge of the Foot, 1970," among others—has been deliberately, purposefully chosen. Each of the stories is a variant on a single universal theme suggested by the book's title, *Will You Always Love Me?*

All my life, I've loved the short story form, the very essence of storytelling. Its relative brevity compared to the novel, its shapeliness, its sharp focus, its mimicry of the human voice. *Here is something you haven't heard before!* a short story seems to be telling us, in excitement. *Not in this way, not like this!*

It might be theorized that, for the writer, a story is a "haunting." Something lodges deep inside us, or springs from memory, or a dream; we can't rid ourselves of it; we become obsessed by it. The strangest story in this volume, to me, is "The Brothers." Though I wrote it, I can't quite understand *why*; I don't know what provoked it; swiftly skimming it, I'm never quite prepared for what comes next. Another strange story, to me, is "The Revenge of the Foot, 1970," which sprang full-blown as a dream out of reverie while driving from Stratford, Ontario, a few years ago; I've visited Toronto numerous times, lived in Windsor, Ontario, from 1968 to 1978, yet would surely not have written this story but for that drive, that day, through that countryside. "You Petted Me, and I Followed You Home" sprang from an experience with a "little lost dog" and from the eerie, unnerving remark made to me by an acquaintance (*You petted me, and I followed you home,* murmured with an air of possessiveness and reproach), but the strangeness of the dog himself and his effect upon a young married couple was a surprise to me. Equally mysterious, to me, is "Mark of Satan"—which seems to have sprung from its very setting, rural Pennsylvania in the heat, a stand of bamboo in a backyard. (Yes, bamboo grows in my own backyard. But what does it *mean*?)

Other stories can be traced to their historical origins with no difficulty, though they have been transposed into fiction. "American, Abroad" happened, or almost happened, in the American embassy in Amsterdam, a few years ago. "Will You Always Love Me?" is based upon a tale told me twice removed, in a very different venue. "The Track" is based upon personal experience; extremely intense personal experience; if I reread the story, I begin to feel apprehension at about the same place each time, just as I did that autumn afternoon, propelled around a dirt track behind a high-stepping harness racing filly, in sudden fear of being killed, in a setting of surpassing beauty at a horse farm in northern New Jersey. "Good to Know You" is a dramatized, succinctly embellished account of a heated exchange of male-female voices to which I was a participating witness, in a Chinese restaurant in Princeton, New Jersey, perhaps three years ago. (I never return to the restaurant without sharply reexperiencing the exchange, and the emotions that led to the story. For the record, the couples are still together.) The visit from a Detroit lawyer, the threat of a subpoena, the melancholy "work-in-progress" of a former student—all provide the very real core of the more mythical "The

Handclasp," with its, to me, unexpected ending. The exquisitely beautiful abandoned fawn of "June Birthing" was my own obsession one evening in early summer a few years ago, here in semi-rural New Jersey where I live. "The Lost Child" and "Christmas 1962" are largely fiction, but set in a region of vivid memory in upstate New York, like "The Girl Who Was to Die." "The Undesirable Table" is a *What if*—? tale for people very like my friends and myself, a parable for our time of sharply divided affluence and poverty almost too painful to contemplate; like "Is Laughter Contagious?" which explores an affluent suburban world identical to our own except for the terrifying fact that the solicitude born of human sympathy and decency has been lost, supplanted by the most primitive instinct of laughter.

Will you always love me? I don't know of a more unnerving question. It's a question we never dare ask unless we believe we know the answer beforehand. It's a question, put to us, which we immediately answer, like the lover in the title story, confronted with the desperate woman in his arms, *Yes*. In assembling the stories, I began to see an unexpected pattern of love relations, some quite ironic ("The Vision," "Mark of Satan," "The Passion of Rydcie Mather"), but some quite forthright. A number of the men and women in these stories discover that they *are* loved, whether they entirely deserve it or not: the emotionally distraught woman writer of "The Handclasp"; the guilt-ravaged husband of "Act of Solitude"; the young divorcée of "June Birthing" so fearful of again falling in love, and being hurt; the lonely middle-aged widow and her difficult stepdaughter of "The Girl Who Was to Die"; the childless married couple of "The Track," who've had a glimpse of imminent mortality; and the hopeful lovers of "The Missing Person," who find themselves in an embrace that might mean love. Even stories that end ironically, like "The Vision" and "Mark of Satan," seem to have brought their distraught protagonists—an aging Catholic who sees the Virgin Mary in his backyard, a paroled sex offender and would-be rapist visited by a similar sort of "grace"—to a renewed definition of self, a surprising renewal of spirit.

"*Ghost Girls*"

"*Ghost Girls*" is one of those stories that originated not in an idea, concept, or theme but purely out of an image: the small country airport with its rotted wind sock flapping in the breeze and a single dirt runway between cornfields. Such airports were part of my childhood in upstate New York; my father, Frederic Oates, and certain of his friends flew small airplanes like the one described in the story (including, in fact, the romantic old Vultee basic trainer, in which I seem to think I flew, though perhaps I didn't). The child Ingrid, her attractive momma, and the absent, possibly malevolent daddy are as vivid to me as my own memories of the past, but are wholly fictional. Ingrid's fascination with the mysterious lives of her parents mirrors my fascination with my parents' lives—the child's fascination with an adult world that surrounds her, entirely out of her control and even her comprehension. After "*Ghost Girls*," there came to me a related story, also narrated by Ingrid, titled "See You in Your Dreams"; then came "Easy Lay," then "Gorgeous"; eventually "Man Crazy"—when I came to see that the stories were evolving toward a single story, a novel built of images and episodes titled *Man Crazy*. Its genesis is the image of the "airstrip at Marsena."

ACKNOWLEDGMENTS

(These pages constitute an extension of the copyright page.)

"Where Is an Author?" appeared in *The Gettysburg Review* (Winter 1999).

"In Olden Times, When Wishing Was Having . . ." originally appeared in *Kenyon Review*, Fall 1997, and was reprinted, in a slightly expanded form, in *Into the Mirror: An Anthology of Women on Fairy Tales*, edited by Kate Bernheimer (Anchor Books, Doubleday, 1998).

"The Aesthetics of Fear," in a slightly different version, was given as the keynote address for "The Aesthetics of Fear" conference at New York University, March 22, 1997; and published in *Salmagundi*, in this form, 1998.

"Art and Ethics?—The F(U)tility of Art" was originally presented as a paper at a conference sponsored by *Salmagundi* and The New School, 1996; and subsequently published in *Salmagundi*, 1996.

"Transformations of Play" originally appeared in *New Literary History*, Fall, 1995.

" 'Zero at the Bone' " originally appeared in *The New York Times Book Review*, July 1993; reprinted in *The Seven Deadly Sins*.

"Art and 'Victim Art' " appeared in *The New York Times*, February 1995.

"On Fiction in Fact" appeared in *The New York Times*, February 26, 1998.

"F. Scott Fitzgerald Revisited" originally appeared, under a different title, in *The Times Literary Supplement*, January 1996.

"Raymond Chandler: Genre and 'Art' " appeared in *The New York Review of Books*, January, 1996.

"After the Road: The Art of Jack Kerouac" originally appeared, under a different title, in *The New Yorker*, February 1995.

"Haunted Sylvia Plath" originally appeared in *The Times Literary Supplement*, July 1991.

"The Enigmatic Art of Paul Bowles" appeared, under a different title, in *So Far from Home* (Ecco Press, 1993).

"Biography as Pathography" originally appeared, under a different title, in *The New York Times Book Review*, August 1988.

"To Bedlam: Anne Sexton" originally appeared, under a different title, in *The New York Times Book Review*, October 1991.

"Saul Bellow's *A Theft*" originally appeared in *The New York Times Book Review*, March 1989.

"John Updike's *Rabbit*" appeared in *The New York Times Book Review*, September 1990.

"Henry Louis Gates, Jr.'s *Colored People*" appeared in *The London Review of Books*, January 1995.

"John Edgar Wideman: Memoir and Fiction" appeared in *The New York Review of Books*, March 1997.

"Exile and Homeland: Brian Moore" appeared, under a different title, in *The Times Literary Supplement*, September 1997.

"Updike *Toward the End of Time*" appeared in *The New Yorker*, December 8, 1997.

"Inside the Locked Room: P. D. James" appeared in *The New York Review of Books*, February 5, 1998.

"A Dream of Justice: Dorothy L. Sayers" appeared in *The New York Times Book Review*, March 15, 1998.

"Lost in Boxing" appeared in *The Los Angeles Times Book Review*, March 1, 1998.

"The Miniaturist Art of Grace Paley" appeared in *The London Review of Books*, April, 1998.

"American Views: Elizabeth Hardwick," appeared in *The New York Review of Books*, November 28, 1998.

"Jeffrey Dahmer" appeared, in a slightly different form, in *The New Yorker*, December 1994.

"Timothy James McVeigh" appeared, in a slightly different form, in *The New Yorker*, May 1995.

"Mike Tyson" appeared, in a slightly different form, in *The New York Times*, July 1997.

" 'I Had No Other Thrill or Happiness': The Literature of Serial Killers" appeared in *The New York Review of Books*, March 1994.

"Tragic Melville" appeared as the introduction to the Signet Classic edition *Billy Budd and Other Tales* by Herman Melville, 1998.

"The Essential Emily Dickinson" appeared as the introduction to *The Essential Dickinson*, edited by Joyce Carol Oates (Ecco, 1996).

"Henry James's 'The Middle Years'" appeared in *New Literary History*, Spring 1996.

"The Riddle of Christina Rossetti's 'Goblin Market'" appeared as the introduction to a new edition of the poem, published by F.L.Y. Productions (San Francisco, 1997).

"*The Damnation of Theron Ware*" appeared, under the title "Fall from Grace," in *The New York Times Book Review*, December 1995.

Introduction to Joseph Conrad's *Heart of Darkness* and *The Secret Sharer*, Signet Classic, 1997.

"Arthur Miller's *Death of a Salesman*: A Celebration" appeared in *Michigan Quarterly Review*, Fall 1998.

"Killer Kids" appeared in *The New York Review of Books*, November 6, 1997.

"Workings of Grace: Flannery O'Connor's 'The Artificial Nigger'" appeared in *Kenyon Review*, Winter 1998.

"Nighthawks, 1942: Painting and Poem" appeared in *Introspections* (University Press of New England, 1997).

Where Are You Going, Where Have You Been? Selected Early Short Stories: Afterword appeared in the book of that title (Ontario Review Press, 1993).

"*Expensive People*: The Confessions of a 'Minor Character'" appeared as the afterword to the Ontario Review Press reprint, 1990.

"*Wonderland*" appeared as the afterword to the Ontario Review Press reprint, 1992.

"American, Abroad" appeared in *The Best American Short Stories*, 1991.

"Why Don't You Come Live with Me It's Time" appeared in *Prize Stories: The O. Henry Awards, 1992*.

"*Foxfire: Confessions of a Girl Gang*" appeared as the preface to the Franklin Library edition, 1993.

"You Petted Me, and I Followed You Home" appeared in in *Prize Stories: The O. Henry Awards, 1995*.

"Mark of Satan" appeared in *Prize Stories: The O. Henry Awards, 1996*.

"*Will You Always Love Me?*" appeared as the preface to the Franklin Library edition, 1996.

"Ghost Girls" appeared in *The Best American Short Stories*, 1996.

To all these, acknowledgments and thanks are due. And special thanks to Barbara Epstein of *The New York Review of Books*.